Susan Lastarria *(signature)*

land reform
land rights
land tenure
customary tenure
land policies
Africa
gendered land rights

...ving
land rights, policy and tenure in Africa

Edited by Camilla Toulmin and Julian Quan

This book was prepared for the UK's Department for International Development (DFID) as part of its *Issues* series. It is based on the papers presented and discussions held at a DFID sponsored workshop on Land Rights and Sustainable Development in Sub-Saharan Africa, in February 1999. The views expressed in this book are those of the various authors involved and should not be taken to represent DFID policy.

Cover photograph: Ploughing in a fertile valley near Dessie, Wollo, Ethiopia
© **Neil Cooper/ Panos Pictures**
Design: Andy Smith, London, UK
Printing: Russell Press, Nottingham, UK
Paper: Sovereign Silk 100 gsm, Chlorine Free (ECF)

Copies of this publication can be obtained from:
IIED Bookshop
3 Endsleigh Street
London, WC1H ODD
United Kingdom

Tel: + 44 (0) 20 7388 2117
Fax: + 44 (0) 20 7388 2826
Email: bookshop@iied.org
Website: www.iied.org

Contents

LIST OF BOXES:

LIST OF TABLES AND FIGURES

ACKNOWLEDGEMENTS

For the editors of a book of this sort, there are many people to whom thanks are due. From the Department for International Development, Michael Scott and Leigh Stubblefield, Rural Livelihoods Department, have provided rapid and valuable feedback on issues of content and approach in the preparation of this book. In the Natural Resources Institute (NRI), Claire Troy and Ruth Burchill have given much support and hard work to ensure both the effective organisation of the Sunningdale workshop and communication with authors during the editing process. At the International Institute for Environment and Development (IIED), Judy Longbottom and Rebeca Leonard have both invested a very large amount of effort in keeping the editorial programme moving, checking text, and preparing the book for publication. Christèle Riou and Nicole Kenton have been highly valued members of the administrative team, while we have been reliant on the keen and experienced editorial eye of Jacqueline Saunders. Eileen Higgins and Andy Smith have provided very supportive, flexible and imaginative approaches to design and production of this book. We owe them all a considerable debt of thanks.

The many participants of Sunningdale generated, through their energy, engagement in land debates, and willingness to share their ideas, the momentum for taking forward this book, as well as the land tenure networking process which is now under way (see Appendices). We gratefully acknowledge their inputs, perspectives and commitment to working together in future on this subject of such importance. We hope that this book, which incorporates much of their material, and illuminates their differing perspectives, will help nourish discussions within their own countries and in Africa more broadly on approaches to consultation, legislative measures and implementation processes. We would also like to thank the many authors of chapters in this book who, despite very tight deadlines, have been cheerful and committed participants in the process of revising material, adding new information and checking details.

With thanks,
Julian Quan & Camilla Toulmin
NRI, Chatham and IIED, Edinburgh, March 2000

ABOUT THE AUTHORS

Martin Adams worked as a soil surveyor and plant ecologist in Africa and the South Pacific in the 1960s. In the 1970s, he became involved in the economic, institutional and tenure aspects of irrigated and dryland agriculture in the Middle East, the Horn and East Africa. Since that time, he has worked in a wide range of land-related fields, including the management and utilisation of protected areas. Since 1990 he has concentrated on land reform in Southern Africa and the Philippines. For the last five years he has been a policy adviser in the South African Department of Land Affairs.

Aninka Claassens worked as an Advisor to South African Minister of Agriculture and Land Affairs, Derek Hanekom, and a consultant to the Department of Land Affairs from 1996-1999. She participated in the drafting processes of various pieces of South African land reform legislation from 1994-1999. She is currently a consultant specialising in land rights in communal areas of South Africa and providing services to farm dwellers threatened with eviction.

Ben Cousins holds the Chair of Development Management at the School of Government, University of the Western Cape, South Africa and directs the Programme for Land and Agrarian Studies (PLAAS) within the School. He has worked in agricultural extension, training and curriculum development in the UK, Swaziland and Zimbabwe, and undertaken research on communal rangelands, livestock production, common property management and land tenure. His doctoral research was on decision making in communal area grazing schemes in Zimbabwe and, since returning to South Africa in 1991, has worked on tenure reform policy and the economic value of common property resources.

Thea Hilhorst completed her MSc at the Agricultural University of Wageningen focusing on tropical crop science, economy and gender studies. She joined the Royal Tropical Institute (KIT) in the Netherlands in 1991 where she wrote a book on women's access to savings and credit institutes. She was based in Sikasso, Mali for five years at the ESPGRN, Institut d'Economie Rurale. Since 1997, she has been a Drylands Programme research associate at the International Institute for Environment and Development (IIED), based in the UK where she coordinates collaborative research programmes on natural resource management.

Philippe Lavigne Delville is an anthropologist working at GRET (Groupe de Recherche et d'Echanges Technologiques) in Paris. He is working on issues of agrarian and social change in rural areas, mostly in West Africa. His particular research interests are rural organisations, irrigation and land development, and land tenure issues.

Patrick McAuslan is a Professor of Law at Birkbeck College, University of London. He has also taught in the Faculty of Law in the University of Dar es Salaam, Tanzania, in the School of Law in the University of Warwick and the London School of Economics, where he was Professor of Public Law. He worked in UNCHS (Habitat) for three years from 1990 to 1993 as Land Management Adviser to and Coordinator of the Urban Management Programme and in 1999–2000, he was the DFID Senior Technical Adviser to the Land Act Implementation Project in Uganda. He specialises in all aspects of land tenure and land use law and policy, environmental law and public law, on which he has published many books and articles. He has acted as adviser on land and environmental legal and policy matters to governments in many parts of the world.

HWO Okoth-Ogendo, is Professor of Public Law at the University of Nairobi, and is Global Visiting Professor, New York University, School of Law. He teaches constitutional politics, agrarian systems, and land law.

Robin Palmer has worked since 1987 for Oxfam GB and is currently its Land Policy Adviser for Africa. Prior to that he was an academic, working primarily in Southern Africa. His areas of research interest include land rights, reform, policy and tenure. He has written and communicated widely on these issues and has recently established an Oxfam GB website on Land Rights in Africa, http://www.oxfam.org.uk/landrights. His most recent fieldwork has been in South Africa, Zimbabwe and Zambia.

Jean-Philippe Platteau is Professor of Economics at the University of Namur, Belgium and is Director of the CRED (Center for Research on the Economics of Development) at the same university. He is the author of several books (including a forthcoming book at Harwood publishers entitled "Institutions, Social Norms and Economic Development") and numerous papers in academic journals. His main fields of study include: determinants of effective collective action; inequality and collective action; management of common property resources, in particular small-scale fisheries; transformation of land tenure systems in sub-Saharan Africa; emergence and functioning of land markets; marriage systems in relation to land availability; role of social and moral norms in economic development; informal risk-sharing and income-pooling arrangements.

Julian Quan is a social scientist specialising in the social and economic dimensions of land and natural resource management and land policy. Following extensive rural development experience in Southern Africa he has been a senior member of the Social Development Group at NRI undertaking consultancies and collaborative research throughout Africa and in Brazil. He currently acts as a specialist adviser on land issues for the Rural Livelihoods Department of DFID, supporting the development of an African programme of networking and capacity building.

Sipho Sibanda left Zimbabwe in 1972 to study in exile at the University of Zambia, Lusaka. He wrote his doctorate at the University of Wisconsin, Madison on comparative experience with tenure reform in six African countries, Zimbabwe being the focus of his work. He moved to South Africa during the transition in 1993 to work for the Association for Rural Advancement, coordinating research on land issues. In 1997, he was appointed Director of Tenure Reform in the South African Department of Land Affairs.

Camilla Toulmin is a development economist who has worked principally on issues of natural resource management in Sahelian West Africa. She directs the Drylands Programme at the IIED, which pursues a range of collaborative research projects in the fields of land tenure, soil fertility management, and broader rural livelihoods. She has a particular interest in examining the role of and limits to national policy in setting the framework for improved incentives more effective land management. She has worked extensively with a number of donor agencies on developing strategies for bilateral support to dryland resource management, and with the UN Convention to Combat Desertification.

Stephen Turner is a geographer who works for the International Cooperation Centre at the Vrije Universiteit, Amsterdam. He works mainly on natural resource management, conservation and rural development issues in Southern Africa. Since 1996, he has been seconded to the Programme for Land and Agrarian Studies (PLAAS) at the University of the Western Cape in South Africa. At PLAAS, he has helped to develop and coordinate a Natural Resource Management Unit and has undertaken a number of studies on land reform and community-based natural resource management.

The following people have also made a significant contribution to this book through their authorship of papers presented at the Sunningdale workshop on Land Rights and Sustainable Development in Sub-Saharan Africa: Lessons and Ways Forward in Land Tenure Policy, subsequent material and summaries of workshop discussions and findings. These other works have been extensively referred to and drawn upon to provide case studies and other material for the chapters that follow. Details are included in the bibliography to this book.

Prof Abdel Ghaffar M. Ahmed, Organisation for Social Science Research in Eastern and Southern Africa (OSSREA), Addis Ababa, Ethiopia

Dr Liz Alden-Wily, Independent rural development and land tenure specialist, Nairobi, Kenya

Prof John Bruce, Director, Land Tenure Center, University of Wisconsin, USA, and currently seconded to the World Bank, Washington DC, USA

Sr Albino Cuna Junior, Coordinator – Land Use and Management Component, National Directorate of Geography and Cadastre (DINAGECA), Maputo, Mozambique

Mr Vipya Harawa, Presidential Land Commission, Blantyre, Malawi

Ms M.H.C. Stella Longway, Commissioner for Lands, Ministry of Lands and Human Settlements Development, Dar es Salaam, Tanzania

Dr Junaidu Maina, Project Manager, National Livestock Projects Division, Department of Livestock, Kaduna, Nigeria

Ms Botshelo Mathuba, Deputy Permanent Secretary, Office of the President, Gaborone, Botswana

Ms Sue Mbaya, Independent consultant, Harare, Zimbabwe

Dr Shem E. Migot-Adholla, Lead Specialist, Rural Development and Environment, Africa Region, The World Bank, Washington DC, USA

Prof Sam Moyo, Director, Southern Africa Regional Institute for Policy Studies (SARIPS), Harare, Zimbabwe

Ms Rose Mwebaza, Uganda Land Alliance, Kampala, Uganda

Sr José Negrão, Land Campaign, Mozambique

Mr Lungisile Ntsebeza, Programme for Land and Agrarian Studies, School of Government, University of the Western Cape, South Africa

Mr Michael Ochieng Odhiambo, Resources Conflict Institute (RECONCILE), Nakuru, Kenya

M Jean René Mambo Okoin, Head, Plan Foncier Rural, Abidjan, Ivory Coast

Ms Irene Ovonji-Odida, Legal Officer, Uganda Law Reform Commission, Kampala, Uganda

Sra Maria Conceição Quadros, National Land Commission, Maputo,
  Mozambique
Dr Desalegn Rahmato, Forum for Social Studies, Addis Ababa, Ethiopia
M Moussa Yacouba, Secretariat Permanent du Code Rural, Ministère de
  l'Agriculture et de l'Elevage, Niamey, Niger

1

Evolving Land Rights, Tenure and Policy in Sub-Saharan Africa

Camilla Toulmin and Julian Quan

INTRODUCTION

> One of the important components of any land use or farming system is the land tenure system. The institutional arrangements under which a person gains access to land largely determines, among other things, what crops he can grow, how long he can till a particular piece of land, his rights over the fruits of his labour and his ability to undertake long term improvements on the land. (Benneh, 1987)

The material in this book arises from a workshop on *Land Rights and Sustainable Development in Sub-Saharan Africa* at which the UK government's Department for International Development (DFID) brought together policy makers, researchers and civil society representatives from across the African continent to debate issues of land rights, tenure and land policy reform, held at Sunningdale, UK in February 1999. This successful consultation aimed to stimulate an exchange of experience and expertise, and mutual learning about issues at the heart of rural development in Africa, concerning the use, management, control over and rights to land. This book, following the Sunningdale workshop, focuses on questions of rights to land and natural resources, the tenure systems which control those rights and the policies which enable, or constrain, secure access to land as a livelihood resource for rural people.

In the last two decades, almost all countries in sub-Saharan Africa have been undertaking land reform in one guise or another. The aims have been to promote economic growth, encourage more sustainable management, and reduce poverty. Land remains an asset of great importance to African economies, as a source of income, food, employment and export earnings. As well as its economic attributes, land continues to have great social value – as a place of settlement, providing a location within which people live and to which they return – as well as symbolic and ritual associations, such as burial sites, sacred woodlands, and spiritual life. In addition, the landscape provides a range of environmental services of considerable value, such as water, biodiversity, and a wide range of wild products. Access to land is of especial importance for many poor people who may have more limited opportunities to obtain profitable off-farm incomes.

The present wave of land policy reforms follows a general failure of earlier approaches to land reform, in which free market models, emphasising the conversion of customary tenure to individualised freehold rights, or alternatively, egalitarian socialist models were dominant. Individual land registration and titling, in particular, came to dominate the land policy prescriptions of international finance institutions in the era of structural adjustment. During the 1990s, mounting evidence of the pitfalls of this approach, in particular its high economic and social costs, and negative consequences for the poor, led donors and African governments alike to re-examine accepted approaches.

Despite common problems, in terms of securing rights to land, harmonising customary tenure systems, and resolving land disputes in a transparent way, Africa's farming and livelihood systems remain remarkably diverse. The countries of sub-Saharan Africa present a complex mosaic derived from past history, colonial legacy, and current economic pressures and opportunities, as well as from their natural and ecological characteristics. This great diversity at continental level is mirrored at lower scales, within each country, region, and district. This makes it difficult to draw comparisons between different parts of the continent, and demonstrates the need for considerable tailoring of national provisions concerning land to the range of conditions found at local level.

Yet within such diverse patterns of experience and situations, there are generic issues relating to land tenure and land reform processes. These are discussed below, and in considerable detail in the different chapters of this book. The common features are a consequence of Africa's experience with colonisation, the imposition of an alien legal system on top of customary rules for managing people and land, and the many common shifts in policy and approach to land tenure which have been pursued since Independence. One major consequence has been the existence of plural systems of law. These often overlap, giving rise to land claims with conflicting sources of legitimacy and contradictory outcomes regarding who can establish access to and control over land.

In this context it will be important for Africa to evolve common and workable approaches, to the challenges and dilemmas involved in land policy and law-making. Yet the changing dynamics of population, economy, culture and environment should always be kept in mind. The need for state intervention and donor co-operation will vary from place to place, so that there are no blue-print solutions.

A consistent feature in Africa's reappraisal of land policy, if not always ex-emplified by governments, then certainly by civil society institutions and pop-ular movements concerned with land, has been a search for approaches which are at once practical, democratic and consistent with enduring African socio-cultural values. In most African customary traditions, rights are established to land by birth, kinship, and the investment of sweat and toil, as well as by social contract. In a continent where poverty, vulnerability and human suffering have been endemic in many regions, the approach to land policy and land rights needs to be strongly human-centred, and less driven by economic prescrip-tions than governments and donors have frequently allowed. Land policy and land law need to be more even-handed in relation to the various stakeholders, particularly the poor. This requires a fundamental recognition that imported western notions of property rights are not the only principles which may be ap-propriate in Africa.

Much of sub-Saharan Africa remains heavily dependent on development assistance. As a consequence, African governments have been particularly sub-ject to the ebb and flow of donor thinking about the importance of the land question and how it should be addressed. This has led to the exposure of African nations to changing views linked to broader shifts in world view as they relate to the role of government, adherence to greater market orientation, and policy and academic debate led by western intellectuals. Greater levels of debate and self-determination within Africa are required in relation to land and other areas of development policy.

At the same time, a new donor consensus reached by the main OECD member states, is facilitating the development of a more human-centred ap-proach to land rights. The OECD now aims to harmonise agency approaches to achieve substantial reductions in the incidence and level of poverty in the developing world, by stimulating patterns of economic growth which are "pro-poor". The UK White Paper on Development issued in 1997 commits the British government to meeting the International Development Targets drawn up by the OECD. Principal among these is that of reducing by half the pro-portion of people living in absolute poverty by 2015. DFID has sought to gen-erate commitment and galvanise action amongst donor agencies and developing country governments to achieve this goal.

Under this umbrella, DFID, with multilateral and non-governmental agen-cies such as UNDP, Oxfam and CARE, have sought to promote a livelihoods approach to development, which seeks to build on the strengths and opportunities open to the poor. It posits three key elements as central to an understanding of the livelihoods of the poor. These are: the capital assets which people require for a livelihood, including land and natural resources, basic infrastructure, human skills, sources of finance, and associative social networks; the institutional and policy environment which enables or constrains livelihood strategies; and the historical, structural and natural conditions which help determine the broader context of vulnerability and opportunity.

In rural Africa, land and the biological resources the land supports are principal livelihood assets. Smallholder farming on plots that households can control and nurture themselves makes efficient use of people's energy and labour. It also can be more productive than large scale commercial farming. Although people are migrating to towns and cities, the majority of poor people in Africa live in rural areas. Without secure rights of access to land, Africa's rural people have scarce hope of escaping from poverty. Land and natural resource rights underpin subsistence oriented farming, smallholder cash crops, animal husbandry, and the gathering of bush and forest products. These activities, together with the development of rural markets, village-based industries and service activities, are central to rural livelihoods.

Past failures with land reform might be attributed to the politics of the Cold War, but the current drive for agricultural modernisation underpins the latest wave of policy reform. African farmers and African nations need not only to feed themselves, they need to produce quality goods for sale, and compete on global markets, while sustaining the productive capacity of the land.

African business people, customary chiefs and, in many cases, politicians and government officials are keen to accumulate and invest in land. They seek land title, hunting and timber concessions, mining rights, and collateral to raise investment. The processes at work may be legitimate, or occasionally corrupt, but they will undoubtedly continue to shape African development. Like small farmers, but on a larger scale, the powerful seek security for themselves and their families, as source of profit for current and future generations. Land has also been a factor in the development of civil and political conflict in Africa. In Congo, Angola, Sierra Leone and Liberia wars are conducted to control the mineral and biological resources which are the foundation of wealth.

The design and implementation of land policy measures must acknowledge the wide range of stakeholders with an interest in land, and its role both as an economic good, and social and political asset. In some cases, governments have failed to consult adequately and have imposed policies which lack popular support and understanding. Donor institutions have also short-circuited debate through a combination of conditionality (strings attached to loans and aid) or manipulation of the policy process. Growing capacity for self determination, in both government and civil society is opening up the dialogue between stakeholders and ensuring that national elites and external interests can no longer combine to dominate policy choice without regard to the interests of the majority of land users.

In many ways, the last few years have witnessed a reassessment of conventional wisdom regarding land tenure. It often appears that the component pieces of land policy have been thrown in the air, and have yet to fall back to earth. This book, the workshop which led to it, and the continuing debate and interaction amongst African practitioners, scholars, policy makers and opinion leaders are intended to help these elements settle down, into workable approaches. A new paradigm is emerging which does not prescribe a specific approach to land reform. The paradigm is based on pluralism and the imperative of African national, regional and local governments, tribal groups, villages, communities, and civil society organisations negotiating their own solutions to securing access to land

An outline of the book

This book follows the overall thematic structure of the workshop. It examines the linkages between land reform, economic growth, and poverty reduction. It discusses the legislative and practical challenges of tenure reform and the harmonisation of customary and formal land rights in both anglophone and francophone Africa; the management of Africa's commons; the opportunities for and constraints on women's land rights; the institutional arrangements for securing and managing land rights; the challenges of decentralisation; and those policy and implementation processes now underway.

In writing and editing the material for this book the editors have sought to represent the key issues debated at the DFID 1999 workshop at Sunningdale. We have reproduced some of the key papers presented by both African and European land specialists. Because of the sheer number and range of papers presented, we have been selective about those papers reproduced in full, but have sought to do justice to the variety of the papers presented by summarising, and presenting them as case study boxes. In addition, in some chapters (for example Chapters 2 and 8), we have summarised the outcomes of working group debates held at Sunningdale.

The disciplines represented in the book are primarily those of social science, economics, and law. In addition, specialists in natural resource management, agricultural systems, surveying, and land administration, as well as policy makers and planners have contributed material. There are, of course, gaps in the subject matter covered. In particular, we are conscious that the book does not do justice to urban land issues, and the complex dynamics of land use change in peri-urban situations. Nor does it address tenure issues in major resettlement or land development and irrigation schemes. These are questions which are also critical to the livelihoods of the poor in Africa. These and other areas for further research and reflection are considered at the end of this chapter.

The material presented at Sunningdale and edited in this book reflects much of the diverse experience gained by countries in sub-Saharan Africa over the last century. The primary focus has been on the English speaking countries of eastern and southern Africa. The UK government's Department for International Development has been closely engaged with land reform processes, notably in Zimbabwe during the 1980s, in South Africa since 1994, and more recently in Uganda. Parallel material is also represented in this book from French-speaking countries. The chapters range from a synthesis of research findings (Chapters 2, 3 and 5), a pulling together of papers on key themes presented at the Conference - gender, common property resources, the registration of customary rights, and decentralisation (Chapters 8 to 12), and reflections on the processes underway regarding approaches to tenure reform from various practitioners actively engaged in various countries both with the consultation process, design of legislation and implementation (Chapters 4, 6, 7, 13 and 14).

The focus of the papers presented here is largely trained on land as a social and economic asset, fundamental to supporting improved and more sustainable livelihood options for the rural poor. Hence, our interest is in examining whether and how land tenure affects agricultural investment and productivity, as well as assessing the impact of different land tenure programmes on poorer and more vulnerable land users. However, it is also clear that economic functions of land cannot be separated from related aspects. For example, the spiritual role played by customary land chiefs helps strengthen their authority more generally. Authority over land, whether vested in the chiefs, or in government officials and political leaders, can in turn, lead directly to private economic benefits for these actors, derived from land accumulation, patronage, and land transactions. The question of who gains access to land and on what terms can only be understood by seeing how control over land is embedded within the broader pattern of social relations. In some instances, land has acquired powerful symbolic value within the political life of a country. For example, in South Africa, the need to be seen to redress a great historic wrong provides continued momentum behind the land reform process.

The 1999 workshop was seen by many of the participants and by DFID, as the beginning of a process to improve understanding and strengthen collaboration amongst governments, civil society and development agencies. The workshop's key recommendation was that DFID and other donors find ways of facilitating the development of African–owned networking on land issues, as a basis for widening and deepening the learning process. Over the following year, workshop participants and others participated in studies and discussions about how to achieve this objective. A further workshop, held in Addis Ababa in January 2000 in collaboration with African regional organisations, agreed on a way forward for land networks in East, West, Southern, and the Horn of Africa. In the appendix to the book we reproduce the final statement of the Addis Ababa workshop.

LAND POLICY APPROACHES

Myths and conventional wisdom

Land tenure is a field in which there have been major changes of view regarding the best means to control access to land and other resources, and promote their development. A number of myths have continued to provide a powerful grip on the thinking of those responsible for land management and administration, whether in national governments or development agencies. The evolution of approaches to land from colonial times to the present forms a common thread through the early chapters of the book. Platteau, in Chapter 3, attempts to refute several areas of myth or conventional wisdom, such as the need for private title to land to encourage investment. Hardin's thesis (1968) on the Tragedy of the Commons is a marked example of how particular myths have dominated policy debate. He argued the tendency for all systems of shared property to lead to systematic over-use and degradation of the resource base, implying the need to enclose common resources, and privatise their ownership. The appeal of the idea lies in its simplicity and the apparently straightforward actions which follow from acceptance of his thesis. Fortunately, the experience of the last 25 years has enabled a sufficient body of evidence from the field to demonstrate the very limited relevance of this conceptual model in practice. In most cases, collective resources are managed by some kind of institution. As a result, such free and open access as described by Hardin rarely occurs, and the argument in favour of enclosing and privatising the commons falls away. This change in understanding about alternative means to manage collective resources has brought about a much more promising set of approaches. This is of great significance because of the enormous importance of common property resources to the incomes and livelihoods of people in many parts of Africa, and especially those of the poor (see Chapter 8). A second myth that has dominated much tenure policy concerns the need to title land. This has exerted a powerful influence on the thinking of many government officials, despite evidence to show its limited relevance to many African rural contexts.

The changing approaches to land in Africa must be seen as part of a broader picture at a global level. There are clear links between the privatisation agenda pursued by many Western governments from the early 1980s with parallel thinking elsewhere about the need to withdraw government from many aspects of economic life. Loud echoes of such thinking can be heard in the design of structural adjustment programmes imposed on African countries in the 1980s and 90s. Several writers in this book note the loosening up of previous dogma concerning privatisation which came about following the fall of the Berlin Wall, and the consequent willingness amongst Western governments to consider a broader range of approaches to land management. Thus, for example, the formal position of the World Bank has changed markedly from its early statement of principles regarding its approach to land tenure. In 1975, the World Bank emphasised the need to move to private titling. It now acknowledges that this may not always be the right approach and the important role which can be played by customary systems (Box 2.3 in Chapter 2).

However, external sources and interests do not by themselves explain the changing pattern of ideas regarding land tenure in Africa. The assertion of the state's right to own and manage land in many countries after Independence constituted not only a political statement about making available the country's resources to its citizens, but also ensured that the state could acquire the land needed for its own development purposes. At the same time, it established a situation of conflicting and overlapping jurisdictions, within which local officials could benefit from rents gained from interpreting the law in favour of wealthy, and more powerful claimants (Chapter 5; Moorehead, 1996). In many cases, governments remain unwilling to hand over property rights to community groups, or private individuals, because of the loss of power and patronage this would imply.

Above all, the chapters presented here demonstrate that changes to land tenure do not just involve a change in legislation. They require a much broader view of how law relates to public attitudes and behaviour, as well as the institutions available to implement provisions of the new laws. It is increasingly recognised that a mechanistic approach to law and society in which legislators draw up a set of rules by which they wish to transform social behaviour has serious flaws. In practice, legal changes need to reflect and support broader changes in the norms and values expressed within society. Of course, such views are unlikely to be unanimous. Hence the importance of gaining a good sense of how different views are spread across society, through a consultation process. Legal changes in a field such as land tenure must also acknowledge the intensely political nature of the debate, since decisions must be made regarding changes to the current distribution of power and patronage. The choice of locating decision-making in the hands of traditional chiefs has very different implications for local political power structures from choosing to grant these powers to an elected local body. Consequently, local, national and international land tenure debates are likely to be strongly guided by the interests of the various groups involved. Some may lobby very vociferously, while others have access to less transparent methods.

What is the purpose of land reform?

The material presented here shows that there are usually a wide range of objectives being sought by a government in addressing land reform. These involve a mix of political, social and economic aims. In some cases, the main aim has been a redistribution of rights and assets (South Africa, Zimbabwe). In other cases, the aim is to promote economic development, agricultural growth, and more sustainable management, through increased security and incentives to develop land (Ivory Coast, Niger). The government may wish to create an inventory of land to identify available areas for allocation to other purposes, and also to provide the potential basis for local taxation (Ivory Coast). Equally, some countries want to encourage inward investment through providing clearer guarantees regarding security of land rights (Burkina Faso, in Ouedraogo and Toulmin, 1999). In several instances, governments have been pressured to bring in legislation concerning land in order to comply with conditions associated with structural adjustment (such as Burkina Faso, ibid), or new legislation has emerged as a result of donor-led packages for wider reforms, taken up by governments (for instances in Tanzania and Zambia).

The colonial encounter, or why history matters

The starting point for understanding current tenure issues in sub-Saharan Africa requires a backwards look at both pre-colonial systems of land and people management, and the ways in which the establishment of colonial authority affected land. This is described by McAuslan for many English speaking countries, and the phases through which law and its administration have passed (Chapter 4). Thus, he notes the passage from the acquisition of territory by colonial conquest, through destruction and denial of customary law, towards the more recent integration which aims to develop a new common law. In every case described within this book, the colonial administration was keen to establish its ultimate right to control the people and resources under its rule, through declaration of eminent domain (a claim of the state's pre-eminent authority over the nation's land), or its various equivalents.

As Okoth-Ogendo notes for Kenya, Uganda, and Tanzania (Chapter 6), allied to this assertion of state power was a parallel contempt for customary power, and the introduction of English Land law as providing the principles and basis for land administration. This created the legal foundation for the alienation of land to settlers and government appropriating land, as required. Indeed, in many cases, colonial administrators considered that they were introducing concepts of law into a situation where no law had existed before. Ignorance, disregard, and even contempt for customary law continue to this day, in various forms. For example, Mwebaza (Chapter 11) notes that Uganda's 1998 Land Act ignores the potential role which might be played by existing customary structures in managing land and resolving disputes, in favour of the creation of new institutions.

Customary power was not always treated with contempt. On occasion, it provided a valuable aid to administration of the colonial territory, but it needed to be re-cast to fit the roles required of it by colonial government. This recasting strengthened the position of traditional chiefs and conferred powers upon them often much in excess of their pre-colonial rights over land and people (Berry, 1993). Thus as McAuslan notes (Chapter 4):

> Colonial officials used and adapted customary law to suit their own ends… Customary law ceased long ago to be part of traditional society - a bulwark against the colonial authorities - and became instead part of the colonial apparatus of rule.

A similar point is made by Olivier de Sardan (cited in Chapter 5):

> Customary law was derived from the way administrators interpreted rights over land and people as described to them retrospectively by the chiefs at the beginning of the colonial occupation… who tended to over-estimate and often invent the fees due to them, the privileges they held, and the land they controlled.

Countries colonised by the French suffered a similar fate. The transfer of French civil law and conceptions of the state remain clearly visible in the post-Independence political and legal regimes. Both Okoth-Ogendo and McAuslan (Chapters 6 and 4) as lawyers recognise the inherent conservatism of legal practitioners and draftsmen. They tend to follow familiar, well-trod paths, and are reluctant to go for innovative and possibly risky solutions. Thus, texts tend to be couched in highly technical language. They often specify all possible eventualities to avoid uncertainty, and thereby attempt to close-off possibilities for corrupt practice. At the same time, Okoth-Ogendo also recognises that

English legal traditions and judgements continue to play an important role amongst East African lawyers because of the lack of published material stemming from legal process in their own countries.

Approaches to land policy following Independence

For many African countries, Independence was achieved four decades ago. South Africa, Zimbabwe and Namibia provide the exception here, which has generated, in these three countries, a rather different set of land related challenges. Most countries have pursued a range of strategies and approaches to land, as summarised by Quan (Chapter 2). These included nationalisation in the early years, followed by a set of policies to grant private title, redistribute land, and more recently, decentralise land management and grant some form of recognition to customary rights.

Nationalisation of land on Independence followed similar objectives to those pursued by the colonial state. It reflected the desire to acquire absolute authority over land allocation to enable acquisition of land for development purposes and, acting on behalf of the nation, to ensure access to land for all. Thus, post-Independence governments gave themselves the role of trustee in the name of their citizens to enable them to carry out the various responsibilities they assumed to accelerate economic development and grant land where needed to a variety of projects and commercial activities. However, experience showed over the years that the ambitions of the state were frequently far greater than their capacity to manage land effectively. At the same time, vesting trusteeship in the state administration did not ensure that decisions were always taken for the good of ordinary people. Conversely, it was used as a source of political power and patronage essential for holding together the various interest groups on which the state depended (Chapter 6). Equally, the contradictions inherent in the imposition of state ownership on a diverse set of customary management practices opened up areas of confusion (Chapter 5).

In the post structural adjustment era, governments have been forced to scale back their ambitions and budgets in favour of a less interventionist role. In many countries, central government has divested itself of certain rights and responsibilities, and handed these over to a variety of lower level bodies. These bodies take a number of forms, such as District Land Boards, which originated, for Africa, in Botswana in the 1970s (Chapter 10), local Land Commissions (Chapter 11) and elected local government bodies (Chapter 12). At the same time, governments have started to recognise customary rights and encourage their registration in a more formal manner, either at village level, as in Mozambique (Chapter 11) or Tanzania (Chapter 14), or as individual plots, as described for Ivory Coast (Chapter 11).

Following state nationalisation of land, a number of governments were pushed by donors in favour of land titling, on the grounds that customary rights would never be able to provide sufficient basis for agricultural development (see Chapters 2 and 3). It was considered that customary rules regarding land did not provide land users with enough security to encourage investment in raising its productivity, nor could land become a freely marketable asset if still hedged about by social constraints. The emergence of land markets was thought necessary to make sure that land could be transferred through sales to more efficient farmers, who would also be able to use the title deed as collateral for raising credit. The example of land titling programmes demonstrates the dominance of economic theory over a careful consideration of how things work in practice. Kenya provides the best known example of such a programme where the overall effects on livelihoods and poverty are summarised by Quan in Chapter 2. The doubtful economic and social benefits gained from titling programmes are further reinforced by Platteau (Chapter 3). He confirms the negative consequences for poor farmers who were unable to pay for titling of their land, the increased vulnerability for secondary rights holders such as women, and the grabbing of land titles by richer, better-educated people.

Titling represents a salutary example of the way in which a process can have results substantially at odds with those anticipated, because it fails to take into account the way in which different groups of people behave and their differential access to information, money and power. The components of the process were systematically biased towards those with access to knowledge, good links with the state administration, and sufficient resources to pay the costs of titling. Rather than increasing the security of those using the land, titling rendered certain groups increasingly insecure (see Chapters 2 and 3).

Nor did titling bring the gains expected in terms of generating increased investment and productivity. The path-breaking research of Bruce and Migot-Adholla (1994) demonstrated that no differences could be found between levels of productivity and investment when titled land and that held under customary rights were compared (see also Chapter 3). Increasingly, people have come to recognise that there are considerable merits in customary systems for land rights management since they provide a relatively secure means for those who are members of the community, at a lower cost than state-run administrative structures. Many arrangements exist within customary systems which provide flexibility and movement of land between different users, through sharecropping, tenancy, short and long term loans (see Chapter 5). Also, customary systems tend to consider the needs of poor members of their community and prevent the alienation of land from the group as a whole.

Some governments have opted for other measures, such as the redistribution or partial collectivisation of land. This occurred in Ethiopia, Tanzania and

Mozambique during their socialist phases. In Ethiopia, governments sought to control access to land through collectives or peasant associations, to prevent the emergence of a rich peasantry, and to enable periodic redistribution of fields to accommodate changes in household size, and land per family. At the same time, control over land allocation by the local political body provided a means of political control over the rural population. The consequences for Ethiopia are described by Rahmato in Box 2.6 (Chapter 2) as having discouraged any investment in land improvement, leading to reduced area available per person, and growing poverty in rural areas. Experience with redistribution of land in Southern Africa has played a very different role from the case of Ethiopia, and is described in a later section.

The end of the Cold War has prompted a new look at the range of policies which can be used to address the land question, combined with experience from ongoing initiatives. Together these have shown that a broad mixture of policies are possible which go beyond market related, or socialist dogma. There has been a shift in global views towards the need for greater participation by local people in the planning and management of natural resources, and greater emphasis on decentralised approaches. It has also become clear that customary structures may be able to carry out many of the tasks related to land rights. At the same time, policy makers have started to recognise the heavy material and personnel costs associated with creating new institutional structures to carry out land reform. Several papers presented therefore, discuss the need for pragmatic solutions, which move progressively towards the implementation of new provisions, in pilot areas and which build on existing structures, rather than setting up entirely new systems (Chapters 7 and 14).

LESSONS FROM IMPLEMENTATION

Discussions at the DFID workshop covered a number of countries in which governments had become involved in major programmes of land reform (see Chapter 14 for a summary of many of these). The papers presented and edited into this volume show that a lot is happening, following different approaches, and encountering a variety of challenges. In general, processes of land reform have become much more open, engaging debate with a wider group of stakeholders than was formerly the case. These have included:

- Consultation processes, through commissions of enquiry (e.g. Zimbabwe, Tanzania, Malawi, discussed in Chapter 14), national conferences (e.g. Namibia, and the case of Niger, discussed in Chapter 11)
- Legislative debate, through drafting of bills for discussion with lobbying from interested parties and NGOs (e.g. Uganda, Tanzania and Mozambique, Chapter 14)

13

- Pilot programmes to test out new institutions and provisions (Land Commissions in Niger and the Rural Land Plan in Ivory Coast in Chapter 11, land redistribution in South Africa in Chapter 7)
- Nation-wide programmes establishing new structures, such as the system of Land Boards in place in Botswana since the 1970s, and now proposed in Uganda (Chapter 10), village land management in Tanzania, pilot programmes for the registration of customary rights in Niger, Ivory Coast and Mozambique (Chapter 11), and the establishment of Communes Rurales in Mali (Chapter 12).

In Tanzania, Zimbabwe and Malawi, there have been Presidential Commissions of Enquiry involving senior public figures, lawyers and academics and based on widespread consultation. In the case of the Shivji report for Tanzania, and the Rukuni report for Zimbabwe, these Commissions generated very detailed analysis and proposals, which have taken several years to find their way towards implementation. Those proposals at odds with major political interests have been shelved by government. Malawi's highly consultative Presidential Commission (Harawa, 1999; see also Chapter 14) presented its report in 1999, but the uptake of its findings through the political and legislative process is expected to take considerable time.

Implementation is thus at different stages, depending on the country concerned (as discussed in Chapter 14). For example, Uganda is currently considering how best to implement the very ambitious set of activities planned under the Land Act of 1998. In Tanzania, the Lands Act and Village Lands Act passed in 1999 are being reviewed to assess how best to carry out their proposals, with the recognition that it may take several decades (Longway, 1999). In South Africa, certain parts of the land reform programme have been initiated, such as the Land Reform Pilot Programme (Chapter 14). In mid-1999, the draft Land Tenure Reform Bill which had been developed in detail, and has been considered both ambitious and creative, was put on one side by the new Minister of Lands (Chapter 13). In addition, it is recognised that the costs of establishing and staffing the various structures envisaged would be a major undertaking, and particularly difficult in a period of very tight pressure on budgets for education and health (ibid).

The Rural Land Plan of Ivory Coast (Chapter 11) is being taken forward into its next stage, building on the basis of the pilot phase. Its work has, however, been made less straightforward as a result of legislation passed in December 1998, which has set a deadline of December 2008 for the registration of all land. The state will take ownership of any lands left unregistered at this date. While it has provided for the possibility of villages being able to register their lands as a whole, all lands registered under customary use by the Rural Land Plan will need to be converted to formal title within the space of three years.

Currently, there is no provision for villages to constitute a legal entity. Thus, it is very unclear what will happen to lands held under collective ownership. In Niger, subject to donor funding, it is planned to extend the work of the pilot Land Commissions beyond the current eleven, which have been running since 1994. In Ghana, plans are underway to develop new land legislation. As a first step, the government is looking to other countries for possible lessons in land registration procedures. In the case of Mali, the newly established elected Rural Communes are starting work, and will be exploring their role in land allocation and resource management over the forthcoming years.

Common findings

The costs involved

Land reform can be a very expensive business. It involves a lengthy consultation and legislative process, and a major programme of institution building, training, and awareness raising, as well as staff and other costs. For example, in the South African case, it was estimated that the annual costs of setting up and running the institutions required by the Draft Land Bill would be 108 million rand, equivalent to around US$30 million (Chapter 13). In Uganda, estimates of the programme envisaged by the Land Bill come to US$400 million (Chapter 14). However, in terms of cost per unit area, such large figures seem more manageable. For example, in the case of Niger, the per hectare costs of the registration process are reckoned to be the equivalent of US$1.60, though it is unclear whether all costs associated with the Land Commissions have been added into this figure. For Ivory Coast, costs per hectare for the pilot phase of the Rural Land Plan are estimated to average US$7 (Chapter 11).

The expense of carrying out such a programme can be very substantial. Some assessment must therefore be made of whether the expected benefits from such reforms justify the expenditure, given alternative uses of public funds. In the case of Niger, such money is judged as well spent, if it affords the land user relief from further worry and conflict regarding the land holding (Chapter 11). Elsewhere, very little discussion occurs regarding the balance of costs and benefits.

Given the heavy outlays required, some writers note the need to look at alternative models for addressing land issues. This could involve a cheaper, second best solution. In the case of Mozambique, the village lands registration programme was able to build on the commitment of a large number of volunteers who were trained as paralegal guides. Also, because the programme has built on existing structures at village level, the additional costs arising from the need to hire staff and set up new structures can be reduced (see Chapter 11).

Similarly, for Tanzania, the likely costs of implementing the Land Act may be kept low by mandating existing village committees to take on the management of land issues. Nevertheless, some reform and development of official or parastatal institutions for land administration is likely to be needed, because their structures, systems and resource limitations can make them ill-equipped to cope with the challenges of the new approaches.

In the Francophone context, Lavigne Delville (Chapter 5) notes the emergence of indigenous innovations for recording land transactions, which provide a greater sense of security to land holders through the adaptation of a legal process – the *procès verbal de palabre*. Following lengthy discussions (*palabre*), a certificate of agreement may be drawn up with the signature of the parties, customary authorities and representatives of the administration, giving the document official validity. In Burkina Faso, "certificats de palabre" were instituted by the French colonial government and have been highlighted in the latest version of the *Réforme Agraire Foncier (RAF)*. Thus, the availability of a *procès verbal de palabre* is required for a permit to develop parts of the state administered land *(Domain National)*. Furthermore, to clarify the validity of land sales, some prefects will not issue title deeds unless a *procès verbal de palabre* is available. Tallet believes "the recognition of the role which these can play in the current law in Burkina Faso merits attention. It is a path which should be explored to respond to the need for security for rural people who search both the guarantee of social networks and the weight of an official stamp" (1999: 96). Rochegude also draws attention to these little known formalisation mechanisms as a means of recognising customary rights without engaging in a long and complicated legal reform (cited in Lavigne Delville and Mathieu, 1999: 34).

Long term process

From consultation, through pilot approaches to implementation – land reform is a long-term process. Land reform programmes involve establishing new procedures for handling an asset which is at the heart of rural life and agricultural production. There are no quick and easy fixes. In the case of Niger, the process of drawing up the Rural Code began in 1986 and, as of the beginning of 2000 is moving from the pilot to the nation-wide phase. The Secretariat involved in the programme recognises that it will be 'a long, long term process' (Chapter 11). In the case of Ivory Coast, first steps in establishing the Rural Land Plan began in 1988, and it is now broadening out from the pilot phase (ibid.). Similarly, in Tanzania, it is noted that it may take several decades to carry through the proposed changes. In Uganda, work on preparation of the Land Bill of 1998 began in 1988 (Chapter 14). The pace of land reform in South Africa was faster, with the process beginning in 1992 and accelerating with the establishment of the new government of President Mandela in 1994. Yet, it is clear that such speed has put very heavy pressure not only on the officials involved but also on the legislature and the institutional framework required for its potential enactment (Chapter 13).

Accompanying measures

Changes in the law may achieve little without a range of accompanying measures. These include ensuring that people can take advantage of what is being proposed. There are useful examples of materials being translated into local languages, setting up district level seminars and national conferences, paying particular attention to groups less likely to hear of the planned changes, such as women and mobile groups like pastoralists.

Where major changes in land ownership are being proposed, such as redistribution of land to those formerly landless, provision needs to be made for support in the early years of their establishment as independent farmers, through credit, extension and input supply programmes (as described by Quan, Chapter 2). Thought will need to be given to improved access to markets as well. Other necessary changes to the law may also become apparent. For example, there may be inconsistencies between the provisions of new land law and existing laws. A particular case concerns the rights of women to hold and transfer property, which may run counter to provisions under laws relating to the family and inheritance (Chapter 9). As noted in that chapter by Ovonji-Odida (1999), it may be unwise to use land law to achieve major improvements to women's status which are not also acknowledged in other fields of legislation.

It is important to gain feedback on the land reform process, so that lessons are learned and changes may be made. This requires flexibility, so that changes can be made to the different provisions, as well as providing opportunities for different stakeholders to feed their views into the evaluation process. This is of particular importance because African economies, like those everywhere, are undergoing rapid change under the impact of local, national and global processes. Consequently, land reform provisions are likely to have to address new and emerging challenges in the years to come.

The list of necessary accompanying measures may seem daunting and lead to inertia. However, a separate but linked approach is probably the best way forward.

Pre-emptive behaviour prior to implementation of the new provisions

In several cases, it is noted that more powerful stakeholders, such as businessmen, the families of politicians and traditional leaders, and former colonial settlers, as well as ordinary landowners may be manoeuvring themselves to ensure they are well positioned to take advantage of the new situation. This is illustrated by the processes of rangeland enclosure, by wealthy cattle owners in northern Namibia, anticipating the ratification of private rights established by occupation. In Niger it is noted that land owners have been expanding the areas they cultivate, even where this involves little more than a rudimentary clearing of the field, in order to be able to demonstrate the size of their holdings once the law had passed. At the same time, cases were recorded of land owners taking back land which had been lent out to others because of the fear that those actually using the land, as tenants or land borrowers would be attributed rights over the land (Lund, 1993). In the case of Ivory Coast, it was noted that although very few cases of contested land emerged during the process of registering customary claims, it is likely that considerable manoeuvring had taken place prior to the arrival of the land registration team (Chapter 11). In Zimbabwe, in less productive areas, the diversification into safari-hunting and tourism by white settlers, has served to avoid charges of inefficiency and under-utilisation of land, and guard against the risk of compulsory land acquisition for redistribution to poor blacks. For South Africa, Claassens (Chapter 13) notes that:

> In many instances, these disputes hardly existed or were latent before land transfer was on the agenda, but the irrevocable nature of land transfer is an effective alarm clock…

In the case of Uganda, the Implementation Study Report notes that "there has been a certain amount of land-grabbing by opportunists in the hope of acquiring a certificate" (Government of Uganda, 1999), suggesting that people are positioning themselves to take advantage of the changes in legislation (Chapter 14). McAuslan also reminds us that there are bound to be losers, as well as winners, from any land reform programme and that thought must be given to ways of defusing likely action by potential losers to block the impact of the legislation (Chapter 4).

Bridging the divide between customary rights and statutory law

Many of the challenges arising from land reform in sub-Saharan Africa stem from the plurality of systems of authority related to land. While the duality of statutory and customary law constitutes the main divide, Lavigne Delville rightly reminds us that the debate should be conceived more broadly. This is because of the contradictions inherent in statutory law, the range of competing interests within customary systems of land management, and the existence of yet other avenues for redress of land grievances, such as religious authorities (Chapter 5).

The competing jurisdictions of customary and statutory systems provide an ever present element in almost all of the case studies and country material presented here, whether it be in the struggle between traditional authorities and elected land management bodies in South Africa, or the attempts by customary chiefs in Burkina Faso to block the new land legislation (Ouedraogo and Toulmin, 1999). Following Independence, many governments attempted to break the power of customary chiefs by the state taking formal ownership of land. In some cases, chiefly structures were considered feudal or archaic, such as during the Sankara regime in Burkina Faso (ibid). In the case of Ethiopia, they were swept away with the fall of the Imperial system and the establishment of the Derg (Rahmato in Chapter 2).

Attempts to do away with customary chiefs were only partially successful, given the weak authority of central government in many countries, and their inability to exert de facto control over land management and allocation. Hence, customary systems remained important in many areas on a day-to-day basis with the state stepping in to assert its rights only in circumstances where it wished to achieve certain aims, such as the alienation of land for government purposes, like urban development, the establishment of an irrigation scheme, or setting up a national park.

Subsequent manoeuvres by government to establish alternative systems of local government have produced a mixed response, such as the Committees for the Defence of the Revolution in Burkina Faso, the creation of decentralised local government in Senegal in 1972, or the new land law in Uganda (Mwebaza, 1999). In some cases, customary chiefs have been able to dominate these new structures through a variety of manoeuvres, by ensuring that they get a representative to sit on the new body and act for them. Elsewhere, such as in Ghana, customary chiefs have retained important powers over land, since paramount chiefs are responsible for administration of land transactions through a register (Kasanga, 1999).

One way in which governments have tried to take over the powers of customary chiefs has been by setting up decentralised bodies to administer and allocate land. The District Land Boards in Botswana are considered by many a good example of how traditional powers can be reined-in by a local structure which draws on a wider set of interests and stakeholders (see Chapter 10). This has led to a more locally accountable pattern of land management, since it involves a mix of elected representatives as well as government appointees. Land Boards are considered by some to operate in favour of the elite, and to pursue the agenda of central government. Currently, there are few channels by which the poor can express their concerns and insufficient checks on the decisions made by Land Boards. Namibia and Uganda plan to follow a similar pattern and set up local land boards, as was also proposed for South Africa (Chapter 13).

Concerns about these local structures relate to the make-up of such Boards, the proportion of elected versus appointed members, and the need to ensure effective representation of less vocal groups. It may be necessary to have a specific number of seats set aside for women and minority groups to ensure their views are heard, and to find ways of strengthening their capacity to intervene effectively within the discussions held. A further concern relates to the cost of establishing these structures and the lack of any clear linkage with existing arrangements for managing land. In the case of Uganda, it has become clear that funds will not be adequate to cover the setting up of the several thousand institutions proposed under the Land Act 1998. As a result, options for simplifying the arrangements will need to be made (Nsamba-Gayiiya in Chapter 10).

A second approach to addressing the need to bring together customary and formal systems of land administration can be seen with the various programmes undertaken to register customary rights. This approach may involve rights both at the collective level, as when a village registers the lands over which it exercises control, and at an individual or household level, such as through registration of plots. The first approach has been followed in Mozambique, and represents a relatively simple measure which maps village boundaries, and attributes rights and responsibilities for land management to a village level body (Chapter 11). This is also the pattern proposed for Tanzania under the Village Land Act. Advantages include its relative ease and speed, since it does not involve the mapping and registering of many thousands of individual plots.

Gestion de terroir (literally "village lands management") found in many Francophone countries, is a variant of this approach, but confers lesser rights over land. Villagers are transferred the responsibility for management and planning land use but without any formal powers to control access. Local conventions are an emerging institutional innovation in several Sahelian countries (see Chapters 5 and 8) which aim for formal recognition of collective rights to manage, control access, fine users, issue permits and make by-laws. There are as yet only a few pilot examples. Governments are often unwilling to transfer too much power to these institutions since it means a loss of power and patronage for local officials, and also leads to a break with the idea of all citizens receiving equal access to resources.

Experience with registering rights at individual or household level is provided from Ivory Coast and Niger (Chapter 11). In both cases the procedure involves the mapping of boundaries and registration of the land owner in a land register. In the case of Niger, however, the subsequent certificate constitutes a formal title to the land, whereas in Ivory Coast, it carries lesser legal weight. All subsequent transactions involving the plots of land which have been registered are meant to be recorded to keep the record up to date. One of the main purposes behind setting up the Rural Land Plan (PFR) in Ivory Coast has been to provide a greater level of security and promote investment in agriculture. It is too early to judge whether the latter goal will be achieved. Regarding increased security, it should be noted that while some people may find their rights made more secure by such a process, others may be adversely affected. Early evidence from Ivory Coast shows the difficulties encountered by the project teams in addressing the complexity of actual practice as regards customary arrangements by which people gain access to land (Chauveau et al, 1996). A simple categorisation into land owner and land user masks the many variants of secondary rights existing, and may have made more vulnerable groups lose out. The PFR has now developed a broader set of categories for recording the rights people claim to land which should lead to a registration procedure which is more faithful to field-level realities. Yet this may not be able to deal with the rights of many immigrants within Ivory Coast, who may have been resident for many years, but do not have Ivorian nationality and, hence, cannot be considered a valid land owner (Stamm, 2000).

Recognising common property resource management systems

Cousins makes clear the great importance of common pool resources for the livelihoods of many rural populations (Chapter 8). In the case of South Africa, it is estimated that such resources provide US$ 1.6 billion to the national economy. Yet, "few policy makers appear to take the high value of common pool resources into account, despite the high costs to society that would be incurred if all the goods and services provided from the commons had to be supplied by the state or purchased from supplies in the market place" (ibid.).

In drier regions, a large part of the land area may be used as common grazing land, of critical significance for pastoral populations who must maintain a mobile pattern of land use to ensure the well-being of their herds. Pastoral and agro-pastoral peoples, often the poorest and most vulnerable to drought and conflict, continue to be marginalised by land policy and by project-led land use change despite the fact that mobile grazing of the commons provides the most rational and successful management and livelihood strategy in Africa's semi-arid rangelands. While Hardin's thesis of the Tragedy of the Commons led to the view that common lands must be privatised to prevent their degradation, much current thinking stresses that solutions are possible by conferring rights and supporting user groups to maintain responsibility for the management of such areas. Nevertheless, there remains some resistance to grant firm rights over common resources which some governments see as being without a proper master and, thus, falling to the state to administer.

Alternatives to the maintenance of state control over these areas have been proposed by the 'new institutionalist' perspective of common property resource management which emphasises the possibility of institutional arrangements and rule-making by local bodies to manage common pool resources effectively (Ostrom, 1990; Chapter 8). Although this approach provides a more positive and realistic perspective on the management of common or collective resources, it has nevertheless come in for recent criticism from academic quarters on several grounds (Peters, 1994; Leach et al, 1997). These include the tendency to ignore the often highly differentiated nature of rural society. This means that "the community" is, by no means, a simple homogeneous grouping with common interests. Some groups may be systematically excluded from decision-making and may not get their views heard. Equally, the emphasis on rules may be over-stated. Rules are not necessarily set in stone, but are subject to contest and negotiation. Also, the boundaries between resource groups are often fuzzy, and much less tightly defined than is outlined by the new institutionalists. There may be the need to consider a range of levels at which different decisions need to be made rather than a single instance. Hence, for example, certain resources such as wetlands, woodland or grazing areas may be shared by several such groupings.

It must be asked, however, whether these criticisms negate the arguments in favour of community-based management arrangements. Rather, such worries help serve as a reminder of the need to try and modify the operation of management systems to ensure their weaknesses are addressed. This might involve encouraging representation of certain groups whose views tend to be excluded, and establishing means by which resources spanning several such groups can best be dealt with. In some cases, it may be appropriate to leave management of the commons to evolving customary practice, while strengthening systems for dispute resolution to ensure that these are equitable and transparent. It may also make sense, in the case of high value and diminishing resources, to introduce formal safeguards to prevent over-utilisation and resource degradation by customary, or other users. The ideal solution must lie in a nested structure of institutions, in which subsidiarity determines the appropriate level for any particular kind of decision.

Taking on the challenge of land redistribution

It was evident from papers and discussions at Sunningdale that certain countries face very particular challenges to tenure reform given past seizure and settlement of the best land during the colonial period. Thus, in Namibia, South

Africa and Zimbabwe, large scale, predominantly white, commercial farmers remain a considerable political and economic force to be reckoned with. The inequality of land distribution is very marked. For example, in South Africa, 80% of the country was previously reserved for white people, while 13% was available for black people (Chapter 13). Equally, in Zimbabwe, Moyo notes that:

> Some 4,500 large scale mostly white commercial farmers dominate Zimbabwe's agricultural sector, denying access to the bulk of the nation's resources for over six million people, who must live in the more marginal areas (Chapter 2).

However it is not only the proportion of the land held by such a small group but also the fact that this usually covers much of the most productive land of the country. These politically powerful groups generate substantial agricultural output for domestic food supplies and export markets. They argue that all this will be put in jeopardy by major redistribution programmes. There is also an emergent black elite in all three countries who see opportunities for gain from taking over these farms in their entirety, rather than seeing them sub-divided into many thousands of small holdings.

The economic arguments in favour of large scale farmers are, however, not well founded. The economic performance of commercial farms in these countries has often been dependent on structures of government support for research, extension, credit, inputs and access to markets, which assured them a preferential position. Once changes to these policies had been brought in, following Independence, the strong economic performance of these farms was shown to be more apparent than real. Equally, it is now generally acknowledged that small farms tend to be more productive than large in terms of output per hectare (Chapters 2 and 3). They also provide a better spread of incomes and assets and promote greater rural employment than a system based on a few large landowners and many farm-workers or tenants. However, there may be need in the interim period following redistribution of holdings, to support new farmers establish themselves and gain experience with marketing, access to inputs, research and extension advice.

Addressing gender and land tenure

Gender issues loom large in the current policy debate, cutting across discussion of customary and formal tenure systems, both of which have marginalised women's rights. Gender equality in land rights will, moreover, involve wider changes in socio-cultural attitudes, and strengthening of women's rights under the constitution, family and inheritance law.

Women tend to have subordinate roles in relation to land in both customary and statutory systems. Under the former, land usually belongs to and is managed by a patrineal group, so that women are always secondary users, whether as daughters, sisters, wives or mothers. Their rights of access are highly dependent on the social ties which link them to those with primary rights over land. Hence, for example, on divorce or widowhood, women may be forced to leave their land behind and to move away (Chapter 9). Even within modern systems, women may have lesser rights to those of men, or have their rights subsumed into the broader household, the head of which is usually assumed to be male. However, conditions are changing. In some customary situations, women are achieving firmer rights and recognition of their major contribution to household incomes and livelihoods.

In formal law, women's situation is improving in most countries, with new legislation ensuring that women's rights are considered on an equal footing to those of men. The question remains how best to improve women's position in relation to land, and the extent to which this should be through formal legal changes, or broader measures. While changes in the law are obviously important as embodying principles concerning the status of women, law cannot by itself achieve improved positions for women without understanding the place of women in society as a whole. Statutory law tends to treat women more favourably than under customary law, yet it is usually very difficult to see these provisions implemented. It may be just as important to ensure that women have good access to services and economic opportunities, such as health, education, credit, markets, etc. In addition, affirmative action may need to be considered, such as taking special care that women have access to information about legal changes, since they tend to be less in touch with formal processes, as well as working with officials to ensure they understand better the perspective of women and take their views into account in a systematic manner.

Other secondary rights-holders

Customary systems provide a wide array of arrangements by which people can gain access to land and other resources, even though they are not land owners themselves. These include sharecropping, borrowing of land, tenancy, pledges, and access for a particular purpose, such as grazing of crop residues. These arrangements are important because they provide flexibility within rural economies and enable land to be made available to those with surplus labour on negotiable terms. They also provide a means by which poor groups without land of their own can nevertheless gain access to resources. The social relations between borrower and lender are usually of significance in terms of ensuring access and the terms of the arrangement. The terms of such agreements may change where the borrower no longer adheres to expected social conventions. The papers presented at Sunningdale and within this book have paid relatively little attention to the position faced by secondary rights holders, suggesting this is a field where further attention is needed.

THE ROAD AHEAD

The papers presented and discussions held at the Sunningdale workshop highlighted a number of important findings, as well as setting the context for an ongoing learning process amongst government officials, donor agencies, researchers, NGOs and other actors. While the historical, political and economic context within which land policy and tenure reforms are taking place differ greatly from country to country, there are several general lessons which can be drawn out, as summarised below in Box 1.1.

Land and poverty

Land has a particularly significant role to play for securing the livelihoods of poorer rural people. A large number of developing countries as well as OECD nations, have pledged themselves to reducing very substantially the number of people living in absolute poverty by the year 2015. National strategies to combat poverty are either being drawn up, or in place in countries such as Uganda, Ghana, and Mali. Such strategies have sought to ensure a more coherent approach to addressing poverty across the different areas of government. In the case of land policy, there are several important means by which a pro-poor agenda might be developed. These include the following:

● Aiming for a more equal pattern of land distribution, to promote both more equitable and possibly higher rates of growth, and improved security to land users operating under diverse forms of tenure;

● Adopting a pluralistic approach, which seeks convergence of customary and formal tenure systems, to avoid overlapping and conflicting sets of rights;

● Identifying diverse ways in which reforms in land relations can be approached.

Comprehensive country-wide reforms may not necessarily bring the best results. A range of other options also need consideration. These include:

● Targeting assistance for the poor to gain access to land and natural resources, such as through brokerage of negotiations between local communities, state agencies and the private sector;

● Creating an enabling policy and legal framework, which promotes sub-

---

Box 1.1: Key findings from the Sunningdale Workshop

1. There are many approaches to addressing land policy and tenure changes in Africa, as well as a growing body of experience with implementing reforms. This provides a sound basis for sharing experience between different countries and stakeholders. A mechanism to facilitate this process of learning lessons would be very valuable.

2. Governments have been forced to recognise the relatively limited role they can play in direct allocation and management of land. Nevertheless, they retain an important set of tasks concerning the framework of law and underlying principles. They must establish the authority of those institutions given the powers to manage land and resolve conflicts. Also, there may be need for a significant redistribution of land between different groups.

3. Law needs to draw upon the values and aspirations held by society, and cannot be drafted in a vacuum. Hence, widespread consultation processes are needed to permit effective engagement by a broad range of actors, in discussion of proposed legal reforms and the institutional options for implementation.

4. Reforms to land tenure and administration have major political implications. Choices must be made about attribution of responsibilities and rights, such as between reliance on established customary systems and the establishment of elected local government structures. In each case, there will be pros and cons, with neither choice offering a perfect solution. Thought must be given to providing checks and balances on the powers attributed, whichever institutional option is chosen.

5. Many land reform programmes have begun with pilot measures to test out their feasibility and need for amendment before launching a nation-wide approach. Use of pilot schemes seems much more appropriate than trying to do everything at once, since it allows for a focus on priority areas where land issues have become acute, as well as learning how best to tailor reforms to fit local conditions.

6. Governments face tight budgetary constraints and need to consider the costs of land reform measures in the light of their likely benefits. There may be considerable advantages to building on existing institutions, modified as necessary, rather than trying to establish a brand new set of structures which require staff, operating budgets, and time to establish their legitimacy.

7. There has been systematic neglect of resource and tenure systems which do not fall into the neat categories of conventional land law. Hence, pastoral grazing rights, common property resource management systems, the position of women, and the wide range of institutional arrangements by which people gain access to resources always appear, if at all, as an after-thought to debate on land policy. This is despite the enormous importance of the commons for securing rural livelihoods, the pivotal role of women in ensuring the food needs of many farming households, and the economic value of the pastoral livestock sector to many African countries.

8. Contempt of customary law remains common in many countries. Even where registration of customary land use is underway, establishing private title to land often remains the underlying purpose of land reform. Yet, registration of collective rights could be a much simpler, cheaper and, potentially far more equitable process.

9. Processes of land policy and tenure reform take time and require an iterative approach. Establishing new systems and implementing new legislation will require a strategic choices to be made, and a feedback mechanism set up to allow amendments to be made as lessons are learned. The many components of civil society have a valuable part to play in helping to guide government position its land policy in relation to social, economic and political objectives.

sidiarity, and devolves authority to local and indigenous institutions, whilst ensuring access and transparency in land administration and tribunal / judicial processes;

● Keeping processes simple, promoting awareness of rights, translation of laws and rights information into local languages;

● Strengthening consultation processes, debates within civil society, and easier access to the official policy and legislative processes.

Land as a cross-sectoral issue

Land policy and tenure reform processes need to be set within the broader objectives and programmes pursued by government, to ensure a consistent approach. Such linkages with other areas of policy should also enable these different activities to build constructively on interventions underway in their respective domains. Thus, for example, as noted earlier, it may be problematic trying to improve the security of women's rights of access to land without opening up a much broader discussion regarding the rights of women within society more generally. Equally, a change in the legal provisions over land in favour of poorer farmers may achieve little without understanding the constraints under which they operate and the limited economic opportunities they face. Many of the participants at the Sunningdale workshop observed that land reform had to be considered a long-term process. This requires a strong commitment from government, a willingness to learn lessons as implementation proceeds, and a clear-sighted strategy for ensuring land reform supports and is supported by complementary measures to address poverty, increase agricultural productivity, and manage land in a more sustainable manner.

Areas for further work

Presentations at a three day workshop cannot hope to cover the full range of issues and concerns regarding land tenure in contemporary Africa. It was decided to concentrate on rural land issues, new legal and policy approaches to land management in different countries, and the challenges now being faced in their implementation. Discussions at the workshop identified areas which have been neglected, as well as those fields in which further work could generate valuable new findings.

As noted in the introduction to this chapter, the Sunningdale workshop did not pay explicit attention to the rapid changes in land values and markets in urban and peri-urban areas. Nor were tenure rights and issues associated with particular kinds of resource given much attention, such as those linked to water, forestry, fisheries, or minerals. Each of these sectors presents a set of challenges which need to be addressed which have characteristics peculiar to the resource in question, the range of actors with an interest in the resource and its mode of exploitation.

The area of secondary rights-holders requires greater thought to identify ways of providing greater security to many such groups, while maintaining the high level of flexibility within the local economy such arrangements permit. Such rights are of particular importance for major groups such as women, pastoralists, fishing peoples and other mobile forms of land user. They frequently lack political power and, hence, risk seeing their rights neglected. The associated field of common property resource management equally would benefit from further work, with the aim of encouraging governments to recognise and confirm collective rights to manage these resources effectively. This would require acknowledgement of their rights to establish by-laws, control access to the resource, impose fines, and so on.

Another area which was discussed at Sunningdale but which would merit much greater attention concerns the rapid growth in land transactions and the evolution of innovative arrangements to provide more secure rights. Markets in land rights are active throughout Africa, whether within customary or formal systems. Under the pressures of market forces and growing land values, many customary systems have come to accept permanent land alienation, particularly in peri-urban areas. Urban development and the growing value of land for uses other than agriculture are major forces driving the development of a market in land ownership rights[1]. Such transactions take place not just between individuals, companies and public bodies but also between social units such as lineages. A robust understanding of markets in land rights in customary tenure system requires such a broad approach (see Box 2.7, Chapter 2). While the number of land transactions is accelerating, many of them are technically illegal. People are trying to assure themselves some level of security, such as by increased reliance on paper documentation described above (Lavigne Delville and Mathieu, 1999). However, it would be helpful to find ways of formally recognising and making more secure the transfer of rights associated with these transactions.

---

1 Pressures for marketisation of land derive not only from demand of rich or powerful elites, landholders in poor regions of Africa may find that selling their land is the only means of obtaining funds needed for unforeseen or large costs. For example, in some parts of Africa, it is increasingly the case that families depleted by illnesses such as AIDS are forced to sell vital productive assets such as cattle, tools or land to pay for medical care, funerals or the hire of additional labour. In the SADC region, it is estimated that around 12 percent of the adult population is now infected with HIV. The implications of this have yet to be fully addressed.

Networks for the future

As noted in the introduction to this chapter, since February 1999, workshop participants and other stakeholders have been reflecting on how to support a more systematic way of sharing experience between the different actors engaged with the land policy and tenure reforms currently under way in many parts of Africa. Four sub-regional groups have developed plans for a set of activities to carry out over the next few years. The overall purpose of such networks is to provide a means to build consensus on progressive, workable and acceptable land policies in the interests of all stakeholders. Objectives include to share experience and lessons from good practice to improve management of land issues, develop institutional and individual capacities in this field, and provide support for different stakeholders to engage with and influence the decision-making and implementation processes related to land. In addition, each group has identified a series of themes on which further work needs to be done, which build on those identified above, such as gender and land, conflict management, land tenure, land use and decentralisation, and the evolution of land markets, particularly in peri-urban areas. The final statement from the January 2000 networking meeting held in Addis Ababa can be found in Appendix 1.

2

Land Tenure, Economic Growth and Poverty in Sub-Saharan Africa

Julian Quan

INTRODUCTION: POVERTY AND TENURE

Poverty and livelihoods

Sub-Saharan Africa is recognised as facing the greatest and most intractable problems in addressing poverty and achieving more sustainable livelihoods for the rural and urban poor. As shown by the UNDP Human Development Index, per capita incomes, literacy and life expectancy are low in comparison with most other developing regions, while the incidence of malnutrition and endemic disease is generally high (see Table 1). The predominant economic activity for the majority of people in most countries is agriculture. Farming systems and food security are vulnerable to drought and external shocks, particularly in semi-arid areas, and in areas of high population density, even where the productive potential is good. In recent decades, the combination of armed conflict, a fragile ecological resource base and climatic uncertainty has led to the displacement of a large number of people, and severe famine in a number of countries.

Table 2.1: Comparison of Human Development Indicators 1997

Developing country regions	Life expectancy at birth	Adult literacy	Real GDP per capita (PPP$)
Latin America & Caribbean	69.5 years	87.2 %	6,868
East Asia	70.0 years	83.4 %	3,601
South Asia	62.7 years	52.2 %	1,803
Sub-Saharan Africa	48.9 years	58.5 %	1,534

Source: UNDP, 1999

Land and poverty

Since land is a primary means of both subsistence and income generation in rural economies, access to land, and security of land rights, are of primary concern to the eradication of poverty. In rural areas, land is a basic livelihood asset, the principal form of natural capital from which people produce food and earn a living. Access to land enables family labour to be put to productive use in farming, generates a source of food, and provides a supplementary source of livelihoods for rural workers and the urban poor. The grazing of livestock on extensive rangelands is a basic livelihood activity for pastoralists and access to pasture land is also important to supplement the livelihoods of arable farmers. Gathering fruits, leaves and wood from common lands is an important regular source of income for women and poorer households, as well as constituting a vital coping strategy for the wider population in times of drought and famine. Land can be loaned, rented or sold in times of hardship, and thereby provides some financial security. At the same time, as a heritable asset, land is the basis for the wealth and livelihood security of future rural generations.

In most parts of sub-Saharan Africa, unlike much of Asia and Latin America, land is relatively evenly distributed. The exceptions are parts of Southern Africa, where colonial settlers concentrated productive land into large private estates and where, as a result, land-related poverty is marked. Most rural African households have access to a plot of land, plus a wider area of common land for grazing, gathering and hunting. Access is guaranteed by customary systems of tenure, in which kinship confers usufruct rights to lands held, and managed by extended family lineages. Customary systems of land tenure and management are changing, however, because of a decline in the availability of agricultural and common land. This results in part from population growth, but also from technical change, the increased level of commercial activity, and the reservation of public lands for conservation and other uses.

Economic growth and poverty

Attempts to reverse the economic decline prevalent in Africa in the 1970s and 1980s have been based upon market-led economic reforms aimed at encouraging export growth and private investment. It is widely accepted that economic growth is a necessary condition for the reduction of poverty. Even where growth does not directly benefit the poor, it can do so indirectly, for instance through improved provision of rural services, employment or safety nets. Statistical studies show that generally, during times of economic growth, the incomes of the poorest sections of society also tend to increase (Deininger and Squire, 1997). However, income is not the only measure of poverty, or well-

---

Box 2.1: Types of land reform undertaken in sub-Saharan Africa

i) Land nationalisation

Most African countries, following independence, vested land rights ultimately in the state or president. The purposes of nationalisation were to assert the power of the state over traditional chiefs and allow the appropriation of land for development, in the belief that the state would be best placed to manage and distribute land in the interests of all. Although the political power of indigenous chiefs and courts has been marginalised by land nationalisation, the impacts have been uneven, depending on the extent to which the state has been able to exert its own authority. In practice, many states have maintained multiple tenure systems, including public ownership, customary tenure and leasehold, and freehold title.

ii) Tenure reform: land registration and titling

The introduction of formal titles, through granting of individual leases or freeholds, has been introduced, notably in Kenya, following processes of land survey, adjudication and registration. A number of other countries have also pursued this approach on a more limited scale. The aim has been to promote farm investment and land markets as a basis for agricultural development and growth. Land registration, and sometimes titling, have also been introduced as a voluntary measure, such as in Nigeria.

iii) Agrarian reform: land redistribution and resettlement

In other cases, where inherently inequitable dualistic systems of land tenure have predominated, such as Zimbabwe and South Africa, the main approach to land reform has been the redistribution of private holdings to small producers, under different forms of tenure and land management. Various approaches have been taken, predominantly state-led, but more recently market-based.

iv) Agrarian collectivisation

Following the overthrow of colonial or feudal regimes, socialist oriented African governments, notably in Mozambique, Ethiopia and Angola, have converted private estates to state farms, while promoting the cooperative association of small producers and forms of communal labour. In Tanzania and parts of Mozambique, rural life was reorganised by villagisation programmes, relocating people and extinguishing pre-existing customary rights to land. More recently, following structural adjustment and political change, state farms and collective production units have been privatised or divided up.

v) Land development projects and protected areas

De facto changes in tenurial relations have also occurred as a result of land development and conservation programmes rather than because of an explicit demand for land reform. For example, project led resettlement or land registration have occurred as a result of major infrastructure or irrigation development. Another example is the creation of parks or reserves where local people have been displaced, or their land and resource rights have been restricted.

(iv) Efforts to reaffirm and recoqnise customary rights

More recent approaches to land reform in sub-Saharan Africa aim to provide customary rights holders with real security. This may involve some form of codification of customary law and or registration of customary rights, on an individual but also a kinship-based or community basis. It may also involve work to support and develop local institutions for the management and zoning of land, for instance through the "Gestion des terroirs" programmes in West Africa.

Source: Quan, 1997

---

being, and growth can also lead to growing inequality, with benefits for the rich at the expense of the poor, whose asset base may be further eroded. The situation of the poor in relation to land and natural resources may require particular attention during periods of economic growth in order to ensure an equitable spread of benefits. Development practitioners now employ the concept of "pro-poor economic growth" to focus greater attention on the need to consider the distributional impacts stemming from economic growth.

Land reform, economic growth and development

Many African governments and international donors have attributed the problems of rural poverty, poor agricultural output, and low levels of economic development to the persistence of farming systems based on customary tenure. This view has inspired a variety of approaches to land reform, whereby tenure arrangements have been formalised, vesting the rights to land in the state itself, or individual farmers, through the issue of titles. Land reform has a chequered history in Africa, however, and the approaches range from land registration and titling – through which those who benefit obtain very strong individual rights – to the collectivisation of production and egalitarian land distribution – through which farmers obtain generally rather weak use rights to plots owned by the state. Box 2.1 summarises the approaches to land reform adopted by independent African nations over the last forty years.

Economic analysis supports the view that the contribution of land to economic growth depends upon the security, duration and enforceability of property rights, since these provide an incentive for agricultural investment, and help develop markets to rent and sell land (Deininger and Feder, 1999). Land markets, in theory, enable the transfer of land from less to more efficient producers, thereby increasing yields and agricultural output. Orthodox economic analysis argues that only individualised tenure can confer certainty in land rights, facilitate access to credit, and foster the emergence of such land markets. Consequently, economic reform, especially during the years of structural adjustment led by international finance institutions, has generally sought to underpin agricultural growth with systems to provide secure individual land ownership. However, recent evidence and critical analysis contests such an approach on the basis that social relations within and between local communities in rural African society have been able to provide generally secure rights to land. Frequently the land rights involved are individual, transferable and enforceable under customary law and practice, approximating Western property rights and conferring similar benefits. Nevertheless, conventional wisdom about rural development in Africa has continued to argue in favour of replacing customary systems of land management with what are considered to be more secure forms of individual tenure, through the issue of land titles.

LAND REGISTRATION AND TITLING

Secure individual tenure, and a free land market, have been promoted in the belief that they will lead to higher levels of agricultural investment and productivity and thus provide a firm basis for national economic growth and development. Customary land management has been perceived as an obstruction to development, because of the *insecurity* of land rights deemed to be inherent under such arrangements, and the view that land is too strongly associated with non-monetary cultural values in Africa (see for example Dorner, 1972; World Bank, 1974; Harrison, 1987). Customary tenure is believed to provide poor incentives for land investment by the farmer, and cannot be the basis for access to credit nor enable a market in land to develop which could ensure its allocation to the most efficient users. Following this line of argument, agricultural growth requires the conversion of kinship-based systems of customary tenure, in which land is not a saleable commodity, to formal, individual land titles which can be traded. Free market theories predict that increased agricultural growth will follow, bringing benefits not only to those receiving title directly, but also to the poor as a result of more employment, cheaper food, and other "trickle down" effects.

However, empirical evidence tends to refute this pessimistic view of customary tenure, which in reality, is more complex and less inimical to economic growth. The introduction of individualised titles, by contrast, has in practice benefited powerful private interests, creating opportunities for land concentration in the hands of political and other local elites, with few safeguards for the non-formalised land rights of rural communities. There is no clear evidence to show that land titling has led to greater agricultural growth. The links between formalised, individual property rights on the one hand, and the emergence of land markets and the availability of credit on the other, are also questionable (see Chapter 3, this volume). In many cases, improvements in the supply of credit, to which land titles supposedly enable greater access, have simply not been forthcoming for smallholders. On the other hand, titling has in some cases led to increasing landlessness and poverty, by undermining the livelihoods of those depending on customary land rights (see Box 2.2 which summarises the impacts of individual land titling in Kenya).

Many aspects of customary tenure arrangements are now recognised as compatible with economic growth, even by analysts at the World Bank, which has for a long time been closely associated with the promotion of land titling in Africa (see Box 2.3). These include:

● Customary tenure frequently includes heritable use rights which can, by their nature, provide incentives for longer term investments in land improvement.

- Customary property rights can be very secure, even if not defined at the individual level; indeed rights defined at the extended family or community level are often the most appropriate arrangement. This is especially true in circumstances of lower population density, more subsistence-oriented production, and without significant market infrastructure and specialisation.
- The social acceptability of customary tenure arrangements is a paramount consideration in the process of their development. The recognition of a variety of different interests in a single area of land seeks to maximise the potential productive use of resources by a number of different stakeholder groups.
- Intra-community land loans, rentals, sharecropping and sales allow customary land users many of the efficiency advantages previously thought to be available only via individual titles and formal land markets (Deininger and Feder, 1999) while providing opportunities for land access for the landless.

The evolution of the World Bank's land policy is of interest because it reflects wider historical changes in understanding amongst researchers and policy makers, and because the World Bank and other Western donors have tended to dominate debate on land tenure, particularly in sub-Saharan Africa. It should be noted however that the new openness in World Bank policy on land is not always or necessarily reflected in practice by its operational divisions.

Key questions which tenure reform must address concern:

- Under what circumstances do existing tenure arrangements (often combining customary practice and formal rules) fail to provide secure enough access to resources to protect the rural poor from absolute poverty?
- Where these fail, what sort of state intervention is appropriate to ensure that land tenure arrangements provide both sufficient security and effective incentives for sustainable farm production, investment and livelihoods?

These questions are best addressed through an understanding of African customary tenure arrangements, their interface with formal systems, and how they can evolve in response to population growth, and wider political and economic changes. Rising population density, access to markets, economic specialisation and land values are all likely to increase the importance of investment, and access to credit, bringing a greater pay-off from formalised land ownership (Deininger and Feder, 1999).

However, in many circumstances a variety of measures are available which can increase the security and productivity of customary land users, without the need for major legislative changes. These include the introduction of simple systems of land rights documentation, boundary definition and support for the

Box 2.2: The impacts of land titling on poverty in Kenya

Land tenure reform in Kenya was originally introduced in the colonial period by the Swynnerton Plan of 1954 with the political objective of counter-insurgency. It was hoped to create a class of "yeoman farmers" amongst the Kikuyu, to help foster political stability. The Plan aimed to provide individualised tenure security and to stimulate farm investment, agricultural growth and the emergence of a land market. The programme was maintained following independence, and expanded nation-wide. Kenyan nationals were granted individual titles to portions of former colonial settler estates and fragmented customary holdings were subject to compulsory consolidation. Further consolidation was expected as a result of market transactions in land while administrative benefits were anticipated from the creation of an organised record of property rights. The titling and registration process remains incomplete and, in principle, is still continuing. The programme has had a wide variety of unanticipated effects, which include the finding that sub-division of holdings and customary patterns of land allocation and inheritance have in fact persisted, despite registration. This has meant that the expected free market in land has not materialised, the availability of agricultural credit has not significantly increased, and registers are becoming outdated, as heirs or lessees fail to renew registration.

In addition, land registration has been accompanied by:
● increased concentration of land ownership, especially in the hands of the recipients of former settler land, and those influential enough to manipulate the registration process in their own interests;
● the weakening of customary rights, within households and between different social groups, resulting in diminished security of tenure for non-title holders, notably wives, children and landless farmers who can no longer rely on secondary claims or kinship ties to guarantee access to resources. Particularly, registration has brought about increased insecurity amongst women, especially widows, those without off-farm incomes, and those with no male heirs;
● heightened inequalities in land ownership and agricultural incomes, leading to increased landlessness through land sales, and growing rural-urban migration;
● rising rural unemployment, caused by reduced opportunities for share-cropping and tenancy opportunities;
● diminished food security and increased vulnerability to drought amongst groups whose access to land has been diminished by the titling process;
● increased level of disputes resulting from individual rights being imposed on pre-existing systems of multiple rights; and
● the inability of poorer farmers to acquire title, since the costs are often greater than the benefits.

For the direct beneficiaries, land titling has provided very secure tenurial rights, and the early phases of the programme were indeed accompanied by increases in farm income for recipients of title. However, it is difficult to disaggregate the impacts of tenure reform from the many other agricultural development programmes, carried out in the post independence period. While debate about the effects of land registration and titling continues, the policy implications of Kenya's long experience with titling show that:
● the process of registration has been very costly, and the net benefits ambiguous;
● tenure reform alone is not likely to enhance smallholder production without a range of associated measures;
● land titling tends to generate damaging impacts on the position of the poor.

The President has now appointed a Land Commission to review the whole system of Kenyan land policy and law, following recognition of the need to accommodate better certain aspects of customary tenure (see Chapter 6, this volume).

Sources: Bruce, 1986; Green, 1987; Okoth-Ogendo, 1982; Migot-Adholla et al, 1994

Box 2.3: Evolution of the World Bank's land policy

In 1975, the World Bank issued a Land Reform Policy Paper which recommended:
- formal land titling as a precondition of "modern development";
- the abandonment of communal tenure systems in favour of freehold title and sub-division of the commons;
- widespread promotion of land markets to bring about efficiency-enhancing land transfers; and
- support for land redistribution on both efficiency and equity grounds.

In the light of practical experience and continuing policy debate since 1975, the World Bank has considerably revised its assessment and guidance, and now recognises that:
- communal tenure systems can be a more cost-effective solution than formal individual title, if transparency and local accountability can be assured;
- the circumstances in which land titling is an optimal solution are much more limited than had been thought. Where credit is not widely available to the rural poor, titling is likely to be biased in favour of the rich and precautions against land-grabbing need to be taken; and
- widespread market distortions limit the effectiveness of land markets in enhancing efficiency and equity; greater benefits should be expected from the development of land rental markets instead.

Following the end of the Cold War, debates about private versus public ownership of land have become less polarised. More flexible alternatives to universal private titling on the one hand, or public ownership on the other, can now be proposed, such as market assisted land reform.

Nevertheless, the Bank maintains that the key principles outlined in the Land Reform Policy Paper remain valid:
- the desirability of owner occupied farms on equity and efficiency grounds;
- the relative inefficiency of farming based either on wage labour or collective ownership;
- the need to promote markets for sale, purchase and rental of land; and
- the desirability of land reform.

The World Bank continues to view a framework of secure, transparent and enforceable property rights as the critical precondition for investment and economic growth. But they now recognise that property rights need not necessarily be individualised, and that security can be provided within customary tenure systems.

Within Africa, the World Bank is now engaged in the promotion of:
- land policy reforms (as opposed to tenure reform, more narrowly conceived) to reflect this new understanding, and to eliminate conflicts between parallel sets of rights;
- pilot programmes to register and adjudicate customary rights and provide titles on a community basis; and
- piloting of negotiated and market-based programmes for land redistribution.

In addition, the Bank now places more emphasis on gender rights, on those of pastoralists, the importance of encouraging stakeholder participation in land policy processes, partnerships with civil society and building capacity of local institutions for decentralised land management.

Source: Deininger, 1998; Migot-Adholla, 1999

---

resolution of disputes at community level. Such mechanisms often evolve spontaneously, and may not need to be introduced by the state. A sensible approach is therefore to facilitate the development of robust and transparent systems for land rights management, building where possible on local good practice.

LAND REDISTRIBUTION

In Africa, land redistribution remains on the agenda in countries with highly inequitable patterns of land holding. In South Africa and Zimbabwe, following the end of white minority rule, political demands for the restitution of settler-acquired land to the descendants of the original occupiers have been particularly strong. In Namibia, Malawi and Uganda, historic inequities in land holdings also still persist. The elimination of inequalities in land ownership which were established during the colonial period has been a fundamental part of the platform on which nationalist and socialist governments have come to power.

Redistributive land reform has delivered clear benefits elsewhere, notably in North Africa and the Far East, for some of the poorer sections of society and for national development as a whole. In sub-Saharan Africa, however, experience with and evidence from land redistribution are more limited.

Land redistribution has often been blocked by the powerful political and economic interests of large landowners (see Box 2.4). As with registration and titling, land redistribution has sometimes provided the opportunity for political elites to acquire land themselves, producing a mixed impact so far as equity is concerned. In cases where land redistribution has been attempted, benefits may not be realised unless the newly resettled poor also have access to markets and to agricultural and other services. Simply redistributing land, without linkages to wider development opportunities, may not by itself lead to improved agricultural production and growth. Radical egalitarian measures, as practised in Ethiopia and Tanzania in the 1970s and 80s, probably undermined overall farm production and food security, leading to increased poverty (see Box 2.5). This was due to the high level of insecurity generated by fears of further redistribution and a consequent unwillingness to invest effort in measures to improve soil conservation and enhance fertility.

The economics of land redistribution and its impacts on poverty

If economic growth is to reduce poverty, then the benefits of such growth need to be distributed equitably within society. In practice, in a number of cases growth has brought negative consequences for equity and has even increased poverty. Hence, explicitly pro-poor strategies for economic growth need to be devised, which may include more direct measures to ensure the poor gain better access to resources. This requires an understanding of the links between economic growth and the distribution of incomes and assets, in particular those based on land rights, as discussed below (see also Box 2.4).

Economic research, using time series data from developing countries has investigated the links between inequality and economic growth. Inequality frequently increases in the early stages of development, but can subsequently decrease as economic growth becomes broader based. In the majority of cases, however, the income of the poorest groups appears to have increased in absolute terms during periods of growth. Growth is as often associated with increasing inequality as it is with decreasing inequality (Deininger and Squire, 1997).

Box 2.4: Efficiency and poverty considerations of land reform in Zimbabwe

The highly uneven distribution of rural incomes in Zimbabwe is a direct consequence of land ownership patterns. Some 4,500 large-scale, mostly white commercial farmers dominate Zimbabwe's agricultural sector, denying access to the bulk of the nation's natural resources for over six million people, who must exist in the more marginal areas of the country. This imbalance in land holdings, reflected in gross income disparities between the two groups, has greatly impeded growth in rural incomes for poorer households.

With such a central economic position occupied by large-scale farmers, attempts to reform land tenure are typically countered by claims which emphasise the substantial costs that such measures may entail, such as reduction in agricultural production and thereby GDP, deteriorating race relations and diminished foreign investment. A key assumption here is that the break-up of large-scale farms into smaller units means a decrease in overall productivity, an assumption which is not borne out by research from elsewhere (Platteau, 1992; Lipton, 1993). This economic argument against land reform has also frequently subordinated claims based on historical grievance and the need to right such long-standing wrongs. Appropriate land taxation could promote more efficient land use within large farms, while the redistribution of some land from commercial farms would increase the number of small and medium-scale farmers, help intensify land use and enlarge the scope for enhancing rural incomes. Thus, land reform needs to consider a combination of ways to address historic claims as well as promote greater land use efficiency.

Source: Moyo, 1999

Economic analysis has also shown that countries with considerable inequality in wealth distribution may experience poor levels of economic growth, and a clear relationship has been found between more equal distribution of land holdings and other assets, and higher levels of economic growth.

El Ghonemy (1990; 1994) argues that reducing land concentration is a more effective strategy against poverty than relying on agricultural growth alone. Statistical evidence shows a link between a reduction in rural poverty and declining land concentration during the land reform periods in Egypt, Morocco and Tunisia. Analysis of data from 21 developing countries which have undertaken land reform also indicates that while agricultural growth can cut poverty levels by 50% over 60 years, a 30% reduction in land concentration, combined with the same levels of growth, could achieve the same results in just 15 years (Tyler et al, 1993). Support for such analysis can be drawn from the case of Egypt, where the proportion of rural people below the poverty line fell from 56% to 18% between 1950 and 1982, as a result of sustained agricultural

---

Box 2.5: Impacts of land reform on rural poverty in Ethiopia

In spite of egalitarian intentions, land reform in Ethiopia over the last few decades has generated an increase rather than a decrease in rural poverty. With the seizure of power in 1974, the Derg military regime abolished feudal land ownership and distributed usufruct rights to peasant associations (kebelle) in an attempt to reverse the long-standing social differentiation found under the imperial period. While ownership of land resided with the state, the right to use it was dependent on residence in a particular kebelle. This use right could neither be sold nor exchanged and land was subject to periodic redistribution. This enabled those coming of age to acquire plots of land, but led to great insecurity amongst other land users, who were moved from plot to plot and lost portions of their holdings to others. Family holdings were further diminished, in the event of either old age or death, by subdivision between children.

While such land redistribution did much to reverse the previous highly unequal distribution of land and wealth, it has also served to exacerbate rural poverty. With much uncertainty as to how long a family's holding would remain its own, there is little incentive to invest in it, nor to manage it carefully according to traditional methods of crop rotation, organic soil fertilisation and fallowing. Moreover, because the right to use land depends on residence (where extended periods of absence from the kebelle could result in land being forfeited), many people have chosen to stay in rural areas to retain these rights, swelling the population to over 47 million. Since their land is subject to periodic redistribution, an increasing number of people have had to survive on a decreasing quantity of land which, in the absence of easy access to capital and improved technologies, has increased rural poverty and destitution.

Despite the fall of the Derg, and the establishment of an elected government, Ethiopia's land policy continues largely unchanged today, prohibiting the selling and mortgaging of land but allowing short-term leasing and hiring of labour. The widespread rural poverty that characterised earlier periods has, however, yet to see significant improvement. One of the principal defects with this land policy lies in the denial of secure rights of land tenure to the user. If established, such rights could provide much better incentives for proper management and longer term investment, and could be based on a combination of private and community-based systems. Yet it must also be recognised that in order to address the problems of rural poverty in Ethiopia in a more comprehensive way, land reform must go hand in hand with the development of new opportunities within an increasingly diverse national economy.

Source: Rahmato, 1999

---

growth plus a major programme of land reform in favour of smallholders. This evidence suggests that the poor are most likely to benefit from a combination of economic growth, increased investment, and redistribution of assets.

One reason for the link between relative equality in land ownership and higher levels of growth in developing countries is the relative efficiency of farm production by large numbers of small producers, as opposed to small numbers of large ones - the so-called *inverse relationship between farm size and productivity*, a feature observed by economists since the 19th century. A large number of smaller farms can produce and earn more than a small number of large farms operating at the same level of technology. This, in turn, can be explained by the combined effects of low labour costs, where farming families work their own land, and the desire to maximise returns to their scarce asset –

land. Large farms depend on hired labour to a much greater extent, which has associated costs, such as supervision to ensure quality of effort. Smaller, family-run farms are generally able to avoid the transactions costs associated with labour markets, by applying family labour or making informal arrangements to gain access to extra labour within the local community, at a lower cost than market wage rates (Platteau, 1992; Lipton, 1993).

The inverse relationship between farm size and productivity runs counter to the theory that agricultural production is subject to significant economies of scale. This theory was based on the notion that large farm size will minimise capital transaction costs and ensure more effective use of indivisible capital inputs, such as large machinery. The problems associated with indivisible capital resources can be overcome through the operation of a hiring system or by group ownership, although there will usually be some associated transaction costs. But, since capital makes a relatively small contribution to agricultural production in many African countries (Platteau, 1992), such scale economies are of minor importance. While larger farms may, in some cases, be shown to be more productive, this is usually due to their privileged access to technology, credit and information, for instance in areas where green revolution technology dominates.

The general implications of these arguments are that the greater and more secure farmers' sense of ownership over small, family-run farms, the greater will be the labour input, and the higher the resulting land productivity. Promoting labour intensive growth, including the encouragement of small farms, and more egalitarian land relations is likely to have a more significant impact on reducing poverty than more capital intensive growth which marginalises small producers and undermines their land rights. Overall, economic analysis provides a powerful argument in favour of land reforms that both improve land distribution and enhance tenure security for small farmers within an overall strategy of labour intensive growth (World Development Report, World Bank, 1990).

An important caveat however, is that labour intensive strategies may also be linked to poverty in that they may promote exploitation of labour. Firstly, labour intensive growth may not benefit women who are already likely to be overworked (Lipton and Maxwell, 1992). This problem, however, can be addressed by strengthening women's own land rights, and their opportunities to control productive enterprises. Second, labour intensive farm activities need not be confined to small holdings, since some cash crops also require labour-intensive production methods, such as on large tea and coffee estates, where private capital has a dominant role. Here, however, there are opportunities to promote community-private sector partnerships, through ethical trading and responsible investment initiatives, which can improve labour conditions, and

Box 2.6: Approaches to land redistribution in Africa

a) Where is redistribution an issue?

Redistribution programmes are currently underway in Zimbabwe, South Africa, Namibia, Ethiopia, and Eritrea. In many countries, redistribution is primarily a political issue. The debate is increasingly framed in terms of restitution of lands lost through state-driven dispossession, rather than transfer from rich to poor producers, as it was prior to the 1990s.

b) What are the objectives of redistribution?

Objectives of redistribution programmes appear over-ridingly political. Bringing more land into production and achieving greater land use efficiency are also considered, but often the land obtained is not of sufficient quality to improve significantly the livelihoods of beneficiary farmers. The economic implications of redistribution are often given less weight than social justice and land restitution arguments. But it should be remembered that costs of redistribution can be very great, if land is acquired at market rates, or full compensation paid for expropriated land. In South Africa, one of main aims of the redistribution programme has been to 'un-pack' very overcrowded Communal Areas, thus reducing the pressure on environmental resources. Programmes elsewhere have often been aiming to resettle refugees, or displaced peoples.

c) What processes have been used?

In the main, governments have expropriated or purchased land for redistribution, but in some cases, direct purchase by beneficiaries has been explored as an option. More indirect approaches, such as imposing ceilings on land holdings, provide an indirect way for the state to prevent unjust or monopolistic land purchase. In South Africa, where one of the objectives of reform is the redress of past discrimination, beneficiaries of redistribution programme can choose to receive cash *in lieu* of land. Market mechanisms can also lead to redistribution of land, though tenure rules may have to be changed to enforce sales. Traditional community land management may also operate an effective form of redistribution. In Kenya, for example, even where titles are held, sales may not be approved by elders if the seller will become landless as a result. Land invasion is a spontaneous, *de facto* approach to land distribution, used by activists to force the government's hand.

d) What lessons have been learned?

● Greater emphasis should be placed on supporting productivity and access to input and product markets following redistribution. There are risks of harvest shortfalls during the transition period, if planning does not take account of short, medium and long-term effects on farm production and socio-economic life.

● Delays in implementation may weaken the political impetus needed to make redistribution work. In some cases, failure to redistribute rapidly generates further tensions and potential for conflict.

● State directed land redistribution can lead to heightened tenure insecurity, as in Ethiopia (see Box 2.5), and if infrastructure and extension services are not available, then the process does not necessarily bring increased production.

● The state has to withdraw at some point from the process, but the extent to which the market mechanism should be allowed to take over the allocative role has not been sufficiently explored.

● There is a need to resolve the aims of redistribution programmes. Are they to provide access to land or to livelihoods? Or to promote resettlement in urban or rural areas? Or, indeed, to provide land or a cash payment to beneficiaries?

● Demand-led land reform often results in sporadic pockets of resettlement and poor overall planning. A systematic approach may be a better option.

● Redistribution programmes are time consuming, expensive, difficult, and fraught with problems.

Source: Workshop group discussion; DFID, 1999

strengthen community shares in the products, and community rights over land alienated to commercial estates.

Reforms which improve land distribution and strengthen small farmers' security, can be justified both as a poverty reducing measure and from the point of view of economic efficiency. There are direct benefits for the recipients of redistributed land, higher levels of production than where land is highly concentrated, and these factors can contribute towards higher levels of growth. Land reform can also promote more equitable patterns of growth which shift both income and power to poorer groups. This can generate important multiplier effects, by stimulating local employment in urban and industrial development, as a result of the growing consumer demands of increasingly prosperous smallholder farmers.

Since land holdings are relatively equitable in sub-Saharan Africa, in many countries land redistribution has not been deemed a relevant approach to land reform. Redistributive land reform is inevitably a highly politicised process, and it is never unproblematic. Box 2.6 provides an overview of some of the issues involved in contemporary land distribution programmes in Africa. However, the persistence of poverty, poor economic performance and growing inequality in countries with inequitable patterns of land holding require renewed attention to redistributive land reforms, and the benefits they can bring.

LAND MARKETS

Whether or not land is registered and titled, the emergence of formal and informal land markets is increasingly apparent in many parts of Africa. This is the case particularly in high potential and peri-urban areas, and those with high population densities. Land market issues were identified as an important topic for further investigation by land tenure practitioners from throughout Africa at the DFID Workshop on Land Rights and Sustainable Development in Sub-Saharan Africa held in 1999. The substance of this discussion is presented in Box 2.7.

Economists argue that market transactions in land are beneficial because they should allocate land from less to more efficient producers. In a rational world of perfect markets, inefficient producers will benefit from selling their land, because the market value should exceed that of the income stream they are able to generate themselves. More efficient producers, on the other hand, should be able to generate greater incomes and should find it profitable to invest in land purchase. Moreover, if small farms are indeed more efficient than large ones, land markets should also promote greater equity, since they should encourage the transfer of inefficiently used large land holdings to more efficient smallholders.

The spontaneous development of market transactions in recent years within

Box 2.7: Findings of workshop discussions on land markets

1. What is meant by a land market?

Markets in land deal in land rights. They are active throughout Africa, in both customary and formal systems, and discussion should consider the whole range of transactions, including:

● the buying and selling of freeholds, as well as temporary transfers such as lease and rental

● long and short term informal land borrowing including land pledging;

● land mortgaging;

● land exchanges;

● land pooling and other informal arrangements.

Land transactions take place not only between individuals but also between companies and public bodies. In customary systems, exchanges may involve social units such as lineages.

2. The relationship between formalisation of tenure and development of land markets

● Customary systems tend not to acknowledge the permanent alienation of land, because underlying rights are held by family and lineage, not individuals.

● However, since customary systems are responsive to new needs and opportunities, and under pressure of market forces and growing land values, many have come to accept land alienation. Urban development and the growing value of land for uses other than agriculture are major forces driving the development of a market in land ownership rights.

● Formalisation of land tenure through titling is neither necessary nor sufficient for the development of a western-style land market. Demands for a formalised land market are generally first voiced by individuals from outside the community, such as officials and merchants who want to acquire land to which they might not be entitled under custom.

● Formalisation can create greater security of tenure for those who purchase land, facilitating exchanges and increasing land values. However, where markets are not well developed, formalisation of tenure will not produce land sales. Equally, where people have few or no livelihood options outside agriculture, little land is likely to enter the market.

● Simple approaches to formalising land market transactions are evolving in the field, such as announcement of agreements at public meetings, providing facilities for written transactions, registration of contracts, and the witnessing of signatures.

3. Impacts of land markets on poverty

● There is no clear correlation between the development of land markets and increasing concentration of land in a few hands. There is also insufficient evidence to assess the impact of land markets on levels of landlessness, in different circumstances. Growing land concentration has been reported from Rwanda and some areas of Kenya, but elsewhere in Kenya and in parts of Uganda land distribution has become more equitable with the establishment of land markets.

● Nevertheless it is possible to identify certain situations where land markets concentrate ownership and accelerate landlessness. This may occur, for example, where land markets develop in chaotic fashion in peri-urban areas. This is sometimes linked to abuse of power by traditional authorities who alienate community lands to outsiders (e.g. cases in South Africa, Ghana). Distress sales by poor households constitute another example. However, in general, poor households that are dependent on agriculture usually try to keep hold of some land.

● There is a need to examine land markets from a gender perspective. Poorer women may suffer in cases where their spouse alienates family land, but the better off may be able to acquire land in their own right when markets in land develop.

---

4. Effects of land markets on economic growth

The importance of land markets as a means to provide better access to credit has been seriously overstated. Only for larger landholders and where banking systems and formal credit markets are well developed does this link seem to hold. For smallholders, borrowing within the community, or micro-credit schemes, provide more reliable and efficient sources of finance, neither of which depend on the existence of transferable land titles.

Theory suggests that land markets should allocate land to more efficient users. However, in rural Africa, purchasers often bank land for the next generation, leaving it unfarmed. Thus, land market development may lead to speculation rather than increased investment.

5. Action needed

Not enough is known about the operation of land markets in Africa. The lack of adequate multi-disciplinary studies seriously impedes a proper discussion of policy options. Areas for further investigation include the *impact of land markets on land concentration and poverty, the role of land markets in promoting livelihood diversification, and the importance of rental markets for the poor and for agricultural efficiency.*

Source: Workshop group discussion; DFID, 1999

---

customary tenure systems bears out the idea that land markets provide net benefits for buyers and sellers. But there is little evidence that such markets encourage the transfer of large land holdings to small farmers, as would have been expected from economic theory, given the greater efficiency of smallholders. More often than not, land markets appear to encourage land concentration. Economists explain this by pointing to market distortions, which prevent the development of perfectly free and fair land markets, as follows:

- In practice the market value of land often exceeds that of the income stream that can be derived from it. In many countries, the better-off invest in land as a hedge against inflation, and speculate on future increases in land values, especially in circumstances which favour conversion from agricultural to residential or industrial use.
- Landlords, or traditional authorities, may have a strong incentive to dispose of land held in trust, at the expense of claims by tenants or community members, who lose access to land and gain few if any benefits from the sale (see for example Kasanga (1999) for a discussion of the land market situation in peri-urban Kumasi, Ghana).
- Alongside the speculative value which land frequently acquires, a variety of hidden subsidies and tax incentives can artificially inflate land values (Deininger and Feder, 1999).
- Fixed transaction costs make it difficult for landowners to subdivide holdings or sell small parcels, and for small farmers to acquire them (Deininger and Feder, 1999).
- In sub-Saharan Africa many small farmers, and especially the landless poor, operate within a partially non-monetised economy, and have no access to

capital or sources of finance. As a result they are unable to enter the land market. Moreover, low levels of literacy, and inadequate market information allow the poor to be exploited in market transactions by the better off.

• Natural hazards such as drought, and the stress and shocks they impose on livelihood systems, bring about swings in the supply and demand for land. Distress sales occur particularly during times of hardship, when market values are low. Buyers subsequently benefit when conditions improve and land prices increase. Although the poor rarely sell all their land, it becomes more difficult to buy it back, once sold (Deininger and Feder, 1999).

Where markets are distorted in these ways, the existence of formalised property rights can accelerate such a concentration of land holdings. Although there may be some economic advantages, for instance in facilitating land transfers to the urban sector or for promoting commercial farming, the benefits tend to accrue to the better off with the poor often losing out. The relationship between the formalisation of land rights and the development of land markets, and between the development of land markets and the livelihoods of the poor are complex and, as yet, poorly understood.

As noted earlier, the growth of land markets does not require the existence of formalised property rights. In customary land tenure systems, especially in West Africa, a wide variety of transactions, including land loans, leases, sharecropping contracts, exchanges, and pledges are well established features of socio-economic life, within and between communities and kin groups. Such transactions are subject to revocation, contest and re-negotiation over time, as conditions change, providing the advantage of considerable flexibility.

Rental markets, including those recognised by customary systems, deserve more attention, because of their low transactions costs and greater accessibility for the poor (Deininger and Feder, 1999). Rentals, leases and loans do not involve the permanent alienation of land, and provide benefits for both lessor and lessee. Land borrowing arrangements provide a mechanism for landholders to dispose, temporarily, of land they cannot utilise, and for in-migrants, the displaced or dispossessed to take up farm production. Moreover, sharecropping, as a form of payment in kind for land access, is not necessarily as exploitative as has been supposed. Sharecropping offers a means by which the poor can gain access to land, and in Africa it often provides an important form of risk sharing and mutual aid in times of crisis, strongly rooted in social and kinship relations. Thus, land rental and sharecropping markets have mixed impacts on poverty and inequality depending on the terms. In promoting land market development, several important areas will require attention, such as the monitoring and regulation of rental markets, encouraging the provision of more equitable contracts, compensation for investments, as well as ultimate possibilities for land purchase by tenants.

CONCLUSIONS: THE RELEVANCE OF LAND TENURE AND LAND REFORM TO POVERTY ERADICATION IN AFRICA

Across the developing world, land reform, whether through land distribution or changes to tenure legislation, has had some success in combating poverty, and in promoting economic growth. This has occurred in cases where:

- the poor have been explicitly targeted as beneficiaries;
- ceilings on land ownership have been effectively enforced;
- marketing opportunities for farm produce have been available and agrarian support services provided alongside a wider emphasis on rural development;
- focused, coordinated programmes have been sustained over a long period of a decade or more;
- there has been beneficiary participation in programme design and implementation, especially in land adjudication;
- flexible design of tenure reform or land distribution has allowed for institutional learning from experience, and adaptation to varied and changing circumstances.

Both historically, and in global terms, the redistribution of large landholdings with provision of secure smallholder rights, often in the form of titles, appears to have been the most successful model for land reform around the world. But this approach has not generally been relevant to much of Africa. In those African nations in which land ownership remains highly skewed, redistributive land reform is a relevant approach, but it can be difficult politically. If the desired results are to be achieved, government needs to be tough in order to overcome the entrenched power of landowners who are often closely linked to the political class. Moreover, land redistribution is no substitute for wider programmes to tackle poverty within crowded communal areas.

Within Africa, land titling and registration, especially on a nation-wide basis, has not proved to be an effective approach against poverty, although there may be specific circumstances where it is relevant. These include cases where there has been a breakdown of indigenous tenure systems, where land encroachment by outside interests is common or increasing, and where defensive registration is needed to safeguard individual and group rights. It may also be of value in areas with a high level of land fragmentation, disputes and inheritance problems, especially in ecologically fragile lands where the intensification of agriculture is unsustainable, and where inter- or intra-ethnic conflicts over land are apparent. Such cases frequently overlap and careful context-specific diagnosis is required to identify specific reforms, targeted to assist the poor in providing land access and more secure rights.

Stepping aside from major programmes focusing on land reform, several other interventions can promote more equitable, efficient land use as a component of pro-poor economic growth, but which stop short of major land reform. Possible measures include:

- recognition and integration of customary rights into the legislative framework and their registration, where appropriate, on a community basis;
- extension of tenants' rights and the development of more accessible rental markets;
- promotion of women's access to land and the reform of inheritance laws to promote greater gender equality;
- introduction of low cost survey and registration procedures for the demarcation and confirmation of community land rights;
- support to community-based natural resource and common property management;
- building decentralised, local institutions for land rights management, including a role for customary institutions, especially in the settlement of land-related disputes;
- land rights advocacy on behalf of the poor;
- promotion of stakeholder participation in land policy development.

This chapter has sought to provide an overview of the linkages between land reform, poverty and economic development, which are also discussed in more detail in subsequent chapters of this book. In particular the gender dimensions of the links between land rights, development and poverty are addressed in Chapter 9.

While all are agreed that secure land tenure is important for both poverty reduction and economic development, it is important to avoid simplistic assumptions about how to design arrangements that can best support agricultural development. Over recent decades, top-down, centralised approaches to land and tenure reform have been attempted based on sweeping assumptions – for example that individual private property is the sole foundation for agricultural development, as in Kenya, or, as in Ethiopia, that all land should be owned and controlled by the state, and the rural populace should be given use rights in equal shares. Both of these approaches have generally failed, often undermining security of tenure, and in some cases deepening poverty and allowing richer groups to gain control over valuable resources.

It is now recognised that, in many cases, customary tenure systems remain quite effective, and capable of evolution to accommodate changing circumstances. With the benefit of hindsight, the more cautious experimentation with less radical, less comprehensive reforms underway in Africa today point the way to more open, participatory and decentralised policies and institutions for land and land rights management capable of delivering lasting benefits for the poor, and for African nations as a whole.

3

Does Africa Need Land Reform?

Jean-Philippe Platteau

INTRODUCTION

It is recognised that land reforms which involve redistribution (radical land re-distribution, land ceilings, transformation of tenants into owners, etc.) are not needed in most parts of sub-Saharan Africa given the relatively egalitarian nature of land allocation mechanisms prevailing at village level[1]. Many argue instead for land reform aimed at consolidating indigenous land tenure rights through a centralised formal procedure of registration and titling.

Two dominant views support such a policy stance. According to one view, the inadequacy of land tenure systems stems from a fundamental disequilibrium or misfit between systems embodying a long tradition of extensive farming practices on the one hand, and the requirements of output growth from a shift to more intensive agriculture on the other (Lewis, 1955: 121; Eicher and Baker, 1982: 98-99; Giri, 1983; Falloux, 1987; Ault and Rutman, 1979; Gourou, 1991: 156). If this view is followed, nothing short of a drastic alter-ation of customary land rights by the public authorities would provide a viable solution.

Another, much more optimistic view denies such a static interpretation of African land systems, and proposes instead a dynamic picture in which in-digenous land rights, under the impulse of market forces, are capable of sig-nificant autonomous evolution in the "right" (efficiency-enhancing) direction. Hence the label "evolutionary theory of land rights" (ETLR) given to this doc-trine (Platteau, 1996c). It should be noted that public authorities still have an

---

1 Major exceptions to this general picture concern areas of white settlement, such as South Africa, Zimbabwe, and Namibia, where extreme disparities in land holding persist.

important role to play under this theory, as autonomous changes in land rights need to be supported by government intervention to formalise and consolidate these newly emerging rights.

This chapter questions the conclusions of this theory on the basis of both theoretical arguments and empirical evidence. It starts by presenting the central thesis of the ETLR. Thereafter, a critique is offered that considers successively the effects of land titling (and greater individualisation of land rights) on investment behaviour, land market activation, and equity. It ends by summarising the main findings of the study and drawing its main policy implications.

THE THEORY

The basic position of the evolutionary theory of land rights is that as land scarcity increases, people demand greater tenure security. As a result, private property rights in land tend to emerge and, once established, to evolve towards greater measures of individualisation and formalisation (Demsetz, 1967; Ault and Rutman, 1979; Noronha, 1985; Feder and Feeny, 1991). Deepening *individualisation* takes place in relation to the range of rights held, and the level of autonomy with which the landholder can exercise these rights. The range refers to the package of rights enjoyed by the landholder, including rights of use and rights of transfer. Typically, rights over a given piece of land begin to be asserted in several ways: by choosing which crop to grow and how to dispose of the harvest; and by preventing others from exploiting the same parcel (e.g., by grazing their livestock). Individualisation develops through a gradual extension of use rights (for example, the right to recultivate the same plot of land even before the normal period of fallow has elapsed, or the right to plant trees and to bring other improvements to the land) and, above all, the rights to transfer their interest in the land to others. The latter may comprise the right to lend the land along traditional lines (as part of a wider relationship of reciprocal exchange between two families or lineages), the right to give it, bequeath it, rent it out for cash and, ultimately, sell it.

Individualisation of land tenure is also reflected in the growing autonomy enjoyed by farmers over how they may use the land and, particularly, regarding their decisions to transfer it. Thus, in the initial stages of individualisation, the rights to rent out or to sell land parcels are seriously circumscribed by the requirement that land ought to remain within the family or the lineage. It is the responsibility of the family or lineage heads to see to it that this condition is duly respected and this is why their permission is explicitly required before any sale of land can take place. Such conditions are however, gradually relaxed as land becomes more scarce, so that at advanced stages of the individualisation process, land transactions become increasingly supported by written evidence. In the ultimate stage of this process, when land becomes extremely scarce and valuable, public sector involvement is called for as there is a pressing demand for legally protected land titles. Maximum security of land tenure can then be achieved.

In other words, the ETLR contends that a spontaneous movement towards individualisation and formalisation of land rights unfolds under the combined pressure of growing land scarcity and increasing commercialisation of land-based activities. Only in the final stage, must this endogenous evolution be aided by a public intervention designed to consolidate and legally sanction the rights that have emerged in the field. In the following sections, we shall examine the two ways in which the theory explains that land rights are transformed.

Endogenous evolution

The considerable flexibility of indigenous land tenure arrangements is emphasised by many scholars. As can be seen by the recent experience of many African countries, growing population pressure and increasing market penetration, particularly since the introduction of commercial crops such as oil palm, cocoa, coffee, cotton, groundnuts, etc. in colonial times, have given rise to gradual but significant changes in land tenure practices. These have involved the enhanced individualisation of tenure, a higher incidence of land sales (first disguised, then increasingly in the open), increased use of money in connection with land loans, and a shift from matrilineal to patrilineal inheritance patterns (Boserup, 1965; Noronha, 1985; Downs and Reyna, 1988; Migot-Adholla et al, 1991; Bassett and Crummey, 1993).

Over time, rules of inheritance have evolved towards increasingly direct transmission of land between father and sons and, as a result of the individualisation of land tenure, younger members of society have started to emancipate themselves (albeit rather slowly) from the authority of their elders. Such emancipation may involve a converse process by which family heads rid themselves of the responsibility of paying tax and marriage costs for their sons. Moreover, customary modes of land transfer through gifts, exchanges, loans, renting, pledges or mortgages have intensified and sales of land, though often redeemable to the seller, have begun to take place in some areas, running counter to one of the most deep-rooted customary limitations on land use. At first, sales were sanctioned only among members of the group (such as those sharing common descent or residence), but later spread to outsiders with approval of the group or its head, and still later even without such consent (Bruce, 1986: 38, 40). In addition, sales may initially be subject to a right of pre-emption by family members or to a right of repurchase by the seller (Bruce, 1993: 42).

With greater integration of rural areas into the market economy and growing population pressure, the above modifications in African customary land tenure arrangements have tended to accelerate during the post-independence period, often in spite of and with few connections to the formal land laws enacted by the state.

Public sector involvement

Let us now turn to the second way in which land rights can be transformed, as a result of government intervention. According to the ETLR, formal private property rights, far from being imposed from outside by public authorities, actually emerge in response to a pressing demand indirectly expressed by increasingly insecure landholders. The story continues as follows.

When land acquires a scarcity value, landholders begin to feel uncertain about the strength of their customary rights, and disputes over ownership of land, inheritance and land boundaries tend to multiply. Landholders will tend to assert increasingly individualised use rights to given plots as population continues to rise, such as the right to resume cultivation of a specific plot after a period of fallow; the right to assign the plot to an heir or to a tenant; the right to prevent secondary claimants (e.g. the right of pastoral herders to graze their animals on crop stubble) from exercising their traditional prerogatives; and the right to dispose freely of the land. This increasing assertion of individualised rights gives rise to numerous conflicts which become more difficult to resolve and entail rising costs. With rising land prices, the expected gain from obtaining specific land rights begins to outweigh the costs. The rising incidence of land conflicts and the accompanying threats to social order provide clear signals for the government to act.

The expected response from national governments to these signals is to carry out administrative reforms to encourage a more effective use of resources and to address the social tensions arising from land disputes. Sooner or later, such reforms include a formal registration of private land rights and fully fledged land titling procedures. As a consequence of such formal adjudication, the theory posits that all conflicts should then be resolved, leaving nothing further to dispute: once adjudicated, well-defined property rights ought to put an end to uncertainties and ambiguities.

The beneficial effects of land titling

Two types of beneficial economic effects are expected to follow from the proper recording of private property rights in land: *allocative effects* resulting in more efficient use of the land available; and *dynamic effects* resulting in land conservation and improvement (Demsetz, 1967; Johnson, 1972; Ault and Rutman, 1979; Feder, 1987, 1993; Feder et al, 1988; Feder and Feeny, 1991; Barzel, 1989; Binswanger et al, 1995).

Gains from more efficient use of the land arise from two distinct sources. First, more efficient crop choices become possible because any bias in favour of short-cycle crops (arising from tenure insecurity) is removed when land titles are introduced. Second, under the same circumstances, land is likely to be transferred from less to more dynamic farmers and consolidated into larger holdings, thereby eliminating the excessive fragmentation and subdivision encouraged by traditional land allocation and inheritance patterns. By putting an end to ambiguity in property rights, land titling greatly reduces transaction costs and encourages land acquisition by those able to make best use of it. The development of the land market is also often supposed to induce a switch from subsistence cultivation to commercial agriculture given its transfer to more dynamic, market-oriented farmers (see, e.g., Falloux, 1987).

Fully-fledged private property rights not only improve the allocation of land for different uses and different users, they also enhance investment incentives. The dynamic impact of land titling on investment behaviour can be broken down into demand and supply effects. Or, to put it another way, landowners whose rights are legally protected can be expected to be both more willing and more able to undertake investment.

They are more willing to invest for essentially two reasons, the first of which stems from a point made long ago by John Stuart Mill. He argued that when farmers are better assured of reaping the future benefits of their present efforts and sacrifices, thanks to secure use rights, they have greater incentive to invest in soil conservation measures, land improvements and other operations that raise productivity in the long term (Mill, 1848). This *"assurance effect"* follows from the fact that when farmers feel more secure in their ability to maintain long-term use over their land, the return on long-term land improvements is higher. Conversely, lack of tenure security creates the risk of land loss, and an associated fall in expected income from investment. Second, when land can be converted to monetary form through sale, improvements made through investment can be better realised, thereby increasing its expected return. Investment incentives are then again enhanced (Besley, 1995c: 910-12; Platteau, 1996c: 36). This second effect may be called the *"realisability effect"*.

Farmers with title to land may be not only more willing but also more able to invest. This is because, when freehold titles are established, land acquires collateral value and access to credit is therefore easier. This *"collateralisation effect"* is especially true regarding formal lending sources which often have imperfect information about the borrower[2].

If we exclude gifts and inheritance, land may change hands in two main ways: through foreclosure on mortgages or through voluntary market transactions. In both cases, greater economic efficiency is the expected outcome, whether in static or dynamic terms.

Beyond the above efficiency effects, land titling has the additional advantage of providing the government with a precious tool for assessing property taxes and thereby increasing its revenue. Furthermore, by identifying the possessors of rights over each and every land parcel, the centralised recording of land rights enables public authorities to bring clear and definite solutions to any land dispute or complaint and to thereby lay down the basis of law and order. From the above presentation of both the predicted evolution of land rights and the expected effects of this evolution on economic efficiency and social order, it is evident that the ETLR assumes that a beneficial mechanism is at work in societies subject to growing land pressure.

To say that the evolutionary process is beneficial does not, of course, imply that it must be trouble-free. The pervasive incidence of land disputes and litigation during the transition period leading to public registration of land rights, also reflects the conflictual process through which a more efficient land system emerges. Moreover, there is a strong possibility that land distribution will become more unequal as this process unfolds.

ASSESSING THE EVIDENCE

The effects of tenure security on investment

The empirical evidence on the relationship between land rights and investment or productivity in African agriculture is inconclusive. This holds true whether the level of investment is compared between lands protected by a formal title and non-registered lands, or between lands characterised by varying degrees of tenure security.

The "assurance" effect

According to the ETLR, assurance is provided both by land titling and infor-

---

2 The "collateralisation effect" is important since credit from informal lenders is typically more costly than formal credit (Feder and Nishio, 1997: 5).

mal individualisation of tenure. Below we will examine the effects of these processes with respect to incentives to invest.

• Land titling

Contrary to expectations, the evidence from Kenya and some other African countries where titling has been systematically implemented shows that there has been no clearly discernible impact from land titling on investment behaviour. The theoretical assurance effect (described above) does not seem to operate under ordinary circumstances, except in cases of resettlement or newly settled areas, and in urban or peri-urban areas (see below). In those cases, the granting of titles is likely to increase the assurance that returns from an investment will accrue to those who make it and thereby promote land improvement and conservation (see e.g., Alston et al, 1996, for Brazil; Moor, 1996, for Zimbabwe; Friedman et al, 1988, for the Philippines).

• Informal individualisation

The evidence regarding the strength of informal tenure security is consistent with the evidence gathered in land titled areas. In customary land areas, basic use rights seem to be sufficient to induce landholders to invest, so that the adding of transfer rights (with the possible exception of the right to bequeath land) does not appear to improve investment significantly (see Brasselle et al, 1998 for a recent survey). Hence, there is no basis for claiming that increased individualisation of land rights will bring forth a higher level of investment. Indeed, a possible alternative process may also be at work, in which investment enhances tenure security, such as through planting trees, and construction of soil conservation measures.

It is also worth emphasising that in agrarian societies in general, and in African rural communities in particular, firm use rights can be held by farmers despite their apparent vulnerability. What appears to the external observer as precarious rights may actually be long-term entitlements in the specific context of these societies. For example, borrowing land may not necessarily expose the farmer to a high risk of losing access to this land and the returns to investments made. This is because borrowing and lending land are often part of a wider relationship between two families or lineages, and the desire to keep such a relationship going ensures that such arrangements are frequently renewed or not easily brought to an end. Use rights over borrowed lands can often be bequeathed to descendants, such as when the borrower and the lender belong to the same lineage and when land has been lent for an indefinite period (Matlon, 1994: 52-54; see also De Zeeuw, 1997).

Tenure security on land that appears to be held under a rather precarious arrangement may in fact be much higher than the arrangement implies. This may explain why, for example, immigrant farmers who have comparatively low levels of tenure security as measured by standard yardsticks, may feel it worthwhile making long-term improvements in view of the stable relationship prevailing between them and the household by whom they have been given land. Such improvements, in turn, may enhance their tenure security further (Brasselle et al, 1998).

Under normal circumstances, the local informal order is embedded in social relations linking different members of the rural community, and guarantees basic land rights to all villagers (including migrants) which are sufficient to induce investment. There is then no need for the state to intervene through centralised procedures aimed at formalising land rights (Atwood, 1990; Migot-Adholla et al, 1991; Platteau, 1992, 1996c, 1997; Bassett and Crummey, 1993; Bruce and Migot-Adholla, 1994). If, however, for one reason or another, the local informal order is absent, has vanished, or is proving unable to regulate access to land, the state may be well-advised to substitute for this missing structure. Resettlement or new colonisation areas, as well as areas subject to acute land pressure (including urban or peri-urban areas) are cases in point.

There are good grounds to believe that, by reassuring owners about the definitive character of their ownership rights, land titling could encourage types of rental contracts that promote increasing levels of investment (e.g., through a lengthening of the contract period). Yet, it is also possible that indigenous tenure systems will gradually evolve institutional innovations that are less costly than registration and titling and serve the same purpose. Letters of occupancy granted by local chiefs to rights-holders, such as are found in Zambia (Sjaastad, 1998: 161), or locally produced documents attesting land rentals or sales in Rwanda (André and Platteau, 1998: 42), provide a good example of the kind of solution that the indigenous order can produce. In Zambia, when a litigant loses an ownership dispute, he is usually compensated for any improvements made to the land during his occupancy (Sjaastad, 1998: 176). To the extent that investment enhances tenure security, it is possible that the incentive to invest is higher under an indigenous tenure system than under the freehold regime. Even if the benefits of investments under indigenous tenure were smaller than those generated under freehold, the relevant comparison is between the difference in benefits and the costs of specifying and enforcing rights, since the establishment of freehold rights is not free of cost. In many cases, the security-enhancing investments undertaken by African farmers are also far from being unproductive (such as tree planting, construction of anti-erosion barriers, building of ditches and furrows).

The "collateralisation" effect

The positive influence of land titling on investment behaviour through the credit supply or collateralisation effect is far from being systematically present, since use of production credit by farmers may remain low in spite of the emergence of mortgageable land. The ETLR predicts, that organised credit sources will spontaneously arise in response to land registration to meet the latent demand of credit-rationed farmers, but this clearly is much too simplistic. Low credit use may be caused by two distinct types of factors. On the one hand, it may result from supply failures that have their origin in various imperfections not only in the credit market itself but also in other rural factor markets, particularly concerning land. On the other hand, it may be determined by demand failures that prevent farmers from tapping available credit sources. Let us consider these two sets of factors in more detail, starting with demand failures.

• Demand failures

Smallholders may fail to apply for loans because they perceive a high risk of losing their land through foreclosure, as the experience of Kenya testifies (Green, 1987: 8; Shipton, 1988: 106, 120; Barrows and Roth, 1989: 9). This may be especially true of subsistence-constrained farmers who fear that their ability to repay loans taken for investment purposes is very low (unless pay-offs are short-term).

Another important reason behind the failure of farmers to respond to the availability of loanable funds is the lack of attractive investment opportunities or the absence of conditions critical for their successful exploitation. This typically occurs when no technological package suitable for intensive agriculture is on offer (Platteau, 1990: 324-335). Alternatively, when investments embodying technical progress are highly labour-intensive (e.g., fencing, digging of furrows and ditches, tree planting, building of anti-erosion barriers, etc) and family labour is sufficient to supply the required effort, no capital is needed for purchase of equipment or advancing wages. It may also happen when the required infrastructure, input-delivery, output-marketing or extension services are not available (Roth, 1993: 316), or when visible wealth is being arbitrarily taxed (a risk to which agricultural investments are particularly vulnerable); or when more entrepreneurial farmers are discouraged from improving their land and accumulating capital because this stirs up jealousy amongst the other villagers (Bruce, 1986: 29, 31, 1993: 39-40).

• Supply failures

Failure of credit provision in spite of titling may arise for different reasons. Clearly, it may result from imperfections in the land market that tend to make registration ineffective. This happens if titled land is not considered a reliable collateral by credit-givers because it poses difficulties of foreclosure or because, the market being thin, it is not easy to dispose of in case of default (Okoth-Ogendo, 1976: 175; Collier, 1983: 163-164; Noronha, 1985: 197-198; Bruce, 1986: 40; Barrows and Roth, 1989: 9).

Difficulties in loan foreclosure may originate in both the official and civilian sphere. The first case occurs when the judicial system is ineffective or partial. This is a widespread phenomenon, particularly in urban and peri-urban areas where official titles are generally granted to private owners of land and buildings. A complaint frequently voiced by institutional credit-givers - not only state finance corporations but also commercial banks and other private credit agencies - is that foreclosure on property belonging to rich and powerful borrowers cannot be legally enforced because the judicial system is under the strong influence of their political allies. Clearly, perverse equity effects result from the operation of a land market when it is combined with a biased legal system. Popular expression of anger and active opposition can also break the link between registration and credit supply. If people do not consider the new system of land rights as legitimate and do not accept the reshuffling of wealth it may imply, they may succeed in blocking the foreclosure on property. Thus, in Kenya, lending authorities have had great difficulty foreclosing on land mortgages chiefly because "the presence of many kin around mortgaged land makes it politically unfeasible to auction the holdings of defaulters" (Shipton, 1988: 120). Governments may not want to run counter to popular demonstrations of this kind lest their political base or the fragile consensus on which their national policies rest should be undermined.

Ineffective operation of the land registration system may also result in the invalidity of the title documents particularly when landholdings comprise numerous, very small, parcels. This is amply confirmed by evidence from Kenya, where failure to maintain a valid record of succession and the absence of updated records constitute one of the major disappointments of the land titling programme (Green, 1987: 11). Shipton writes: "So the emergent land market is largely unregistered. It is likely to remain so. The government does not have the resources to monitor, let alone control, the many kinds of land exchanges that happen every season in the farm neighbourhoods. By their very nature, these defy recording and classification: for the most part they are *ad hoc,* unnamed, individually tailored agreements in which land is only one of many mutually interchangeable goods;... the lines blur between loans, rentals, barter, swaps, and sales" (Shipton, 1988: 123).

More generally, people's failure to register transactions may be ascribed to the continued strength of customary tenure rules. As a result, customary law (such as subdivision of land among all the sons) "in fact continues to govern the way in which most people deal with their land, making tenure rights ambiguous. The land law (in Kenya) failed to gain popular understanding or acceptance, individuals continued to convey rights to land according to customary law, and a gap developed between the control of rights as reflected in the land register and control of land rights as recognised by most local communities" (Barrows and Roth, 1989: 7).

To sum up, as a result of glaring failure to build up and update reliable land records, titles shown on the register are increasingly at variance with the facts of possession and use, creating considerable confusion over legal property rights. The impact of land registration is therefore undermined and, since credit agencies are not able to rely on titles as evidence of land ownership, the collateral effect fails to materialise.

Besides difficulties in repossessing land used as collateral and realising its value on the market, there are supply constraints arising from the strategy of credit-givers. First, commercial banks and financial institutions are often reluctant to lend for land purchases because they are unwilling to tie up their capital, raised largely through short-term deposits, for long periods of time (Dorner and Saliba, 1981; Stringer, 1989). Moreover, bankers usually prefer lending against more reliable streams of income than those found in agriculture. Second, considerations of administrative costs may lead banks and other credit agencies to set a minimum size of loans which often exceeds the capital needs of smallholders (Barrows and Roth, 1989: 9), or to refuse to lend to them on the ground that their property is costly to dispose of in the event of foreclosure due to the tiny size of fragmented landholdings. Following titling, distribution of credit is thus likely to become more unequal. The above analysis, it must be noted, suggests policy implications which widely differ from those usually associated with the ETLR. To the extent that land titling affects investment behaviour only through the credit-supply effect, it may be better to address the collateral problem directly (perhaps through the formation of informal co-operative borrowing groups) than to resolve it through expensive titling programmes (Carter et al, 1994: 156). Special attention ought to be paid to market access problems, particularly with respect to capital, that tend to disadvantage smallholders who constitute the bulk of the farming population.

It is wrong to think that the collateral effect can only occur if land is duly titled. As is documented in the next section, informal land market transactions can be supported by written evidence that is sufficiently reliable to allow the use of land as collateral by local credit-givers. In Rwanda, for example, credit-cum-savings associations known as *tontines* are able to seize the land of a defaulting member (André and Platteau, 1998). The fact that formalisation of land rights does not often appear to encourage investment may therefore be due not only to the lack of assurance effect but also to the kind of factors that we have just analysed in connection with titling (e.g., an absence of investment opportunities requiring credit or the fear of losing family land through foreclosure).

The effects of tenure security on land market activation

The analysis here centres around two main points. First, in ordinary circumstances the land market does not appear to be activated by the provision of greater tenure security, through titling. As a result, the "realisability" effect predicted by the ETLR is generally insignificant. Second, even when a land market is active, most land transfers do not seem to promote increased efficiency of resource use. The empirical facts underlying each of these statements and the explanations accounting for them are examined below.

Lack of land market development

Evidence from Kenya shows that land sale transactions did not increase following land reform except during the earliest stages, that is, before registration had been completed. Indeed, in the knowledge of pending registration, the educated elite took advantage of the situation to acquire additional land. Furthermore, it has been shown that subsequent transfers remain unregistered. The majority of plots continue to follow the path of customary channels (lending, gifts, inheritance or non-registered sales) among which inheritance stands foremost (Haugerud, 1983: 80; Collier, 1983: 156-158; Bruce, 1986: 56; Green, 1987: 13-18; Barrows and Roth, 1989: 10-11; Migot-Adholla et al, 1991: 160-164; Mackenzie, 1993: 200). Evidence from many other African countries confirms the important role of inheritance as a mode of land acquisition.

Supply considerations largely explain why land sale markets are thin. Landholders are typically reluctant to sell their land, even when they are employed outside the agricultural sector and reside in town. Land continues to be perceived as a crucial asset for the present and future subsistence of the family, all the more so as it is a secure form of holding wealth and a good hedge against inflation ("It is our bank and we will not part with it" said the member of a founding lineage in a village close to Matam, Senegal). Considerations of social insurance generate a deep attachment to land which is understandable in a context of scarce alternative employment opportunities and risky labour markets. For many people working in urban areas, land serves both as insurance against uncertain employment, as a pension fund for their old age, and as a means to avoid landlessness in the next generation of the family

(Bruce, 1986: 56; Green, 1987: 27; Lawry, 1993: 58)[3].

Such social security considerations often underlie the apparent persistence of indigenous control over land transfers even when they are duly registered: thus, in Kenya, many owners of titled lands do not consider that they are entitled to transfer their lands outside the lineage or to make permanent transfers without having previously obtained the approval of their family or community. Such interference with the free play of market forces is justified in so far as these communities are ultimately responsible for the subsistence of their individual members, and will therefore be called upon to assist any member who has become destitute due to bad luck or wanton behaviour.

In the case of Kenya, this situation of a constrained land market is reinforced by the fact that District Land Control Boards in charge of approving land sales are frequently reluctant to permit transactions which would leave families and their descendants landless and destitute. That is why they insist that all adult members of the title-holder's household, including women, are present at the hearing to indicate their agreement with the sale. The government has actually sanctioned this *de facto* situation since a presidential directive aimed at minimising land disputes requires the agreement of family members in addition to that of the title-holder prior to any sale or use of land as collateral (Haugerud, 1983: 84; Mackenzie, 1993: 200; Pinckney and Kimuyu, 1994: 10).

There is a remarkable lesson to draw from the above: under the pressing need to prevent land disputes and family conflicts from multiplying too rapidly, the state has decided to retreat from the most radical interpretation of freehold tenure and to revert to some customary principles of land allocation. Contrary to predictions, central registration of land has not served to reduce land disputes but, if anything, to exacerbate them. Consequently, public authorities are well-advised to rely on decentralised, customary mechanisms of intra-family negotiation and dispute settlement. Economic considerations are not the only rationale for keeping family land. Other more symbolic motives that belong to a traditional realm of values also seem to play a role. In tribal societies, the collective identity of a people is strongly tied to its ancestral land. Since its value is embedded in the social structure and history of a particular community (Riddell et al, 1987: 82-83), land represents far more than a mere input into an agricultural enterprise and it is impossible to abstract it from all the social, ritual, affective and political meanings associated with it.

To sum up, market transactions cannot be expected to be automatically triggered by the establishment of secure private property rights in land, even when they are legally backed and centrally registered. This is because supply

---

3 In this respect, an interesting informal contract is that whereby a widow who is without family and lacks the minimal resources for farming, leases out her land and designates the lessor as heir to it provided that the latter provides her with all basic subsistence requirements, including food and clothing (Lawry, 1993: 70).

of land to the market is limited owing to social security considerations and symbolic reasons. Thus, it can be seen that land titling is not a sufficient condition for land market activation. We will see now that it is not a necessary condition either.

Lack of efficiency-enhancing market transfers

Under conditions of acute land scarcity, and in the absence of land-saving technical innovations and new income-earning opportunities outside the agricultural sector, land sale transactions tend to multiply, even when they are illegal and land is not titled. This is even more likely to happen if customary social security mechanisms are weak or have eroded under the pressure of individualistic tendencies (Baland and Platteau, 1996: 279-83). Distress sales are then the mechanism through which a shortage of voluntary supply is overcome and the land market is activated (a high incidence of migratory flows is another circumstance which will activate land sale transactions).

Spontaneous individualisation of land rights, unassisted by any process of titling or registration at the state level, can be extremely effective in activating the land market even when land sales do actually violate the law. In this respect, it is quite revealing that, in countries such as Rwanda, Uganda, Benin and Zambia, land sale transactions are typically attested by written documents established in the presence of witnesses, thereby ensuring the validity of land transactions. This demonstrates that what matters are *de facto* rather than *de jure* rights. In Rwanda (and in some other parts of Africa), relentless population pressure and a history of much more individualised settlement patterns, making for the absence of genuine community life, have caused the land tenure system to evolve so radically that *de facto* private property rights have emerged even in the absence of state-led registration. The same observation can be made with respect to Uganda.

In order that land sale transactions can lead to efficiency gains, land must be transferred from less to more dynamic farmers. This does not appear to be the main case, however. In fact, the large incidence of distress sales (e.g., in Rwanda see André and Platteau, 1998) suggests that those who abandon ownership are not relatively inefficient farmers, but smallholders who face a comparatively high level of risk exposure and dispose of their land when compelled to do so.

The presence of multiple rural market failures - arising, in particular, from absent insurance markets, wealth-differentiated credit markets, and declining self-insurance capacities on the part of poor rural dwellers - may determine individual wealth trajectories that are highly dependent upon initial endowments. Thus, a succession of bad shocks may drive poor farmers to sell land parcels while better-endowed farmers are able to insure against such shocks through access to credit, temporary depletion of accumulated non-land assets, diversification of income sources (including access to non-agricultural incomes), and a strong social network through which help can be sought.

Are land purchasers likely to be relatively more efficient farmers? There are many grounds to believe that there is no systematic tendency for transacted lands to fall into efficient hands. This is essentially because, in many cases, the motives behind land purchases are not driven by efficiency. To begin with, demand for land may be guided by non-economic motives, such as social prestige and political power. It is common practice not only for the traditional elite to penetrate the modern network of administrative-political power but also, conversely, for the new urban elite to try their best to get elected, co-opted or appointed to traditional chieftaincies after having acquired a significant acreage of local land.

In addition, land purchases may arise out of economic considerations that have nothing to do with efficiency *per se*. Under conditions characterised by the underdevelopment of capital markets and a lack of sufficiently safe investment opportunities, investment in land is very attractive for people with significant savings, usually people with regular incomes from non-agricultural sources (Haugerud, 1983: 80-83; Bruce, 1986: 56; 1993: 42; Green, 1987: 27; André, 1989; Mackenzie, 1993: 209-210). Also, the same social security and insurance considerations that motivate landholders to stick to their land may operate to make other people wish to buy land even though it is not immediately required for subsistence. The land thus acquired may not be brought into efficient cultivation, at least in the short or medium term, a particularly obvious feature of land which is worked by poorly supervised tenants.

Given the above, it is not surprising that absentee ownership is widespread in areas where the land market is active, and that holdings acquired by the educated urban elite "go largely uncultivated" or "tend to be poorly managed and less productive than smaller farms around them" (Bruce, 1993: 42; see also Collier, 1983: 152-153, 159; Green, 1987: 9; Golan, 1990: 15-16; Leservoisier, 1994: 181-82).

The equity effects of land rights formalisation

It has been argued above that advanced systems of individual tenure - including its most extreme development in the form of titling and centralised registration - do not necessarily enhance efficiency when introduced in societies characterised by dynamic, informal institutions at village level. In fact, complete transfer rights do not yet seem to be required for increasing efficiency in present-day Africa, which still exhibits relatively low levels of agricultural technology development (Migot-Adholla et al, 1991). Deepening individual-isation of land tenure, in the sense of adding these rights to a core set of fun-damental use rights and a few important transfer rights (particularly, the right of bequest), is, thus, likely to be premature. This conclusion is reinforced when the adverse distributive consequences which often follow from the establish-ment of freehold tenure are taken into account. These adverse effects may take place through two distinct mechanisms: the adjudication of land rights, on the one hand, and the land sale market, on the other hand.

Equity problems raised by the adjudication of private property rights

Empirical evidence from several African case studies shows that "registration can create rather than reduce uncertainty and conflict over land rights" (Atwood, 1990: 663). This confirms Boserup's diagnosis that "each new step on the road to private property in land may well create less and not more se-curity of tenure, and a vast amount of litigation is the obvious result" (Boserup, 1965: 92). Two sources of increased uncertainty accompanying the establish-ment of fully-fledged private property rights in land deserve to be mentioned here: the loss of derived rights by vulnerable categories of people, and the unfair assignment of rights to the powerful.

• Loss of derived or secondary rights
The idea that land registration is based on an adjudication procedure that does nothing more than recognise and accurately record existing land rights is a gross simplification. If titling can reduce risk and transaction costs for some categories of people, it simultaneously creates new uncertainties for other cat-egories which rely on customary or informal practices and rules (Atwood, 1990: 663-64). In other words, as the experience of Kenya reveals, particular local groups face a serious risk of being denied legal recognition of their cus-tomary rights to land during the registration process (Green, 1987: 6, 22-23). This is especially true of women, pastoralists, hunter-gatherers, low caste people, former slaves and serfs, and people belonging to minority tribes, etc., who have traditionally enjoyed subsidiary or derived rights to land.

Ultimately, if an equity problem arises, it is because traditional tenure rules and rights which determine access to land, water and other resources in such a way as to assure employment for the able and social security for the poor, the old and the disabled, defy recording and classification[4]. Put in another way, it is impos-

---

4 In Senegal and in Gambia, for example, women, older relatives, poor relations, and other 'marginal' compound mem-bers all have rights to compound land under the stewardship of the head of the 'compound' (Von Braun and Webb, 1989; Golan, 1990: 53-54).

sible to bring to the adjudication register all the multiple rights claimable under customary law (Barrows and Roth, 1989: 8). The complex bundle of rights associated with given plots of land are extremely hard to sort out (where one person's bundle of tenurial rights stops and where another's begins is often very difficult to determine). Equally, the landholding unit (such as the 'compound' in West African societies) is rarely under a single management rule (if only because women manage "their" fields fairly independently), so that the cost entailed by comprehensive registration can be prohibitively high. The bureaucratic machinery is confronted by a considerable information gap, and has much less information and knowledge of land tenure history of rural communities than these communities themselves (Riddell et al, 1987: 30-31).

When customary group rights and community control are extinguished by a procedure of registration or titling, there is, in effect, a shift of transaction costs from local land authorities to the state and it is the inability of the state to bear them that explains the failure to adjudicate and register all rights existing under the customary system (Barrows and Roth, 1989: 21). It must also be added that traditional systems of land tenure involve a great deal of flexibility, and recording all the adjustments implied would prove extremely difficult.

To sum up, due to high information and other transaction costs, governments in poor countries are typically unable to record accurately all existing land rights. Such a failure is likely to have two effects: firstly, to create new uncertainties for vulnerable sections of the local population, and secondly, to reduce the efficacy of traditional institutions or mitigating factors that used to provide economic security for all members of village communities and to help hold economic differentiation in check. The latter effect is particularly worth pondering over when economic opportunities in the outside economy are few and no alternative insurance systems exist.

• Unfair assignment of rights to the powerful

In a social context dominated by huge differences in education levels and by differential access to the state administration, there is concern that the adjudication or registration process will be manipulated by the elite in its favour. Experience with land registration and titling schemes has shown that well-informed, powerful and usually educated individuals often compete successfully for land not previously registered in their own name, while the mass of rural people are generally unaware of the new land provisions or do not grasp the implications of registration[5]. It is often the ability to use both statu-

---

5 See, for example, Coldham, 1978: 99; Le Roy, 1979: 72-73; Gastellu, 1982: 275; Wolf, 1982: 247-249; Koehn, 1983, 1984; Noronha, 1985: 145; Engelhard and Ben Abdallah, 1986: 61; Feder and Noronha, 1987: 156-157; Green, 1987: 7; Hoben, 1988: 216; Berry, 1988: 68; Goheen, 1988: 301-305; Shipton, 1988: 106-107; Kerner, 1988: 179; Bruce, 1988: 44; Atwood, 1990: 662-663; Roth, 1993: 317; Firmin-Sellers, 1996.

tory and customary law that enables powerful individuals or groups to enhance their interests. Customary systems are manipulated by those individuals or groups to claim firm rights over large tracts of land which are then registered under the freehold system of tenure (Glazier, 1985: 231; Berry, 1993).

Given the high level of politicisation of wealth allocation and the highly unequal chances of getting access to strategic information or influencing bureaucratic and judiciary decision-making (see, for example, Sklar, 1979; Hyden, 1983; Berry, 1984; Young, 1986; Bayart, 1989), registration can be said to supply a mechanism for transfer of wealth in favour of the educated, economic and political elite (Barrows and Roth, 1989: 8). Insofar as it encourages the assertion of greedy interests with powerful backing and is likely, wittingly or not, to reward cunning, land titling opens up new possibilities of conflict and insecurity. This evolution can have disastrous consequences for vulnerable sections of the population if loss of land is followed by outright eviction (see, e.g., Doornbos, 1975: 60, 66, 73, for Uganda).

One final remark is in order. If titling is not fully subsidised and a charge is therefore levied on landholders, the strategies of powerful individuals is all the more threatening as lack of access to credit and low wealth levels prevent smallholders from registering their land. The cost of registration thus acts as an important rationing mechanism, with smallholders highly vulnerable to attempts by the elites to grab their untitled lands while the latter can protect their own. In other words, titling increases tenure insecurity for the poor because it places a formidable weapon in the hands of the rich who have both better ability to pay the price of registration and superior knowledge of government bureaucracy and procedures (see, e.g., Roth, 1993: 318-319).

• Inequitable distributive effects from the land sale market

Discussion in the previous section has shown that, in countries subject to growing land scarcity, the land market is likely to be activated by poor smallholders who are driven to distress sales.

Traditional systems of social security could, in principle, provide an alternative to land sales as a way to cope with these adverse shocks. However, there are good reasons to believe that such systems are gradually eroding under the combined impact of population pressure and land market development, a process which Carter (1997) describes as the "individualisation of risk exposure" (see also Reardon et al, 1992, for Burkina Faso). Under such conditions, relatively well-endowed households are able to accumulate land and increase their self-insurance capacity, as a result of which they become ever more independent of the reciprocal logic of customary risk-sharing networks. As they pull out, leaving behind those with smaller asset bases, the effectiveness of such networks diminishes to the disadvantage of smallholders. Similarly, individualisation of land tenure tends to threaten informal sharing and risk-pooling arrangements customarily made within extended family households.

To assess the equity effect of land market development properly in densely populated areas, the role of non-agricultural income-earning opportunities must be brought into the picture. If access to rural labour markets is sufficiently open to poorer households, off-farm incomes may provide them with a self-insurance mechanism that reduces the need to sell land under distress conditions. Such incomes also enable them to buy land, thereby enlarging their initially low endowments. If, on the other hand, access to off-farm income opportunities discriminates against poor households, the development of rural labour markets is likely to reinforce the tendency of the land market to increase inequality. To the extent that richer households are usually better educated and better connected, the latter scenario tends to be more common.

Titling, as we have seen earlier, is not a necessary condition for land market activation. Yet, superimposed on an active land market, it may reinforce the disequalising process at work in this market. This is because there is a strong possibility that land titles enhance formal credit supply only for large-scale producers who enjoy a privileged position in terms of market access, as argued above.

As a result of rural market imperfections, titling has more economic value for privileged farmers owning comparatively large amounts of land and having other forms of wealth. The incentive to acquire title is therefore stronger for them and, as we know, this incentive may be compounded by other strategic advantages in terms of access to the government bureaucracy. What must be added now is that, in the same logic of differential market access, titling raises the value not only of the initial land endowment of relatively well-endowed farmers, but also the value to them of the land of less advantaged neighbours. If a free land market exists, therefore, registration of land "may have the unintended consequence of boosting the relative land acquisition incentives and economic power of the already well-endowed" (Carter et al, 1994: 155). By addressing the credit supply problem directly, as suggested earlier, the adverse distributive consequences, and the considerable costs of a titling programme would be averted.

CONCLUSIONS AND POLICY IMPLICATIONS

Where the evolutionary theory of land rights fails and why

The ETLR represents an important attempt to predict how land rights become transformed in countries where land is becoming increasingly scarce due to population growth, market integration and agricultural commercialisation. When its relevance to African experience is examined, two important points emerge:

- Land arrangements and practices, far from being static, are indeed evolving autonomously under the pressure of growing land scarcity, and;
- The significant shifts taking place are, as predicted, geared towards increased individualisation of tenure rights, including enhanced transferability of land assets.

The theory meets serious difficulties, however, when the critical step of formalisation of private property rights under the form of land titling and central registration is considered. This is because the expected effects of formalised land rights on productive efficiency have not materialised. Whether examining the effects of land titling or less formal modes of individualised tenure, the evidence from sub-Saharan Africa shows that interventions to try and increase tenure security in this way do not encourage increased investment, a growth in land market activity, or the availability of credit through the use of land as collateral.

It would seem that basic use rights possibly accompanied by a few fundamental transfer rights (most notably, the right to bequest) provide sufficient security to induce farmers to invest in many parts of sub-Saharan Africa. These rights are typically well-guaranteed by a common set of values and knowledge held by village communities. Also, demand for investment may remain rather low because of a variety of non-tenurial constraints that can often be ultimately ascribed to various market and state failures. At least some of these constraints nevertheless are likely to be gradually relaxed as population density rises and markets develop due to a gradual lowering of transaction costs.

For the ETLR to be valid, evolving factor endowments must simultaneously induce technical advances suitable for the intensification of agriculture while yielding pressure for change in the land rights system. Attractive new investment opportunities will then be available for private investors who, thanks to enhanced security of property rights in land, would now be more willing and able (through the credit supply effect) to invest in agriculture. Unfortunately, this theory of induced technical change cannot be expected to work properly in a context of extremely rapid population growth and severe structural constraints of a physical nature. When challenges arise too abruptly and are massive, it is indeed unreasonable to believe that decentralised processes of spontaneous technical change will suffice to ensure proper supply of technical innovations.

Under such circumstances, technical advance will only arise from deliberate, intensive and prolonged efforts by specialised public agencies, rather than from spontaneous market forces. As a result, there is no guarantee that new technical packages will become available when farmers are ready to invest.

The problem is further compounded by the fact that in sub-Saharan Africa the natural environment is very fragile and diverse, population is widely spread, and the functioning of state bureaucracies is hampered by organisational, financial, ideological and other complex problems which affect their ability not only to foster technical change but also to provide essential inputs and services to agriculture.

As for the failure of the collateralisation effect, it may result from imperfections in the land market that contribute to maintain foreclosure costs at a high level. But it may also reflect the fact that lack of collateral is not the only problem constraining rural credit supply. As is evident from experience elsewhere, rural financial markets often remain fragmented, so that the positive impact of titling on credit appears to manifest itself only for large farms enjoying privileged market access conditions. Registration of smallholder land does not allow them to gain more effective access to credit.

Finally, land titling is neither a necessary, nor a sufficient, condition for the activation of the land market, as the contrasted experience of Kenya (where the land market is rather inactive despite titling) and Rwanda (where the market is quite active despite the illegal character of most land transactions) reveal. The "realisability" effect does not require titling since sales take place whether or not land is titled. The equity effects of land titling also raise important problems. The most perverse effects generally occur at the times of adjudication, since educated and politically connected people are in a better position to benefit from formalised procedures. The operation of the land market does not appear to work in favour of allocative efficiency, nor do land markets seem to be activated by procedures such as titling, contrary to the contentions of the ETLR.

The importance of community-based solutions

As a rule, comprehensive land titling is not a cost-effective operation in most of sub-Saharan Africa today. This is all the more so as landholdings are typically highly fragmented (an important self-insurance device in areas subject to considerable environmental risks) and African governments face tight budget constraints. As a result, it makes sense to explore "community-based solutions to tenure insecurity and a "state-facilitated" evolution of indigenous land tenure systems" (Bruce, 1993: 50-51).

Experience shows that direct state intervention in land matters is better minimised - state intervention is indeed a major source of farmers' insecurity – and since village systems are frequently able to evolve to meet new needs, one may conclude that indigenous land tenure arrangements still have a dominant role to play. What is required is a pragmatic and gradualist approach that re-institutionalises indigenous land tenure, promotes the adaptability of its existing arrangements, avoids a regimented tenure model, and relies as much as possible on informal procedures at local level (Bruce, 1986: 64-68; Atwood, 1990: 667; Migot-Adholla et al, 1991: 170-173).

Reliance on local communities offers significant advantages. First, in contrast to formal procedures such as land titling which are costly and impose definitive land rights, informal practices at village level are cheap (they economise on information costs) and flexible. Second, even though social differentiation is not to be underestimated, African village communities tend to provide social security to all their members and to ensure that everybody can participate in new opportunities. Such considerations of social security and equity usually dominate pure efficiency concerns, which should be regarded as a positive contribution in a generally insecure economic environment. Third, even today, customary systems continue to generate a remarkable degree of consensus, in particular on the norms and values justifying land claims.

Emphasising a crucial role for village communities does not mean falling into the snare of romanticism. Recognising their role is rather a pragmatic attitude grounded in a realistic assessment of sub-Saharan Africa's present predicament. The fact of the matter is that the top-down approach has failed miserably all over Africa, and these communities form dynamic systems which have at their disposal many effective means to pre-empt or subvert any external change which they do not like. Opposing village communities in land matters is all the more difficult as tenure rights are embedded in socio-cultural systems that are not easily bypassed (they embody rules about virtually all aspects of social life, such as marriage, inheritance and power).

What is therefore needed is an approach based on cooperation rather than confrontation. This implies, whenever feasible, a strengthening of local capacities for management, information, and dispute settlement rather than imposing from above the mechanisms of a formal state legal system (Atwood, 1990: 667). In most cases, it also implies recognising the rights of original occupants to "vacant" land located in their ancestral territories (Bassett, 1993). Owing to the persistent influence of traditional concepts of corporate land ownership and identity, it is indeed a more effective strategy for the state to negotiate acceptable compromises with village communities, if the objective is to open pockets of abundant land to stranger cultivators or to improve village lands that are not optimally exploited. Such compromises can, for example, lead indigenous communities to rent out land to landless people in a peaceful atmosphere, so long as their original rights are not disputed or subverted by the state.

This said, when informal institutions and practices are no longer reliable methods of adjudicating land rights and ensuring land tenure security, African governments may have to undertake a formal registration procedure. There are special circumstances where titling may thus be worthwhile, such as when indigenous tenure systems are absent or very weak (e.g. in new settlement areas), or when traditional lines of authority have been severed and loyalties to lineage and communal groups eroded (Migot-Adholla et al, 1991: 170).

Yet, even when uncertainties and tensions prevail that cannot be adequately resolved by local communities - particularly with respect to inter-community relations - or when local practices involve efficiency or equity costs which are deemed excessive, the government does not necessarily need to have recourse to the most costly solution. Thus, short of registration, it could lay down a number of basic, well-publicised principles aimed at validating certain kinds of land claims or transactions (Migot-Adholla et al, 1991: 170; 1994a: 114-17). Through appropriate institutions where government representatives sit side by side with customary authorities, it may be possible to negotiate the best ways of implementing these principles in any given locality, and to verify that they are duly abided by.

As Weitzman (1993) has pointed out in another context, conventional economic theory that draws on the property rights literature may be inadequate because it misses a critical dimension, namely the ability of groups or communities to solve potential conflicts internally, without having recourse to explicit legalistic rules of behaviour. Since such an ability depends to an important extent on the history or culture of the society concerned (an element of social life that cannot be easily changed), this literature may be misinterpreted to suggest that all cultures and societies have the capacity to manage land without the need for titling or other individualised forms of tenure. However, when communities have a good problem-solving potential, to which many experiences in Africa are testament, trying to impose formal rules and procedures on them is counter-productive and involves a considerable waste of resources.

4

Only the Name of the Country Changes*:
The Diaspora of "European" Land Law
in Commonwealth Africa

Patrick McAuslan

INTRODUCTION

This chapter will attempt to assess the impact of "European"[1] land law on policy-making and legal reforms in Commonwealth Africa. It will concentrate on the impact of "old" English land law (as explained below) on English speaking countries in the Commonwealth, since this is where most of my practical and intellectual experience stems. Thus, it looks particularly at eastern and central African states – Kenya, Tanzania, Uganda, Malawi and Zambia. The chapter will also look at the experience with Roman-Dutch law in Southern Africa, drawing on the extensive South African scholarship on this topic and my work on land law in South Africa, Namibia, Swaziland, Lesotho and Zimbabwe. Developments in civil law from other civil law countries in Africa are less well covered and rely on second hand sources.

Issues to be addressed include:

(i)   the impact of concepts and ideas drawn from English and other European land law on perceptions of who owns and controls land in traditional African societies;

(ii) the effect of old English land law as an impediment to innovative approaches to land management in Africa and, the conservatism of the legal profession in Africa on land issues;

---

* The title is based on the well-known sentence from Italo Calvino's book *Invisible Cities* (London 1997) whose theme is that all cities are basically the same: "Only the name of the airport changes." p.128. My thanks to Professor William Twining for drawing my attention to this sentence.

1 The word 'European' is in inverted commas to denote that it is referring to the law of different European countries. Increasingly, in legal discourse, European law is taken to mean the law of the European Union.

(iii) the impact of the introduction of town and country planning law on land tenure, especially in urban areas;

(iv) the divorce between customary tenure and state land law, and the effect this has on land management;

(v) the way forward; the future of European land law in Africa and lessons to be drawn from other parts of the common law world.

In the last decade, a considerable amount of work has been done on the culture clash between Roman-Dutch land law and customary tenure in South Africa and ways to integrate them. But little or no work has been done on the clash between English land law and customary tenure in Africa and the effect of English land law – dominant by virtue of its state backing – on systems of land management in African states[2]. This chapter attempts to fill this gap and contribute to a better understanding of the constraints and opportunities involved in the use of law to secure land rights and manage land in Africa on a sustainable basis[3].

THE RECEPTION CLAUSE

Every story has a beginning, a middle and an end, and this is no exception. The beginning is the reception clause, a legal phenomenon well-known to lawyers in English-speaking Africa, but perhaps less well known to non-lawyers. Since it provides the foundation for the application of English-derived and Roman-Dutch law in those countries – and there are equivalent legislative provisions in civil law countries in Africa – it is necessary to explain it at the outset of this chapter.

Throughout colonial English-speaking Africa, the reception clause provided that, as from a specified date, the common law, the doctrines of equity and statutes of general application applying in England[4] as on that specified date would apply also in the particular country named in the reception clause. In the Southern African dependencies – now Botswana, Lesotho, Swaziland and Zimbabwe – the "received" law as it was called, was Roman-Dutch law from South Africa, which was applied also in Namibia after 1919. Different reception dates applied to different colonial dependencies.

---

2 An honourable exception to this is the work of Martin Charnock (1991). I have to admit that I had not read his paper until after I had committed myself to this paper and then found that my views had been more or less anticipated by him. It seems right to recognise that at the outset of this paper.

3 A good deal of work has been done on this topic in France and in French-speaking African countries but my command of French is not so good that I have been able to go very deeply into the French literature on this. There is some English writing on the subject of the clash between civil land law and customary tenure, not all of it based on African examples, and this will be drawn on in this paper.

4 There are different legal systems and bodies of common law for England and Wales, Scotland and Northern Ireland. A certain uniformity is applied by the final appellate court of the House of Lords but the systems remain distinct. It was the common law of England and Wales that formed the basis of the reception clause; not Scottish law nor the law of Ireland.

All these reception clauses have survived and indeed were confirmed at independence either in the new Constitutions or in an Act passed at the same time as these Constitutions came into force. They have continued to survive and have been reconfirmed in every constitutional change which has taken place in every country since independence. Thus, for periods varying from 77 years (Tanzania) to over 100 years in many other cases, the basic principles of old English Land Law (the land law applicable in England prior to the fundamental reforms of 1925) have been applied to some or all of the land in many English-speaking African countries outside the Roman-Dutch sphere. In very few of these countries has this basic received law been replaced in its entirety by a new country-specific basic law, although in most countries there have been piecemeal reforms. A similar process took place with the reception of Roman-Dutch law; the basic principles as developed in South Africa have continued to apply to the Southern African states where Roman-Dutch law is the received law. Likewise, the two civil law countries in the Commonwealth, Mozambique and the French-speaking half of Cameroon[5], have retained the basic principles of the received Portuguese law and French law respectively.

In the common law and Roman-Dutch legal systems, the development of the law relies very heavily on judicial precedent. Decisions made by judges of the higher courts, which are fully reported in law reports, are then used in later cases to support and justify those later decisions. The effect of the reception clauses allied to the doctrine of judicial precedent has been to import into the legal systems of English-speaking Africa not just the law of England, or South Africa, as it was on the date of reception but, to some extent, as it continues to be interpreted and developed by judges in England and South Africa. Thus, for good or ill, English and South African land law continues to have a major influence, via judicial decisions, on the development of national land laws and thus on national land policies and practices. In some respects the influence has grown since independence; with the collapse in so many countries of a system of national law reports, judges rely on precedents from English and South Africa law reports which continue to be received in the law court libraries in lieu of local reports. The position in civil law countries is rather different since judicial precedents are not nearly so important.

---

5 The "reception clause" arrangements for these two countries were not exactly the same as for English-speaking countries although the effect was the same.

THE BASIC CONCEPTS AND PRESUPPOSITIONS OF "EUROPEAN" LAND LAW

Land law derived from the colonial powers of Europe is based on certain philosophical principles, and uses certain concepts, ideas and techniques which are derived from the specific historical evolution of those European countries. In order to show the effect of these laws on the evolution of land law and policy in African states, it is necessary to have some understanding of these basic principles and concepts. The case of English land law will be examined here.

English land law has always been based on the two fundamental principles of divided rights of ownership and the separation of what is owned from the physical substance of the land itself. In common law countries, which still base their land law on the English system, what is owned is not land in itself but an *estate* or *interest* in the land; a bundle of rights which at its highest confers on the owner of the estate all the powers over a piece of land which a layperson would associate with "ownership". This bundle of rights may be thought of as a bundle of sticks and, like a bundle of sticks, it can be split up into lesser bundles all of which can be owned. So, at any point in time, English land law may recognise several people as having different degrees of ownership or property rights in the same piece of land. The ultimate owner of the land in England is the Crown; 'subjects' own estates in land held from the Crown.

The historical reasons for this position go back to the 11th century. Briefly, William the Conqueror declared all land forfeited to him when he invaded and conquered England in 1066. He drew no distinction between conquest of a country and acquisition of the land of that country. To reward his supporters, he handed out land to them but consistent with the notion that conquest and land ownership were inseparable, his supporters did not get ownership of the land; they held their land from him in the form of an estate – an abstract tenure concept.

By the late 19th century, when reception clauses began to be applied to British colonial dependencies, English land law had evolved into an immensely complex body of law with a huge variety of estates which people could own in the land. These included not only the freehold and leasehold estates which most lay people know of but also future estates, estates for a life or lives, estates that could spring up in the future or shift to another person on the happening of a future event, legal estates and equitable estates based on the concept of a trust. The reason for all this complexity was the desire of the landowning classes in England to keep land in the family by making it as hard as possible for land to be sold or taken away.

During the 19th century, a "long wave" of land law reform began which had as its aims the freeing of land from the family fetters, and the facilitation of a market for land. This was hoped to be achieved through simplification of the law, the introduction of a system of title registration and the elimination of the rights of family members to block commercial transactions in land. Significant reforms took place in 1882, however substantial powers were left in the hands of traditional landowners and the basic rules of land law unchanged. Major reforms which totally altered both the legal framework and the whole philosophical basis of the land law did not take place until 1925. The philosophy changed from a land law geared to protecting the interests of large landowners to one geared towards facilitating a market in land; indeed commentators have suggested that the total body of land law enacted by the reforming legislation of 1925 can be seen as one large Vendor and Purchaser Act.

Thus, without exception, the English land law imposed on countries in Africa via the reception clause was and, with very few exceptions remains, old land law stemming from the pre-1925 reforms; in a few cases in West Africa such laws date from before 1882. This law was complex and wholly geared to English social and economic class relations in existence in late Victorian England. At the same time, it was also in the process of being reformed to become more market-orientated. In no case was any attempt made to tailor the received land or any other law to the circumstances of the colony to which it applied.

The imposition of civil law and Roman Dutch law was, in essence, no different. The law that was imposed was that of late 19th century France and 'European' South Africa. In the latter case, the law was itself an imposed law and geared to supporting the carving out of large estates from African occupied land. The major differences were that these laws reject any notion of divided rights of ownership, and use philosophical or methodological terms not found in English law. While English common law has developed on a case by case basis, civil law develops based on a strictly deductive approach applied within a broader conceptual framework. In relation to property, the civil legal approach leads to one and only one basic right of ownership – *dominium* – with other lesser rights being either limited real rights, acknowledged in Roman-Dutch law, or purely personal rights. The matter is put thus by van der Walt:

> Ownership and only ownership is conceived in terms of the traditional definition of dominium, and therefore becomes the most important and valuable property right in terms of which all other rights (both personal rights and limited real rights) are defined and evaluated. Personal and limited real rights are described in terms of how far they fall short of ownership, thereby subjecting them to ownership as concepts and as rights. (van der Walt, 1996: 177)

On the basis of this admittedly very limited introduction to the basics of the imposed land laws, we must now turn to consider ways in which they have been used in traditional societies and within states in Africa and their impacts on indigenous land relations and land law.

FIVE PHASES IN THE USE OF RECEIVED LAND LAW

The argument advanced here is that, taking the imposition of English land law as the model, we can see five interlocking phases, in terms of the relations between received and indigenous land law. An alternative analysis would see the phases as representing a layering of the law; one approach to law being laid on top of another, rather than displacing it, so that what looks at first sight like a new approach to the law might be disrupted at any time by an older approach breaking through. This is particularly likely to occur with English common law and Roman-Dutch law, where judicial precedents from one phase may be used to subvert or displace a later phase or layer. The five phases are: acquisition; destruction; reconstruction; substitution; and integration. They are discussed in sequence below.

Acquisition

The phase of acquisition commenced in the 19th century. It involved the reversion to the feudal approach to land law; acquisition of territory involved acquisition of the land of which the territory consisted and its availability thereafter to be allocated to supporters of the new sovereign. Specialists in British colonial constitutional law will protest that this analysis overlooks the careful and subtle gradations which existed in that law between conquered colonial territories, ceded colonial territories, protectorates and protected states. Each of these groups experienced a slightly different impact from the application of law. However, on the ground in colonial Africa, the subtleties of colonial constitutional law were not of great importance. Thus, without exception, the British colonial authorities assumed full rights of jurisdiction over all land in every dependency as far as land matters were concerned. All existing customary land laws were subordinated to the received law and so all existing rights in land were at the mercy of the incoming power.

The courts played their part in this charade by helping portray the exercise of political power disguised as the objective application of rules of land law. Commentators have drawn attention to key decisions of the Judicial Committee of the Privy Council – the final court of appeal for the Empire – in the first two decades of the 20th century which culminated in the decision of *Sobhuza II v Miller and others* in 1926[6], the key sentence of which is worth quoting:

The true character of native title to land throughout the Empire including South and West Africa with local variations the principle is a uniform one…The notion of individual ownership is foreign to native ideas. Land belongs to the community not to the individual…The title of the native community generally takes the form of a usufructuary right…Obviously such a usufructuary right, however difficult to get rid of by ordinary means of conveyancing *may be extinguished by the action of a paramount power which assumes possession of the entire control of the land.* (p 525) (italics added)

Conceptually, the view that "the true character of native title to land" did not embrace individual ownership was aided by the fact that freehold title as developed by the common law did not appear to exist in Africa (or Oceania or Asia for that matter) but could readily be introduced once the new legal regime was in place. The Crown as the allodial owner of the land, as in England, was able to obtain freehold title. Naturally, those who did not acknowledge freehold could not obtain it unless they left the system, as some did in the dependencies in West Africa and in the very special case of Buganda in Uganda. In other parts of Africa, and this included the Roman-Dutch dependencies and South Africa, land as divided up into that available for settlement via freehold, leasehold or ownership and that set aside for Africans, where customary law applied, by virtue of the fact that it was allowed to apply by the "paramount power".

The notion that the received land law as a superior law permits and justifies the unrestricted acquisition of land held under customary law dies hard. It was at the root of the Tanzanian case of *Akonaay v A-G* in 1994 where the government argued that those holding land under customary tenure did not own any property and therefore were not entitled to compensation, when in pursuance of Operation Vijiji – the policy of villagisation – they were forcibly removed from their land and made to settle elsewhere, their land being allocated to others. The Government's argument was rejected. As the Chief Justice remarked, such a proposition involved the notion that most Tanzanians were squatters in their own country (see also Chapter 5, this volume). This is, however, exactly the position that the colonial approach to customary land law had involved. A further illustration is provided by a draft Communal Land Tenure Bill prepared by consultants for Namibia in 1995 which perpetuated the notion that those occupying land under communal (customary) tenure did so only by permission of the government and could be moved off their land with minimal

---

6 [1926] AC 518. Miller was a major landowner in Swaziland. His name still graces the main street in the capital, Mbabane. The other leading cases were *In re Southern Rhodesia [1919] AC 215 and Amodu Tijani v Southern Nigeria (Secretary) [1921] AC 399.*

notice at any time. Constitutional rights to security of property applied apparently only to those holding land under Roman-Dutch tenure.

Destruction

Destruction followed naturally from acquisition. Acquisition involved the displacement of indigenous law by the received law so facilitating the displacement of indigenous landowners by incoming landowners as in East, Central and Southern Africa. In West Africa, the alienation of land was less marked but nonetheless helped to facilitate the growth of a market in land, an essential aspect of the growth of a cash economy, based on crops grown for export.

Destruction involved the denial of the rules and practices which governed land rights amongst Africans as a form of law. They certainly were not law in the Austinian sense of "orders backed by threats" which was the foundation of the colonial system of law. Denying the status of "law" to rules of customary tenure made it much easier to set the rules aside and so set the people living under those rules aside, or at least accord them lesser status in respect of their land rights. Here too, the Privy Council cases noted earlier were relevant, but statutory examples abound in which the superiority of received land law over customary land law is asserted. There are the obvious examples from what might be called the settler colonies of Eastern and Southern Africa but it is the less obvious examples which are, perhaps, the more telling.

Thus, in Uganda, outside the *mailo* land in Buganda, all land was declared to be Crown land and available for allocation, via freehold or leasehold. Those actually occupying Crown land under customary tenure, that is, all Ugandans except those on *mailo* land, could be moved off when it was leased. This received law trumped customary law, and Ugandans became tenants at will of the state. This position was retained after independence and in fact the position of customary land-holders worsened after the passage of the Land Reform Decree of 1975. It was only with the enactment of the Constitution of 1995 that those occupying land under customary tenure were accorded equal status in law with those occupying land under freehold, leasehold and mailo tenure – this last being a variant of freehold tenure[7].

In Tanganyika, it required the intervention of the League of Nations in the 1920s to ensure that customary rights were given the same legislative status as statutory rights – the basic land-holding right in Tanzania to this day and governed by the received law. But as numerous commentators have pointed out, the position in practice has always been to accord customary right of occu-

---

7 Constitution of Uganda 1995, Article 237. See too the Land Act, 1998 which fleshes out the general principles enshrined in the Constitution.

pancy a lower status[8]. Nowhere is this more overt than in the case of urban rights of occupancy, where the extension of the Town and Country Planning Ordinance to areas governed by customary law, instantly imposes development standards geared to English planning standards which customary occupiers cannot meet. The consequence is that their occupation becomes illegal. In rural areas too, the independent government of Tanzania continued the colonial approach to customary land tenure by purporting to abolish it and replace it by statutory laws on several occasions in the 1970s and 1980s.

Customary law was also set aside in relation to vacant and unoccupied lands. Colonial authorities everywhere in Africa claimed a right to such land. Bentsi-Enchill refers to it as a prerogative entitlement and states: "The claim was everywhere met with the counter-assertion by indigenous peoples that there was no land without an owner" (1975: 69). But that was to pose notions of customary tenure against the common law and the civil law and in that contest there could be only one winner. Bentsi-Enchill defends the colonial expropriation of "vacant land" as being in reality a "legislative device for preventing land from being unduly alienated to foreigners [a.k.a Europeans] and thus ensuring its use to local people. The model for this kind of legislation was the Land and Native Rights Ordinance 1916 of Nigeria," reproduced elsewhere in West African dependencies. It is an odd form of reasoning that justifies a government of foreigners imposing its own law on land occupied by Africans so that the land becomes subject to the superior power of that government, to prevent those Africans from disposing of their land to those same foreigners. It should be realised that to foreign governments, their law did not *replace* customary law; it applied law where there had been none before. As Bentsi-Enchill puts it:

> The colonial powers took surprisingly few positive steps to reform or modernise [African] systems of law…The noteworthy fact is that very little legislative assistance was given during the colonial period to the necessary process of adapting and modifying the indigenous systems of land tenure to enable them to cope more efficiently with changing circumstances. (1975: 70)

On the other hand, the fact is only noteworthy if it is assumed that the colonial powers saw these as systems of law which could be and should be reformed by legislative means. If there was a policy at all, it was one of benign neglect. Customary law was thought of as a stage in the evolutionary process and it would gradually be replaced by the received law. In civil law Africa, this

---

8 See Twaib, 1996, for a good summary of the whole debate on the subject.

was to be hastened by *immatriculation*, a formal process whereby a person could opt out of customary law and become subject to the received law. In common law West Africa, market forces and judicial decisions gradually helped freehold tenure to make headway over customary tenure. In East, Central and Southern Africa, on the other hand, customary land tenure was increasingly used as a tool of governance, as described below.

There was another reason why land law reform via legislation was not considered to be a possible way forward, at least in common law Africa and in the early decades of the 20th century. Old English land law was perfectly suited to the circumstances of colonial society in East, Central and Southern Africa and could readily be adapted to the hierarchies of traditional societies in West Africa. The social basis of Africa tenure systems comprised a few large landowners who were able to tie their land up in such a way as to prevent others, eg, governments and 'the people' getting their hands on it. Large numbers of people with no secure title to their land were thus available for work on terms fixed by the large landowners. Land law reform in England involved a shift in a democratic direction: a new land law to reflect and assist into being a new society where it would become easier for ordinary people of limited means to acquire land with secure tenure. This was not an approach favoured either by colonial authorities or the new common law landowners.

Reconstruction

The use of the term "reconstruction" here to describe the third phase of relations between colonial and customary law may not be quite apt, but it is designed to draw attention to the 'new scholarship' on law in Africa. This seeks to show how colonial officials used and adapted customary law to suit their own ends; and how customary law in fact long ago ceased to be part of traditional society – a bulwark against the colonial authorities – and became, instead, part of the colonial apparatus of rule.

There has always been a close connection between land law and public law in Europe, as the rules which regulate the manner in which people may acquire, deal with, use and lose land greatly affect political stability in any state and therefore must be of prime concern to governments. This connection between land law and political stability was also made an important basis for the system of indirect rule which characterised British colonial rule in Africa and was not entirely absent from other colonial systems. In areas set aside for Africans in British dependencies in East, Central and Southern Africa, traditional authorities were accorded significant powers over the allocation of land which were used to police and control populations.

Essentially, what was at issue here was the question of rights versus administrative discretion. Received land law dealt with rights and in particular the rights of individuals to own and deal with their land as they saw fit, subject to fairly general common law restrictions, such as nuisance and trespass and a few statutory restrictions. As the American legal philosopher, Cohen, put it in a famous piece written in the 1920s, ownership of land enables one to put up a sign at the boundary addressed to the world: "Keep off". But this was not an attitude that Africans were permitted by the colonial authority. Thus, not only were the benefits of received land law denied to the majority of inhabitants in colonial dependencies but strenuous efforts were also made to prevent the infiltration of ideas from received land law into customary tenure.

Charnock (1991) summarises the position as follows:

> The question of how to respond to the growing assertion of individual rights and especially to the sale of land, became the crucial terrain of conflict over customary tenure. For it seemed fairly plain that this was not customary behaviour and therefore not legitimate for Africans to engage in. It appeared to be against both the legal and the socio-political regimes of colonialism and against the views of African social institutions sanctioned by both conservative administrators and liberal anthropologists…This process of assertion of individual rights has also generally been reproved by historians. Typical is Boahen's summation: "the commercialisation of land…led to illegal sale of communal land by unscrupulous family heads.
>
> [There were] fundamental concerns of colonial governments about [developments in the areas of leasing, mortgage and sale]: a fear of social dislocation, often cast in a protective framework of concern over the creation of an indebted peasantry and a landless class…Extensive legal intervention by the state was consistently proved to be necessary to maintain the customary regime. Native authorities and district officers were given wide powers to check dispositions of interests in land. (pp. 68, 71)

Reconstruction was the dominant approach to customary tenure in what might be called the middle era of colonialism: the 1920s to the 1950s. This reconstruction of customary tenure by, for example, the deliberate suppression of any cross-fertilisation from the received land law and the imposition of administrative controls on the operation of customary tenure, has had a profound effect on approaches to land tenure and land law reform in the era of independence, at least until very recently. In virtually all countries in English-speaking Africa, the dominant approach to land tenure was one of the maintenance of the dual system and the imposition of tight administrative controls on the customary system. In some countries, e.g., Tanzania in the 1960s and Zambia in

1975, controls were based on the principle that customary tenure did not recognise a market in land and that such a tendency must be prevented from developing. In Nigeria, a more or less unrestricted land market in the southern part of the country was subjected to the administrative controls long imposed on land tenure in the northern part of the country via the Land Use Decree of 1978. In Swaziland, one of the bases of the King's coup in 1973 was to reassert full politico-administrative control over the land and use that power the better to assert control over the population. Even where a land market was accepted and provided for, it was on the basis that customary law had to be replaced.

Substitution

The era of substitution may be dated from the mid 1950s. A defining document was the report of the Royal Commission on East Africa (1955) with its firm espousal of a rapid move towards security of tenure based on freehold tenure for the indigenous populations of the three East African countries of Kenya, Tanganyika (as it then was) and Uganda. Kenya was the first country to take such a step, impelled as much by political factors associated with Mau Mau as by the economic factors which lay behind the Royal Commission's recommendations. The aim of Kenya's policies and laws developed in the 1950s and refined via the Registered Land Act 1962 and the Land Adjudication Act 1968, is to record the customary rights and interests in land which exist, metamorphose them into 'equivalent' rights and interests recognised by the common law, register them and provide a legal framework for the operation of a market in these newly minted rights and interests. The legal framework created in Kenya – the Registered Land Act – was the first piece of land legislation in English-speaking Africa which consciously and deliberately was modelled on the 'new' 1925 English land law, suitably adapted and simplified for the circumstances of Kenya. It promoted the growth of a property owning democracy via a simplification of the process of acquiring and dealing in land.

These aims may now seem naïve some forty years on, with the advantage of hindsight and our knowledge of the imperfections of the land market in Kenya (see Chapter 3, this volume). However, they have influenced and continue to influence policies elsewhere. Malawi provided for adjudication and conversion of customary tenure as far back as 1967. Zanzibar, in a series of major reforming laws in the early 1990s, has gone most of the way down the Kenyan route, though not to the extent of permitting freehold tenure (Jones, 1996). The Tanzanian National Land Policy, following the recommendations of the Presidential Commission on Land Matters, committed the Government to permit persons holding land under customary tenure to obtain, via a process akin to adjudication, a customary right of occupation of indefinite duration – though they stopped short of using the politically incorrect term "freehold"[9]. Uganda's Land Act 1998 also provides adjudicatory mechanisms for the acquisition of individual customary titles and the conversion of these titles to freehold, governed thereafter by the received law (McAuslan, forthcoming). Zambia's Land Act 1995 provides for the conversion of customary use and occupation rights into leases of 99 years, also governed thereafter by the received law.

There are some differences between the Kenyan model and more recent developments. The Ugandan Land Act and the Tanzanian laws make more attempt than did the Kenyan law to assimilate customary law and the received law and so come closer to the integration model discussed below. But they also adopt the fundamental principle that the overall aim of the reforms is to move towards individual ownership of land or rights in land. Another difference between the Kenyan model and the Ugandan and Zambian model is that the latter two countries have, to date, retained much of the old English land law rather then developing a more country-specific land law[10].

An alternative variant to the Kenyan model has been what might be called the *immatriculation* model, although it is to be doubted whether there has been any conscious borrowing from civil law countries when this model has been introduced in English-speaking Africa. Under this model, the received law is "opened up" to the whole population so that those who want to can obtain land under a lease or right of occupancy without any restrictions and this could be land which was hitherto governed by customary tenure. Thus, the Land Act 1979 of Lesotho introduced leasehold as the main statutory system of landholding in Lesotho and it is clear from the Act that it was designed to replace customary tenure, at least in the urban areas of Lesotho. No formal system of adjudication was established, however, and the Act has proved unpopular and virtually unworkable since its enactment, as it was perceived as an attempt to cut the chiefs out of the land allocation process and to facilitate foreign (South African) acquisition of land in Lesotho (Franklin, 1995).

Another example of this model is the Agriculture (Commercial Land Reform) Act 1995 of Namibia, which sets up a programme for the resettlement of Namibians from the overcrowded communal lands in the north of the country to the sparsely populated ranch lands in the south. Those who move will be governed by Roman-Dutch law as modified by strict ministerial controls on transactions. No allowance is made in the Act for the application of custom-

---

9 This is provided for by the Land Act, 1998 and Village Land Act, 1998. Both these Acts were enacted in 1999. For two views on the Tanzanian reforms, see McAuslan (1998)

10 Interestingly, one of the areas where both Uganda and Zambia have tackled old English land law is trusts. Uganda introduced a variant of the English Trustee Act 1925 via the Trusts Ordinance in 1954, the relevance of which to the majority of the population was absolutely nil, while Zambia via the Trusts Restrictions Act of 1970 repealed the old English law of trusts, settlements and future interests, replacing it with a more restrictive regime. See Kaunda (no date) on the Zambian law.

ary law at all.

It is perhaps appropriate to mention here the matter of registration of title. Title registration is an integral part of the Kenyan model of substitution and, as such, finds a central place in the new Zanzibari laws. But provisions for the registration of title have long been a part of the received law all over Africa and it must be admitted fit rather uneasily into the framework of analysis offered here. They were mainly concerned to provide for the registration of non-African owned land, but not exclusively so. Where they had a wider remit, they can be seen as an early form of the substitution layer. A good example of this is the Registration of Title Act of Uganda passed in 1922 and a strong contender for the title of the worst drafted statute on land law in English-speaking Africa[11]. Based on the registration statute of the State of Victoria enacted there in 1916, it provides for the registration of, amongst others, *mailo* land in Uganda with dealings thereafter having to comply with the statutory code rather than customary rules. Kenya too in 1908 introduced a registration law designed to bring order to the chaos, as it was perceived to be, of titles in the coastal strip – the old and original Protectorate of Kenya, leased from the Sultan of Zanzibar. Ninety years on, there is still confusion relating to titles at the coast.

The history of registration in Ghana is quite instructive in this respect (Agbosu, 1990; Woodman, 1988). Registration was first introduced into the Gold Coast (as Ghana then was) in 1883. The Land Registration Ordinance of that year and its successor Land Registry Ordinance of 1895 were basically laws to register deeds rather than title. They were introduced to try and bring about some order and security of title in the rapidly growing land market which was developing in the southern parts of the Gold Coast via an amalgam of customary and common law. As successive Commissions over the years testified, the Ordinances were gravely deficient and did little to lessen land disputes or increase security of title. The Land Registry Act 1962 did little to rectify matters. In Agbosu's words:

> The Land Registry Act inherits substantially the same defects from which its predecessors suffered. The Act retains the deeds registration system which falls short of a title registration system…It falls short of making the attachment of accurate plans to registrable instruments a *conditio sine qua non* for their acceptance for registration…The Act makes no positive provision for the establishment of an adjudication tribunal and its supporting staff for the purpose of final determination of title to land. (1990: 120-121)

---

11 See the splendid critique of the Act in Henry West's Land Policy in Buganda, Cambridge 1972, pp. 166 et seq.

The Law of 1986 however made a decisive break with the past. It provides for the registration of titles and as a corollary, for processes of adjudication. Unlike the Kenyan model however, the Law provides for the registration of existing customary rights in the land without any changes to the nature or content of those rights. As Woodman (1988) points out, this marks this system off from those, argued for consistently and strongly by Simpson, a former Land Tenure Adviser to the British Ministry of Overseas Development, and his successor Lawrence. They were of the view that title registration must be seen as part and parcel of tenure reform, which should lead to the replacement of customary tenure by English-type tenure. While Woodman sees the 1986 Law as neutral in its effect on possible future developments in tenure, Agbosu argues that:

> The introduction of a system of title registration at this time is not motivated simply by a desire to secure titles so as to prevent costly litigation. It is intended to satisfy the demands of the business community by confirming, consolidating and crystalising in legal form the private landed rights acquired in the last hundred years through the commercialisation, usurpation and privatisation of communal land... (1990: 124)

Agbosu sees the introduction and use of English land law and doctrines of contract over the same period as being directed to the same end. Thus, he would argue that the maintenance of the form of customary tenure in the Law of 1986 should not blind one to the fact that the Law is part and parcel of a policy of changing the substance of the law to facilitate the operation of the market economy – the same *raison d'être* of the Kenyan model.

Integration

Integration, the fifth phase, refers to the attempts to develop a new common land law of a particular country from the disparate parts of the existing law – received law, customary law, statute law. The basis for this approach is a rejection of any notion of a hierarchy of land laws within a country; there is just one land law derived from different sources and it is the function of the legislature and in particular of the judiciary to fashion from these diverse sources, based on different philosophies one law based on one philosophy which can apply to all land and all people.

In terms both of articulating this approach intellectually and applying it in practice, the land reform programme of South Africa leads the way here, though this programme is by no means the first attempt at this approach. That position must be accorded to Botswana and its pioneering Tribal Land Act of

1968 (Frimpong, 1986; Ng'ong'ola, 1992)[12]. This law aimed at modernising customary land tenure by democratising the process of allocation of land through the establishment of Land Boards. These make allocations on the basis of applications for land, developing a more formal approach both to allocation and cancellation of a grant. The Land Act also provides for the possibility that boards may grant leases and freeholds which would be governed by the received Roman-Dutch law, subject to the overriding powers of the Land Boards as lessors of the land. Integration here was to be a function more of administration than of legal rules since both common law and customary law tenures have been retained but in the eyes of some commentators the stage has been set for increasing legal integration in the future.

The South African land reform programme stems from the Constitution which mandates the government to "take reasonable legislative and other measures, within its available resources, to foster conditions which enable citizens to gain access to land on an equitable basis" (Constitution, Art 25(5)). The programme has three aspects to it; land redistribution; land restitution; and from a legal perspective, most complex and far-reaching, security of tenure. Legislation on all three topics has been enacted but what may be regarded as the centrepiece – the Land Rights Bill – has still to be brought forward and its future is uncertain in the light of changes in land policies consequent on the general election in June 1999 (see Chapters 7 and 13, this volume). It is this law which will be making the greatest strides towards integration – attempting a reconciliation between the norms and practices of customary land tenure, the rather austere and rigorous concepts of Roman-Dutch law and the requirements of the Constitution.

There has been a considerable amount of legal writing on the land reform programme, much of it addressing the issue of the extent to which Roman-Dutch law can accommodate the new approaches. Some of the most thought-provoking writing has come from van der Walt who highlights some of the legal aspects of the programme as follows:

> A number of new rights completely unknown to Roman-Dutch law have been introduced to improve access to and strengthen the security of 'Black' land rights.
>
> Many reforms are aimed at providing statutory security or backup for traditionally insecure or weak rights and others are characterised by strong policy-orientated efforts to change the current distribution of land rights. Both these categories amount to efforts to change the relative position of 'Black' land rights vis-à-vis 'white' Roman-Dutch land rights.

---

12 See also the Report of the Presidential Commission on Land Tenure, (Gaborone, 1983).

The constitutional arrangements around land reform, especially in the 1996 Constitution, demonstrate a clear intention to break down the paradigmatic primacy and inviolability of existing (mostly 'white') land rights and create a new, constitutional, balance between the protection of existing rights and the promotion of land reform.

Some land reform measures demonstrate a tendency to privilege traditional, Roman-Dutch property structures (where full ownership is regarded as the strongest and most secure right); others demonstrate a tendency to opt for a greater fragmentation of land rights (where a wider range of differentiated rights is promoted and, where necessary, bolstered by statutory security of tenure). (Van der Walt, 1998)

There seems to be general agreement amongst commentators that Roman-Dutch law will be able to accommodate the new approach to land tenure but only, according to van der Walt, if it adopts an alternative approach to property which fits in with the values espoused in the Constitution:

Such an alternative approach to property would require a very decisive move away from the civil-law tradition, both with regard to its methodology and its substance. What seems to many to be the strongest point of the civil-law tradition, its conceptualist methodology, poses perhaps the greatest threat to the new legal order. The new legal order cannot afford to use 'tradition as a substitute for value choices' while covertly relying on the seedy and seamy underside of the seemingly respectable pre-1994 civil-law tradition. Property lawyers will have to 'search for social conditions, including cultural understandings of law, legality and rights, under which collective determinations of aspects of social life are consistent with personal freedom.' (Van der Walt, 1995)

This challenging statement could well be taken as a general text for lawyers concerned with land tenure reform in Africa. For too many of these lawyers, at least in English-speaking Africa, a little bit of tinkering with old English land law, bringing in a bit of new English land law, represents the height of their ambition[13].

---

13 See, eg, Kludze (1974) "It [the Decree] brings the law in Ghana generally into line with the current English law and makes the modern standard works on English law more helpful" (at p. 2).

SOME GENERAL CONCLUSIONS

On the basis of the foregoing analysis some tentative conclusions may be drawn which may be of use to policy-makers and lawyers thinking about land reform via law.

First and foremost, and perhaps obviously, no country starts with a clean slate when it comes to land law reform. This point is not just about the existing legislative texts. It refers to the contending philosophies which lie behind the texts and the existing vested interests which support them. The principal thrust of this chapter is that one cannot avoid the past; the baggage of negative attitudes towards customary land tenure bolstered by statutes passed in colonial times, and still applied, remains an impediment to the kind of land reform which Botswana, South Africa, Uganda and Tanzania have embarked upon and hopefully, other countries will follow.

What the past also tells us is that land laws in African countries, as in all other countries, have been first and foremost the products of politics, not of "objective" considerations of what is best for economic or social or sustainable development. Being products of politics, they have been enacted by and are directed to benefiting the ruling group in each country. It might seem obvious that a simpler land law or a land law that integrates the people's law with state law would be a positive good to be aimed for, but it might not be seen that way by the political and administrative elites. A complicated law and a law which denies rights in the land to the majority of people, leaving them at the mercy of administrative discretion, provides opportunities for accumulation of land and rent-seeking behaviour by those elites. Independence was three or more decades ago for most countries in Africa; why has there not been a greater effort to develop more relevant people-friendly land laws all over the continent?[14]

The attitudes of the legal profession cannot be ignored. They often have a vested interest in the status quo. Recent scholarship has shown how the English legal profession had a powerful role in shaping the final form and substance of the English property law reforms of 1925. It would be unwise to assume that the legal professions in countries in Africa will put the national interest before their own professional concerns. For many of them in English-speaking Africa, and I would suspect in French-speaking Africa as well, law reform which departs from the metropolitan model is instinctively regarded with suspicion[15]. The formal superiority of the received law is allied to a con-

---

14 For a critique along these lines of urban planning policies and laws in African countries, see McAuslan, (forthcoming).
15 In Uganda, for instance, in connection with the Land Act 1998, there were not wanting lawyers who were unhappy at the notion that freehold tenure in Uganda could be different to freehold tenure in England. In Namibia, the legal profession were very unhappy at attempts to develop a new intermediate urban tenure to facilitate the urban poor gaining access to land and made plain that they would not recommend it to the banks as a safe form of security for lending. See also Kaunda (no date) who recommends the re-introduction of trusts and settlements into Zambian land law and Kludze (1974).

cern to perpetuate the law they practice and know best.

Allied to the conservatism of the legal profession is the question of language. There are two aspects to the language of the law; the technical legal language which lawyers write and speak in; and the European language – Afrikaans, English, French, Portuguese – in which even now most laws are drafted and most of the higher courts conduct their proceedings. The combination of technical and "foreign" languages represents a barrier to most landowners' ability to make use of the law in acquiring or protecting rights in the land. More important has been the problem of how to 'translate' the concepts and ideas of customary land tenure into received law. In the past, the "solution" has often been to ignore interests which could not be accommodated within the confines of received law; this has tended in particular to affect the interests of women adversely. A greater awareness exists in other parts of the world of the importance of the language in which law is expressed and the need to accommodate indigenous rights within statutory systems.

There should therefore be a much greater willingness on the part of land law reformers to look beyond the colonial models. The common law world, for instance, has a wealth of experience and models to draw on, many of them of infinitely greater relevance to land reform in Africa than the products of the English Law Commission. One matter can however be learned from the English and the South African experience: land law reform is best not done piecemeal (cf Chapter 7, this volume). Tenure reform needs to be accompanied by reform of the law relating to transactions; a new tenure reform law aimed at simplifying the means of obtaining title and directed to small-holders will be frustrated if the law dealing with land transactions remains rooted in an older tradition.

This broader process of reform is needed for several reasons. First, there would otherwise be a mismatch between a law on tenure that attempted to accommodate the integrationist perspective and a law on transactions that did not; it might be difficult for some persons with "new" statutory rights to buy or sell these rights. Second, the old law is couched in language even more difficult to understand than much modern land law. Third, there is a greater willingness to make use of standard forms in modern land law, so greatly simplifying and reducing the costs of transactions. Fourth, just as tenure change must be geared to the needs of the country, so should any law on land transactions. There may, for example, be a need for some restrictions on dealings or special procedures that have to be observed before a dealing can be valid which are relevant to the circumstances of a particular country. Such provisions exist in England, rooted in the particular historical circumstances of the land law of England. However, there is no reason for such provisions to be replicated elsewhere, as is too often the case, where English law has been adopted uncritically.

The integration of the received and indigenous law is now widely recognised as the way to go. Other ways have been tried and found wanting. It is always tempting to think that the present generation has found the answer to problems that have proved so intractable in the past. In this case, however, it is difficult not to believe that an approach that seeks to marry the law recognised as legitimate by the populace at large – customary law derived from local concerns and needs – with state law – a law that can and should take account of the wider national and international interests – is indeed the most appropriate way forward for those involved with land tenure reform. Such an approach does not dictate any particular solution, but is rather concerned with the method of analysing and developing possible solutions.

Two pathways to achieving this marriage of laws may be identified. The first is the enactment of a national land law which attempts to integrate local laws and certain imported laws into one unified law. This must be preceded by a thorough study of the existing land tenure situation. Part and parcel of any such an approach, must be the duty given to dispute-settlement bodies to help develop a common land law through the decisions they make which should aim to blend the local with the national. This may be seen as a top-down approach, informed by experience and views from the grass-roots[16]. The second pathway involves leaving it all to the grass-roots and replicating the evolution of common law. Such an approach must accept that it will be many generations before a national integrated land law emerges from a multiplicity of local decisions and local law making. Whatever the theoretical advantages of adopting such a bottom-up approach, the practicalities of governance in the modern world suggest that the former approach is more realistic.

A further point must be made about law reform that goes a little beyond the strict confines of this chapter. Alongside any programme of law reform, there must be a plan for implementation of the new law which includes a budget. Opposition to implementation must be foreseen and a response planned. This was not done in Uganda, so that it was only after the enactment of the Land Act, 1998 that the relevant Ministry began to realise the implications of what had to be done. This involved the huge financial costs, a revolution in styles of land management and a shift in the balance of power between the Ministry and local authorities; the training needs of new land management authorities; the organisation of the new judicial system requiring over 1000 Land Tribunals; and the need for a plethora of rules, regulations and forms. Overall, the Land Act required a major programme of capacity building. It is not to be wondered that things moved very slowly even with external assistance from the British government. A great deal of tension was generated within the relevant Ministry

---

16 For a discussion of this approach applied generally, see Sachs and Welch (1990). The approach to land law reform in mainland Tanzania also approximates to this.

as officials tried to come to grips with their new roles – more guidance and facilitation than command and control – and the need to operate in partnership with local government and institutions of civil society.

So too in South Africa, a good deal of work took place in 1999 in preparation for the implementation of the Land Rights Bill. But there must remain a doubt as to whether the politics of implementation – the loss of political control over land which many traditional rulers will face as a result of enactment of the Bill – might not yet derail the whole process.

Will the wheel then come full circle? The diaspora of land law from Europe to Africa was to facilitate the grabbing of land from Africans by colonial officials and settlers. The idea that the law relating to land was also part of the law relating to governance, and existed for the benefit of the ruling class, was embedded in the culture of colonialism. But it was also part of the culture of many African societies, so that there was an easy transfer of the colonial approach to the new independent governments. Liberalising the law, removing the central organs of the state from management of land, and allowing a market in land to develop thus pose fundamental governance and power challenges to African governments. Both liberal market reformers and those espousing reforms aimed at conferring land owning rights on the people may then be disappointed as, whatever the form of the new laws, the temptations of the old approach will be too powerful for governments to resist completely.

5

Harmonising Formal Law and Customary Land Rights in French-Speaking West Africa*

Philippe Lavigne Delville

INTRODUCTION

The complexity of land tenure in West Africa is the result of the coexistence of several systems (whether customary - sometimes with Islamic influence - or state), none of which is completely dominant. Modern tenure legislation, designed in accordance with the model of private ownership and registration, takes no account of the legal principles underlying local land-holding systems, so that, in the eyes of the state, most rural people's landholding status is precarious, if not actually illegal. This legal pluralism, deriving from the colonial era causes a degree of uncertainty about land rights and leads to conflicts for which the many different arbitration bodies (customary, administrative and judicial) are unable to find lasting solutions. The gross inadequacy of colonial tenure legislation, which was largely retained after independence, resulted in legal reforms being adopted by African states during the 1980s. The reforms aimed to incorporate local land rights into the national legal framework, although the approaches differed widely. This chapter summarises current thinking on rural tenure issues in West Africa, then describes and analyses recent experiences before drawing some conclusions about ways to harmonise customary rights and formal law.

---

* This paper is based on the work of a team of specialists led by the author on behalf of the French Ministry of Co-operation as part of the "Plan of Action on Tenure". The programme of work links with the Franco-British Initiative on tenure of the UK's Department for International Development (see Lavigne Delville, ed, 1998; Lavigne Delville, Toulmin, and Traoré, forthcoming; and Lavigne Delville, 1998a). However, the analysis and interpretation offered here are the responsibility of the author alone. An earlier revision of this chapter was first published in Politique des structures et action foncière au service du développement agricole et rural, proceedings of the seminar in Réunion, CNASEA/AFDI/FNSAFER, 1998.

STATE LAW AND LOCAL LAND-USE SYSTEMS: LEGAL PLURALISM AND "MANAGING CONFUSION" IN WEST AFRICA

Socially-determined land-use rules

Any attempt at an overview of local systems shows the wide variety of situations on the ground and the profound transformation that they have undergone. Nevertheless, where customary tenure principles and local regulatory mechanisms still prevail it is possible to point out some common features. These include the fact that rules governing access to land and resources are an integral part of the social structure, tenure being inseparable from social relationships and that the use of land confers certain rights. These principles are implemented and arbitrated by customary authorities, whose legitimacy usually derives from prior occupancy (they are the descendants of the community founders) and the magic/religious alliance with the local spirits, or from conquest (Chauveau, 1998). These authorities (the land chiefs) then control the territory, exercising their political power to allocate land to other lineage groups and carrying out the rites required for them to clear it for cultivation (Bouju, 1998). Families settled in this way have control over the bush areas allocated to them, and these can become family landholdings with transmissible cultivation rights. Individual farmers may themselves delegate cultivation rights to "outsiders", in the form of short-term loans or, quite often, loans of unlimited duration with restrictions on the permanent investments allowed. There may even be various types of rental or share-cropping arrangements allowed (Le Roy, 1998b). Such "outsiders" may marry into the community and become full members of it, thereby changing their status, and rights to claim access to land.

The distribution of rights is, therefore, based on the socio-political system (the political history of the village and region from which the alliances and hierarchical relationships between lineages are derived) and on family relationships (access to land and resources depending on one's social status within the family), so that social networks govern access rights (Berry, 1993). Far from being the result of a series of precise rules, rights held by individuals are the fruit of negotiations in which the local land authorities act as arbiters; customary law is by nature "procedural" and not codified. It does not define each person's rights, but the procedures by which access to resources is obtained (Chauveau, 1998).

These basic principles continue to apply in most of rural Africa, even though the authorities, socio-economic conditions and the rights themselves have profoundly changed over time. Researchers prefer to talk about local landholding systems, and "socially-determined land-use rules" *(logiques sociales du territoire)*, rather than customary systems *(système coutumier)*, since the latter term could suggest something "traditional" or "ancient" with roots in the past (Mathieu, 1995). As is demonstrated by many field studies, local landholding systems do not consist of the rigid rights so often described in earlier academic literature. They are flexible, and evolve in accordance with customary practice whereby rights are negotiated with the authorities on the basis of a number of shared principles. For example, new land-use rules may develop for valley bottom land *(bas-fonds)* in response to new ways of farming, market opportunities and alterations to social relationships. Tenure rules also evolve in the face of major changes in the conditions of production, or when the pressure on resources increases. There is no system that is "traditional" or customary in itself, but there are forms of land management based on customary principles.

Legal pluralism: the state and society

Colonial governments, and the independent states which followed them, enacted legislation on land and renewable resources. The colonial state was motivated by the desire to assert its power and to transform farming into a sector geared to development, but its action was based on profound ignorance of the local system, both in terms of tenure and production. Some of the mechanisms imposed (e.g. public registration, derived from the Torrens system developed in Australia to distribute land among the settlers) involved the dispossession of local landholders in favour of colonial settlers (Comby, 1998). In French-speaking regions, the urge for centralised authority led the colonial state to seek to break the power of the customary authorities and replace them with state management, particularly regarding forests, fisheries, etc. In English-speaking regions, the system of indirect rule left more room for customary authorities. These colonial "traditions" were based on a different conception of the relationship between the state and its citizens.

A lasting mark has been left on the legal and institutional culture and land-holding systems of the English and French speaking regions by the English Common Law and the French *Code Civil* respectively. These imported legal precepts and the different objectives of the colonising powers coloured the interpretation of existing rights within indigenous legal systems. This distorted interpretation was then built into local handholding systems.

> Strictly speaking, customary law was derived from the way administrators interpreted rights over land and people as described to them retrospectively by the chiefs at the beginning of the colonial occupation. It was filtered not just by the chiefs and leading figures who tended to over-

estimate and often invent the fees due to them, the privileges they held and the land they controlled, but also by administrators seeking to express what they heard in terms familiar to Western law and bring it into line with the demands of the colonial system. (Olivier de Sardan, 1984: 223)[1]

In the main, the post-Independence states retained the colonial legal system and sometimes reinforced its centralising tendencies with the stated aim of binding the nation into closer unity. In the French-speaking regions, land was often nationalised, which amounted to formal abolition of customary systems. Use rights, however, have normally been tolerated and sometimes recognised in so-called *terroirs* (village community land), as in Senegal, but the customary authorities have usually been denied any official responsibilities (except in conflict management, for instance in Niger – see chapter 11). Legislation in these countries remains generally based on legal principles and a conception of law which are profoundly alien to the customary principles and landholding practices of rural communities (Le Roy, 1987; Keita, 1998). This dichotomy creates a situation of legal pluralism in which different, incompatible rules overlap[2].

The effects of legal pluralism

Areas governed locally by socially-determined land-use rules (i.e. the vast majority of land) fall within the scope of national legislation, in theory, if not always in practice. Within the same village or the same farm, areas governed by different legal systems may coexist. This can happen, for example, when part of the village land is removed from customary authority for an irrigation scheme in which plots are allocated by the state based on the labour power available to the household. The result is individual appropriation of irrigated plots held within a broader system of customary tenure (Mathieu, 1991). Legal pluralism causes uncertainty over rights, not because land-use rules and rights are ambiguous as far as local stakeholders are concerned, but because they can be challenged - and cancelled - through resort to state law or state authorities.

---

1 On this subject, it is somewhat surprising to see the term "customary" used in Southern Africa to describe the way tenure and local society currently operate in the former reserves (pseudo-independent Bantustans or reserves tactfully renamed "Communal Areas"), where the African population was restricted to marginal and currently overcrowded areas, and used as labour pools for white industry or agriculture. This often involved forced villagisation, compulsory restructuring of land use, the imposition of new cropping methods, manipulation of the "chieftancy" and the establishment of new, 'tame' local authorities. Not only that, there is virtually no farming in these areas now. There are undoubtedly local social rules and rules governing access to land, resulting in partial social autonomy vis-à-vis state power, but this is far less a reflection of historical continuity than a product of the situation. To speak of "custom" in this case obliterates political and economic history and the fact that social and political reality in the Bantustans is shaped first and foremost by the domination to which their populations have been subjected.
2 Legislation designed in the interests of the colonial power has also been carried over in English-speaking African countries (see this volume, chapter 4).

Thus, rights which are legitimate according to local rules, are often not legally recognised. Rural people find themselves in a position of permanent illegality and insecurity, especially in forest areas, where the gap between formal law and local practice is greatest. This exposes people not only to the imposition of fines levied by the Forestry Service, for example, for bringing fallow land back into cultivation, but also the risk of having their land allocated to other people via the registration procedure. In all cases, this situation has favoured urban elites (or people close to the regime in power), who have been able to exploit the legal system to acquire land or other renewable resources (forests, fisheries, etc.) to the detriment of holders under customary rules.

The fact that tenure legislation is rarely, if ever, applied does not prevent it from having an impact. Political slogans such as "the land belongs to those who can develop it" *(mise en valeur)* speed up the rate of clearance, both by migrants seeking to appropriate virgin or fallow land and also by customary landholders using evidence of tillage to protect their rights. Loans of land also become less common, for fear that borrowers will try to appropriate the loaned field. Stakeholders pick and choose opportunistically between the different systems to further their own interests. The authorities responsible for enforcing the law (territorial administration, courts, etc.) and urban elites, for example, may have a strategic interest in using the law to claim rights to which local rules do not entitle them.

Box 5.1: Legal pluralism in Cameroon

Since the introduction of the Land Ordinances in Cameroon, in 1974, only 2.3 per cent of rural lands have been titled. The principal beneficiaries of registration and the subsequent exploitation of forestry resources have been the educated local elite, civil servants, politicians and town dwellers.

The spirit of the present land tenure reforms in Cameroon has been to put all lands, except lands covered by certificates of title, under the control of the state by classifying them as national lands (Ngwasiri, 1984). Thus the strategy from 1974 onwards, has been to reduce the interest of traditional communities in land to greatly restricted 'use rights'. The registration procedure is cumbersome, expensive and time-consuming and communities have been barred from registering unoccupied forests. To mobilise village communities and provide them with an incentive to engage in resource management, they must be given firmer and more permanent rights. At present, the Forestry Law is violated on a daily basis in many areas, and local people act as if such laws are non-existent.

Part of the problem lies in the fact that the Forestry Law is drafted in such a way that many key tenets are open to a high degree of administrative interpretation. Most studies within Cameroon suggest that when bureaucrats enforce the Forestry Law, their over-riding consideration is to interpret this in such a way as to vest themselves with power and privilege, or at least establish their standing with their peers and local communities. As a result, the local population view state laws as accumulative, arbitrary, oppressive and alien to their customs, from which a confrontational situation has emerged.

Source: Egbe, forthcoming

Box 5.2: Occupation of land to pre-empt Niger's Rural Code

Niger's Rural Code was introduced in 1993 to formulate clear and binding rules for land distribution and use which would give agricultural producers legal security, thereby according locally established customary laws the same legal status as modern laws. The aim has been to avoid changing the actual distribution of land while clarifying the conditions under which land is held. In particular, the Code has sought to encourage investment in land by according rights to those able to make good use of it *(la mise en valeur)*. This has led to some land owners taking back land formerly loaned out to others, since they fear that the "tiller" of land will acquire firmer claims as a result of the new code. Since "making good use of land" is interpreted to mean cultivation (rather than grazing), there is evidence of many farmers seeking to expand greatly the area which they can claim to be cultivating. This usually involves no more than a rapid clearing of former grazing lands, a quick chopping down of bush vegetation, and a brief acquaintance between the land and a plough.

The announcement of the Rural Code has constituted an invitation to have customary rights in land recognised now in order to secure irrevocable private property rights later. "Get customary rights in your land recognised before your neighbour does" seems to be the main message which people have retained from the Rural Code.

Source: Lund, 1998

Finally, far from doing away with the patron-client aspect of customary tenure systems, both colonial and independent governments strengthened it by reorganising socio-political networks governing access to land around the state machinery as discussed below (Berry, 1993).

Hybrid practices

Evolutionist theories of land rights tend to cite causes such as demographic and market pressure for changing local practice and increasing tenure conflicts (see chapter 2 this volume; Lavigne Delville and Karsenty, 1998). However, these changes and conflicts may themselves be the product of state-led policies in conjunction with legal pluralism. The uncertainty surrounding rights is directly responsible for some conflicts as people take advantage of the dichotomy between the rules. One can no longer contrast "traditional" local practices with official legislation; rural communities have been faced with state interference for almost a century and have incorporated external concepts in their landholding practices. Stakeholders are often opportunistic, and make use of various systems to back up their land claims. Current local landholding practices are not "traditional". As Le Roy stresses, they also borrow from state law, resulting in hybrid contemporary systems which do not follow a linear progression from "traditional" to "modern"[3].

---

3 The term "modern" law is particularly inapt to describe West African legislation and state procedures, in the sense that legislation remains still founded on colonial legislation from the beginning of this century. The land registration policies derive from this period. From this point of view, they can, on the contrary, seem particularly archaic.

Arbitration problems: the multiplicity of authorities

Recent studies show that legal pluralism need not be a problem in itself (Chauveau, 1997). The real problems arise not from the coexistence of different systems but from the multiplicity of arbitration authorities. There are unclear links between authorities such as customary chiefs, imams, *préfets* who do not stay long in one post, project technicians, interfering politicians and so on (Lund, 1995). This leads to considerable uncertainty over who may deliver rulings, such that no arbitration can ever be accepted as final, because a decision by one authority may be overruled by another. As a result, outcomes cannot be predicted and all forms of arbitration may be challenged, so conflicts escalate and lasting solutions are harder to achieve.

This problem is compounded by the complexity of interrelated legal texts, which are unfamiliar and poorly understood even by members of the local administration, and by the absence of clear political directives. In this situation, presenting the authorities with a *fait accompli* tends to stand a good chance of success (see Box 5.3).

Box 5.3: Straying fields and straying livestock in the Ferlo, Senegal

A twofold process is bringing about a major shift in land from grazing to cultivation in the Ferlo region of Senegal. The scale of degradation and poverty of the soils in the old groundnut-growing area are such that groundnut producers are urgently searching for more fertile lands. This means that the open areas set aside for grazing, including those which have been legally allocated as rangelands by rural communities, are either taken over illegally by farmers, or simply reallocated by the rural councils.

However, such settlement is not undertaken in an anarchic, disordered manner. It is often a carefully thought out operation, and prepared by the group concerned, such as the powerful Mouride brotherhood. Taking advantage of their demographic and economic and political weight (at both central and rural council level), this community presents the administrative authorities with a *fait accompli*.

The colonisation technique consists of setting up farming hamlets in grazing areas and then settling permanently by encouraging the establishment of a village around the original hamlet (Traoré and Ka, 1996). Having colonised the land in this way, the farmers gradually claim tenure rights, a dynamic process whereby they gradually restrict the area traditionally given over to livestock and reduce fodder resources and access to water points. While reference is usually made to straying livestock and the damage caused to fields, the phenomenon of "straying fields" and the damage they cause to pastoralists must also be taken very seriously. In addition, livestock chased out of the best grazing are always tempted to return, causing damage to fields, a direct consequence of rangelands having been ploughed up. Such crop damage results in increased disputes and the risk of heavy fines.

Once again, we see the consequences of legal marginalisation for pastoralism. Pastoral use is, wrongly, not considered "making good use of land" (or "mise en valeur"). Nor are Peuhl encampments considered to have a similar status as villages. Thus farmers can claim that the land they have colonised was not previously occupied and can ask the rural council to make their settlement official.

Source: Juul, 1999; Traore, forthcoming

Managing confusion

It is the possibility of contradictory claims being out forward, rather than any uncertainty about customary rights as such, that is responsible for the unpredictable nature of disputes over land. The inadequacy of legislation has also been denounced repeatedly, but the various adjustments and reforms have had little real impact. It is no longer possible, more than 30 years after Independence, to blame the situation entirely on the colonial past, or on legal training that is biased towards the French Civil Code.

> Wherever access to resources is highly politicised and the rules are confused, it is generally those who have the most financial resources, or those who have privileged access to political power and strategic information (including simply the ability to understand and use the complexity of the laws) who draw the best advantage for themselves from the coexistence of different rules and the resulting regulatory confusion. Hence, this confusion and the non-application of land rules are not simply accidents or unfortunate imperfections, and their role is not a negative one for everyone. (Mathieu, 1995: 56)

While it facilitates change and thus plays a relatively functional role in rapidly evolving contexts, the confusion surrounding land rights favours powerful players, particularly the political-administrative class and some local elites who are the only ones able to master the legal and administrative complexities. They take advantage of the situation to varying degrees: using their influence to acquire land, arranging allocation of land in irrigation schemes to civil servants, using the concession procedures to transfer state-owned land to political elites, and gaining various advantages from charging for arbitration. Forestry Commission staff throughout the region have been known to receive bribes from granting logging permits or imposing arbitrary fines on local people forced into permanent illegality.

Finally, as access to land is related to social identity, the land rights of some social groups are frequently contested by challenging their national and ethnic identity, opening the door to the political exploitation of ethnic tensions. It is a volatile mixture; politicians play on competition for land and on social identity, which leads to challenges to national allegiances against a background of ethnic divisions. Such tensions have recently become very apparent in the case of Ivory Coast, the Democratic Republic of the Congo (Mathieu et al, 1997), and Kenya (Médard, 1996).

There is, in fact, more logic than disorder in the current situation, which leads Mathieu to agree with Piermay (1986) when he refers to African land

---

Box 5.4: The Nigerian Land Use Decree: evidence from English-speaking West Africa

The Nigerian Land Use Decree of 1978 vested all land in the hands of the government, 'in trust' for the people. It was based on the view, prevalent in the 1960s and 70s, that customary tenure systems were by their very nature backward and not conducive to the development of a dynamic agricultural sector, and that, by contrast, the state was able to act impartially to identify opportunities for economic development and growth. The decree provides for the appointment of rural Land Allocation Advisory Committees by the governor of each state. All previous forms of title were replaced by 'rights of occupancy' that could be granted by local government, and revoked where such land was needed for public purposes.

The government used the Decree as the means to acquire major areas of land for a variety of purposes, including housing for government staff, building of universities, as well as for irrigation schemes and other development projects. Equally, significant areas of land were turned over, with minimal compensation, to large scale commercial producers, at the expense of smallholder farmers and herders. Far from creating a greater sense of security and reducing land speculation, the Decree has helped prompt a movement towards the acquisition of land through whatever means people can exploit, while distribution of land holdings has been a very important form of political patronage for those in power. Increased uncertainty also has been created around tenancy, since the government's claim to now own all land has led to some tenants refusing to pay rent to the person they consider their former landlord.

Source: Francis, 1984; Knox, 1998; Kolawole, 1997

---

tenure systems as "managing confusion". A similar point has been made by Moorehead (1996) when he speaks of "structural chaos" to describe processes for administering access to resources in the inner Niger Delta of Central Mali.

HARMONISING FORMAL LAW AND CUSTOMARY LAND RIGHTS: RECENT EXPERIENCE IN FRENCH-SPEAKING WEST AFRICA

We have seen that legal pluralism lies at the heart of the tenure issue. The assertion of state ownership gives an ambiguous legal status to local landholding systems (rights and regulatory mechanisms), oscillating between denial and mere tolerance. Having recognised this, the challenge for new policies is to do away with the gross inadequacy of tenure legislation, to give legal recognition to existing rights, and to build links between local landholding systems and formal law. Using different approaches and strategies reflecting their political history, the French-speaking West African countries have, since the mid-1980s or early 1990s, engaged in comprehensive debate about the tenure issue, leading to legislative reform (ongoing or under preparation) and/or innovative interventions at local level, all aimed at harmonising the two systems. We shall give a brief overview of these before drawing some lessons.

The principles of the post independence legislative reforms

Senegal anticipated these issues with its very innovative 1964 law on State-administered Property *(Domain National)* although it was only fully applied in 1980. While retaining the principle of national property owned by the state (all non-registered land), in rural areas the law distinguishes between "pioneer areas" which remain under state control and *terroir* areas where land management is the responsibility of the rural councils set up in 1972. The existence of local use rights is recognised in the latter areas, but the land may be taken over by the state for development projects or allocated by the rural councils to whoever can "develop and use it productively"[4]. Such allocation mirrors the registration procedure, on a local scale and with fewer legal guarantees, as land may be allocated to individuals without taking existing rights into account. In practice, however, the rural councils rarely make allocations without the agreement of customary holders.

Another major reform was the Agrarian and Land Reform of 1984 in Burkina Faso. The revolutionary regime of Thomas Sankara hastened to enact a very complex legal code, bringing in a "modern" tenure system centred on ownership of cultivated land by those who worked it. Given its "revolutionary" aims, the reform rejected any role for the customary authorities, which were regarded as representing "feudalism". The reform law, which denied all customary rights, was so complex that not even the local officials responsible for its enforcement could understand it. Two successive versions followed (1991 and 1996), which allowed for private property and recognised existing customary rights in undeveloped areas (although providing no legal safeguards to support such claims). In essence, the government tolerates customary claims, so long as they do not compromise the state's own development plans. At the same time, traditional chiefs have been brought back into the consultation process for re-formulating the RAF and have successfully delayed the subsequent legal revisions of the legislation (Ouedraogo and Toulmin, 1999).

In Mauritania, the development objectives of a private irrigation scheme in the Senegal river valley led to a 1983 land law (amended in 1990) clearly favouring private ownership and based on the concession system which, for political reasons, remains very centralised and retains cumbersome colonial registration procedures (Crousse, 1991).

In the 1980s, pressure from structural adjustment programmes encouraged the privatisation of land in West Africa but, with the exception of specific contexts such as noted for Mauritania above, the political authorities resisted this. The state always retained ultimate rights to land, so there was never a question

---

4 On the ambiguity of the concept of "productive use", see Traore, 1997.

of issuing full private land ownership to citizens. However, privatisation, whose appropriateness for rural Africa is hotly disputed by most observers, was not the only response to emerge from the widespread questioning of state management of land. A better understanding of local landholding systems encouraged the clearer recognition of local rights. International debates, particularly those held under the auspices of CILSS and the Club du Sahel, put forward the idea of decentralised management of land, based on recognising the rationale and efficacy of local land-use practices.

Le Roy (1998a) notes three main trends in the legislative reforms of the 1990s aimed at harmonising the different landholding systems:

- codification of local land rights and national laws;
- the registration of local rights with the aim of giving them legal status;
- subsidiarity within public land administration authorities and the introduction of 'common heritage' management principles.

Codification follows earlier colonial attempts to classify customary rights and seeks to provide legal definition to land-use rules applied in practice. The aim is to integrate customary systems into formal law, with rules clearly spelled out. The recent Rural Code of Niger follows this trend, drawing on in depth studies of local farming, pastoral and forestry practices. However, the desire to take local practices into account in this way comes up against the obstacle of their great diversity. Customary practices are not a series of precise rules applicable to everybody in a given area that just need to be formalised. They are the particular expression of general principles, in accordance with local socio-political history, the social status of individuals and negotiation with other stakeholders and the land authorities. Even within units which are homogeneous from an agro-ecological or socio-cultural point of view, the identification and formalisation of customary practices can only result in the simplification of a complex body of otherwise flexible and variable rules[5].

This failure to reflect the diversity of local practices means that the Rural Code in Niger is in danger of being perceived as inappropriate or illegitimate, although less so than the legislation it is slowly replacing. Codification still follows a positivist approach, which assumes that the purpose of law is to define how things should be, with the aim of transforming reality accordingly. The Rural Code also makes provision for the setting up of "Land Commissions" at district level (currently, on a pilot basis), with the task of receiving applications for land title, recording land rights, and issuing title deeds. Existing rights may be formalised through simplified procedures, on request. Yet as the concept of "ownership", cited in the basic statutes of the Code is not defined, conflicts are likely to ensue over who may be recognised as an "owner" (Lund, 1993; Gado,

---

5 For a discussion of codification approaches in rural France, see Assier-Andrieux, ed., 1990.

1996). A key part of the approach embodied in the Rural Code is to carry out detailed surveys and to hold public debates. However, the difficulties in organising these, coupled with fear of the potential risks of the reform, sometimes gives the impression that the whole process has become bogged down in detail and consultation.

In view of the difficulties and political implications of legal reform, Ivory Coast has been pursuing since 1990 an instrumental approach, through the Rural Land Plan *(Plan Foncier Rural)*, which attempts to identify and map all existing land rights. A flexible and effective survey and mapping method has been devised, with the intention of producing a simplified land register. The aim has been to record existing rights and arrive at a local consensus; the subsequent land reform would then define all the recognised forms of tenure and give legal status to the local rights recorded. The approach is intended to be politically neutral since it seeks merely to give concrete expression to actual existing rights rather than seeking to transform them. In practice, the approach and methods followed by the Plan create difficulties of a different order. During the current pilot phase, emphasis has been placed on mapping. Consequently, the analysis and understanding of existing rights and their social dimensions have been superficial (Chauveau et al, 1998). Despite the declared intention not to fall into the trap of "ownership-based" simplification, the different levels of interlocking rights that actually exist have been reduced in the surveys to a simple differentiation between "land managers" and "land users". Secondary rights, such as those of women and rights to grazing land are superseded in the records in favour of the right to cultivate. Finally, in the interval between the start of the pilot project (1990) and the adoption of the law relating to land reform (1998), uncertainty has remained over the legal categories to be established and formally recognised. For example, it is not clear where collective rights would fit in. Overall, in reading the new legislation, one has the impression that it draws very little on information and experience generated by the *Plan Foncier Rural.* Instead, it aims to promote private land ownership and is pushing in favour of rapid titling of registered land rights.

In Mali, the transitional government set up after the overthrow of Moussa Traoré's dictatorship suspended the Forest Laws (one of the causes of an earlier peasant uprising) and launched a debate on the links between tenure issues and decentralisation (Diallo, 1996). The aim was a substantial revision of the 1986 *Code Domanial et Foncier,* and a specification of the powers to be devolved to local government bodies *(communes ruraux).* Following the *Conférence Nationale et aux Etats généraux du Monde Rural,* an innovative plan for a land charter was launched. The Land Observatory *(Observatoire du foncier)* was set up in Mali to encourage debate on tenure issues and to provide support to those development projects which were involved. Its brief was

> **Box 5.5: Rural firewood markets in Niger**
>
> Legislative reforms in Niger brought in during 1993 have allowed for the formal transfer of powers from central government to local people, over the management and use of woodland resources. These have established rural firewood markets, which consist of a site where firewood can be sold by a local body which has been recognised by both customary and state structures. This permit to sell firewood is linked to the existence of a plan for the conservation and sustainable management of the woodlands from which the wood has been cut. Firewood sold through these markets is taxed at a lesser rate than that stemming from unregulated sites.
>
> There are now more than one hundred such firewood markets in Niger, each one associated with an area of woodland where increased control over offtake is being exercised, with the benefits being reaped by local people. It is reckoned that they now provide at least 10% of the fuelwood needs of Niger's towns. They have been an excellent means of bringing together a number of actors who, in the past, have not found it easy to work together – such as forestry agents, traders in charcoal and firewood, and local people.
>
> These firewood markets demonstrate clearly the need to combine the interests and functions of many different actors. For example, despite their emphasis on local management and incentives, the establishment of this system would not have been possible without government support and action by setting a differential rate of tax, by changing the legislation to provide formal legal backing to their operations, and setting up a more effective, transparent way of monitoring supplies and transport of firewood.
>
> Source: Bertrand, 1998

to study land-use practices and their dynamics in the various agro-ecological regions and to put forward proposals in respect of the charter. The approach was both ambitious (rejecting a land and property code in favour of a land charter recognising rights and local tenure rules) and cautious (launching a series of field analyses). This approach fitted in well with the reforming ambitions of the transitional government, but now, this radical approach has been set aside in favour of a more straightforward revision of the existing legislation. One problem is that elected local government authorities are being set up without adequate prior clarification of the tenure issue. Although a "communal estate" is established within which the rural commune has jurisdiction, the issue of how village and communal decision-making structures are linked together and their respective powers has not been resolved.

Initiatives focusing on managing the common heritage *(gestion patrimoniale)* (Le Roy et al, 1996; Weber, 1998), have recently begun to be implemented in Madagascar, but not in West Africa. The principle of *gestion patrimoniale* rests on the concept of common heritage which has been put forward as a new legal concept to move away from the idea of state ownership of natural resources, which is seen as too closely connected to state management. To say that land is the patrimony or heritage of all citizens with respect to existing rights is to give them the legitimate right to manage these resources. In effect, this concept does not challenge ownership, but is aimed at taking into account the actual use of land and resources by different groups, and exploring joint management through negotiation. Furthermore, it explicitly introduces the well-being of future generations as a concern for whoever manages the common heritage whether it be the state, a community or an individual. In Niger, some experiments with regard to timber resources have applied similar principles (see Box 5.5).

Major issues

Most surveys and expert studies advocate decentralised management of land and resources, restoring decision-making powers to local communities and seeking alternative methods of settling conflicts. Legislative reforms, however, range from privatisation through registration to recognition of local rights. There are also different degrees of recognition: from mere tolerance, as in Burkina Faso, where local rights are limited, to the attempt by Ivory Coast's Rural Land Plan to map all existing rights in order to give them legal status. In between lies Niger's recognition of existing farming rights and the possibility of registering these on request. Although we have little benefit of hindsight so far, given the short period of time within which these programmes have been underway, comparison of the approaches and analysis of their initial results allow some of the major issues in these processes to be identified.

The question of interlocking rights

Under customary systems, apart from the territorial control exercised by the land chiefs, cultivation rights are exercised at different interlocking levels. All bush land cleared by a lineage makes up its landholding, under the overall responsibility of the head of the lineage. However, depending on inheritance rules and the degree of operational autonomy enjoyed by individuals, the actual division of land and cultivation rights may be managed at the level of the compounds (residential units) or directly by the production units, with the higher levels of the kinship structure playing only a minor or formal role. Even when land is managed at farm level, the compound head may sometimes arrange reallocation to offset demographic imbalances between units. A distinction can thus be drawn (Schlager and Ostrom, 1992; Le Roy, 1996a) between management of administration rights and management of use rights, which may both occur at different levels of the lineage social structure[6].

---

6 It is only when the two coincide at production unit level that the term ownership may be used. As a result of dynamic changes in family structure (fragmentation of lineages, splitting up of production units and so on - cf. Raynaut, and Lavigne Delville, 1997; Quesnel, and Wimard, 1996), there is no single model per region and different scenarios may be found in the same village.

Another dimension to this interlocking system is the existence of derived rights *(droits délégués)*. Also known as secondary rights, these may be temporarily delegated by a holder of cultivation rights to an individual. The head of a farm may allocate plots to his dependants (young people and/or women), in accordance with social rules and land availability; various types of agreements exist to allow an "outsider" or someone who is not a member of the family to cultivate a plot, such as short or long term leases, sharecropping, pledging, etc. (Le Roy, 1998b).

Finally, when the same piece of land supports different resources (e.g. crops, pasture and timber), each resource is usually covered by specific rules of appropriation and use. For example, a field cultivated individually during the growing season becomes common grazing land after the harvest and until it is needed for the following growing season. Also, the use and ownership of trees may be separate from the use and ownership of the land on which they grow. However, this obviously may change as cropping patterns shift. Examples include the exclusion of transhumant cattle from areas taking up cotton cultivation, since the cotton harvest comes much later than those of cereals, and farmers want to avoid risks of crop damage. Equally, where farmers become more dependent on mineral fertiliser for maintaining soil fertility, relations of exchange with transhumant herders whereby farmers gain access to dung provide less and less benefit to them.

This complexity and diversity clearly illustrate why a perspective based on ownership, which considers that all administration and management rights are in the hands of a single person, and distinguishes only between owner and user, cannot reflect the reality of local systems. Indeed, such an approach may invite or exacerbate many contradictory claims to the same area. At each level, stakeholders can claim to be the "owner" or main holder of all the different rights. The use of the term "owner" which redefines the nature of rights over land may then trigger a struggle between different claimants to gain recognition as such. The head of a lineage may seek to become the "owner" of the land he is managing on behalf of the family group, thus reducing the other members of the family to the status of mere tenants or sharecroppers. On the other hand, attempts by farmers or household heads to have full rights of ownership recognised (i.e. including rights of sale and transfer), would be tantamount to breaking off ties with the lineage. The secondary rights of women or young people are also liable to be marginalised in this process. As regards derived rights, conflicts between parties often hinge on whether or not payment of a symbolic fee is made since this marks the holders acceptance of a higher authority. In many cases, willingness to pay such symbolic fees falls off after some years, with migrants considering themselves absolved of further claims, as can be seen from Mossi farmers moving into south west Burkina Faso (Hagberg, 1998). Encouraging the recognition of exclusive ownership rights may be a political choice, but it is important to realise to what extent social relationships and land-use are thereby transformed, and to weigh up the social and economic issues and risk of conflicts[7].

Any operation to register land rights comes up against the difficult question of status. One could devise categories to reflect realities on the ground, by specifying the lineage to which each plot belongs, who has the right to allocate the farming rights, who holds the farming rights and on what terms, the different encumbrances on the plot (common grazing, rights to the trees on the plot), specific arrangements applying to the plot, etc. This would, however, produce a most unwieldy system, which would in any event lose the flexibility and capacity to evolve provided by customary rules.

The question of the authority system

> Every ownership system is based on a system of authority. Only an efficient authority can guarantee the effective and lasting application of the relational fabric of rights and reciprocal obligations on which the ownership system is based. (Mathieu, 1996: 41)

In the debates on land in West Africa, *"an unspoken, fundamental question is that of the relationship between the power of the state and that of the customary authorities"* (Mathieu, 1996: 41). In formal law, the recognition of "customary rights" is most often limited solely to the right to cultivate. This is the case in Ivory Coast, Burkina Faso and, more ambiguously, in Niger, where the "traditional chiefs" have been granted a right of arbitration. This restricted field of application disregards a fundamental element of customary regimes: the role of local authorities, who have the task of implementing and regulating rights, which provides an essential component of local land-use systems. Even though the state has sought to acquire a monopoly of power over land, these local authorities usually remain legitimate in the eyes of the community or continue to enjoy considerable political power[8].

This is, therefore, a debate about local land management bodies, their status (state, local or equal representation), composition and prerogatives. As centralised state management has proved inadequate, consensus currently favours "local" management. However, the apparent consensus around the loose term "local" hides a split between those who advocate continued control by the

---

7 A similar process occurred in France: depending on the balance of power, either the peasantry succeeded in consolidating their rights and wiping out the remaining feudal power or, as in the West of the country, the landed aristocracy became owners and peasants became their sharecroppers. Similarly in Scotland.
8 Even where the customary authorities may be discredited by their involvement in competition over land, the communities may look for regulation along customary lines, albeit implemented by new bodies.

state's technical services, in consultation with local people, as compared with supporters of decentralised management that provides real powers to the community (Bertrand, 1996). These questions about levels of authority and types of management body encompass important political debates about the relationship between the state and local communities and between the state, the customary authorities, and the new local elites. When harmonising legal systems, consideration must be given to the role of customary authorities. One should also not overlook the fact that local land chiefs are also involved in the competition for resources. Lineage chiefs sometimes sell parts of the lineage holdings over which they hold only management rights. Outsiders seeking access to land may find it increasingly difficult, as competition for land grows fiercer, with the motives for excluding outsiders overriding those for their inclusion[9]. Where the population is heterogeneous and the number of "outsiders" is significant, the choice and representivity of the local body with authority over land raise several political and economic issues. Endorsing "customary" power could sustain exclusion of outsiders by strengthening the "ownership" rights of the indigenous population at the cost of undermining or even withdrawing rights granted to migrants, in some cases decades ago. Conversely, installing "democratic" or elected bodies could give much greater power to migrants than under customary systems and trigger strong reactions on the part of the indigenous population. Each of these institutional options are linked to political choices[10].

One of the difficulties in harmonising customary rights with formal law is that while they are both of a highly political nature, each is based on radically different principles of authority. The land prerogatives of customary authorities (land chiefs) are founded on territorial and spiritual control. At the same time the state aims to retain and strengthen its powers to control and allocate land as part of its broader mandate to promote the development of the nation as a whole. What room can then be found for common ground?

The power to allocate land

The right of eminent domain and the power to allocate land rights are fundamental to customary systems and the power of the local land authorities. In es-

---

9 Even if local systems limit the rights of "outsiders" (who may still be considered "strangers" after several generations), they can be considered as "inclusive": when space is not rare, new family groups may be welcomed as a way to reinforce the chief's political influence, and access to land is quite easily granted.

10 It is inevitable that national policy will have differentiated socio-political effects depending on the local balance of power. The imposition of private property on feudal systems at the time of the French Revolution had differential effects. Where de facto peasant ownership had already been consolidated, this completed the eviction of the land-owning aristocracy and the establishment of a class of small farmers owning their land. Conversely, in Western France, the aristocracy successfully secured the acknowledgement of its ownership rights, thereby transforming tenants into mere sharecroppers.

tablishing state control over land and concession procedures, both the colonial and post-Independence governments took to themselves such powers to allocate, which in Senegal were then delegated to elected rural councils. While the power of land chiefs to allocate land was generally confined to uncleared bush and was thus exhausted when the entire territory had been allocated to lineages, governments gave themselves the right to allocate land that was already occupied. The power to allocate land is a fundamental component of all landholding systems, and the associated patronage and political power at both national and local levels[11].

Harmonising two legal systems: by registration or authority systems?

Private ownership cannot be imposed from the top, as can be seen from attempts to transform practices radically through law, which have proved ineffective. Landholding systems have their own dynamics that are subject to changing economic forces and power relations. The state may influence them and provide them with guidelines but, save in exceptional situations, it cannot swim against the tide. It is also acknowledged that local landholding systems are not the expression of an unchanging "traditional law", but the fruit of a process of social change, which incorporates the effects of national legislation. The relationship between ownership, land title and productivity has recently been reassessed, demonstrating that customary systems rarely hinder agricultural intensification (Bruce and Migot-Adholla, 1994; Platteau, 1996). Consequently, the issue is no longer one of substituting a "modern" tenure system[12] for a "traditional, ineffective" system, but of getting away from the unregulated coexistence of contradictory tenure rules. Thus, state ownership of land and resources and the allocation of concessions "from the top down" should be replaced by granting legal recognition to local landholding systems. Even if the aim is eventually to promote private ownership, this will not come about through the spread of registration procedures, but rather through gradual evolution of existing rights, facilitated by the law. The paradigm is thus one of "adaptation", rather than "substitution" (Bruce et al, 1994).

As discussed above, to recognise the existence and legitimacy of rights is not the same as going back to some idealised notion of "traditional" systems. The local context in Africa has changed; landholding practices and rights to land have progressed. The existing reality, with all its complexity and hybrid forms,

---

11 See Blundo, 1996 for an analysis of clientalist, factional land management by rural councils in the Kounghel area of Senegal.
12 Those who employ this term often forget that registration is a colonial procedure designed to grant considerable rights (stricter than French civil law) to settlers and that it is therefore particularly archaic from the point of view of states which have been independent for 30 years.

must be taken as the starting point, rather than taking a neo-traditionalist stance, and advocating "customary" rules which are no longer enforced, or simply allowing customary authorities complete control[13].

How, therefore, can legal systems be harmonised? Recent initiatives in Africa are based on recognising the current duality of the land authority system, namely the legitimacy of both local practice and state intervention. By approaching such harmonisation from the status of both use rights and allocation of responsibility, the two systems can be combined in varying proportions.

Registration

Those in favour of registration propose the harmonisation of the two legal systems through legal recognition and registration of ownership and other existing rights in order to bring them under formal law. It is still up to the state to put land rights on a secure footing but, by adopting a lighter approach, it is possible to break away from formal titling procedures. This lighter approach requires the mapping of plots, the creation of a land tenure register and a system for recording changes in rights over time. As this comes close to the cadastral approach, promoting private ownership of land is often an implicit or explicit goal of such policies. Nevertheless, although technically more complex to implement, the lighter approach could acknowledge other sorts of land appropriation, and this does not amount to adopting a simple system of individual private ownership. There are various procedures possible, such as creating new, innovative legal categories matching local socio-tenurial categories; issuing titles in collective names; recognising various forms of derived rights; and acknowledging any restrictions on the right to alienate land or "encumbrances" connected with other use rights over the same area. All of these provide a better "fit" with existing rights. Deciding which types of rights should be acknowledged is therefore more a political or legal choice than a technical question even if the practical complexity of implementation should not be underestimated. However, this type of arrangement does call for complex tenure information systems and an administration responsible for managing and updating them, which raises the problem of its cost for both the government agency involved as well as and for holders of rights (transfer fees, etc.).

Moreover, in this model, security of tenure is based on land title and the state, superimposed on local mechanisms and the steps taken by stakeholders to secure their rights in a world governed by many different rules (Koné et al, 1999). Land tenure management becomes an administrative act, linked to

---

13 Experience in English speaking countries has shown problems associated with this; that chiefs sell land over which customary system allows them only a right of administration, thus dispossessing farmers of their land (Abudulai, forthcoming).

recording transfers, rather than a socio-political mechanism in which the customary authorities act as arbiters. These authorities are left with practically no role to play, except perhaps as mediators in cases of conflict during a transitional phase before the registration system has become fully operational. Registration implies a radical transformation of the *ways of managing* land rights and hence the very nature of local landholding systems with implications for the whole social structure of local society.

Where land values are so low or tenure so secure that rural communities do not see the need to register land transfers, where procedures are complex and costly, or where accepting formal arrangements means breaking with long-standing principles of local land-use management, it is highly unlikely that information will be updated. In these cases, the tenure information system will rapidly become obsolete and be overtaken by informal ways of achieving security. This leads to further confusion surrounding rights rather than clarifying the rules of the game.

Managing the common heritage

This concept takes regulation as the starting point and aims to provide security of tenure by clarifying rules and forms of arbitration, so as to reduce ambiguity. The aim is not to formalise all rights as such (except when customary rules are no longer sufficient to ensure security of tenure), but for stakeholders to adopt a system of shared rules so that, at least at local level, the rules of the game are the same for everyone. The approach is based on a concept of the land and its resources as forming part of the common heritage. Le Roy (1996b: 311) explains that "heritage is, by definition, non transferable (which is what distinguishes it fundamentally from property) and it is inter-generational by nature (it must be handed on undamaged to subsequent generations). It has a permanent character and is intimately related to its holder's identity of which it is an essential component". The concept of heritage management also recognises local arbitration mechanisms, operating in accordance with principles laid down at national level. Rules can change partly through negotiation and partly through jurisprudence. In this way, there is substantial reliance on mediation and judicial process, but the important role of the customary authorities is recognised. Rather than suppressing legal pluralism by absorbing one system into the other, the aim is to retain the most dynamic aspects of each. At the same time they are linked together within a national legal framework and a hierarchy of arbitration bodies, in order to avoid the perverse effects of the current situation. This means improvements should be made to arbitration processes, whereby the local authorities are approached in the first instance and joint authorities are set up at regional level where need be. The role of the latter would be to define national land tenure principles in accordance with specific regional features, or to settle conflicts by coming up with solutions which are acceptable according to both systems. Forums may be organised to help reach consensus over the principles to be used in a given area, and these may also be used as a vehicle to enforce these principles (Le Roy et al, 1996).

Attempts have been made to find a middle road or a hybrid form for land tenure administration, borrowing from both systems to varying degrees. Different elements can be found in recent literature, including:

- subsidiarity, which gives genuine powers to the community, without challenging the principle of state administration;
- allowing land titles to be issued on demand, with the state providing additional security on top of local mechanisms for safeguarding tenure;
- legal innovations that move away from excessive reliance on the French Civil Code, for example registering land in collective names[14], and registering village lands to protect them against expropriation;
- considerable delegation of land tenure management power to bodies being set up by the process of administrative decentralisation;
- provisions aimed at directing change towards greater individualisation of tenure, and greater circulation of land rights by, for example, allowing registration on request.

In any event, emphasising rights (via registration) or rules is more a matter of making political choices about systems of authority and regulatory mechanisms than a technical issue. Discussion of the system of authority allows one to focus on the institutional coherence of a particular framework for managing land tenure. Is it realistic, for example, to think that village level committees can provide an open, neutral forum for the regular updating of a tenure information system whose essential purpose is to profoundly alter the nature of local landholding systems?

In all cases, clarifying tenure necessarily involves clarifying multiple claims to land. Claims based on "prior occupancy" or "indigenous occupancy" are particularly problematic. While they are an issue for legitimisation, they are often the basis used to justify the revival of "ancestral" rights that may have been lost, or to challenge open-ended loans of land that have, over time, been transformed into de facto ownership. In some cases, the intervention of the Rural Land Plan in Ivory Coast has enabled local people to reclaim ownership of land that had been made available to a group of incomers several generations

---

14 Where specific legal status is given to collective appropriation rights to cultivated land, careful attention must be paid, when defining such legal forms, to internal rules and methods, especially as regards decision-making. In particular, it is important to ensure that the various holders of rights are involved in any fundamental decisions (e.g. the alienation of a portion of the land), otherwise the transaction will not be valid. Appointing an individual to speak for all stakeholders is not sufficient to prevent abuses of power, and could, on the contrary, serve to obscure any such abuses behind a veil of legitimacy.

Box 5.6: Local conventions: institutional innovation for managing collective resources

A local management convention is a contract between villagers and the administration to regulate the use of land and other natural resources. It is signed by village representatives and the administration and both parties are responsible for it being carried out. Since 1993, several programmes in Southern Mali have assisted villages with the development of local conventions in anticipation of the new forestry law.

In the case of the Siwaa programme, lengthy and sometimes difficult negotiation resulted in a local convention between six villages, the local authorities and the government technical services on a mutual understanding of each other's role in the sustainable exploitation of the forested areas. The initial formulation of the convention took two years. This was partly because one village was afraid that the convention would mean loss of control over their land given that it was the only village which had an abundance of land. Only through direct dialogue with village leaders, explaining that no long term effect on land rights was intended, could agreement be reached.

Conventions touch on sensitivities concerning customary property rights. Understanding the nature of disputes and conflicts over resource use and land rights, was very important to the formulation process. The Siwaa experience showed that feedback mechanisms, information exchange and communication need special attention. The forestry services accepted most regulations proposed by the villages after some discussion. Initially, they did not want to give villagers the possibility to impose more stringent restrictions than those found within the forest legislation. The villagers' list of trees to be protected, for example, was more detailed than that of the Forestry Service and they also insisted on the obligation of all households to use improved wood stoves. However, the Forestry Service could not allow higher levels of fines, nor permit the village to receive a significant share of the proceeds, as these were strictly governed by the forestry legislation. The resulting convention makes reference to respect for both customary rules and forestry legislation, providing a clarification of how and when, each of these systems of rules should apply.

Involving villages and the local administration in this form of co-management is a major breakthrough, given the rather conflictual relations of past decades. It is clear however that it requires a serious commitment on the part of the government departments and the local administration to ensure the rules decided on are subsequently respected.

Source: Hilhorst and Coulibaly, 1998

---

ago (Chauveau, pers. comm). To avoid such injustices, there needs to be a statute of limitations, such that legally indisputable ownership or appropriation rights may be granted to those who have actually exercised them for more than a certain period, such as 20 years, or a generation[15].

CONCLUSION

Once the allocation of formal land title is no longer seen as absolutely vital to the process of agricultural intensification in Africa, the tenure issue shifts from

---

15 I am grateful to J.P.Chauveau for drawing my attention to this point. A sufficiently long period of effective occupation is needed to consolidate de facto situations and avoid the perverse effects of slogans such as "the land belongs to those who work it", where cultivation for a few years, even on the basis of derived rights, is considered sufficient to claim ownership of land.

the economic to the social arena. Although an *economic* impact may be achieved by putting land transactions on a more secure basis and allowing freer trading in land rights, the challenge for any tenure reform is to meet a *social* goal: to ensure that the rural population is not left in a legally precarious position. Providing adequate security of tenure to rural communities is increasingly seen as a condition for, and means of, establishing effective local government and the rule of law.

In current circumstances, choosing a tenure policy is mainly a political choice about the system of authority - customary, state or mixed - and the geographical level at which land management should take place. Irrespective of any judgement about these options, it seems over-ambitious to seek to register all land, bearing in mind the cost of maintaining a systematic tenure information system. It is unlikely that the state has the resources to ensure the systematic registration of transfers, so that land registers become out of date very quickly, as has happened in Kenya (see chapter 3, this volume).

The converse policy of giving communities the right to define management rules in their own areas (observing the general principles laid down by the state), encouraging legal recognition of local arrangements and facilitating negotiation processes undoubtedly constitute necessary steps. However, when it comes to managing agricultural land, can ambitious approaches based on the common heritage idea really operate effectively on a large scale? What are the conditions needed for regional level "forums" to come up with common rules which are acknowledged by everyone and which clarify multiple claims?[16]

A hybrid and perhaps more realistic option consists of combining community and state safeguards. Some rural communities are attempting to do this, by validating local regulatory mechanisms and providing all stakeholders with the opportunity to apply for state endorsement of locally-recognised rights. One way of doing this, sticking more closely to existing practice, would involve providing an opportunity for administrative and legal recognition of land transactions. Where the parties involved feel the need for it, because their membership of the community does not offer sufficient safeguards, or where they do not share enough social ties to regulate their relationship, they could formalise their arrangements and set them down in writing for endorsement by the administration. In fact, apart from the risk of having one's land taken by the state for its own purposes, most cases of insecure tenure relate to transmission of rights (inheritance, loans, sales, etc.). Land transactions could be put on a more secure footing by ensuring that the person transferring the rights has the

---

16 The question must be framed differently when it comes to renewable resources which are taken rather than cultivated (wood, pasture, fish) in a given area; stakeholders may negotiate joint rules governing access and use for themselves. Government intervention could give the inhabitants a legal, exclusive right and validate the management rules by making them binding on third parties. See Bertrand, 1998, on the rural wood fuel market in Niger and Lavigne Delville, 1999, for an analytical overview.

power to do so and by specifying the content of the transaction. This would guarantee that the beneficiary of the transaction receives the transferred rights from someone who actually held them and was legally entitled to transfer them. Such a 'contractual approach' has the advantage of relying to an increasing extent on written documentation to which rural people have become accustomed (Lavigne Delville and Mathieu, 1999), and on local ways of ensuring security of tenure (Mathieu, 1999; Koné et al, 1999). It provides for great flexibility, covering the whole range of derived rights and market transactions ("outright" sales, lifetime sales of cultivation rights, reimbursable "sales", etc.[17]), providing that the clauses are clear. It is also far less cumbersome than a systematic registration system, since it only needs to handle those situations felt to be "insecure" by one or other of the parties, without implying changes in regulatory methods as a whole. It seems wholly unrealistic to try and eliminate legal pluralism in the short term. These approaches clarify and stabilise a limited but crucial aspect of tenure dynamics and the problems of providing secure tenure. They define procedures which are both legitimate and legal, flexible and in line with local practices, but sufficiently clear and unambiguous, and introduce written tools based upon local arrangements.

This is only a hypothetical approach for the moment and it is too soon to assess its feasibility and how it could be put into practice. It would probably, like any other approach, involve delicate legal and institutional choices. Various studies are under way on this topic, which should allow progress to be made and lessons learned[18].

Debate and experimentation on approaches to security of tenure are still ongoing and it is not certain that clear solutions to the challenges posed by the tenure issue are yet available. However, even though the desire to take local landholding systems into account still often clashes with a broadly administrative conception of land management, recent experience in French-speaking West Africa has opened up a better understanding of what is at stake and which points must be debated. There is now opened up a better understanding of a range of varied tools to bring about appropriate legal, technical and institutional solutions, depending on the political choices made by governments. There can be no universal solution, as the choices necessarily reflect the historical traditions of the various states, the current balance of power and their political options. There remains, however, much to do to in the struggle to construct an overall approach which links together the three essential aspects of land management (legal, institutional and technical) in a coherent framework. Accu-

---

17 See Lavigne Delville, 1998a, 45-47, for a summary of the debate on sales.
18 See Lavigne Delville, 1998a, 115-117 for an initial formulation, and Lavigne Delville and Mathieu (eds.) 1999, which gathers together various papers on the way rural people put land transactions down in writing. Research into the dynamics of derived rights and ways to provide security is under way, coordinated by GRET and IIED. A study on land transactions in Burkina Faso is also in progress.

rate, meticulous legal work is needed, based on a rigorous analysis of social and tenure issues. Recognition must also be given to lineage rights over land and their importance for maintaining security. A great deal of attention must be paid to practical choices, to define the prerogatives of the various bodies involved, the links between them, and the social repercussions of particular technical or institutional choices. The difficulty lies in defining the components and links within this framework, while taking existing practices into account. At the same time, care is needed to anticipate how the different players, depending on their interests and room for manoeuvre, will try to use that framework (and its legal or institutional loopholes) to pursue their own advantage.

The greatest difficulty lies ahead. The need to clarify political choices often seems to be left on one side since such choices imply possible risks, and because the current confusion favours some sections of Africa's political and administrative class. Beyond the fine rhetoric about decentralised natural resource management, few countries seem ready to abandon the doctrine of state ownership or even to recognise genuine subsidiarity, and to delegate land management responsibilities to structures that represent the population. The question of drawing up a coherent, effective policy is further complicated by the "features specific to the contemporary African state: mixing up authoritarian government practices and notions of common heritage, together with a degree of inability to control the national territory, thereby leaving local society some freedom of action" (Constantin, 1998). Many factors reinforce the uncertainty about the purposes of a tenure policy - the multitude of different stakeholders, with contradictory agendas; the interaction of various government departments; resistance within the political and administrative class, some of whose members see their interests threatened; and the conditionality imposed by funders and experts. A way forward must be found which is acceptable to both the political/administrative class and the wider population.

6

Legislative Approaches to Customary Tenure and Tenure Reform in East Africa

HWO Okoth-Ogendo

LAND POLICY IN EAST AFRICAN HISTORY

The colonial phase

Colonial land law and policy in Kenya, Uganda and Tanzania reflected the needs and concerns of imperial authority by vesting absolute land rights in the British Crown. Despite divergences in the constitutional development of each of the three countries, in every case there was no attempt to incorporate the customary rights and practices of the indigenous inhabitants into the legal system.

When Kenya was formally declared a British colony in 1920, all land was regarded as Crown Land, available for alienation to white settlers as private estates (Okoth-Ogendo, 1991). Attempts to create areas reserved for each ethnic group offered no real protection in the face of settler advance. In 1938, a distinction was eventually drawn between Crown Land, for which titles could be granted, and *native lands*, held in trust by the Crown for those in actual occupation. In Uganda, the British authorities made a series of agreements with traditional rulers granting private estates to them and their functionaries (called *mailo* in Buganda and *native freeholds* in Toro and Ankole), broadly equivalent to English freeholds, but subject to certain obligations in respect of customary tenants. The remainder of the country was regarded as Crown Land. Subsequent legislation regulated the payment of rent and tribute to landlords by *mailo* tenants, creating a system of land tenure not unlike that of feudal England. In Tanzania, the German imperial authorities assumed all land without documentary evidence of ownership to be ownerless, and made a series of freehold grants to settlers (Okoth-Ogendo, 1969; 1993). At the end of the First World War, Britain assumed control of the country. Because of restrictions under the League of Nations mandate which prohibits further transfers of land occupied by indigenous people to settlers, Britain declared all land, occupied or unoccupied, to be public land (Chidzero, 1961).

The post-colonial phase

These different circumstances, and their underlying juridical commonalities, have continued to dominate land policy and law. Following Independence, rather than restructure land relations in accordance with new development imperatives, these countries simply entrenched and sometimes expanded, the scope of colonial land policy and law. However, Uganda and Tanzania have recently undertaken radical tenure reforms through their respective 1998 and 1999 Land Acts. These new pieces of legislation provide for some recognition and protection of customary rights, in the case of Tanzania, setting the stage for the eventual integration of customary and formal tenure by legislative means.

Nyerere's Tanzania expanded the domain of "public land" by abolishing all freeholds extant in 1962 and converting all existing government leases into 'rights of occupancy' under the 1923 Land Ordinance. The location of radical title[1] in public land was never identified and the juridical nature of the right of occupancy as the basic tenure system was far from clear. Nevertheless, this Land Ordinance remained, until 1999, the basic land tenure and land use law in Tanzania.

Similarly Uganda, despite its traumatic political history, has stuck to the same tenure regime categories defined by British colonialism, namely feudal tenures interlaced with public and customary land holdings. The Land Reform Decree 1975 which had sought to abolish all feudal and private tenure and to convert all land in Uganda into "public land" was never really implemented. Indeed, after some twenty years of dormancy, that Decree was rendered defunct by Uganda's 1995 Constitution and finally repealed by the Land Act 1998. Thus, until very recently land tenure systems in Uganda have progressed no further than they were immediately after the 1900 and 1901 Agreements.

In Kenya, despite its long experience with comprehensive land tenure reforms, little effort has been made to design innovative land rights systems and complementary infrastructure for the country. Private ownership rights derived

---

1 The term 'radical title' is feudal in origin. It means the final or ultimate root from which all other land rights recognised by the juridical system of a given polity are derived. Under English feudalism, that root was the Lord of the Manor, and in colonial Africa it was presumed to be the colonial sovereign.

from the sovereign (now the President) remain as legitimate as they ever were in colonial times. Native lands (now called trustlands) are still held by statutory trustees rather than directly by indigenous occupants. Unalienated land remains the private property of the government[2], and as such no obligation exists in law to consider the public interest when allocating land. In other words, government conduct in respect of such land is not subject to a public trust. Although attempts to convert trustland into individually held absolute ownership rights have thrown the country's tenure system into confusion, in general terms, however, not much has changed since 1938.

TRENDS IN LAND POLICY DEVELOPMENT

Commonalities beneath divergence

A number of common issues have influenced contemporary land policy development in East Africa, three of which are of special significance. The first is *the role of the state in the property law regime* introduced by the colonial powers and perpetuated by the post-colonial state. In all three countries, the state became, in law, the ultimate authority in matters of control and management of land. Whatever differences there may have been, they were essentially of degree rather than substance. Thus, while the role of the state was much more directly and clearly entrenched in Kenya's land law, the position in practice was in fact no different in Uganda and Tanzania.

In Uganda, since *mailo* and similar estates held by traditional rulers were regarded in law as "freehold" interests, some sort of residual or radical title was always retained by the protectorate power. Radical title to all land in Uganda, and not simply to "Crown Lands", therefore rested with the colonial power up to Independence in 1962, and did not finally change until the Land Act 1998 came into effect.

In Tanzania, while the Land Ordinance 1923 vested radical title to all land in the public at large, control and management of that land supposedly in the public interest was expressly vested in the Governor (later the President), rendering the public virtually powerless to assert their rights and protect their interest in the land. In practice, the Governor, (and later the President), proceeded to deal with land in Tanzania as if he were both trustee and beneficiary and therefore free to dispose of land virtually at will.

As if those powers were not in themselves sufficient, in all three countries

---

2 Under current law, the concept of private property is unknown, however the government holds private property to the same extent as individuals may own.

the power of eminent domain, that is the authority to expropriate land rights should public interest require it, was expressly reserved, either in constitutional instruments, as in Kenya and Uganda, or in ordinary legislation in the case of Tanzania. This remains a powerful instrument of public policy. The availability and exercise of this power in all three countries has meant the state has always had an overriding interest over access, control and management of land, irrespective of the tenure category under which it is held or owned.

The second commonality is *the general contempt for customary land tenure* evident from the legal texts in all three countries. The most extreme case of this has been in Uganda where, as late as 1975, customary land users were regarded in law as 'tenants at will', at risk of eviction by the government or of those individuals holding leasehold title from the state. Indeed, even though the 1998 Land Act purported to reinstate customary tenure as a basis for property holding, this was done in terms which make it clear that the state would be happier if the system was phased out of the juridical landscape altogether. For example, provision is made in this Act for the conversion of customary tenure into freehold through simple registration, but without any possibility of the converse process of transforming freehold to customary tenure.

In Kenya, contempt for customary land tenure has been widely documented. Even before the 1954 Swynnerton Plan laid down procedures for the conversion of customary tenure into individual freeholds, official policy always contemplated the ultimate disappearance of that system. Even today, the official policy of the Kenya government is to achieve the extinction of customary tenure, through systematic adjudication of rights and registration of title, and its replacement with a system akin to the English freehold tenure system.

In Tanzania, contempt for customary tenure is evident from the deliberate refusal by the legislature and the courts to develop customary land law as a body of jurisprudence supporting an important system of land relations. For example, the classification of customary modes of landholding and use as "deemed rights of occupancy" has never been followed by a clear definition of content, or an indication of the legal regime which should be applied to land held under different customary regimes.

It is important to explain that contempt for customary land tenure has its origins in two assumptions, one ideological and the other historical. Except for Tanzania where explicit attempts were made from 1957 to resist the introduction of a private property regime as the basis for social and economic development, in Kenya and Uganda this has always been and remains the dominant ideology. This can be seen from many policy documents and laws, including the recently enacted Uganda Land Act 1998. Examining the dynamics of land relations in Tanzania also shows that land has always been treated as a commodity in that country, despite state ideology. The 1995 National Land Policy now expressly acknowledges that land in Tanzania is a commodity, subject to individual expropriation and control.

The second basis for contempt towards customary tenure stems from the assumption that customary land tenure is merely a stage in the historical evolution of societies as they move from "status to contract" (Maine, 1861). Fuelled by the conclusions of legal anthropologists, colonial administrators did indeed believe that customary land relations would wither away as Western civilisation became progressively dominant in African social relations. There was, therefore, no need to acknowledge, let alone develop customary land law as a viable legal system. It was even thought that simply by enacting a new system of land law - usually based on Western property notions – customary land law would atrophy and disappear.

Consequently, in all three countries, customary land tenure and land law was systematically misinterpreted and undermined by the judiciary, ignored by legislatures and manipulated by administrators, as and when this served their purposes.

The third commonality is *the essentially administrative character of land law* in these jurisdictions. Not only was customary land law neglected and undeveloped, the substantive content of imported English property law was not developed either. The reason for this was that the corpus of English common law was presumed to be so well developed that proprietors would have no problem understanding the nature and content of rights conferred by that regime. Instead of enacting property law statutes, therefore, the colonial government concentrated rather on the development of an administrative infrastructure around land relations. The result is that much of what counted as land law was, in effect, the law of land administration. The link between land law and administrative law being thus firmly established, colonial authorities proceeded to deal with land, especially in the African areas, in exactly the same way as they would have dealt with issues of public administration.

In Kenya, for example, no consolidated body of land law was enacted until 1963 when a Registered Land Act came into effect. Up to that point, and for a vast number of ex-settler properties, the applicable regime remained the common law of England as modified by the doctrines of equity and statutes of general application. Similarly, in Uganda and Tanzania, land administration institutions (including land, survey and registry offices) grew at the expense of clarity in the substantive content of land law. Consequently the content of "mailo" freeholds or of the "right of occupancy" have remained undefined, decades after Independence.

These commonalities have, in the course of time, created serious problems for the evolution of land rights and land relations in all three countries. First, as regards the role of the state, and its administrative bureaucracy, serious doubts have emerged regarding competence in matters of land management and stewardship. In all three countries, the state simply appropriated to itself a vast array of land rights, including those in respect of which the law designated it a trustee. In Kenya, for example, trust land was often administered as just another form of government land, even though relevant legislation required that the interests of customary land occupiers should override all decisions to alienate or otherwise deal with such land. In Tanzania, the state system granted "rights of occupancy" over vast tracts of land to private investors, without due regard to the "deemed rights of occupancy" of customary land holders. In Uganda, the declaration of all land as "public land" under the Land Reform Decree 1975 should have conferred a duty of trusteeship on the state. However, leases were often issued to private individuals in utter disregard of the occupancy rights of customary land users.

Second, the institutions set up by the state to administer land have become a serious impediment to land development throughout the region. This administrative structure has tended to strengthen the already considerable powers of the state. Furthermore, ordinary land users found themselves subjected to administrative decisions emanating from a host of offices and political functionaries, all of whom had some sort of jurisdiction over land matters. As a result, conflicts and contradictions became endemic in land use decision-making, and inefficient management by these bureaucracies tended to further frustrate decision-making by land users. And, as the bureaucracy grew and remained unchecked, abuses became routine and entrenched. Indeed, throughout East Africa, the land bureaucracy became corrupt, inefficient and largely insensitive to the ordinary land-using public, which they were nominally designed to serve. Because most conflicts and disputes over land use including those involving substantive rights tended to be processed through the bureaucracy rather than the courts, no organised body of property jurisprudence ever really emerged. Instead, legislative policy appeared to support the institutionalisation of administrative and quasi-administrative mechanisms of conflict resolution in the form of tribunals, mediators and elders in matters both of substantive law and land administration.

Third, the fact that statutory attempts to eradicate customary tenure have focused on issues of title, rather than on the dynamics of tenure relations as a whole, has created further confusion in the property systems of these countries. For such a focus misses the fact that the transmissibility of land rights between one generation and the next is a fundamental tenet of customary land tenure. Experience from Kenya and Malawi suggests that as long as succession to land is governed by customary law, it does not matter what other laws govern the determination of land rights in general. Uganda is bound to experience similar effects should the conversion of customary tenure to freeholds occur to any significant degree under the Land Act 1998. That effect is likely to spread beyond areas of land originally held under customary tenure, so as to encompass those governed by other systems of property law. The lesson to be learnt is that in all three countries, despite the constant attempts to legislate them out of existence, customary land tenure institutions and systems persisted. However, the juridical content of customary law remains obscure, control mechanisms ineffective and transactional procedures generally inconclusive. What exists is a body of social practices regarding land which are not likely to die quickly, but which may well be ill-adapted to the challenges of contemporary land development.

Issues in land policy development

The problems outlined above have evolved over a considerable period of time. Given the rapidly changing economic, social and political conditions in the region, reform of land rights and development of complementary infrastructure have become inevitable and urgent. Five issues have become the focus of discourse in East Africa and beyond:

i. *Governance: the role of the state and its agents in land matters.* Under existing legal regimes, the state is both an inefficient administrator as well as a predator on land that in law, and/or in fact, belongs to ordinary land users. Changes in policy and law are therefore needed to institutionalise a more effective framework for access to and protection of land rights. This issue has become especially important given the pressures for economic liberalisation currently sweeping through Africa. Uganda and Tanzania have approached this issue by revisiting the doctrines of radical title and eminent domain so as to protect the public from abuses of public trust. Although no explicit attempts have been made in Kenya to follow a similar path, political activism in defence of 'public' land rights is likely to crystalline along these lines as the constitutional review process gets underway.

ii. *The continuing search for tenure security.* The simple assumption that customary land tenure is inherently insecure and that salvation lies in its replacement with a regime of individual property modelled on English tenure systems is clearly untenable. What policy and legal changes are required to ensure that tenure regimes confer social security and equity, and permit economic efficiency? This is especially important since each of these values - security, equity, efficiency and sustainability - are not always mutually reinforcing.

iii. *How best to maintain social stability through revolutionary changes in land relations?* The issue here is how and when changes in land rights, whatever their propriety, should be introduced. Should they be incremental or comprehensive, cautious or revolutionary? How are established social systems to be protected against adverse consequences of change, or compensated for loss of accrued rights and interests? As a policy matter, this issue has been handled in terms of the search for a comprehensive corpus of law that would establish a complete land rights system. This is what Kenya thought it was doing in 1963, Uganda appears to have done in 1998, and Tanzania hopes to accomplish through the 1999 land laws.

iv. *The nature, objective and limitation of the powers of the state as trustee of the public good.* In recent times, this issue has become central to the discourse on the sustainable management of land resources at national and international levels. The main concern is to design policies and laws that would ensure proper supervision of the exploitation of resources without presenting obstacles for the development or continued enjoyment of property rights. In the East African countries, this issue has been dealt with in terms of the design of policies and laws for the comprehensive and integrated management of all environmental resources (Okoth-Ogendo and Tumushabe, 1999). Uganda has gone farthest in this direction followed by Tanzania, with Kenya still at the stage of designing legislation.

v. *The support infrastructure and services necessary for a land rights system to operate effectively.* This is not an issue to which designers of land policies and laws often refer. The general perspective has always been that changes in the technical description of title *per se* is all that is required for a new land rights system to function. Experience from Kenya and those countries where experimentation with new tenure regimes has been conducted, indicates clearly that reform of complementary institutions relating to physical infrastructure, supply of agricultural inputs and services are important levers in the operation of a land rights system. Although such infrastructure exists to various degrees in each country, they have not always been effectively co-ordinated or fully activated.

Land policy development processes

Each of these countries has dealt with these issues in ways which reflect the pre-eminence of social, economic or political pressures in their land reform agenda. In general, two processes have been adopted in the formulation of policies and design of laws around these issues. The first is essentially bureaucratic in nature and assumes that policy and legal development can be undertaken in the usual course of administration. This means, in practice, that state organs are quickly mobilised to produce policy and legal instruments, which may or may not be radical in content and consequence. The second has been to rely on expert panels, task forces, investigating teams, or comprehensive commissions of inquiry with a mandate to generate and derive policy principles and programmes through extensive discussions and negotiation (Okoth-Ogendo, 1998a). All three countries have, at one stage or another, adopted one or a combination of these processes.

Bureaucratic processes of land policy and legal development have a long history in Kenya. There is a long list of policy papers going back to the Swynnerton Plan of 1954 that attests to the use of this modality. At the same time commissions, task forces and investigations have been used in land policy development on many occasions. Examples of these include the Kenya Land Commission of 1934, the East Africa Royal Commission of 1953-5 and the Lawrence Commission of 1965-6. In November 1999, a Presidential Commission was appointed to review the whole system of land policy and law, with the intention of recommending a new legislative and institutional framework, including the incorporation of customary tenure into statute law.

In Uganda, the approach followed was to include land policy development in the agenda of constitutional reforms which took place between 1990 and 1994. The land component was then passed on to the National Assembly in the form of a constitutional obligation to enact laws designed to incorporate certain principles, within a specified period of time. These principles were that:
- radical title over all land be vested in the citizens of Uganda, not in the state,
- the state should exercise trusteeship over fragile ecosystems,
- proprietary land use should conform to existing or future legislation on sustainable management,
- *mailo*, freehold, leasehold and customary land tenure systems should be restored, and
- the security of actual land users under any tenure regime should be guaranteed.

The Land Act 1998 has sought to incorporate these principles even though a broad policy framework still does not exist.

Tanzania is perhaps the only country in the region that has adopted a fully systematic process of inquiry. Here, a Presidential Commission of Inquiry on Land Matters submitted its report in 1991 after two years of extensive investigation and public consultation (Government of Tanzania, 1991). This report made radical proposals on the first four of the issues identified above, most of which were accepted by the government in a National Land Policy instrument published in 1995. There were some points of disagreement with the Report, concerning matters of location of radical title and the structure of land administration. The National Land Policy forms the basis for the new land laws of Tanzania.

The ultimate aim in land policy development in all three countries is to clarify all matters concerning access to, control and use of land. It is to be expected that even in Uganda and Kenya where authoritative statements of land policy do not exist, some such formulation will eventually emerge. That is the direction which other countries outside East Africa are actively pursuing, such as Malawi, Zimbabwe, Swaziland, Lesotho and South Africa. Apart from providing a basis for legal development in this area, such statements are important pointers towards the direction of future land development in each country. They also afford an opportunity to adapt global principles of land development as these evolve to domestic circumstances.

LAND POLICY CHALLENGES IN THE 21ST CENTURY

The range of issues covered by the policy and legal instruments discussed above go beyond the five issues identified earlier. The manner in which these are treated, however, is not always satisfactory or rigorous. A number of land policy challenges, therefore, still remain and are likely to dominate public debate in the twenty-first century. Four of these are readily apparent.

The first challenge is to design truly innovative tenure regimes to suit the variety of complex land use systems that characterise the African landscape. It is wrongly assumed by policy makers in Kenya that a tenure system suited to agricultural communities can also serve pastoral and nomadic economies. Attempts have been made to provide for the management of pastoral areas through the establishment of group ranches in Kenya, communal land associations in Uganda, and village sovereignty over land in Tanzania. But these do not appear to have provided a satisfactory solution either. Much more thought and design will be needed in this area of policy.

The second challenge is to provide a framework within which customary land tenure and law can evolve in an orderly way. Past strategies based on replacement of customary tenure must give way to a more evolutionary and adaptive approach (Bruce and Migot-Adholla, 1994). Even though individual rights to land exist alongside community rights in all customary tenure regimes, no serious attempts have been made to address this issue within land tenure legislation in the region. The position of individuals relative to the communities in which they live therefore needs clarification in the design of new land rights systems (Government of Zimbabwe, 1994). The various regimes of customary tenure in existence in each country will also require harmonisation into a common regime for all land held under customary law. *This would make land administration and development more integrative and universal.* The tendency to emphasise the unique features rather than commonalities in customary land tenure must therefore be abandoned.

The third challenge concerns ways to democratise land administration systems and structures. Existing land rights systems are characterised by a heavy administrative overload which is by and large inefficient and extractive. Land policy development must seek to install a simple, accessible and broadly participatory framework for land administration, irrespective of tenure category. Although Uganda's Land Act 1998 attempts to do this by transferring power over land matters to directly and indirectly elected boards and tribunals, only time will tell whether this approach can cure the maladies of bureaucratic overload (Okoth-Ogendo, 1998c). Similarly, the jury is still out on attempts in Tanzania's Village Land Act 1999 to transfer most land administration functions to village councils and committees.

The fourth issue which needs addressing is the design of a framework to codify customary land tenure rules and integrate them into statutory law. Although customary rules are largely unwritten, there is no reason why this should always remain so. Most intractable will be the codification of rules relating to the inheritance of land rights and their modification to suit a statutory system of administration. This challenge must, however, be approached with caution. Customary land tenure rules form part of community norms, which govern behaviour in many spheres, not just land matters. Customary land tenure is an organic system, which responds to a range of internal and external pressures, such as technology, population growth, and new economic opportunities just like any other. Thus, the process of codification and integration must not assume that customary land tenure is static or immune to change and should allow for a degree of flexibility and customary legal development.

No satisfactory attempts have been made, thus far, to confront these challenges in any of the three countries. One hopes, however, that as more regional experience becomes available, appropriate lessons can be drawn and used in the design of appropriate land rights regimes in the region. Kenya, especially, is poised to confront these challenges as the constitutional reform process, whose mandate includes the review of land rights, gets underway.

CONCLUSION

The last two decades have seen an unprecedented preoccupation with land policy development in sub-Saharan Africa (Okoth-Ogendo, 1998a). In Eastern and Southern Africa, for example, all countries except Angola and the Democratic Republic of the Congo (former Zaire) are currently engaged, at various levels of detail, in the re-evaluation of their land policies, laws, agrarian structures, and support services. While experience emerging from such reviews do not suggest a spectacular breakthrough in the design of new land rights systems, considerable gains have been made in learning about the process of formulating land policy and the clarification of legislative goals. Land rights systems are being consolidated and rendered more rational, while the corpus of land law is being made less complex and pluralistic.

Further, recognition has been granted to the central role of a clearly stated policy on land in the management of sustainable development in Africa. For this reason, pressures for reform are unlikely to subside. Experience from all three countries reviewed here suggests that policy responses to these pressures must not be regarded as a one-off effort. Even in conditions of relatively stable land relations, such as appears to have been the case in Tanzania, pressure for reform which lies hidden will eventually explode into demands for fundamental change. How each country will respond depends on context, commitment and resource availability.

7

Land Tenure Reform and Rural Livelihoods in Southern Africa

Martin Adams, Sipho Sibanda and Stephen Turner

This chapter reviews land tenure reform on communal land against the background of the repossession of private land occupied by white settlers[1]. The purpose and scope of the proposed tenure reform in the former homelands of South Africa are described, as well as the attempts by South Africa's neighbours to resolve tenure problems in the Communal Areas.

Box 7.1: Land rights

Land rights may include:
- rights to occupy a homestead, to use land for annual and perennial crops, to make permanent improvements, to bury the dead, and to have access for gathering fuel, poles, wild fruit, thatching grass, minerals, etc.;
- rights to transact, give, mortgage, lease, rent and bequeath areas of land;
- rights to exclude others from the above-listed rights, at community and/or individual levels; and
- linked to the above, rights to enforcement of legal and administrative provisions in order to protect the rights-holder.

What is land tenure reform?

Land tenure may be defined as the terms and conditions on which land is held, used and transacted. Land tenure reform refers to a planned change in the terms and conditions (e.g. the adjustment of the terms of contracts between land owners and tenants, or the conversion of more informal tenancy into formal property rights) (Adams, 1995). Two fundamental goals are to enhance and to

---

1 This chapter is based on an ODI paper written by the authors for the *Natural Resource Perspectives* Series in February 1999. For full reference see Adams et al (1999b).

secure people's land rights (see Box 7.1). Reform may be necessary to avoid arbitrary evictions and landlessness; it may also be essential if rights-holders are to invest in the land and to use it sustainably. In South Africa, tenure reform is a component of a broader national land reform programme which also embraces the restitution of land to people dispossessed by racially discriminatory laws or practices, and land redistribution to the poor.

In Southern Africa, tenure reform must address a range of problems arising from settler colonisation and dispossession. Many of the areas referred to as Communal Areas (CAs) were created to further colonial policies. They served as reservoirs for cheap migratory labour and have become seriously overcrowded as a result of the forced removal of blacks from areas reserved for whites. One of the factors complicating attempts to dismantle the apartheid map in South Africa and Namibia is the complex and unstructured nature of the legislation governing the CAs, much of which has yet to be repealed. The differing systems of property rights pertaining to private and communal land are a related problem. Resources for establishing and/or revitalising land administration will have to be procured from increasingly hard-pressed government budgets.

The dual racially-based system of land rights introduced by colonial regimes continues to prevail in southern Africa. Laws involving arbitrary racial distinctions have been repealed, but land in the former "reserves" continues to be registered in the name of the state. This creates the risk of exploitation by traditional leaders, officials and politicians and extortion by "warlords' which must be addressed. Table 7.1 shows the very extensive areas which are classed as communal lands in Southern Africa. Most of these lands are the subject of current tenure reform proposals.

Table 7.1: Proportion of land held under different forms of tenure

	Private/freehold/ leasehold	Communal/tribal/ customary land	Conservation/ minerals/catchment reserves/other state land
South Africa	72	14	14
Namibia	44	43	13
Zimbabwe	41	42	16
Botswana	5	70	25
Swaziland	40	60	-
Lesotho	5	90	5

Source: Numerous sources, based on research by the authors

An "across-the-board" conversion of customary or informal rights into more secure property rights would not be possible as overlapping rights must be clarified and boundary disputes resolved, before land rights can be confirmed. Tenure reform must propose ways of recognising the multiple uses of land rather than simplistically conferring formal recognition on established occupants and/or resource users. In Botswana, considerable progress has been made through the integration of traditional tenure with a modern system of land administration for both customary and commercial forms of land use. The changes proposed in South Africa are consistent with the pragmatic and gradualist approach recommended by Platteau (1996; see Chapter 3, this volume) that re-institutionalises indigenous land tenure arrangements (where appropriate), promotes the adaptability of existing arrangements and avoids a regimented tenure model.

Tenure reform in the context of land reform

In all countries of Southern Africa which have experienced enforced land alienation at the hands of Europeans, the repossession of land by African citizens remains a central national and agrarian objective. Land acquisition for redistribution and restitution has been given priority while tenure reform in the CAs has had to take second place to the redistribution of white farms. So dominant is the imperative to repossess land, that insufficient attention has been devoted to post-settlement planning and support. Thus, the livelihoods and land rights of incoming settlers have too often remained insecure.

Tenure reform is, in most cases, a complex and uncertain undertaking. The economic and other benefits flowing from it are difficult to predict, and the necessary administrative costs therefore difficult to justify. It invariably threatens powerful vested interests: land owners and commercial farmers on private land; and traditional leaders or other institutions in the CAs. Yet, the costs of taking no action may be high. For local people, tenure reform may be a more acceptable and realistic measure than resettlement in some far-off government project. Measures to tackle insecurity of tenure in the CAs should not be seen as a substitute for land redistribution, but a complementary initiative by which tenure reform can be linked to the acquisition and settlement of neighbouring private land.

A common dilemma is finding the funds for tenure reform. The funding of an effective system of land rights management is a precondition for securing the land rights of poorer citizens, both in the CAs and on private land. While communities can be expected to allocate their own resources for this purpose, government should ensure that adequate measures are in place to protect people from exploitation by elites. From the outset of the reform planning stages, therefore, it is essential that funds also be found for public information, the training of officials, community facilitation and dispute resolution.

> **Box 7.2: Critical tenure-related livelihood questions**
>
> Given the inherent complexity of land tenure systems, the limited capacity of the state and the costs of tenure reform, the following questions should be asked: Is reform necessary for reducing poverty and securing sustainable livelihoods? What kinds of reform are appropriate? How should tenure reform be phased?
>
> **Political:** Is land ownership distinct from governance? In other words, is the holder of usufruct in a feudal relationship with the landowner who has power to extract a surplus and cancel usufruct rights? How is tenure reform linked to land reform in the wider sense? Do political conditions favour tenure reform? How effective is the administration of land tenure at national, regional and local levels?
>
> **Economic:** How do tenure systems affect agrarian and other sources of production and income? What economic use is made of common property resources? How does the land tenure system intersect with markets for land, capital, labour, inputs and outputs? Does a lack of clarity about land rights discourage investment?
>
> **Social and cultural:** How are rights to land embedded within wider social and cultural relationships? What is the impact of the structure of land rights on gender inequality? Are tenure systems associated with class, racial ethnic and/or other forms of inequality? Are rights to land an important source of asset-based security for the poor? How have indigenous tenure forms been affected by colonial and post-colonial laws? How do reform policies interact with informal evolutionary processes?
>
> **Legal:** Do constitutional and legal frameworks affect tenure? Are there appropriate and legally secure options for rural and urban situations? What is the legal basis of common property arrangements? When and where are titling and registration programmes appropriate? Do group forms of ownership require titling and registration?
>
> Source: Cousins, 1997

Sustainable rural livelihoods

The sustainable livelihoods framework put forward by Carney (1998) helps the analysis of the strengths of particular systems of land tenure, and of their evolution (see Box 7.2). The framework is useful when considering options for change and their likely impact on people's asset status. Their access to capital assets, including finance, land, natural resources and social capital, determines how and how far livelihoods can be enhanced. Where financial resources are lacking, social capital can provide the basis for a range of livelihood opportunities, including customary access to land and natural resources and opportunities for the poor to sell their labour.

For those relying largely on local rural resources for their livelihood, a secure place to live, free from threat of eviction, with access to productive land and natural resources is essential for rural livelihoods in the region. These elements are broadly located in the customary land tenure categories: "the holding" and "the commons" (see Box 7.3). However, many people in the region continue to obtain their livelihood from places far apart. The reform of residential tenure may be more important for households whose main source of livelihood is pursued outside a rural area but who return regularly. Tenure reform in peri-urban areas becomes more important as populations migrate longer term to informal settlements, often on communal land (Box 7.4). The poorest households may not be involved in migratory labour and may benefit more from the reform of tenure arrangements for arable land and the commons in the village-homestead setting. In all these cases, tenure security, sustainable economic opportunities and good governance are the components that tenure reform should aim to deliver.

Box 7.3: Customary tenure categories

Many African land tenure settings can be divided into two broad categories:

'The holding': land possessed and used relatively exclusively by individuals or households for residential use, farming, or some other business activity;

'The commons': land shared by multiple users for grazing and for gathering field and tree products (fuel, construction poles, medicinal plants, etc.) which may be broken down into:
   Controlled access – commons over which a group exercises control, at a minimum having the ability to exclude non-members; possibly also regulating use of the resource by members; and
   Open access – where there is no control, or access to a given resource and no group with the rights and duties to manage these resources.

NB 'Holdings' may be transformed into the 'commons' during the dry season, once the crops have been harvested and livestock are brought to graze the stubble.

Box 7.4: Tenure needs in informal settlements on Communal Land

Individual family needs include: assurance that they will not be evicted without compensation; assurance that they can improve their house to protect themselves against weather, thieves, etc; assurance that their children can inherit the property; the ability to sell or otherwise transfer the property; the ability to borrow money using the property as collateral; a reduction in property related disputes; properties to be serviced with such things as water, electricity and the upgrading of roads; and an inexpensive and easily accessible system of administering property rights.
The government needs the system to be: nationally uniform and sustainable; a basis for implementing local taxation, land use and building control and for the provision of infrastructure; a flexible means of administering property rights, e.g. the ability to accommodate individual and group rights, the rights of the middle class, business and poor people; a basis for land titling which is accessible, user-friendly, not perceived as inferior, and capable of upgrading to freehold; a basis for delivering social justice in relation to land reform and resource allocation.
Source: Alberts et al, 1996

The case for tenure reform in the Communal Areas

A major issue in debates surrounding the case for tenure reform has been the relative merit of indigenous customary tenure systems and those based on western concepts involving the registration of individual ownership. In the

1980s, the policy debate on the individualisation of tenure focused on the benefits this would provide for the stimulation of productivity growth and economic development. In the 1990s, the focus has turned to the sustainable use of land resources.

Both of these arguments tend to underestimate the importance of customary land tenure systems as an integral part of the social, political and economic framework. Above all, they overlook the unintended effects that undermining land tenure systems have on poor and vulnerable members of the community. They also tend to disregard the empirical evidence that traditional tenure systems can be flexible and responsive to changing economic circumstances. With population pressure and commercial-isation, individualisation has occurred autonomously (Migot-Adholla et al, 1994b; see also Chapter 3, this volume).

The case for government intervention undoubtedly varies greatly throughout Southern Africa. The extent to which rural people are able informally to adjust tenure to suit their livelihood purposes is likely to depend on whether land rights have been disrupted by past interventions and by enforced overcrowding under colonial and apartheid regimes. In parts of South Africa, the 'informal' situation on the ground is getting out of hand and effective reform is urgently needed. On the other hand, in rural Lesotho, where there are more modest expectations about the efficacy of official systems and the rule of law, all kinds of arrangements are made. The informality of customary tenure systems does not appear to be a significant constraint on rural livelihoods, though this does constrain urban and peri-urban livelihoods. There is need for more information about how people around the Southern African region are 'muddling through' and the extent to which each situation is functional or dysfunctional.

There are undoubtedly "tenure hot spots" where, if the rights of the more vulnerable members of society are to be protected, change must not be allowed to take place in a legal and administrative vacuum. Moyo (1995) describes how, in Zimbabwe, competing and ineffective attempts by both government and NGOs, frustrated by weak local administration and disingenuous central government interventions, have failed to resolve land tenure problems in the absence of constitutional and legal principles governing land in the CAs. Studies in South Africa demonstrate the increasing breakdown of customary management arrangements and the often dysfunctional mixture of old and new institutions and practices. People are often uncertain about the nature of their rights and confused about the extent to which institutions and laws affect them. Matters are further clouded by local and national political conflicts over land management roles in the CAs and by continuing corruption. Tribal commons are developing into open access resources and rights to homestead plots and fields are increasingly insecure. Studies in the Eastern Cape have shown that productive small farmers wishing to expand have faced increasing difficulties in borrowing under-utilised arable land from others who are fearful of not getting it back. An increasing area of potentially productive land is not used.

Tenure insecurity is most acute among those using land to generate income, especially women. The rights to make profits from agriculture and other small business activity in the CAs are not clearly established. As soon as informal land markets become accepted, people with allocation authority – usually men with connections to those in power – emerge as squatter patrons or warlords. Mounting uncertainty makes economic land use too risky for many (Cross, 1998). In peri-urban areas in Southern Africa the land market is open to exploitation by unscrupulous administrators and chiefs who sell off communal land, which brings them into conflict with adjacent urban councils.

In South Africa, private investment projects on State Land, part of the government's Spatial Development Initiatives, have been delayed two years because of uncertainty over land rights. While local communities demand the recognition of their rights and wish to enjoy some of the benefits – instead of being just landless employees – potential investors require the assurance that their investments will be secure. Throughout the former homelands, agricultural, forestry and eco-tourism projects are on hold because it is not clear who can authorise such developments to proceed, or who should benefit. Currently, proceeds from the sale or lease of nominally-owned State Land must go back to the state treasury (Adams et al, 1999a).

Box 7.5: Benefits of tenure reform in the rural CAs of Southern Africa

Tenure reform can contribute to economic development and sustainable livelihoods by strengthening rights in the CAs, by removing uncertainty, and by encouraging:
Actions by rural households to: increase production of agricultural goods; lease, rent and share crop land; manage and use natural resources for household provisioning (food and fuel), medicinal plants, craft production, building; invest in local economic development via small enterprises; participate in development projects jointly with private investors; adopt peaceful and legal means for resolving land related disputes rather than resort to land invasion and violence;
Actions by government at different levels to: provide infrastructure and services, and invest in development projects, particularly housing; and, on the understanding that their investment is secure, encourage actions by the private sector, to invest in eco-tourism, forestry and agricultural projects.
Source: Adams et al, 1999a

TENURE REFORMS IN SOUTHERN AFRICA

South Africa, Namibia, Zimbabwe and Swaziland, countries of widespread settler colonisation, encounter tenure problems different from those in Botswana and Lesotho, which have profited from a more flexible and gradualist approach with regard to the role of the traditional authorities. The experiences of land tenure reform in these countries are discussed below.

South Africa

The Restitution of Land Rights Act was the first law to be passed after the elections in April 1994. Land redistribution kicked off promptly in late 1994 with a national pilot programme. By late 1999, some 50,000 households had acquired rural land in the former white areas by means of government subsidies. The government has introduced tenure reform primarily on privately held land. Land tenure reform in the CAs has lagged behind.

In 1996, the Interim Protection of Informal Land Rights Act was passed as a short-term measure to protect people with informal rights and interests from eviction, until more comprehensive tenure legislation, i.e. the proposed Land Rights Bill (DLA, 1998) was in place. The proposed law aimed to provide for far-reaching tenure reform in the rural areas of the ex-homelands by repealing the many and complex apartheid laws relating to land administration, by recognising customary tenure systems and by bringing tenure law into line with the Constitution. The Bill was expected to benefit 2.4 million rural households by providing for a broad category of protected rights-holders with established occupation, use or access rights to land. It was to provide for the transfer of property rights from the State to the de facto owners and devolve land rights management to them. Rights would have been vested in the people, not in institutions such as traditional authorities or municipalities. The proposed law would have recognised the value of both individual and communal systems and would have allowed for the voluntary registration of individual rights within communal systems. Where rights existed on a group basis, they would have been exercised in accordance with group rules and the co-owners would have been able to choose the structures which managed their land rights. The envisaged law would have been neutral on the issue of traditional authorities, supporting them where they were popular and functional, and allowing people to replace them elsewhere.

In June 1999, the new President of South Africa, Mr Thabo Mbeki, appointed a new Cabinet including a new Minister for Agriculture and Land Affairs who brought to a halt the work on the tenure proposals within the draft Land Rights Bill. However, in February 2000, the Minister instructed that "…. the Ministry and the Department must draft overarching legislation which will deal with all the problematic legislation on the statute books and provide for the consolidation and rationalisation of the land tenure systems in terms of freehold ownership and statutory rights" (Didiza, 2000). The extent to which the proposed legislation will depart significantly from the principles of the draft Land Rights Bill remains to be seen.

Namibia

As in South Africa, the need to resolve tenure problems in the CAs, particularly in informal settlements, has been overshadowed by a debate about the restitution of ancestral lands and the redistribution of white-owned ranches. Namibia is a sparsely populated arid country, about 44% of which is made over to freehold, fenced ranches, mainly white-owned in central and southern Namibia. Another 43% of Namibia is communal land, most of it unsurveyed and unfenced, mainly in the fertile north of the country. The more fertile land to the north, where at least half of the population lives, was not occupied by white settlers. Pastoral and mixed farming systems remained more or less intact, but the CAs in the north were seriously disrupted by the war preceding independence (Adams and Devitt, 1992).

On coming to power in 1990, the SWAPO government announced its intention of transferring land to the landless majority but agreed to a constitution in which the property of citizens could not be taken without 'just compensation'. With the support of the opposition, it conducted a national consultation on the land question, culminating in a National Conference in Windhoek in June 1991. Broad agreement was reached that the restitution of particular areas of land to specific tribal groups was not feasible because the land used by the various pastoral groups had overlapped for centuries and could not be identified with accuracy. With regard to the inequity of freehold land ownership, the meeting recommended that foreigners should not be allowed to own farms, that absentee landlords should be expropriated and that ownership of very large farms and/or several farms by one person should not be allowed (Adams, 1993).

Almost half the recommendations relate to the resolution of land-related issues in CAs: *inter alia* the need to guarantee land to local people; to abolish land allocation fees demanded by chiefs; to grant land to women in their own right; to establish a system of land administration; to control "illegal fencing" of grazing areas; and to move the herds of wealthy farmers to commercial farms. Neither the national conference nor the briefing papers by NEPRU (1991) gave guidance on the options for a future land tenure system.

In the years following the conference, land reform received little attention. The Ministry of Lands, Resettlement and Rehabilitation (MLRR) remained weak. Contrary to the recommendations of the conference regarding the fencing of grazing in the CAs, the Ministry of Agriculture (MoA) went ahead with a credit scheme to help farmers subdivide the communal land.

In 1995, shortly before the general election, the Agricultural (Commercial) Land Reform Act was hurried through. It provided for the acquisition of very large, under-utilised and foreign-owned freehold farms for redistribution, but with inadequate attention to how they should be identified or settled.

Unlike this Act, the National Land Policy and the proposed legislation for the CAs have been through a process of public consultation. As Werner (1997) observes, the Communal Land Bill touches on issues that are sensitive among a large and powerful rural constituency, including traditional leaders and the Ovambo people who have their roots in the relatively densely populated CAs in the north and provide the bulk of SWAPO support. However, when the Communal Land Act was finally pushed through the National Assembly on 17 February 2000, the input on the bill from communal area farmers was ignored. They believe that the law does not deal adequately with illegal fencing carried out on communal land prior to the enactment of the law (Maletsky, 2000).

The law provides for the allocation of rights in respect of communal land, for the establishment of Communal Land Boards and sets out the powers of Chiefs and Traditional Authorities and boards in relation to communal land. It remains to be seen whether the Communal Land Act will prove effective for tenure reform in peri-urban areas, outside local authority areas, where the resolution of tenure problems is most pressing, and whether resources for its implementation will be forthcoming.

Zimbabwe

A highly skewed pattern of land distribution was inherited on independence in 1980, with 1% of farmers holding nearly half the available agricultural area and the bulk of the fertile land. How far the tenure system in the CAs is indigenous or was created by the colonial government, to facilitate indirect rule, has been much debated. It is clear, however, that governments have periodically interfered with it, transferring the authority to allocate land to and from the chiefs. The Communal Land Act of 1982 shifted the authority from the chiefs to District Councils and to Village Development Committees (VIDCOs). In 1996, Cabinet accepted the advice of the Rukuni Commission (Government of Zimbabwe, 1994) that this should be reversed (Box 7.6). However, the recommendations on the CAs that were endorsed by Cabinet were never followed through.

In 1998, a team led by Professor Shivji drafted a land policy document which drew on the work undertaken by the Land Tenure Commission, but came up with more comprehensive and far-reaching proposals (Government of Zimbabwe, 1998). The report recommended that all lands in Zimbabwe should be either "customary" or "statutory" and that the radical title of customary lands should be vested in their respective Village Assemblies to be held for the benefit of the villagers. This was to replace the existing arrangement under which customary land is vested in the President. Inhabitants, as families, individuals or groups or any other association recognised under cus-

> **Box 7.6: Zimbabwe: Cabinet's response to the Rukuni report**
>
> Cabinet accepted the advice that the communal land tenure system be maintained, and that legislation should be amended to accommodate existing practices, including the inheritance of land rights. It did not accept that the state should relinquish de jure ownership of communal land, but agreed that village communities should instead have perpetual usufruct. Cabinet accepted that authority to administer land should be shifted from the VIDCOs to a formal local land, water and natural resources board, to be elected by the village assembly. Members of traditional villages, under a traditional village head, would be recognised as the basic unit of social organisation in the CAs. Cabinet also supported the proposal that village boundaries be surveyed to minimise boundary disputes, that Land Registration Certificates be issued to households for all arable and residential land, and that village grazing be held in trust by the kraalhead.
>
> Source: Adams et al, 1996

tomary law, were to 'hold their land of the village assemblies' (1998: 49). The recommendations of the team have been published for public comment but have yet to be codified in law.

A solution of the tenurial problems of the CAs is inseparable from an extensive programme of land acquisition and resettlement of adjacent private farms. But the proposed resettlement raises concerns about the tenure security of the many farm-worker families already living on commercial farms. The long running controversy surrounding land acquisition has not been favourable to the search for integrated solutions.

Systematic research on resettlement schemes has established that the performance of small farmers has generally been good, both in terms of farm production and household income. Incomes have been higher than those left behind in the CAs (Kinsey, 1999). The tenure rights of settlers have, however, remained weak. In recent years, the system of settlement permits has fallen away. Names have simply been entered in a scheme register, with no record being given to the settler. While the Cabinet accepted the advice of the Rukuni Commission that long term leases (minimum of 10 years with options to purchase) be issued to settlers, this proposal has yet to be introduced, leaving settlers with no legal rights to remain on the schemes.

Swaziland

Since the settlement which followed the Anglo-Boer war, a central objective of the Swazi monarchy has been the return of land lost through alienation to settlers. At the beginning of this period, Swazis held only one third of the land. By the 1980s they held two thirds. It had been repossessed with funds raised by taxes on Swazis and with grants from the UK. Land which has been acquired in this way is held by the king "in trust for the nation".

There are two main types of land tenure in Swaziland: freehold, or Title

Deed Land (TDL), and Swazi Nation Land (SNL). This can be subdivided into: land held under customary tenure, which may not be sold, mortgaged or leased and is under the control of the chiefs; and land which is leased, or held in trust by private companies controlled by the monarch. As Levin (1997) points out, there is considerable ambiguity surrounding the legal definition of Swazi Nation Land. In his carefully documented study of land tenure in Swaziland, he charts a history of depressed smallholder farm production, exploitation – particularly of women – and forced removals on SNL, with the tacit support of those in power. He argues that, while in the abstract, 'communal tenure' may have allowed for democratic involvement, in the tribal context it has proved a misnomer because it conceals the power relations which underlie it and control land use and allocation.

Careful steps – in the Swazi tradition of gradual adjustment – are being taken to move forward from this feudal position. Whether or not the recent draft National Land Policy, including its thinly disguised proposals for reining in the powers of the chiefs, will be accepted by the monarch is not clear. Much will depend on progress with wider democratic reforms in the Kingdom. In this respect, the Swazi Administration Order of 1998, which extends the sentencing powers of the chiefs, is a setback. It reinforces the link between land ownership and jurisdiction.

Lesotho

The "Mountain Kingdom", a constitutional monarchy, suffers from an acute shortage of arable land. By 1986 such land had shrunk to 9% of the total area, and 25% of the rural population were landless. Taking into account continuing peri-urban sprawl and land degradation, the arable area is estimated to be far less. Claims for the restitution of ancestral lands pose international relations problems, since these fall within South African territory.

Land is owned by the "Nation". Tenure reform is the subject of debate between those in favour of the traditional system and modernists who believe that land should be tradable. Box 7.7 sets out the former view. In line with the Land Act, 1979, all land in urban areas is eventually to be converted to leasehold at the point of transaction. Urban leases are allocated by committees appointed by the Minister of Local Government (with the exception of the Principal Chief who takes the chair). Rural land is allocated by each of the 1,600 Village Development Councils, comprising the chief of the area (ex officio) and seven other members, elected in a public meeting. Thus, Lesotho has moved one democratic step beyond Swaziland, as chiefs are no longer alone responsible for land allocation.

> **Box 7.7: Land in Lesotho – some basic principles**
>
> At a workshop to discuss the future of land tenure in Lesotho, traditionalists argued that:
> (a) Access to land is a birthright of the Basotho people.
> (b) Land shall remain inalienably vested in the Basotho nation, administered by the State for the Basotho people.
> (c) The provisions for a leasehold system established in the Land Act 1979 and subsequent legislation are currently sufficient for Lesotho, and an adequate basis for improved land use and agricultural and rural development.
> (d) 'Freehold tenure', as such, may not be necessary at the present time.
> Source: UNDP, 1993

The Land Act of 1979 introduced the principle that, while land in urban areas should be in the form of leasehold, land in rural areas, with the exception of residential and commercial land should remain "under allocation", although provision was made for voluntary conversion into agricultural leases. In addition, the inheritance rules were modified for arable land, giving stronger rights to individual families.

In 1987, a Land Policy Review Commission was established to investigate and review land tenure and land administration, and to advise on necessary legal changes. Although some deficiencies highlighted by the Commission were rectified, the legal, policy and institutional frameworks have not been modified. Solutions await a wider political settlement within the country.

Botswana

In Botswana freehold land covers only about 5% of the land area. It originated in the colonial period and still offers the only exclusive rights of agricultural use in Botswana. Tribal land comprises about 70% of the total land area. However, government continues to make purchases to augment tribal land as freehold becomes available.

The Tribal Land Act of 1968 transferred the authority over land from the chiefs to Land Boards, with the aim of reducing discrimination between tribes. District Land Boards were placed under the nominal political direction of the District Councils and comprised representatives of both traditional leaders and councillors. Freehold titles, originally granted by the Protectorate Government to European farmers, were excluded from the jurisdiction of the Land Boards.

The conditions endured by farm-workers employed on freehold farms and cattle posts in the CAs are reported to be miserable. Many of them are drawn from the Basarwa (San or Bushmen) who have been consistently denied their traditional rights by other races occupying their ancestral lands. This failing apart, the land policy that has been pursued by Botswana may be described as one of careful change, responding to particular needs with specific tenure innovations (Box 7.8).

Box 7.8: Botswana's customary land tenure system

The Tribal Land Act, 1968, provided for the establishment of representative Land Boards and transferred all the land-related powers of chiefs to these. The functions of the Boards include the allocation of land; imposing restrictions on the use of land; authorising change of use and transfer; and the resolution of land disputes. Tribal land belongs to the people. Individuals are granted rights to use some parts of the land. It may be held by the Land Boards, or by individuals or groups as customary grants, or under leasehold. The land may also be allocated to the state for public purposes. Although land holders do not 'own' land, they have exclusive rights to their holdings which can be fenced to exclude others. Grazing land and land not yet allocated are used communally. The Land Boards grant land rights under both customary and common law.

The holders of **customary rights** for residential and ploughing purposes enjoy a variety of rights guaranteed by a customary land grant certificate which are exclusive and heritable.

Common law leases for non-customary land use (i.e. residential, commercial and industrial) are limited in time and subject to eventual reversion to the community. They can be registered under the Deeds Registry Act and are mortgageable and therefore transferable without the Land Board's consent.

Key changes which have been introduced since 1970 include: the exclusion of other people's animals after harvesting and the fencing of arable lands; relaxation of the restrictions on land allocation to allow independent allocations of land to all adults; the charging of a price (agreed between seller and buyer) for transfer of developed land; the introduction of common law residential leases for citizens, foreign investors, commercial grazing, and for commercial arable farming.

POLICY CONCLUSIONS

The sensitivity and complexity of tenure issues and concentration on land re-distribution have caused some governments in the region to neglect tenure reform. Land tenure reform is a time-consuming process requiring thorough public consultation and careful preparation. It should be recognised that the necessary institutional development is likely to take decades. Long-term budgetary commitment is therefore needed from governments and (political sensitivities permitting) from donors. External support is likely to be conditional upon the development of appropriate constitutional and legal frameworks.

In the interim, interventions may have to focus on the more densely settled areas and be phased to give priority to situations that are a direct threat to livelihoods or political stability. Tenure reform proposals must be built on a thorough understanding of the livelihood strategies of those intended to benefit. It should not be assumed that the inadequacies of tenure laws and/or administrative support constrain livelihoods in practice.

Land tenure reform must pay special attention to the legal status and economic activities of women and the poor, who are often disproportionately dependent on the commons. Despite the complexities involved, tenure reform is essential if the access of such groups to common property resources is to be sustained. Policy to reform land tenure must be developed alongside policies, resources and financial incentives to help the building of more sustainable livelihoods, including non-land based activities.

Tenure reform measures for communal land should underpin the adaptability and responsiveness of existing customary systems and not constrain local coping strategies. Policy should be flexible with regard to the role of traditional authorities and introduce reforms on a gradual basis. As far as possible, responsibility for land rights management should be devolved to the rights-holders.

8

Tenure and Common Property Resources in Africa

Ben Cousins

INTRODUCTION

This chapter discusses rights to the most ubiquitous natural resources in Africa, those located on the commons. Comprising both high value (e.g. wetlands) and low value (e.g. extensive rangelands) resources, these make a vital contribution to the livelihoods of many rural households. Clarifying and strengthening these rights should form a central component of programmes of tenure reform. One potential outcome of reform is greater security of livelihoods; another is more effective and sustainable management of common pool resources. Despite its evident desirability, however, tenure reforms which result in these kinds of outcomes have thus far proved somewhat elusive. This may be due, in part, to over-simplified conceptual models and the inappropriate policy approaches to which they give rise.

The chapter emphasises the importance of common property resources to African livelihood systems, and their wider significance within the range of institutional arrangements by which people gain access to resources. The rapid incorporation of rural African economies into "globalising" world markets and the economic opportunities which this opens up, may exclude as well as include local people, and pose new problems for those who have rights to the commons and depend on them for their livelihoods. The dynamism, variety and complexity of rights to common pool resources provide a major challenge for tenure reforms, examples of which are vividly illustrated here by case study material from different parts of the continent.

Understanding the strong interlinkages between institutional arrangements for accessing resources and the broader political economy has profound im-

151

plications for the conceptualisation of common property. A number of views will be presented below which seek to modify the current approach to understanding common property resources and their management, known as the "new institutionalist" paradigm[1]. The chapter ends with an analysis of the implications of both empirical research and theoretical perspectives for tenure reform policies, drawing on discussions during the DFID workshop on Land Rights and Sustainable Development in Sub-Saharan Africa.

COMMON POOL RESOURCES AND LAND TENURE SYSTEMS IN AFRICA

Communal tenure and the commons

What is common property? In the "new institutionalism" (Bromley, 1989; Ostrom, 1990) *common pool resources* are public goods which are used simultaneously or sequentially by different users because of difficulties in claiming or enforcing exclusive rights, or because they are so sparse or uncertain that it is not worth doing so (Ostrom, 1990: 30). Many are subtractable in character such that one user's offtake will affect the availability of the resource to other users. When the rights and duties of groups of users in relation to these resources are defined and enforced, the resources become common property, as distinct from open access. In the latter, which Hardin (1968) famously confused with *common property*, rights and duties are not well-defined, and a "tragedy" of over-exploitation is a possible, and likely, outcome. Other types of property, conceptually distinct from common property and open access, are private and state property (Bromley, 1989).

Most land tenure systems in Africa are "communal" in character, although, as Bruce (1988) points out, this is in some respects a misnomer, since it is sometimes taken to imply common ownership of *all* resources, and collective production, which are rarely found. "Communal" means, in the great majority of cases, a degree of community control over who is allowed into the group, thereby qualifying for an allocation of land for residence and cropping, as well as rights of access to and use of the shared, common pool resources used by the group (i.e. the commons). Groups often restrict alienation of land to outsiders, and thus seek to maintain the identity, coherence and livelihood security of the group and its members. However, allocations of residential and arable land usually result in strong rights for individuals or families, or both, who sometimes

---

1 There have been major changes in approaches to understanding common property resources and their management, from the Tragedy of the Commons (Hardin, 1968) which presumes that such resources will always be exploited beyond their capacity, since open access regimes imply no system for management, to the "new institutionalist" perspective which argues that a variety of institutional arrangements are possible within which common property resources can be managed effectively.

Box 8.1: Tenure policy and land use change: competition and conflict in Sudan

Competition over natural resources has become a major issue for the pastoral populations of the African Sahel and the Horn. Current land tenure policies favour sedentary crop production, and often attempt to transform migratory pastoralists into settled farmers. Most tenure systems neglect common property regimes - despite their significance for pastoral livestock economies, thereby contributing to their increased vulnerability.

Nomadic pastoralism in the Sudan is a specific economic adaptation to conditions characterised by rainfall which is highly variable both spatially and temporally. Mobile and flexible herd movement allow marginal resources to be most efficiently utilised. The pastoral livestock economy has always been an integral part of a wider socio-economic system which includes sedentary cultivation - with long established exchanges between crops and livestock and the circulation of people between the two interdependent and complementary forms of production.

In precolonial times, the rangelands were managed by communal ownership. Access was by membership in fluid structures, so-called "tribes", organised around a power-centre controlling a strategic resource. Given the comparative advantage of pastoralism in a region of highly variable rainfall, the tribal rulers (of both sedentary and nomadic populations) tended to be drawn from the more affluent pastoralists.

The British colonial administration issued its first Titles to Land Ordinance in 1899, by which all riverain land in the north of the country which had been continuously cultivated in the preceding five years was considered the private property of the cultivator, and was registered. In other parts of Sudan, however, individual private ownership was not recognised, and land, whether under crops or grazing, was declared to be government-owned, and either subject to no right, subject to rights vested in a community, or (as in the Nuba Hills) held by individuals.

Regulation of pastoralism in the British colonial period: the central Sudan is characterised by seasonal fluctuations in the availability of water and forage. This means that herds must move between the wetter southern region in the dry season, and the drier north, during the rains. From 1904, the British sought to regulate these movements, through the system of Native Administration.

This was achieved through the enforcement of "grazing lines" beyond which no farming was allowed; the delineation of nomadic corridors; and annually issued Local Orders which laid down the timing and direction of movement and the latest date by which crops should be harvested. To limit and contain tribal intermingling, "tribal homelands" (Dar) were declared, which were divided into common and reserved grazing areas (which contained the permanent water points). The former areas were available for use by outsiders in the rainy season, whereas reserved areas were more tightly controlled. Water points were also opened and closed as a means of regulating rangeland use.

The marginalisation of pastoralism in the colonial and post-colonial periods: under the British, the limited usufruct rights of pastoralists on government-owned land began to be withdrawn in favour of large-scale, mechanised and irrigated agricultural schemes. This process continued after independence with the establishment of the Gezira and New Halfa Schemes. Initially, pastoralists were compensated for the loss of dry season pastures by free access to crop residues; but recently, plot-holders have withdrawn this right and begun to demand payment. Plot-holders, backed by government, have seen their economic and political power increase considerably over the years.

The administrative vacuum: in the 1970s, irrigated and rainfed agriculture expanded greatly. The government abolished the system of Native Administration and stopped issuing Local Orders to regulate grazing. Range management and water policy were dissociated, and the sole government department concerned with pastoralism was marginalised. In the early 1980s, the government declared all unregistered land to be the common property of all Sudanese.

Grazing lines are no longer enforced. Government tends to settle disputes in favour of farmers, which has led to an expansion in mechanised crop production, disrupting nomadic routes and blocking access to watering points. Crop damage by herds has increased and consequent disputes have intensified, but disputes are settled by courts controlled by sedentary interests. Rules concerning "tribal homelands" and intermingling of groups have fallen away as Local Orders are no longer issued, provoking increased levels of inter-group conflict.

The condition of water points has deteriorated, with very few new water points established since the mid-1970s. Water scarcity, exacerbated by droughts, has become a major problem. This has led to the digging of many private wells by wealthier herd owners and merchants, raising the costs of watering to pastoralists, and reducing the distances covered by herds of cattle and sheep. This has in turn led to increased dependence on crop residues, which must usually now be purchased.

Source: Ahmed, 1999

---

also exercise rights over land which contains common pool resources such as water points, or wetter areas with dry season grazing. These can also be controlled by sub-groups (kinship groupings, or clans) within larger groups.

The net result is a "communal tenure" system which is in fact a *mixed* tenure regime, comprising individual, family, sub-group and larger group rights and duties in relation to a variety of natural resources. The precise definition and articulation of these vary between ecosystems, areas, cultures, countries and regions, and can evolve quite rapidly in response to social and economic change (e.g. increasing population density, technological change, new economic opportunities, or degradation of resources). Box 8.1 describes the changes experienced by pastoral peoples of the Sudan from pre-colonial times onwards. Herders have suffered major and continuing losses due to the establishment of irrigation schemes and mechanised farming in former grazing areas. Pastoralists have become economically and politically marginalised, and cannot fight for their rights. As a result, livestock corridors which formerly guaranteed a herd's mobility through farmed areas, have been ploughed up, and conflicts between farmers and herders are always settled in favour of the latter.

Definition of what constitutes a common property resource changes over time, both between seasons and as a consequence of growing resource scarcity. In many parts of Africa, family-held fields are defined as individual property in the cropping season, but become a grazing commons in the dry season or when fallow. However, as grazing has become scarcer and crop stover in turn more valuable, fields in the dry season can be redefined as family property not available to other members of the group, with access requiring payment of a fee (see Box 8.1). In other circumstances, a commons, or part of it, can degenerate into open access under certain kinds of pressure, such as population growth, changes in production systems, or the erosion of local institutions formerly responsible for commons management (Lawry, 1990; Ainslie, 1998).

These tenure regimes may also be viewed as "mixed" for another reason: in most African countries, land held under communal tenure is legally owned by the state and the occupants have, in law, only a secondary right of access and use. When resources become more valuable (e.g. wildlife in the context of lucrative ecotourism, or land newly under irrigation), or new high value resources are discovered (e.g. minerals), then often the state asserts its primary rights to benefits or to allocate (sometimes to powerful members of the political elite, see Box 8.2 for an example from Kenya). However, this assertion of state ownership may be contested by the long term occupants. While many indigenous forests are formally state property, the government may in practice find it difficult to regulate their use (Matose, 1997). At the same time, these forests in practice are being used and managed by local communities even though they have no formal rights to do so.

The commons may thus be considered both community and state "property". Similarly, some areas of state-owned communal land may be effectively privatised, or alternatively have become open access, since no formal allocation of rights to a definite group of users may have taken place. Communal tenure regimes may then be "mixed" because they comprise complex combinations of *de jure* and *de facto* rights of ownership, use and access. However, land law in many African countries does not take proper account of common property management systems, preferring to deal in simple concepts of individual property. In Kenya, for example (see Box 8.2), the Constitutional Review process may provide a valuable opportunity to introduce concerns regarding sustainable resource management and the importance of common property systems for many rural people.

Multiple use of the commons and bundles of property rights

Mixed tenurial regimes also result from the character of many commons and their use by diverse groups. These often provide a wide variety of resources to a range of different users, with differential rights and duties. Bruce (1986) refers to these as tenure "niches". For example, because communal rangelands comprise a range of habitats and micro-environments, they can provide grazing and browse, wild foods, medicinal plants, fuel, building materials, and water points for both domestic and livestock use (Williams, 1998; Cousins, 1999). The resource tenures for all these uses may vary considerably, and can be analysed as "bundles of rights and duties", disaggregated by:

- *resource type* (e.g. grass, shrubs, trees, stream water, ground water, wild animals);
- *resource use* (e.g. grazing, cutting of thatch grass, harvesting of fruit, tree felling, lopping of branches, livestock watering, irrigation, hunting);

Box 8.2: Land tenure, common property and constitutional change in Kenya

Kenya has embarked upon a process of constitutional reform, in order to "ensure the provision of basic needs of all Kenyans through the establishment of an equitable framework for economic growth and equitable access to national resources". This process provides an opportunity to rethink a key issue of governance in Kenya: the creation of an appropriate policy, and legal and institutional framework for the sustainable management of natural resources. Land and common property resource tenure are central to this framework.

The existing situation: the current constitutional order is, by and large, the same as that inherited at independence in 1963. Its major concern is the distribution of political power. Although land formed the main focus for the struggle for independence, the land question did not feature very prominently in the drafting of the constitution, on account of its sensitivity.

Section 75 in the Bill of Rights deals explicitly with land as the major form of property rights in Kenya. It seeks to elevate the individual interest above the collective interests of Kenyans in their natural resource base. As a result, both the constitution and the overall legal framework for the management of land and natural resources have failed to make provision for common property resources, and in underwriting a drive towards privatisation, have undermined their sustainable management. Section 75 of the constitution also protects property against compulsory acquisition by the state, except where needed for public purposes, and it requires payment of full compensation by government. This provision was prompted primarily by fears of the departing colonial administration that the newly independent government would nationalise the lands of white settlers.

In the post-independence era, the constitution has served the interests of the new political and economic elite, who have been given individual title deeds to land taken from public lands or forests. Public land in urban centres has virtually disappeared in this "land grab", and the elite have now turned their attention to forest land, which is being degazetted, subdivided and allocated to individuals. These allocations, once made, are then defended by reference to section 75 of the constitution.

Chapter IX of the constitution makes provision for lands held on trust, which are vested in county councils "for the benefit of ... residents on that land", whose rights and interests must be taken into account. However, the wide powers bestowed on councils, the absence of mechanisms for beneficiaries to check the manner in which the trust is administered, and the fact that customary land tenure has been viewed as an intermediate stage in the evolution of tenure systems towards private tenure, have had negative effects on common property resource management. Trust lands have increasingly been sub-divided and then allocated to individuals who register it under individual title.

Common property resources and the land question: the land question in Kenya is still unresolved. Major policy documents over the past two decades have urged government to establish a Land Commission. Reforms initiated in the 1950s have proved inadequate as population pressure has built up in both urban and rural areas, and conflicts over natural resources are becoming increasingly common.

The underlying issue is security of tenure. Despite policies in favour of privatisation and individualisation, customary tenure has persisted over most of the country. Thus, communities and individuals have continued to relate to one another on the basis of custom, even where individual titles have been issued. Most land disputes derive from the conflict between, on the one hand, expectations and ideas regarding property relations under customary systems and, on the other, the rights and privileges flowing from individualisation, titling and registration.

Conflicts over land and natural resources are threatening to tear the country apart, as can be seen, for example, in the mass eviction of Kikuyu farmers by the Maasai who need the land for

---

grazing. Consequently, there is an urgent need to rethink the policy and legal framework for tenure and land management.

The constitutional review process: there is a serious danger that the constitutional review process may not give sufficient weight to the need for a proper basis within the Constitution for a policy to manage natural resources. Only one civil society organisation represented in the review process (the Kenya Pastoralists Forum) can be identified as a natural resource organisation - the rest are pressure groups interested in political rights. Furthermore, many Kenyans are unaware of the existing constitution and its shortcomings, while very little time has been allowed for the review process.

Nevertheless, this commitment to review the constitution does provide a significant opportunity for Kenyans to redefine their system of governance. Civil society organisations in the natural resource management sector have an important role to play in mobilising and facilitating public opinion to ensure that communities who are dependent on natural resources for their livelihood can make an effective input, and that their interests are taken into account in the new constitution.

One of the objects of the constitutional review process is to promote devolution of power to the local level. This should enable natural resource management to be done by local institutions comprising members of resource dependent communities, and ensuring their effective participation.

Source: Ochieng Odhiambo, 1999

- *resource users* (e.g. individuals, families, sub-groups; primary rights-holders, secondary rights-holders or temporary users, men, women);
- *season of use* (e.g. dry season, wet season, in drought years only); and
- *nature and strength of rights and duties* (e.g. exclusive use, shared use, permanent rights, temporary rights, rates of use, boundaries of resource use).

This image of claims to property and access as a bundle of rights and duties in relation to natural resources is well illustrated by the examples in Boxes 8.3 and 8.4. which show the large number and diversity of user groups. They also show the wide range of institutional arrangements under which access to these resources is made possible, and the associated hierarchy of resources and user groups.

Box 8.3: The multiple use commons and property rights in the Sahel

Resource use in the Sahel involves a multiplicity of users: an annual pasture is often accessible to many users from different directions who remain for an indeterminate time; valleys or *bas-fonds* may be exploited and jointly controlled by several agro-pastoral village communities, or by smaller groups with family fields within the *bas-fonds*; family fields will be controlled by households. These fields may be opened at certain times of year to passing herders in exchange for the manure from their animals. Non-exclusive rights, such as to water points, may involve priority usage rights held by a restricted group, who also allow access to other pastoralists, in accordance with strict rules aimed at controlling grazing in the surrounding area. Pastoral land use involves a duality between vast rangelands and more limited home areas which often contain strategic resources: deep wells, areas around lakes, rivers, streams or permanent water holes or *bas-fonds* rich in woody species.

Source: Thébaud, 1995

> **Box 8.4: Tenure niches in pastoralist systems**
>
> Multiple resource use in pastoral Africa is traditionally regulated by informal or formal rules based on the priority claimed by different user groups: "primary users" have highest priority within their home territory, "secondary users" have seasonal access, and "tertiary users" have infrequent access in times of need, such as drought years. Five territorial units within a hierarchy of tenure regimes can be distinguished: the customary *territory* belonging to the "tribe"; flexibly defined *annual grazing areas* within the territory, with priority use by several clans, sections or sub-clans; *dry season bases* where a specific group, such as a sub-clan, is the primary users and other groups are secondary or tertiary users; *key sites* within the dry season base; and *group or individual resources/areas,* such as trees in Turkana, where a household or group of households are primary users.
>
> *Overlapping territories*, managed jointly by neighbouring groups, allow some room for expansion and function as fall-back areas in difficult years. *Buffer zones* between groups, maintained for similar reasons, are more extensive and often used by more than two groups. The latter require *ad hoc* negotiations over use between the different groups when the need to use these areas arises.
>
> Source: Niamir-Fuller, 1994

Exclusion and boundaries

According to both legal and social science approaches to property, a fundamental feature of all regimes, including common property, is the possibility of excluding those without property rights. According to Ostrom (1990: 91) "defining the boundaries of the common property resource and specifying those authorised to use it can be thought of as a first step in organising for collective action". However, for a variety of reasons, the boundaries between territories under common property regimes in Africa are often not clearly defined. Lack of clarity, or "fuzziness", poses problems for management of resources, but also has certain advantages.

Key resources (e.g. wetlands), often of critical importance for production systems, are usually spatially concentrated, allowing close monitoring of access and use. Extensive resources at the margin are less valuable, so the high transaction costs of defining and maintaining clear boundaries are often not justified by the benefits. Thus, boundaries are usually clearly established only in relation to key resources. Behnke (1994) provides examples from Bedouin Libya of hierarchies of rights to water, arable land and pasture resources based on variations in their productive value and costs of control. This results in varying degrees of exclusive control of resource use.

Spatial and temporal variability of resource availability mean that a degree of mobility on the part of resource users may be necessary (e.g. in pastoralist systems). Behnke and Scoones (1993: 13) show how mobility increases the overall carrying capacity of rangelands within regions which incorporate a wide range of seasonal difference in grazing resource availability. This assumes a pattern of predictable environmental fluctuation which movement of livestock may exploit along regular transhumant routes. A similar argument is made by Sandford (1983: 33-36) for situations where stock movement takes place in response to unpredictable rainfall fluctuations, disease outbreaks, borehole breakdowns and range fires. In this case, movement is more contingent and depends on herd-owners negotiating access to fallback areas (see Box 8.4).

For pastoralists, "opportunistic" herd movement over long distances is thus essential, across territories in which boundaries are flexible and negotiable, rather than clear and unambiguous. This allows them to maintain the large herds which constitute their main source of livelihoods (Behnke and Scoones, 1993). Variability occurs at both the macro-scale (e.g., contrasts between clay-soil savannas and sandy-soil savannas), and at the micro-scale (e.g., between riverine areas and uplands), and thus modified forms of opportunism are found in agro-pastoral systems (where producers are sedentary rather than mobile) as well (Scoones, 1995; Cousins, 1992).

Swallow (1996) distinguishes between a *flexible* boundary (here the spatial location of the boundary is identifiable but subject to change as a result of negotiations) and a fuzzy boundary (where it does not separate territories into discrete land units that are the property of mutually-exclusive groups). Both flexibility and fuzziness have the advantage that they maximise the number of landscape patches to which people can have access, which is particularly important when environmental conditions are highly variable.

Lack of clarity in the definition of physical boundaries is often mirrored by a comparable "fuzziness" in the definition of social boundaries. This can derive from the multiple social identities of resource users (Peters, 1994), or from the nesting of smaller social units (such as kin-networks, villages) within larger groupings (clans, wards, chiefdoms) (Devereaux, 1996). These create a complex web of social identities, which are often deliberately and strategically manipulated by diverse sets of natural resource users, who are highly differentiated, rather than constituting a homogeneous group (Moore, 1996).

As Frost and Madondo point out for rural Zimbabwe:

> The underlying communities themselves are inherently heterogeneous in terms of ethnic composition, power relationships, politics of affection, preferences, interests, socio-economic standing and livelihood strategies.... this heterogeneity occurs at a range of scales: ethnic groups, clans, discrete household clusters, family units within these clusters, and even within families. These can act both independently and interactively within the broader social and political units in which they are nested. (1997:7)

Recognition of the flexibility and fuzziness of boundary definition in relation to common pool resources in Africa has contributed to an emerging view of common property tenure which significantly modifies the "new institutionalist" paradigm.

RURAL LIVELIHOODS AND THE CONTRIBUTION OF COMMON PROPERTY RESOURCES

Debate about policies to secure people's land rights often focuses on residential or arable land and those components of communal land tenure systems which are generally allocated to families or individuals. Here the argument has mostly been on the desirability of registration and titling, implying a transition from customary or communal tenure to individualised private property (Shipton, 1989; Bruce and Mighot-Adholla, 1994). Somewhat neglected in the past, but now beginning to feature more centrally, are the common property components (Baland and Platteau, 1996). This has been accompanied by an increasing recognition of the vital role that common pool resources play in multiple livelihood systems (of the rural poor in particular) and of their surprisingly high economic value (IIED, 1995; Campbell et al, 1997; Arnold and Townson, 1998).

The variety of livelihood options provided by the commons

A wide variety of habitats and resources can constitute common pool resources - grasslands, forests, mixed savannahs, wetlands, mountain sides, lakes, rivers, coastal areas, marine fisheries. These ecological bases contribute to rural livelihoods in Africa in diverse ways (see Figure 1). They can provide:
● water for domestic use, livestock, and irrigation;
● grazing and browse for mixed herds of livestock;
● habitats for wildlife, providing food, cash, medicine;
● building materials;
● medicinal products;
● fuel;
● edible plants;
● fish and other aquatic/marine resources; and
● raw materials for tools, products and handicrafts for use and sale.
The list comprises livelihood components that are "traditional", but have often involved long standing engagement with both local and more distant markets (e.g. the urban market for charcoal in Zambia) and are thus often partially commoditised. It can be extended by including newer forms of economic activity which involve interactions with private sector enterprise, and can take the

form of sub-contracts, joint ventures, leasehold agreements, or other arrangements. The most notable are:

- ecotourism of the non-consumptive kind;
- safari hunting or other wildlife-based enterprises; and
- commercial or semi-commercial forestry.

In Southern Africa, the apparent success of high profile community wildlife management programmes, such as CAMPFIRE in Zimbabwe or LIFE in Namibia, have focussed attention and debate on the latter forms of common property management (IIED, 1995; Rihoy, 1995; Murphree, 1996). These have underlined the need to understand the current and potential role of private capital in common property management. Adding external investors to the list of potential stakeholders does allow additional options for commons use, but it also complicates efforts to develop effective institutional arrangements for management of the resources (Fabricius et al, 1999).

The variety of livelihood contributions from the African commons can be understood in terms of the key characteristics of rural livelihood systems in all their multiplicity, diversity and dynamism. Common pool resources often play a key safety net function in times of drought or family disaster, providing wild foods, products such as building materials which can no longer be purchased, or products (e.g. Acacia pods) for sale (Scoones et al, 1996). Hence they help rural people manage risk, reduce vulnerability and enhance security.

The significance of common pool resources for livelihoods varies significantly by social identity and position within social structure; class, gender, age, ethnicity, political status and affiliation, spatial location and other identities can all be important (Clarke et al, 1996; Campbell et al, 1997; Kepe, 1997; Arnold and Townson, 1998). Some common pool resources form the major resource base for large numbers of people, such as communal rangelands for pastoralists in the Sahel or in the Horn of Africa, but others (e.g. wild foods as a nutritional supplement for agriculturalists) are clearly secondary. However, research indicates that many common pool resources are particularly crucial for the livelihoods of the rural poor who have low cash incomes through the formal economy (Cavendish, cited in Clarke et al, 1996; Shackleton et al, 1999).

In addition to their economic contributions, common pool resources fulfil other important functions for rural people through indirect or non-use:

- aesthetic, ritual and spiritual functions; and
- ecological service functions e.g. watershed protection, erosion prevention.

These are often of great value to rural people themselves. A number of studies (IIED, 1997; Campbell et al, 1997) have indicated that non-market values such as rain-making functions, water retention, inheritance value, aesthetics, shade, initiation sites, sacred areas, and the prevention of soil erosion are rated highly by rural communities. In some cases these functions may be ranked higher than direct use (Campbell et al, 1997). Work in Namibian communal conservancies has indicated the high value that rural communities place on the presence or existence of game; in some cases this is as important an incentive for conservancy formation as the direct returns from tourism and safari related activities (Jones, 1999). These non-use values are important for social, cultural, economic, and ecological sustainability.

The economic value of common property in Africa

In recent years environmental economists have elaborated a number of concepts and methods for assessing values gained from the natural environment. Much of this innovation has been motivated by a desire to provide sound economic arguments for biodiversity conservation (Edwards and Abivardi, 1998), but many of the analytical tools which have emerged can also be used to underpin policy advocacy for multiple rural livelihood strategies (IIED, 1995), or for enhanced common property management (Cousins, 1999).

Some of the key concepts are summarised in Table 1. *Direct use* values are those that derive from human consumption, either directly (such as wild foods or building materials) or via livestock products (milk, meat, draught etc.). Some may be marketed, but many are not. Many direct uses involve consumption, but some, such as tourism, do not. Some resources have important *indirect* values e.g. "ecosystem service functions" such as waste assimilation, photosynthesis, flood control, or nutrient cycling. *Non-use* values include the cultural, spiritual, ceremonial, aesthetic and "existence" values of resources.

Attempts to measure the significance of common property resources need to focus on *local-level valuation* which draws on local people's knowledge and

Table 8.1: Economic values of common pool resources

Use values		Non-use values
Direct	**Indirect**	**Existence/cultural values**
Plants and animals consumed by people or domestic livestock, or marketed Examples: grazing, wild foods, medicines, fuelwood	Support for other economic activities via ecological service functions Examples: flood control, nutrient cycling in agricultural lands promoted by grazing areas or woodlands, pollination of crops by wild species	Species or systems which are valued in their own right without reference to an economic use Examples: cultural appreciation, beauty, motivation to bequeath resources to future generations, sacred groves

Source: adapted from IIED, 1997

combines this with economic and ecological analysis. Local knowledge is crucial because many resource uses are site-specific and seasonal, vary between social groups, are used opportunistically or even illegally, are marketed though informal markets or consumed directly, or are valued for indirect uses or non-use (IIED, 1997). Using these methods, a number of case studies from different parts of Africa illustrate the surprisingly high economic value of common pool resources (e.g. Arnold and Townson, 1998; Bishop and Scoones, 1994; Campbell et al, 1997; Clarke et al, 1996; Shackleton et al, 1999). A recent estimate for the aggregate value of common pool resources in the communal areas of South Africa by Adams et al (1999a) yielded a total of R9.5 billion (or $US 1.6 billion).

The high values obtained in these studies are premised on conceptual and methodological advances which take into account the livelihood objectives of resource users (which include self provisioning as well as production for the market, risk aversion, etc), and understanding that common pool resources have multiple uses and functions. However, few policy makers appear to take the high value of common pool resources into account, despite the high costs to society that would be incurred if all the goods and services provided from the commons, such as medical services, housing, energy and welfare payments, had to be supplied by the state or purchased from supplies in the market place.

Figure 8.1: Rural livelihoods and natural resources in Africa

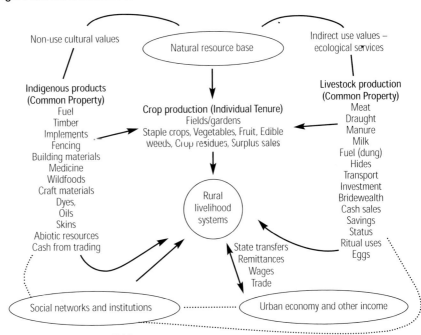

Source: Shackleton et al, 1999

EMERGING VIEWS OF THE COMMONS: CRITIQUES OF THE NEW INSTITUTIONALISM

Growing recognition of the importance of common pool resources for rural livelihoods has been accompanied by innovative conceptual and theoretical work on the institutional dimensions. The critique of Hardin's influential "Tragedy of the Commons" model (e.g. Ciriacy-Wantrup and Bishop, 1975; Runge, 1981) has contributed to a substantial body of work in recent years which offers an alternative understanding of common property (Berkes, 1989; Bromley, 1989; McCay and Acheson, 1987; National Research Council, 1986; Ostrom, 1990). Research has been both theoretical and empirical in character, and has engaged scholars from a variety of disciplines. Much of it has been from within a "new institutionalist" paradigm, which is concerned with questions of "how do institutions evolve in response to individual incentives, strategies and choices, and how do institutions affect the performance of political and economic systems?" (Alt and North, in Ostrom, 1990: xi).

Emerging views are critical of some aspects of this approach to understanding common property. One important contribution has been to recognise that the boundaries of common property regimes are often less clearly defined than theory suggests is necessary. Another is to question the centrality of the notion of "rules" for resource management. In the new institutionalist approach, institutions are usually defined as "the rules of the game in society" (North, 1990: 3), as distinct from organisations, which are conceived of as "the players of the game", or "groups of individuals bound together by some common purpose to achieve objectives" (ibid: 5). This emphasis on rules is perhaps the defining feature of the new institutionalism. One of the most influential outcomes of this emphasis is the set of "design principles" developed by Ostrom (1990). She suggests that these underlie the success in securing compliance by resource users to the rules found in robust, long-enduring common property regimes (see Box 8.5).

Ostrom (1990: 51) clarifies that rules include informal norms and practices; her emphasis is on "working rules... those actually used, monitored, and enforced when individuals make choices about the actions they will take", and they may or may not resemble formal laws. Close alignment is possible; so is a situation in which *de facto* operational rules are contrary to the *de jure* rights and duties of legal systems.

Leach et al (1997) have elaborated a disaggregated view of institutions which mediate access to and use of natural resources. They move from a critique of much of the new institutionalist economics as functionalist, and hence tautologous in its premises, towards a perspective which distinguishes between rules and practices and explores the relationships between them. Points of de-

---

Box 8.5: Design principles for long-enduring common property institutions

1. Clearly defined boundaries: Individuals or households who have rights to withdraw resource units from the common property resource (CPR) must be clearly defined, as must the boundaries of the CPR itself.
2. Congruence between appropriation rules [governing the withdrawal of resource units] and provisioning rules [governing the building, restoring or maintaining of the resource system], and between provision rules and local conditions: Appropriation rules restricting time, place, technology, and/or quantity of resource units are related to local conditions and to provision rules requiring labour, material and/or money
3. Collective-choice arrangements: Most individuals affected by the operational rules can participate in modifying the operational rules.
4. Monitoring: Monitors, who actively audit CPR conditions and behaviour by users, are also accountable to the appropriators to them.
5. Graduated sanctions: Appropriators (or users) who violate operational rules are likely to receive graduated sanctions (depending on the seriousness and context of the offence) by others, by officials accountable to them, or by both.
6. Conflict-resolution mechanisms: Appropriators and their officials have rapid access to low-cost local arenas to resolve conflicts among users.
7. Minimal recognition of rights to organise: The rights of appropriators to devise their own institutions are not challenged by external governmental authorities.

For CPRs that are part of larger systems:

8. Nested enterprises: Appropriation, provision, monitoring, enforcement, conflict resolution, and governance activities are organised in multiple layers of nested enterprises.

Source: Ostrom, 1990: 90

---

parture include Gore (1993), who analyses the "unruly social practices" which often challenge legal rules of entitlement to resources. They emphasise the contested, and more indeterminate nature of institutional orders, and their embeddedness within unequal and dynamic social relations.

Formal and informal institutions can co-exist within common property regimes, but also interact in a complex and dynamic manner. Moore (1975), asserts that *reglementory processes* ("all those attempts to organise and control behaviour through the use of explicit rules") take place at a multiplicity of levels within society, and within a variety of social fields. Numerous conflicting or competing rule-orders exist, characterised more often than not by "ambiguities, inconsistencies, gaps, conflicts and the like" (Moore, 1975: 3).

These dynamics can only be understood by referring to the rule/practice distinction, and in terms of an analysis of power and the politics of meaning. Rules, whether formal or informal, do not determine behaviour, but are a field or context for strategic action and interaction undertaken by diverse social actors. Moore refers to the "continuous making and reiterating of social and symbolic order… as an active process.... existing orders are endlessly vulnerable to being unmade, remade and transformed" (ibid: 6). Institutional analysis must therefore include both a structural analysis of complexes of rule-orders and also a processual and actor-oriented analysis of action which is "choice making, discretionary, manipulative, sometimes inconsistent, and sometimes conflictual" (ibid: 3).

Vandergeest (1997) explores the implications of understanding property as practice rather than as rules. In contrast to the practices preferred by the state, local property often takes the form of informal and flexible practices, which are generally not recorded in writing, with all the ambiguities and inconsistencies removed. Because of long histories of relations between state agencies and locals, and the inability of the state to completely take over administration and enforcement, most property is in fact a mix of formal and informal practices. Property practices are thus complex, some recognised by the state and some not; they are also contingent and dynamic as people continuously renegotiate them with each other and with state agencies. For this reason:

> A study of 'rules' is a very limiting approach to understanding property. One can learn more about property by following people to see what they are doing, and asking them about it, than by asking them about rules. If we begin by understanding property as everyday practices, then the idea of common property as a clearly specified and bounded set of rules set off from the state and from private property becomes limiting. (Vandergeest, 1997: 6)

The shift in analytical focus from rules to practice, social process and social embeddedness is evident in the work of scholars who emphasise fluidity and negotiability in property rights as central features of African tenure systems (Berry, 1993; Peters, 1994; 1998; Moore, 1998; Okoth-Ogendo, 1989). In Berry's influential analysis, (1993: 101-134), despite attempts in many parts of rural Africa to clarify land rights and regulate processes of allocation, inheritance and transfer, access to resources remains subject to contest and negotiation. Access has continued to hinge on social identity and status, and hence on membership of groups and networks; land is subject to multiple interests, and to "a dynamic of litigation and struggle which both fosters investment in social relations and helps to keep them fluid and negotiable" (*ibid*: 133). This has had the effect of making it difficult to enforce legislation on tenure rights, or to institutionalise exclusive control of land by either individuals or corporate groups. "Security of tenure" is in practice secured not through law and administration, but maintained through open-ended, on-going processes of negotiation, adjudication and political manoeuvre (Berry, 1994: 35). The policy implications of this perspective are explored further below.

THE COMMONS UNDER STRESS: CURRENT PROCESSES AND PROBLEMS

The embeddedness of common pool resource use within complex livelihood systems and the diverse social, cultural, economic and political contexts of rural Africa mean that tenure reform policies and programmes are devised and implemented in extremely challenging conditions. This section outlines these conditions and the dynamic processes of change to which they are currently subject.

Socio-economic change and increased pressure on the commons

The significant contributions that common pool resources make to rural livelihoods are under threat from a variety of pressures on the commons. These result from inter-related demographic and socio-economic processes which influence patterns of resource use and are changing the composition of rural livelihoods in many African countries. Some of these processes are extremely contradictory, and their outcomes are not yet clear. While they undoubtedly increase the difficulties of tenure reform aimed at enhancing common property management, they also underline the urgent need to do so - particularly from the perspective of the rural poor, the great majority, who have thus far derived little benefit from decades of "development".

   Dynamics on the commons are shaped by processes in the wider political economy. Most African economies continue to perform poorly and are becoming ever more marginal within the global capitalist system, now characterised by increasingly mobile capital, the "rolling back" of the state, closer integration of some economic sectors and populations and the effective exclusion of others. Problems include an export sector still dominated by the sale of primary commodities (including agricultural goods), whose prices continue to decline in real terms, and the failure to develop a substantial manufacturing sector. Trade balances are negative and the debt burden overwhelming. Formal sector employment is in decline, and the illegal or "second" economy is estimated to account for a third to two thirds of economic activity (Leys, 1994). Population growth has proceeded apace but per capita incomes have fallen at over 2 percent a year since 1980. Widespread and deepening poverty and inequality are the context of rural resource use in most of Africa.

   In this context "natural capital", including common pool resources, is increasingly important in rural people's struggle to stay alive, as: (a) a source of food and materials for immediate consumption, but also as (b) a source of goods which can be sold for cash, either in the form they are harvested (e.g. logs of hardwood sold to timber merchants) or as transformed by labour (e.g. trees into charcoal). The African commons is thus subject to two contradictory processes: increasing use for subsistence, and increasing commoditisation. The latter is being undertaken by both the rural poor who are desperate to earn whatever cash they can to purchase consumer essentials, and by elites and entrepreneurs who see the potential for a quick profit. Both kinds of pressure create problems for attempts to develop appropriate common property management regimes.

Two other processes combine to exert pressure on common pool resources: increased urbanisation, with a resulting demand for marketed food, and agricultural intensification, partly to supply the urban market, partly as a survival option given the poor performance of the formal economy. In some African countries this is leading to a reduction in the area of common pool forest, bush and grazing, and resulting in tensions between sedentary agriculturalists and mobile pastoralists (Lane, 1998; IIED, 1999) or between neighbouring communities. Government policies can produce or exacerbate these conflicts (see Box 8.1).

Two common survival strategies, adopted as responses to the processes described above, also impact on the commons: diversification of livelihood sources, including a turn away from reliance on farming towards "rural non-farm employment" (Bryceson, 1997; Ellis, 1999), and migration, either voluntary or involuntary. Diversification contributes in part to the commoditisation of common pool resources, through people attempting to develop small enterprises based on raw materials from the commons (e.g. craft work, fodder sales, beer brewing from wild fruit, firewood sales), and increases the heterogeneity of commons user groups. Migration can lead to rapid population growth in the targeted area and intense pressure on the commons (e.g. the Zambesi Valley in Zimbabwe - Derman, 1990), and to the recomposition of social and political formations in ways which fundamentally alter patterns of resource use and the institutions which mediate them (IIED, 1999: 19-21).

Involuntary migration often results from civil or military conflicts. These are widespread in many regions of Africa, and millions of refugees have flowed across national borders in recent years (Leys, 1994). Refugees are often forced to turn to the natural environment for part of their subsistence.

In sum, rapid socio-economic change, partly as a result of new modes of interaction between the local, rural economy and the global, capitalist economy, is fundamentally altering the context of common pool resource use in many parts of Africa. Institutionally regulated patterns of resource use in small, stable, relatively homogeneous social units are becoming rarer. Highly differentiated socio-economic contexts in which the commons is used by many of the poor as a last defence against starvation, and by entrepreneurs to initiate or advance a process of capital accumulation, are increasingly evident.

Rights to common property and their weak legal status

The state continues to hold legally defined *de jure* ownership rights over land (including the commons) in much of rural Africa, while rural communities and individuals exert *de facto* rights which are partly defined in terms of "custom" and partly by ongoing adaptations of practices and rules to changing circumstances and shifting relations of power. There is increasing recognition of the problems created by this dualism in tenure, and the need for tenure reform, as other chapters in this book note. One of the key dimensions of tenure reform in Africa is recognition of the centrality of common property rights, and the difficulties that multiple and overlapping rights to land create for programmes aiming to formalise, codify or register land rights and thus overcome the colonial legacy of dualism. This is challenging given the underlying assumption in most Western legal systems, which tend to be the source of suggested reforms (see Chapter 4, this volume), that property implies complete excludability (Peters, 1998).

However, some formidable problems need to be confronted. The state's interests are often seen as primary by policy makers and officials, who therefore resist attempts to give legal recognition to the rights of communities or user groups. Governance and property rights in communal areas are enmeshed and confused as a result of the colonial legacy of indirect rule (Mamdani, 1996), which means that "trusteeship" of land is often confused with "ownership" in the state's right of eminent domain (see Chapter 6, this volume). This can lead to government entering into agreements with foreign investors for the use of communal land. This may include use for tourism or large scale agricultural schemes as in southern Mozambique and, potentially, in the development corridors known as Spatial Development Initiatives which are a key thrust of development policy in much of Southern Africa.

External investment may create new opportunities for wealth creation, but these are unlikely to benefit the rural poor unless the agreements reached explicitly make provision for an appropriate distribution of benefits. One means to achieving this end is the recognition in law of the land rights of the people on whose land development takes place (Ntsebeza, 1999a). As Murphree has emphasised, in relation to community-based wildlife management, "the communal contexts created by colonialism are not communal property regimes, since they have been stripped of the necessary entitlements required" (Murphree, 1993: 12). He suggests that a "sweeping agrarian reform" is required to create "legally titled collective and communal property right holders", but recognises that this requires the mobilisation of political will.

The fact that private property is still seen as preferable by many policy makers, and that common property rights are not generally recognised in national constitutions, is another problem area (see Box 8.2). In certain contexts processes of constitutional review may open up strategic possibilities for advocacy in relation to common property, but here a problem will be the lack of political "voice" experienced by rural groups who rely on the commons for their livelihoods, and the relative weakness of organisations of civil society which represent common property user groups such as pastoralists (Lane, 1998).

The poor status accorded the land rights of women generally are also of concern in relation to the commons, since women often play key roles in the harvesting of natural resources from the commons (e.g. medicinal plants, edible wild fruits), and are therefore important *de facto* "resource managers" (Fortmann and Nabane (1992: 1). Yet their rights and claims to resources, given that they are closely linked to those of the men with whom they are associated in family, kinship, voluntary groups or communities, "are 'nested' or partial, and often unarticulated in, or invisible to, the public domain" (Peters, 1997: 10). As pointed out for West Africa by IIED (1999: 31-32), interventions aimed at improving women's rights of access face difficulties such as the deeply entrenched nature of cultural and religious norms. Similar problems are found elsewhere (Devereaux, 1996; Meer, 1997).

Inappropriate and ineffective systems of land administration

Land administration structures in Africa suffer from the same weaknesses as other components of the state; they are often highly centralised in structure and attempt to implement decisions in a top-down manner, yet are ineffective in practice because of resource constraints, corruption and "capture" by private interest groups. In many countries land administration is "bifurcated" (Mamdani, 1996), another legacy of the colonial era: land registries and land officers keep records and provide administrative support to title deed holders, and chiefs and other authorities administer land in "customary" systems, often without effective checks and balances.

Neither system is particularly accountable to rights holders. Neither provides effective support to the users of common pool resources - or to those groups wishing to develop innovative or more effective common property institutions. Land administration reform is thus a crucial aspect of the many decentralisation initiatives now being undertaken across Africa (IIED, 1999).

Other features of state administrative structures in rural areas that mitigate against enhanced capacity for common property management are their lack of capacity effectively to co-ordinate programmes of development (Shepherd, 1999; Carney and Farrington, 1998: 24), and the tensions that exist between locally elected bodies, traditional authorities and national line departments. Another is the tendency for district administrations to see common pool resources as sources of revenue for themselves rather than for their constituencies, another symptom of the confusion between governance powers and ownership of land and resources (see Murombedzi, 1991 for the case of wildlife management in the communal lands of Zimbabwe). A key role of administrative structures is conflict mediation - a role that is poorly performed at present (Swift, 1995).

Widening conflict over access to common pool resources

As pointed out earlier, the boundary conditions of common pool resources in Africa are often characterised by a degree of fluidity, ambiguity and negotiability. Systems which allow multiple and overlapping rights have real advantages, but one consequence of this is their propensity to generate tension and conflict. In addition, in some areas ecological boundaries (e.g. of grazing areas, or water catchments) do not correspond to political boundaries, which tends to exacerbate conflict (Frost and Madondo, 1999).

Given the processes of socio-economic change described above, and the current incapacities of most African states and their administrative structures, it appears that competition and resource-related conflicts are on the increase, and in certain regions, such as the Sahel, are endemic and widespread (IIED, 1999). In the absence of effective institutional arrangements for their resolution, or at least management, these can undermine regimes of sustainable common pool resource use (Cousins, 1996). It is also clear that individualisation would not resolve these conflicts.

Misunderstanding the commons

Hardins' Tragedy of the Commons thesis is still influential in many quarters, including amongst African policy makers (Peters, 1998). The fact that common pool resources make vital contributions to rural livelihoods and thus to national economies is generally poorly understood, contributing to their low profile with policy makers and state officials. A common policy response has been to attempt to enforce a radical alteration in livelihood systems and land tenure e.g. through sedentarisation of pastoralists or through promoting commercial ranching models of livestock production (see Box 8.6). These have generally failed, but attempts to "modernise" production continue. This example from Nigeria demonstrates the weaknesses in approach, which involve establishing grazing reserves to which pastoralists have no legal title, nor management powers. As a result, the land is frequently encroached upon, and decisions are made by a committee composed of local government staff, with no pastoral input. The idea of trying to get herders to settle also runs counter to their interest and need in movement, and close association with farmers, with whom they exchange goods and services.

Box 8.6: Pastoralists and grazing reserves in Nigeria

Background: Livestock contribute 20 percent of Nigeria's agricultural GDP. Pastoralism is the main system of livestock production in Nigeria, comprising 90 percent of the national herd. Within the pastoral sector, cattle herds are concentrated in the arid and semi-arid zones, with rangeland forage supplemented by crop residues, browse and lopped trees. Transhumance is another dominant feature, herds generally moving from Northern Nigeria southwards in the dry season in order to access water, fodder and crop residues, and then northwards in the wet season to avoid tsetse fly.

While there are recognised grazing areas and stock routes, pastoralists have no rights to the land they use for grazing. With increasing pressure from other land users (e.g. crop farmers, expanding urban settlements), and increasing levels of conflict, the pastoral production system is under growing threat. This has led to a review of policies aimed at protecting and developing grazing reserves.

Grazing reserves: Demarcated grazing areas and stock routes have a long history in Nigeria, dating back at least to the Fulani conquest of Northern Nigeria at the beginning of the 19th century. A government study in the 1950s recommended the "stabilisation" of pastoralism as a means to expand and "modernise" livestock production. This included the establishment of grazing reserves and the allocation of land rights.

A 1965 grazing reserve law gave regional governments the power to acquire native land for the reserves, and the 1978 Land Use Decree extended this law and specified categories of land use. The National Agricultural Policy of 1988 indicated that a minimum of 10 percent of national territory (9.8 million ha) would be put into reserves for lease to herders.

However, the policy has not been fully implemented, and by 1998 only 313 reserves covering 2.8 million ha had been acquired, of which 52 have been gazetted. Almost all have been encroached upon by crop farmers and others, while *fadama* land (floodplain land of particular value for dry season grazing) has been systematically exploited for cropping. The institutions set up to manage the reserves are dominated by government personnel with very poor representation of herders' interests.

Resource conflicts: Encroachment by crop farmers onto grazing areas and cultivation of stock routes are the main causes of conflict, provoking loss of life and property in recent years. The state authorities are reluctant to enforce legal provisions for protection of grazing lands and stock routes while several government projects have been active in ploughing up *fadama* land. Conflicts are caused when farmers deliberately block access to pasture or water, cultivate next to water points, or deliberately leave crop residues unprotected. Pastoralists are eager to let their herds graze and may not seek approval first, or allow their herds to damage growing crops, or migrate in from neighbouring countries. Resentment of pastoralists by others has increased and led to demands for their settlement in designated reserves. However, this is not a feasible option.

Past policies and lessons learned: Private ranching occurs on a small scale in Nigeria but has largely failed as a development strategy for the livestock sector. Various projects have attempted over the years to improve the security and productivity of pastoral production systems. Many of these attempted to provide incentives for permanent settlement by investing in infrastructure, such as water supplies and veterinary services in designated reserves. They also envisaged issuing leasehold titles to pastoralists, although very few have in fact been issued. But in practice, only a small number of reserves have benefited from investment in infrastructure.

> Experience with these projects shows that many pastoralists have continued to prefer transhumance to sedentarisation, leading in recent years to the financing of a comprehensive stock route development programme.
>
> There are five reasons for the failure to persuade pastoralists to settle in grazing reserves:
>
> Exclusive zones which separate pastoralists from crop farmers ignore the former's need for access to markets, and aggravate hostility towards pastoralists, who are perceived to be receiving preferential treatment.
>
> Most grazing reserves are situated on the fringes of semi-arid zones with low carrying capacity, so that nomadic pastoralists must continue to migrate southwards in the dry season, as before.
>
> Some reserves are sited in areas which are ecologically or economically unsuitable for grazing.
>
> Settled pastoralists do not invest much in the land because they see the reserve as owned by government; this is particularly the case when they have not been issued with leasehold titles, or where government has failed to prevent encroachment on the reserve.
>
> Infrastructure has not been maintained due to lack of adequate funds, and pastoralists have not been involved in management or maintenance of this infrastructure.
>
> The way forward: Identification, gazettement and development of more grazing reserves and stock routes are essential. At the same time, pastoral organisations need strengthening so that they can take control over the reserves. Consultation with local communities will ensure that the resources are not violated through encroachment by other users. Management of the reserves, maintenance of infrastructure and establishment of social amenities will have to be done with the active participation of pastoralists. Rights to these areas will need to be secured through legislation, so that the reserves become legally defensible common property, rather than an open access resource. This will allow pastoralists to invest in the development of their rangelands. This should be accompanied by a capacity building programme for pastoralists, focused on functional literacy, resource and organisational management.
>
> Source: Maina, 1999

Inadequate statistical data on the economic value of common pool resources mean that they are not properly accounted for in national accounting procedures, such as estimates of Gross National Product (IIED, 1995; Cousins, 1999; Shackleton et al, 1999). This means that valuation of the commons and re-assessment of their significance for development policies constitutes an important research agenda in many countries. Social science research on common property regimes in Africa has tended to focus on broad "communities" of resource user, with insufficient attention paid to socio-economic differentiation within rural society (Murombedzi, 1991; Peters, 1994; Shackleton et al, 1998). The gender dimensions of the commons in Africa are also inadequately documented (Fortmann and Nabane, 1992; Nabane, 1994).

Research on the African commons has tended to focus on certain resources or habitats (e.g. wildlife, grazing for livestock, water, or forest resources) in a "sectoral" manner and to neglect the multiple-use character of most African commons. In contrast holistic analyses enable the identification of key strategic entry points for enhancing common property resources more generally - Frost and Madondo (1999) for example, hypothesise that in semi-arid regions of Zimbabwe this could be by making more efficient use of water points.

TENURE REFORM AND MANAGEMENT OF THE COMMONS

Given the difficulties outlined above, how can policies, programmes and advocacy seek to enhance the sustainable use of common pool resources in Africa, and in so doing advance the interests of the rural poor? In particular, what contribution can programmes of tenure reform make, and what are the implications for current government policies? Tentative answers to these questions are provided below in Table 8.2. This table summarises the various problems facing common property resource systems, and identifies a range of policy options which might serve to address these. It shows the many ways in which the management of these resources could better be supported at local and national levels.

Table 8.2: Tenure reform and common property

ISSUE OR PROBLEM	POLICY RESPONSE
Inadequate legal status of common property rights	● national legal reform to recognise and secure rural people's rights to the commons ● devolve powers to manage the commons from the state to local communities ● create a menu of organisational and tenure options, to allow for diversity ● implement rights-based support programmes which provide access to legal redress and protection against abuse
Multiple and overlapping rights to common pool resources are held by a variety of actors, with ambiguous boundaries between territories	● create enabling frameworks for negotiation and conflict management ● allow variable definitions of group boundaries depending on decision or issue
Gender inequalities in access to the commons	● rights based laws and support systems ● support to national and local organisations, and social movements supporting women's rights
Authority to manage the commons is contested (e.g. traditional leaders vs elected bodies; local community vs district government bodies)	● distinguish between property rights and governance; create strong property rights for members of user groups ● allow rights-holders to select the governance body of their choice ● restrict role of state in "co-management" to facilitation and support
Role of the state in common property management	● subsidiarity stance: devolve decisions to lowest appropriate level ● create enabling framework of law, policy and programme to support devolution ● programmes to provide support to local decisions, via information, facilitation, capacity building, conflict management services, access to legal redress
Contribution of multiple common pool resources to livelihoods and their full economic value, particularly to the poor, not well understood	● undertake studies of economic value of multiple use commons by differentiated users to promote better understanding within society and by decision makers

Source: adapted from Sunningdale discussion group, 1999.

Recognition and advocacy

A first step is to promote adequate recognition of the importance of the commons to the rural poor of Africa, amongst the chief stakeholders in the development arena (governments, NGOs, donors and international agencies). This requires supportive research, building on the many impressive studies carried out to date, but focussing now on those issues which are still poorly understood: economic values, social differentiation, and holistic analyses of 'multiple-use commons', in the context of the fluidity and uncertainty that increasingly characterises rural social formations. Some emerging frameworks of analysis and planning, such as the Sustainable Rural Livelihoods approach adopted by DFID, facilitate this kind of research (Carney, 1998; Quan, 1998).

Equally, it is important to engage in advocacy on behalf of and together with the rural poor who depend on the commons for their livelihoods (Lane, 1998). Where different groupings within the ranks of the poor are themselves in conflict (e.g. farmers and pastoralists in the Sahel), advocacy is by no means straightforward - whose interests should be supported? This underlines the need to understand adequately the changing character of livelihoods and shifting patterns of poverty and inequality, and to locate these issues in a larger political economy perspective.

Murphree's (1997: 30) formulation in relation to CAMPFIRE in Zimbabwe applies more generally:

> [resource management].. is about power, about centre-periphery relationships, about resource and value allocations. It is, in other words, about politics.

The need to confront explicitly questions of interest and the distribution of benefits, and to seek to secure equitable outcomes, is especially acute in those contexts where external actors (investors, wildlife entrepreneurs, donors) are beginning to play a central role. However, it is equally important when differential interests are entirely local in origin too.

Clarifying and strengthening common property rights within flexible boundaries

One clear thrust of tenure reform is to recognise and secure people's rights to the commons, and to devolve powers to manage the commons to local communities (Lane and Moorehead, 1995; Lane, 1998; IIED, 1999; see Chapter 7, this volume). Rights-based programmes could create a menu of tenure options (as proposed in South Africa - see Chapter 13, this volume), with variability in the degree of group versus individual control, and thus allow for the diversity of the commons. Strengthening the rights of rural people to the commons will usually be at the expense of state control, and political support will have to be mobilised - here too advocacy is required. Constitutional reform processes may open up opportunities for lobbying, and land reform is also back on the agenda of many African countries at present (IIED, 1999; see also Chapters 6 and 7, this volume).

In the light of emerging views on common property, and on land rights in Africa more generally, legal reforms should be seen as necessary but in themselves insufficient (Cousins, 1997). As suggested by analysts of land rights in Africa who see these rights as constituted by socio-political process (Berry, 1993; Moore, 1998; Okoth-Ogendo, 1989; Peters, 1994), equal attention is required to those institutional arenas, both formal and informal, in which negotiations take place and power relations are manifested. This has implications for how rights are defined and where they are vested, for how boundary issues are approached, and for incorporating institutional issues (e.g. decision making, conflict resolution, and administrative support to rights-holders). Moore (1998: 47) emphasises the importance of "practical institutional possibilities" because "rights without remedies are ephemeral"; the need is to "create an appropriate space where legitimate claims [can] be acknowledged and acted upon".

As suggested above, allowing flexible and negotiated definitions of boundaries will be more productive than attempts to adjudicate fixed boundaries. Allowing self-definition of "community", together with flexibility in the definition of rights, is one approach which has been attempted in South Africa (Claassens, 1999; Claassens and Makopi, 1999), with interesting parallels in Namibia's conservancy legislation (Jones, 1999) and Mozambique's new land law (Kloeck-Jensen, 1998).

These ideas resonate strongly with perspectives emerging from the re-thinking of pastoralist ecology, production and tenure in Africa which took place in the early, 1990s. Thus Behnke (1994: 8) suggests that in "non-equilibrium" environments, non-exclusive forms of rights to use resources are complementary to opportunistic stocking and herding strategies. Indeterminate social and territorial boundaries provide "a degree of fluidity which suits everyone's requirements". Complexity and flexibility mean that close regulation by administrators is inappropriate and generally ineffective, and devolution of administration and management to individual pastoralists and communities is more feasible (see also Swift, 1995; Sylla, 1995).

Gender and rights to the commons

Gender inequalities in relation to access to and control over common pool resources is a major problem (Meer, 1997; Nabane, 1994), not resolved by legislating rights (however necessary this step may be). Substantive shifts in social and power relations are also required, and perhaps all that tenure reform can accomplish is help to create an enabling framework, a legally defined "political space" for endogenous movements of change - which often reach out to NGOs for organisational and resource support (Rocheleau and Ross, 1995; TRAC, 1994).

Administrative reform: decentralisation and "good governance"

The many and varied attempts across Africa to decentralise governance and reform local government (taking the form of either deconcentration, or devolution) create both opportunities and threats for tenure reform in relation to the commons. As IIED (1999: 37) points out:

> The potential advantages... - increased participation, greater pragmatism, finding local solutions to genuine problems, resolving conflicts - are largely predicated on local government being both accountable and transparent. A local government within which an unelected executive holds most of the power is unlikely to be as effective as one where elected assemblies, tied to their constituencies, make the key decisions. There are also legitimate concerns that local elites will "capture" local government to serve their private interests.

Most commentators emphasise that local government reform is necessary but not sufficient to ensure good governance; equal emphasis should be on facilitating the emergence of effective institutions at even more local levels, such as villages and communities, where the day to day decisions over resource use are made. This is the "subsidiarity" stance, increasingly favoured in relation to natural resource management (Swift, 1995; Rihoy, 1995).

In some places these efforts amount to strengthening existing institutions which have legitimacy, but in others they will require new institutional arrangements. Concern about elite capture often leads to an emphasis on accountability to the commoners (IIED, 1999). This is effectively an agenda for the democratisation of rural resource management; diverse histories and conditions mean that the institutional forms of democracy are likely to vary widely in structure and effectiveness.

Democratisation requires that the confusion and ambiguities over the relationship between elected organs of governance and "traditional" institutions (chiefs, tribal councils etc) be confronted. Governance powers and property rights need to be clearly distinguished. Clarification of the roles, powers and obligations of different institutions is unlikely to be uncontested (Ntsebeza, 1999a).

177

Some have argued that traditional institutions have an important role to play in conflict resolution, since customary mechanisms for managing conflict are still effective in many contexts (Rugege, 1995; Bradbury et al, 1995). However, there are potential difficulties involved too: sometimes traditional authorities are part of the problem (e.g. by being party to land sales - IIED, 1999: 36); they are no longer the sole source of authority and people may pursue alternative routes, such as the courts, and play the different forums off against one another (Lund, 1998); and new situations have arisen not covered by customary law (e.g. when conflicts occur between local resource users and multinational corporations or international conservation organisations).

As a result, neither the state nor traditional authorities can be relied on for effective conflict resolution, and the piloting of new approaches based on "locally-constituted consultative bodies", as in Niger, might be worth exploring (IIED, 1999: 36). In pastoralist settings, Sylla (1995) and Vedeld (1992) advocate a central role in conflict resolution for pastoral organisations, and Swift (1995) highlights conflict resolution as a central function of pastoral administration at different levels.

In general, efforts to achieve "good governance" at the local level are important for tenure reforms focussed on common property resources. The role of the central state is to create an enabling framework of laws, policies and programmes which promote accountability and transparency, and support the decentralisation of resource management. These must include provision of support services to local decision makers in the form of information on rights, facilitation of local processes, education and capacity building, access to law, and promoting appropriate conflict resolution mechanisms.

The need for a continued role for government is clear in the light of experience with the *gestion de terroirs* (GT) approach in francophone Africa, which has devolved certain kinds of decision making over natural resources to the village level. This can lead to the exclusion of "strangers" whose needs and rights also need to be taken into account (see Chapter 5, this volume), and to neglect of resources (such as wetlands) which fall under several jurisdictions (IIED, 1999: 38). Complementing village level decisions with higher level regional planning mechanisms thus requires attention.

CONCLUSION

The future of the commons in Africa is critically important for the millions of Africans who depend on common pool resources for their livelihoods. These livelihoods are under continuous change and recomposition in many contexts, given the ongoing crisis of most African economies, and the processes of social and economic transformation set in motion by globalisation. Increasing commoditisation and renewed dependency for subsistence are contradictory trends which create both threats and, in some instances, opportunities. In the face of these processes, tenure reform policies and programmes must seek to secure the common property rights of rural people as *effective* access and control rather than as mere abstractions, or paper realities.

This will require a dual emphasis on giving real powers to people at local level recognising their rights, devolving decision making and enhancing the capacity of the state to create enabling frameworks and provide support to local institutions. This is a challenging programme given the incapacities of many African states (Moore, 1998). However, as Leys (1994) suggests, it is difficult to see any answers to the pressing problems of rural Africa which do not include the state playing a central role.

9

Women's Land Rights: Current Developments in Sub-Saharan Africa

Thea Hilhorst

The need to improve women's rights to land and property is now widely recognised in the debates for legal reform. This chapter examines the position of women in customary rights systems and the changes they are experiencing. It goes on to discuss the impacts of tenure and legislative reform on women's land rights and concludes by reviewing the options for adopting a more 'gender' aware approach to land policy. This chapter has been written with reference to several papers presented at the DFID Workshop on Land Rights and Sustainable Development in Sub-Saharan Africa, 16-19 February 1999, Sunningdale, UK on gender rights, particularly those of Irene Ovonji-Odida, Stella Longway and Karen Dzumbira which present recent experience of reform processes in Uganda, Tanzania and Zimbabwe respectively. Reference has also been made to the discussions at the workshop itself and to a number of case studies from other regions.

INTRODUCTION

In most customary landholding systems, community level decisions about land are taken by chiefs or headmen on behalf of, and in trust for the clan or family. Chiefly authority is generally ascribed to a patriarchal lineage, and most major decisions are taken by men (Ntsebeza, 1999). While women have ways of bringing their views to the attention of such authorities, they usually do not participate in decision making.

Women's claims to land within customary systems are generally obtained through their husbands or male kinsfolk and hence may be considered 'secondary' rights. The constraints which women face with respect to their access to, and control over land resources are similar to those faced by other holders of secondary rights, such as migrants, pastoralists, and young men. Such rights, for example, are often of uncertain duration, may not be well defined and subject to change, and are usually subject to the maintenance of good relations between the parties involved. However, while such use rights may seem precarious to the outsider, they may be considered sufficiently secure by local people involved.

The particular issues which affect women relate to the fact that their rights to land are determined by their marital status, by the laws on inheritance and divorce and by institutions that are themselves deeply embedded within local perceptions of the role that women should play in society. A married woman may gain access to land, if she has her husband's authorisation but is likely to lose this in the event of a breakdown in relations, divorce or widowhood. Her rights may also change if her husband remarries within a polygamous arrangement. In the discussion below, these issues are examined in relation to a woman's right of access to land and her rights to exploit, manage or control the products of her labour on the land. This section will also discuss aspects of the various inheritance systems which are found in many parts of sub-Saharan Africa and the impact these have on the rights of women, whether as widows, mothers, sisters or daughters.

A field of her own: rights of access to land

Many rural women, particularly in areas of low population density, have access to plots of land where they can invest any remaining time after their household chores and work on the family fields are done. Although they control the cultivation of their own plot, they do not have complete liberty to dispose of the produce as they might wish. They are often obliged to contribute part of the harvest to supplement the household's food stocks, particularly in years of poor rainfall. A woman's matrimonial status and age tend to influence the degree of freedom she enjoys in deciding how the products of her labour are used. An older woman has greater independence in deciding on her enterprises and may even be in a position to accumulate a private store of wealth.

The rights of women under customary systems vary from place to place. In certain societies or families, women's access to their own fields may be constrained by fear on the part of the menfolk of the perceived independence that this access may generate. In Uganda, for example, some consider that a woman who owns land will never have a stable marriage and, as a consequence, such women will be little respected within the community (Ovonji-Odida, 1999).

Some men in Cameroon refuse to give land to their wives, since they fear that they will lose a wife's labour on their own fields or else may not like the idea of women earning their own money (van den Berg, 1999). By contrast, elsewhere, men may be eager for their wives to work on their own land because of the benefits this brings to their family group as a whole. It should be noted that permission for a woman's access to land generally resides with the husband or his family, but is sometimes in the gift of her mother-in-law.

The matter of location plays an important role in women's choice of fields. They prefer fields located close to the homestead or to the main fields of the household, which makes it easier for them to combine farming with care of young children, working on the family fields and the round of household chores. The fertility of the allocated plot and the duration of the usufruct rights differ from place to place, and can range from almost permanent rights to those which are limited to one season.

Many reports suggest that women face discrimination with respect to the allocation of individual fields (NEDA, 1997a). When access to a plot is granted, this may be on land which other male relatives do not want because, for example, it is not very fertile, difficult to work, or not suitable for animal traction. In northern Cameroon, it was found that women could get relatively easy access to bush field land, given its abundance, but were mostly excluded from fertile former 'kraal' fields and compounds, which were in shorter supply and perceived to be of considerably greater value (van den Berg, 1999). In Niger, women are typically excluded from the higher value riverbed soils, which are used for cash crop production, particularly in the dry season (Cooper, 1997). A study in Burkina Faso comparing the position of women and younger men with regard to access to land, confirmed that women generally received plots that were further away and were less well-protected from erosion than the land gained by young men. The study also revealed, however, that there was fairly equal access for both women and younger men to the clayey, fertile plots found in lowland bas-fonds areas (Kunze et al, 1998).

In general, customary systems often allocate plots to women and other secondary right holders, as long as they are not required by the household. If a man or his family find themselves in need of extra land, a woman's field may be taken from her for reallocation. Constraints on women's access to land are heightened when land becomes increasingly scarce, and men's land holdings come under pressure.

A related development is the trend towards "individualisation" of customary rights, accompanied by an erosion of traditional obligations which often constitute a social security value for certain sections of society. As resources become more strictly administered and obligations to other members of the community are eroded, the ability of secondary rights-holders to assert their customary rights to land, trees and other resources is weakened (Ovonji-Odida, 1999; van den Berg, 1999; NEDA, 1997b). Various studies show that this reinterpretation of customary rights can result from both increasing pressure on natural resources but also from changes in statutory law (Ovonji-Odida, 1999).

A woman may have to explore alternative means of access to land for cultivation when she cannot obtain land through her husband. Access to land can also be obtained through a woman's male relatives (father, uncle, brother, son, etc.) if they live close by and have sufficient land available. A case study in northern Cameroon shows that women may also rent land from local village chiefs, although they might have to ask permission first from their husbands. Women are even allowed to clear bush land. Within the study area, 50% of the women work on land allocated by their husbands, 28% have cleared land themselves and 21% have rented land. It was found that a woman's most important strategy is to ask her husband for a piece of land which is generally granted, assuming the marriage is stable. Clearing bush land entitles the worker to permanent land rights, for women as for men, but this is considered to be very hard work. Nevertheless, it is renting that is considered the least favoured option by the women in the study, as access is temporary, costs money and the soils are often exhausted (van den Berg, 1999).

In parts of southern and eastern Africa, where husbands go on migration for long periods, women may become the *de facto* household head, and take responsibility for farming and managing the land. In such cases, they are allowed

---

Box 9.1: The impact of migration on women in the Sahel

This study examined the impact on women of outmigration by their husbands and sons in various Sahelian settings. Migration from the Sahel does not usually create a vulnerable category of *de facto* women heads of compound. In the three West African cases described in the study, in the absence of their husbands, most migrants' wives continue to live in their husband's compound, or under the charge of his extended family, and are normally supported by the male head of the family (typically the father-in-law). In cases where all the men in the compound have migrated, as was found for the Diourbel region of Senegal, a migrant's wife continues to live in the compound with her sisters-in-law under the supervision of her husband's mother. In this case, the mother-in-law becomes the *de facto* head of the compound and, as such, she is often relatively well-off. Not only can she call upon the financial support of all the migrants who have left the compound but, because of the proximity of Dakar (where many of the men have gone to work) she can also ask for advice from her husband.

Only where much smaller conjugal units (rather than extended families) are the basic unit of production and consumption, do some women become *de facto* heads of household and are more vulnerable as a result. However, even in these cases, this affects only a minority of households (approximately 20 percent of the sample) and because of the tight-knit relations within villages there is a great deal of inter-household support.

Source: David, 1995

---

to use the land of the husband or the family but have no formal tenure rights, and may be restricted in terms of taking certain kinds of management decision. Elsewhere, even though a man may be absent for several years, his wife and children are frequently incorporated into his broader extended family (David, 1995; see also Box 9.1). These women will have to fulfil their obligations towards the work on the family-managed fields, which assures their own and their children's food security while also working on their own plots, if possible.

Working the land

While women's choice of fields is restricted, in general they can decide for themselves how they manage the plot. Nonetheless, like other secondary rights-holders, they must refrain from actions which may be interpreted as trying to establish a long term claim to property. Furthermore, if usufruct rights are temporary, there is little scope to benefit from long-term investment strategies to increase productivity. In some cases, this can lead to women feeling reluctant to spend too much energy on improving and fertilising their plot, since this will make it more attractive for her husband's family to take back. Here again, practice varies amongst different societies. While one study in Burkina Faso suggests that women's "investment" (in terms of inputs of labour, finances and other resources) differed little from those of other farmers working on their own account (Sawodogo et al, 1998), another, in Uganda, reveals that women refrained from planting trees and similar long-term productive investments because they would not be able to control the profits resulting from their efforts (Ovonji-Odida, 1999).

On the whole, where land is relatively abundant, the extent of women's agricultural activities seems to be limited more by their overall heavy workload, rather than by access to land (Sawodogo et al, 1998). Lack of scope for the application of their own labour time and limited access to external inputs and extension services similarly affect their opportunities for increasing productivity. Age and marital status, as indicated above, may influence this situation, so that older women with daughters-in-law, and women with unmarried teenage daughters will have more time and resources available. Equally, a woman in a polygamous marriage may find more time for farming, since domestic tasks can be shared amongst a broader set of female members of the household.

Inheritance patterns

Most customary inheritance laws try to ensure that family and clan land remain within the control of the lineage. Thus, they commonly seek to prohibit or prevent alienation of land to third parties. The most common inheritance systems in Africa are patrilineal, whereby succession and inheritance of property are determined through the male line, and normally only sons or other males inherit land from the family estate. Daughters are prevented from inheriting family land. This is often explained with reference to the practice of virilocal exogamy, by which a newly married woman will leave her parental home, move to her husband's village and become part of another family. If her children were allowed to inherit land from her natal family, it is argued that there is a risk that the strong community links with the land would become fragmented and weakened.

The position of widows differs from society to society and even within families. In many cases, once widowed, a woman is expected to return to her own family group. In Burkina Faso, a widow may continue to use the land of her late husband until she remarries assuming, that is, that the relationship with the family-in-law is convivial (Sawodogo et al, 1998). In some societies, where women's labour and child-bearing capacities are highly valued, the man's family may have paid a considerable bride-price at the time of her betrothal and marriage. Women are thus considered, in effect, to be the property of the family and for this reason, a widow, who will often still be young, may be kept on by the dead man's family. This usually requires that the widow be taken as a wife by her husband's younger brother or cousin. Where the woman refuses such a re-marriage, she may find her access to land revoked (Toulmin, 1992).

In societies where polygamy is practised, the share of family land received by children on their father's death will often depend on the status of their mother within the marriage. For example, the eldest son of the most senior wife is likely to receive the largest share (Longway, 1999). Widows without sons or those with no children at all are likely to be very vulnerable.

In many other societies, widowhood may result in the woman finding herself destitute. Where the dead man's family inherits the land, the widow may be evicted, unless the husband had made a will to the effect that his widow should keep possession of the farm or homestead. (Ovonji-Odida, 1999; Jacobs, 1999).

Islamic law recognises a woman's right of inheritance, although her share is usually smaller than that of a male relative. On marriage to a man in another village, women are often obliged to leave land in the hands of a male relative. In Niger, Cooper (1997) describes cases where land is thus transferred in the form of a rent-free loan, for which the woman may receive part of the harvest, as token recognition of her ownership of the land. Nevertheless, due to her absence, she may find it difficult to exercise her rights over her land, a fact which may be abused by her male relatives (Cooper, 1997).

A few matrilineal societies exist, such as those in Ghana, Nigeria, Zambia, Tanzania, Malawi, and Namibia, in which land and other inheritance claims are passed on through a woman's descent group. In Tanzania, for example, 20% of the ethnic communities follow matrilineal systems of inheritance. There are many variations in the functioning of these systems however, in general, females in matrilineal society tend to have better access to land than those in patrilineal society (Longway, 1999). Commonly, a woman has obligations to and may expect assistance from her brothers and maternal uncles. In Malawi, land is transferred from a mother to her female children through the heads of the matrilineage (who, generally, are the senior maternal uncles) and sub-divided accordingly. Generally, the rights and interests a person may have in land are similar to those in patrilineal ones. Any person to whom the land is allocated may lease his/her land, but in the case of a husband residing uxorilocally (i.e. with or alongside his wife's family), he must first seek the consent of his wife's senior maternal uncle or his representative. Men involved in cash crop production complain about the insecurity of land use and rights they face in this position. This insecurity is compounded by the fact that the land they farm will subsequently be inherited by their wives' brothers and nephews rather than their own relatives. However, strict adherence to matrilineal rules seems to be on the decline, as in Namibia and Malawi, possibly due to increased commercialisation and market development which has increased the value of land (Quan, 1998). This would corroborate Mair's claim (1974) that matrilineal descent is rare in cases where there is any significant property to inherit. In Tanzania also, inheritance patterns in matrilineal societies seem to be changing towards the patrilineal model (Longway, 1999).

Although customary systems of inheritance rights are usually well understood within the communities involved, the situation can become very complicated if account has to be taken of other legal systems operating at other levels. In Tanzania, for example, inheritance is governed by different laws of succession including customary, Islamic and statutory laws. Both customary and Islamic law discriminate against women in ways described above, whereas reforms to statutory law are tending towards giving equal recognition to women's rights. In deciding which law should apply to a particular case, courts tend to base their judgement on what is known as the "mode of life test", whereby the ethnicity and religious affiliation of the heir, as well as the intent of the deceased are taken into account. Customary law is taken to apply to African Christians, unless they can prove that the family has abandoned the "African" mode of life in which case, statutory law applies. For African muslims it is assumed that Islamic law applies, unless it can be proven the deceased had other intentions. (Longway, 1999).

DEVELOPMENTS IN STATUTORY LAW

The customary rights of women and men are continuously evolving as changes occur in the way land is used, new rural livelihood opportunities develop, and social institutions are transformed. The implementation of national policies and statutory reforms also have a significant impact on the rights that local people may exercise in regard to their landholdings. This section examines the effect that policies such as land titling, registration and resettlement programmes, have had on women's rights. It also reviews the recent attempts to improve the status of women within constitutional law and other legislation in relation to their rights to land.

Titling and land registration

In areas subject to land titling programmes, women and other holders of secondary rights, run a serious risk of being denied legal recognition of their customary rights (see Chapter 2, this volume; NEDA, 1997b). There are several reasons for this. First, the land-owner may fear that titling will attribute "rights to the tiller" and, hence, will take back the land from any "temporary" land user prior to the registration process. Second, registration programmes are frequently designed as a rapid, simplifying procedure in which the wide variety of secondary claims surrounding access to resources are collapsed into a single category of tenant (Stamm, 2000). In the case of the Rural Tenure Programme of Côte d'Ivoire (*Plan Foncier Rural* - PFR), despite the clearly expressed ambition not to fall into the trap of oversimplification, the different levels of interlocking rights have in fact been reduced to a simple distinction between "land managers" and "land users". The secondary rights of women and younger men, including rights to collect fruits, fuelwood and other forest products and rights of access to grazing land, have been neglected in favour of the right to cultivate which is now often claimed by the land managers (see Chapter 5, this volume). This is in part due to the time pressures under which the PFR has been operating, as well as an underlying bias in favour of establishing individual title.

NEDA (1997b) argues for the need to issue titles to the actual user of land during the land registration process. However, a piece of land is rarely used by one person alone. Platteau considers it impossible to bring to the adjudication register all the multiple rights which may be held under the customary system (see Chapter 3, this volume). Moreover, due to the high costs involved and difficulties of obtaining full information, governments in poor countries are typically unable to record existing land rights accurately or keep these updated.

The registration process may also run the risk of maintaining and reinforcing the traditional male dominated control over access to land. This may create new uncertainties for more vulnerable sections of the local population. Registration of land rights in the name of individuals may also weaken local institutions and mechanisms that used to provide economic security to all members of village communities, and hold economic differentiation in check. Recognising customary secondary rights requires that forms of legal ownership must be devised which make room for "collective" use rights and overlapping claims. In conclusion, the potential ensuing social transformation, as well as the impacts on methods of land use and on the economic stakes involved, must be carefully considered before embarking on a land registration programme (see Chapters 3 and 5, this volume).

Constitutional provisions and land reform

Improving land rights for women not only requires "gender aware" land tenure policies, but also, in many cases, changes in women's constitutional rights reforms in the marriage and inheritance laws. Gender inequality used to be entrenched in the constitutions of various countries, defining women as "minors", and thereby restricting their ability to make important decisions without the appropriate authorisation of their husbands or male kin (Ovonji-Odida, 1999).

Some countries have passed legislation which assures gender equality with respect to access to natural resources and land, and have given particular attention to the position of women in the process of drawing up land reform. In some instances, these provisions have formed part of the constitution, while in others they have been included in legislation specifically relating to land. For example:
- The Constitution of Uganda includes a commitment to gender equality and affirmative action (Ovonji-Odida, 1999).
- In terms of the constitution, women in South Africa have the right to equal treatment with men (Tenure Newsletter, 1998).
- Equal rights of access to natural resources without discrimination by sex or social origin are provided for in Niger under the provisions of the Rural Code (Yacouba, 1999).
- Legislation in Mali allows women to register land independently of men (Ouedraogo and Toulmin, 1999).
- The right of both men and women to use and benefit from land is enshrined in the Land Act of Mozambique (Quadros, 1999).
- Women's rights to land have become part of the National Land Policy in Tanzania (Longway, 1999).

Progress regarding the reform of marriage and inheritance laws has been slow.

The initial draft of the Land Act of Mozambique included a proposal to change the order of succession to a man's estate, placing the widow in equal position with, rather than behind, his descendants. This has been criticised on the grounds that a Land Act is not an adequate vehicle for altering the more fundamental provisions of the civil law on inheritance and customary practice. As a compromise, the Land Act now expressly declares both men and women as equal subjects in relation to land rights, which dismisses the ambiguities of the term "family household", used in earlier drafts of the legislation (Quadros, 1999). In Uganda, sons, rather than widows, are still the legal heirs to the matrimonial home and land, leaving the widow only with rights of occupancy, which are forfeited upon re-marriage. While inheritance rules remain unchanged, even when women manage to gain title, there is no guarantee that their daughters will be able to inherit (Ovonji-Odida, 1999).

Statutory law may offer more protection to women than customary law but is not always easy to enforce. For instance, in Uganda, the customary practice by family heads of evicting a widow on the death of her husband is regarded as untenable in a "modern society" by some groups, but they think that it is difficult to enforce statutory rights without upsetting customary norms and practices (Mutyaba, 1999; Ovonji-Odida, 1999). Although addressing women's rights in statutory law is a first step, their translation into actual practice, particularly in rural areas, is quite another matter. While there are laws in various countries which assure that wives and all children, including daughters, are entitled to inherit property and titles, specific socio-cultural factors may reduce the possibility of a woman to claim her rights and hold on to individually acquired land. In some cases, women have had to go to court in order to access land which had been denied under customary law. In Uganda, social pressure and coercion are often used to force women to surrender their titles to male relatives, sell land cheaply or relinquish their inheritance rights. In other cases, a man may stop contributing to the basic necessities of the household when his wife acquires a plot of land, or title, and thus a source of revenue. Unsurprisingly perhaps, a considerable number of widows are involved in land disputes with male relatives and neighbours (Ovonji-Odida, 1999).

Where statutory law has become more important than customary norms, such as in peri-urban and urban areas, more formal means of legal administration and dispute settlement are favoured. But even here, perceptions of the role that women should play in society, as well as their access to information, hinder their ability to take claims to court and tend to influence the outcome of legal proceedings (Zimmermann, 1999). In Uganda, for instance, socio-cultural perceptions habitually bias legal rulings against the interests of women (Ovonji-Odida, 1999), although there is also evidence from Zimbabwe to show that some magistrates have used their power to rule in favour of women (Jacobs, 1999).

Box 9.2: Legal reforms against gender discrimination in Tanzania

Historically, land holding in Tanzania was based on the customary practices of the different groups, with access to land based on an individual's association with a family, clan or tribe. Chiefs, elders or headmen had the power of land administration in trust for the larger group, but these were abolished by the African Chiefs Ordinance (Repeal) Act, no.13 of 1963. Nevertheless, despite the legislation, chiefs and headmen remain very important, although they now have no formal institutional role.

The Germans had introduced the concept of leasehold and freehold for settlers who acquired land for commercial farming and in townships. The Land Ordinance of 1923 introduced by the British respected these arrangements, and it was not until Independence in 1963 that freeholds were converted into 99 year leases. Legislation in 1969 further converted these leases into Rights of Occupancy.

The new National Land Policy and the new Land Acts, such as the Village Land Act of 1998, retain this dual system of tenure, comprising the customary right of occupancy and the granted right of occupancy. In the gender field, statutory laws of inheritance, the Marriage Act, and various statutory land laws stand alongside customary and Islamic laws. The choice of which legal system should apply in any instance depends on ethnicity and religion. Both customary and Islamic law tend to discriminate against women.

Customary inheritance law is perhaps the subject of most discontent, as it is considered to be gender inequitable and outdated. In patrilineal communities in Tanzania, clan or family land is protected against alienation outside the family or clan. Daughters are not entitled to inherit land since they marry away from their parental base. The need to protect clan land has operated to the prejudice of women heirs. Even the operation of village councils continue to put women in a secondary position, by always allocating land to household heads, who are usually men.

The National Land Policy which has been developed over recent years has produced two Land Acts of particular relevance to women. It is proposed that women's rights should become part of the Fundamental Principles of the National Land Policy. Family land should be protected by a presumption of co-ownership in favour of both spouses. In cases where land is disposed of (through mortgage, sales, or leases), married women must give their consent before the disposal can be carried out. Appointment of members to the National Land Advisory Council shall endeavour to ensure a fair balance of women and men. Equally, women should constitute not less than half the minimum number of members of the Village Adjudication Committee, and they should also be represented in the Dispute Settlement Machinery. Whenever a Village Council determines an application for a customary right of occupancy, discrimination against women is prohibited.

Thus, overall, the new land laws represent a major change in comparison with the 1923 legislation. It remains now for the provisions to be implemented through the district government machinery, and the 9,000 Village Councils. A programme to promote public awareness will also be needed to ensure that people are better informed about this new legislation.

Source: Longway, 1999

Introducing gender issues in land policy

The position faced by women is receiving increasing attention in land policy reform processes. Successful incorporation of their priorities in subsequent legislation has, however, proved elusive. Box 9.3 describes in further detail at-

---

Box 9.3: Influencing policy in Uganda

In collaboration with the Uganda Land Alliance, a coalition of women working in the Parliament, in NGOs, civil service, development agencies, and in the media undertook a campaign to influence the land law reform process. The coalition included the NGO Uganda Women's Network (UWONET) and the Ugandan Women's Lawyers Association. The coalition lobbied for various measures which would protect women's land rights. These included: the recording of women's claims when registering customary rights; improved accessibility to law; mandatory consent by spouses and dependent children to transactions concerning land; co-ownership by spouses of family land and affirmative action to increase the number of women represented in land management bodies to at least one-third. They raised their concerns at public forums, produced and circulated information to Members of Parliament and other key persons and advanced proposals to improve the draft Bill.

To their disappointment, however, when the Land Bill went before Parliament in 1998, most of the women's recommendations were excluded, contrary to informal indications by members of the Sessional Committee. They then decided to focus, in the ensuing debate, on the key proposal of co-ownership of family land. In spite of comprehensive lobbying and publicity, the new law which emerged still excluded co-ownership. This was very surprising because journalists and some Members of Parliament considered the proposed clause had in fact been adopted, since it was noted in the parliamentary record (Nsamba-Gayiiya, 1999). It is not clear whether the omission was deliberate or inadvertent. The coalition of women's groups is now seeking a formal correction of this error.

The experience of engaging in this campaign has, nevertheless, had a valuable empowering effect on the individuals, organisations and alliances involved. Women have learnt that they can be a significant political force with the capacity to influence policy-making processes, and men, particularly those holding political power, will have to come to terms with this. Women's involvement in government processes should promote the development of more democratic institutions which can work towards enhanced security of tenure for women and consequently other marginalised sections of society.

Source: Ovonji-Odida, 1999

---

tempts by women's groups in Uganda to lobby for joint titling and to influence other provisions of the Land Act. Most research on the subject describes how alliances of various groups have tried to insert gender issues into the formulation of policy, but often without the desired result.

In Malawi, for example, this process started with a Presidential Commission of Inquiry on Land Reform. The terms of reference proposed that the Commission would hear evidence from women and other interest groups such as traditional leaders, and estate owners separately before organising a joint meeting. This format was rejected by the Commission because it was considered too time-consuming, and "the idea of sitting in camera with other people's wives did not go down well". As a result, the Commission met with all concerned parties at one sitting (Harawa, 1999; see also Box 14.9). It is highly likely that this procedure hindered women's freedom to express their views.

In Tanzania, various organisations have brought gender issues to the attention of policy makers on land tenure reform by organising a "public awareness campaign". This has resulted in changes in the new 1999 Land Law which is regarded as a significant step towards more equitable treatment for women (see Box 9.2). Provisions of the new law include:

- Family land is protected by the presumption of co-ownership which in principle favours both spouses.
- A married woman must first give her consent if her husband intends to alienate matrimonial landed property (e.g. through mortgage, sale or lease)
- Affirmative action in favour of women, by making them members of the National Land Advisory Council and of village adjudication committees to ensure that women can contribute to the settlement of disputes.
- Prohibiting village councils from discriminating against women when allocating land or rights of occupancy.

The current challenge is to establish the administrative structure at all levels, including villages, to provide training for committee members and to raise public awareness of the changes in such laws, in order to facilitate their implementation in everyday rural affairs (Longway, 1999)

Gender and land resettlement

Under land resettlement programmes, the rights of women have, for the most part, been limited to issuing title deeds for widows with dependants. In South Africa, the rights of married women under the land resettlement policy are currently being discussed which, according to Jacobs (1999), would constitute a radical departure from previous approaches.

It is noteworthy that in Zimbabwe married women in resettlement schemes have expressed a sense of insecurity not so much in terms of claims to land, but in terms of a lack of security in marriage. In resettlement areas, divorced women lose access to resettlement land since, upon divorce, it is the woman who is evicted, never the man (Jacobs, 1999). Since the law also does not provide for women to be registered as leaseholders, permit holders are invariably men which leaves women particularly disadvantaged in the event of widowhood, divorce or polygamous unions (Quan, 1998).

In Zimbabwe, resettlement officers seem to have played an important role in improving the position of women. They have intervened after the death of a husband, stipulated that the widow should inherit the land and have even awarded land to married women. This may be partly motivated by their perceptions of how family members should behave in relation to each other (Jacobs, 1999). It has also been observed that various improvements in women's position in resettlement schemes can stem from the goodwill of male actors (husbands, resettlement officers) rather than the authority of formal legal provisions. Women's groups in Zimbabwe have campaigned for more secure access to land for married and single women and joint-titling. Jacobs (1999) regards this as notable in itself since the women's and feminist movements in Zimbabwe have tended to be urban-based and less interested in rural land issues. Others have observed however, that the focus on joint-titling is primarily an issue for urban and resettlement scheme lands, and is of limited relevance to rural women living in areas governed by customary law (Quan, 1998). Box 9.4 presents experience from elsewhere with regard to joint titling.

Box 9.4 Experience with joint titling in Latin America's land reform programmes

Joint adjudication and titling of land to couples (married or consensual) are regarded as a significant advance for gender equity for it establishes explicitly that property rights are vested in both men and women. Some Latin American countries have included this principle in their civil codes and both husband and wife can represent the family and administer its property. In countries where it forms part of the agrarian code, joint titling serves to protect women from losing access to land in the event of separation, divorce or death of the husband. Joint titling is mandatory in Colombia, Costa Rica and Nicaragua but optional in Honduras and Brazil. In Honduras it only applies to married couples, while in all the other countries, it also applies to consensual unions which are not formalised by marriage.

In practice it has not been easy to enforce joint titling since it goes against patriarchal norms. It has required major efforts in 'awareness-raising' among those carrying out titling programmes, as well as amongst intended beneficiaries. However, available information suggests that mandatory, joint titling has made a significant difference in expanding women's access to land and is considered a crucial step toward assuring gender equity.

Source: Deere and León, 1999

POLICY CONCLUSIONS

In the development of land laws or constitutional revision, increasing attention is now being given to the status of women. While there have been some achievements, overall gains remain limited, despite the energy invested in advocacy and lobby activities. More affirmative action is needed to ensure that women's voices are properly heard. It is important to include women in committees preparing land reform proposals and to ensure that consultation methods deliberately target women respondents in a way which enables them to contribute their points of view with confidence. This may require sustained advocacy and monitoring. Donors could provide special funds to assure that priority areas such as gender are taken into account when revisions to the nation's legal framework take place (Nsamba-Gayiiya, 1999; Dzumbira, 1999).

Lack of information regarding their rights under existing land laws or of the possibilities offered by reform processes may also weaken the position of women in these matters. In many countries (e.g. Botswana, Malawi and Mozambique), lack of information on the part of the rural poor, especially women, frequently means that they stand to lose in legal and quasi-legal processes to reform legislation (Matowanyika, 1999). In Mali, for example, it became clear that women were less well-informed than most men about the purpose of an inventory on land rights (Ouedraogo and Toulmin, 1999).

In Mozambique special efforts were made to inform women about the new Land Bill. The Land Campaign in Mozambique, which was set up to raise awareness about the Bill, focused on six items, one of which has addressed women and land. The Campaign sought to reach in particular those women whose right to land had been violated (e.g. in cases of eviction following widowhood, divorce or extra-conjugal maternity). These women were advised to apply for individual title deeds or to unite with other women in similar situations so as to obtain a collective title deed (Negrão, 1999). In order to be able to exercise their rights, women must be given sufficient support to assert what rights they have, including being able to resist strong pressure to relinquish them. It is suggested that provisions could usefully be made to inform women of their rights in relation to land and provide training in "legal literacy" (Quadros, 1999; Dzumbira, 1999). While political lobbying and campaigning can be useful in some circumstances, women will also require access to contacts with sufficient authority and influence to gain acceptance of their claim by the relevant authorities (NEDA, 1997b).

Awareness-raising of gender issues amongst civil servants and those responsible for land administration will be equally important. Affirmative action is required to ensure that women are represented in commissions which are set up to advise on land issues, land administration bodies, resettlement scheme authorities and land dispute mechanisms (Longway, 1999; Ovonji-Odida, 1999). Where the "gender balance" has not been achieved, a more considered analysis should be made in order to reveal hidden constraints which prevent women from coming forward as representatives, and making their voices heard within policy making.

As we have seen, ensuring implementation of women's rights within the village setting is one of the more intractable problems of "gender balancing" policies. Revisions of the constitution, land laws and other laws will not automatically change practices; law merely provides a framework within which rights and relationships are to be negotiated. A stronger legal status does not automatically afford women more independence but it may provide a stronger bargaining position (NEDA, 1997b).

A dialogue is also needed with customary authorities. Organisations concerned with gender issues tend to regard customary institutions as outdated and a major obstacle to change, preferring to approach reform through legislation. However, some bridges are needed between the "old" and the "new", especially since customary rules and authority continue to play a very important part in many rural areas. Adherence to a straightforward implementation of statutory law may generate a new set of problems and tensions. Analyses of customary rights have revealed their considerable flexibility and adaptability. Experience from many countries (see Chapter 3, this volume) have shown that ill-advised registration of landholding rights or titling risks strengthening the male dominated status quo. Thus, rather than seeking to override, dismantle or ignore the customary legal systems, an adaptation of the rules could be encouraged within rural community institutions. Many organisations working on issues such as education, health, and local development have a wealth of experience on how to improve the status and image of women in rural society. It is important to build on such lessons when seeking to improve women's status in a viable and sustainable way.

10

Land Boards as a Mechanism for the Management of Land Rights in Southern Africa

Julian Quan

INTRODUCTION

This chapter discusses the role of Land Boards as decentralised institutions for the management of land and land rights in Africa at local level. In principle, district-level land boards provide a mechanism for decentralised decision making for land allocation and land use planning. On the one hand, they can take account of local conditions and provide a platform for the interests of local stakeholders, including civil society groups and traditional authorities. On the other hand, land boards can also be used as a vehicle for implementation of policies on land and rural development, drawn up by central government, since their membership is usually determined by government.

The best known and most successful Land Boards in Africa are those which were set up in Botswana in the 1960s, as the principal institutions responsible for land administration, a role in which they continue today. More recently, other countries such as Namibia and Uganda have looked to the Botswana example in planning to institute land boards of their own. Similar approaches are also underway in French-speaking West Africa (see Chapter 12, this volume)

The discussion presented in this chapter draws partly on a paper presented at the February 1999 DFID Workshop on Land Rights and Sustainable Development in Sub-Saharan Africa by Botshelo Mathuba, a presidential adviser in Botswana, and partly on a more critical summary of Botswana's experience. The current proposals for setting up a system of Land Boards in Namibia and Uganda are also reviewed. It concludes by considering the prospects for other African countries in implementing equitable land tenure policies through the institution of land boards.

LAND BOARDS – BOTSWANA'S EXAMPLE

It is worth noting at the outset that Botswana was less affected by colonial rule than any other country in South Africa, due to a combination of factors including low rainfall, an absence of known mineral resources, and the existence of powerful and well organised traditional chiefdoms. Botswana became a British protectorate in 1885, and Britain's policy of indirect rule resulted in minimal interference in systems of customary law. Colonial settlement was limited, with no more than 5.5% of the land area alienated to white-owned farms (White, 1999) .

Over 70% of Botswana's total land area (582,000 km2) is held under customary tenure, the rest being state and freehold land, which cover about 23% and 6% of the land area respectively. Customary land formerly comprised about half of the total land area, but this has been increased over the years through conversion of state and freehold land to tribal lands. Under customary law, traditional chiefs controlled the distribution and use of customary land, allocating land for residential, ploughing, grazing and other purposes (Mathuba, 1999).

In 1968, two years after achieving independence as a parliamentary democracy, the government enacted the Tribal Land Act, which provided for the establishment of Land Boards as new institutions with responsibility to administer customary land.

In general, land policy in Botswana has shifted away from individual and state ownership of land in favour of more locally accountable ownership of land. In 1983, the Presidential Land Commission recommended against instituting any major changes in the system of customary tenure.

However, a range of contrary forces are at work, which raise questions about the performance of the current system. Thus, for example, the Land Boards have been criticised for not being sufficiently democratic or locally accountable (White, 1999). Elected members are not chosen by secret ballot, but by a meeting of people actually present in the *kgotla* (traditional assembly or forum), who tend to be the wealthier community members and large cattle owners. The Minister for Local Government, Lands and Housing then appoints five from a slate of ten elected candidates. Five further members are appointed by the Minister, and two members are appointed by the Ministry of Agriculture and the Ministry of Commerce and Industry respectively (see Box 10.2).

Although the functioning of the Boards has improved over recent years, and they have become more independent of both the Minister and the vested interests of local politicians and chiefs, some changes appear to have had a negative impact on some customary land users, because of increasing central government interference in local decision making (White, 1999) which may

---

Box 10.1: Structure and function of Botswana's Land Boards

The Land Boards were established in 1970 as local institutions, but governed by broader national land policies. There are 12 Main Land Boards and 37 Subordinate Land Boards. The latter were created in 1973 to assist the Main Boards. Land Boards are one of four local government bodies in Botswana - the others being local Councils, the Tribal Administration and the District Administration. While Land Boards have sole authority over land, they work closely with other local authorities and relevant departments. The Boards fall under the Ministry of Local Government, Lands and Housing - which controls and coordinates their activities and other parts of the local administration. The Ministry provides them with financial support, in the form of grants, and provides logistical and technical support.

With the aim of improving land administration, the Tribal Land Act (TLA) 1968 vested in the Land Boards all the former powers of the chiefs in relation to land. The powers of the Main Land Boards include the following:

a) granting rights to use land;

b) cancellation of rights to use land, including grants made prior to operation of the TLA;

c) imposing restrictions on the use of tribal land;

d) authorising any transfer and change of use of tribal land;

e) determining land use zones, and

f) hearing appeals from Subordinate Land Boards.

Land may be granted under both customary law and the formal national law. Those granted land rights under the former are issued with a Certificate of Customary Land Grant while those granted land rights under the latter sign a lease. While most people still acquire land under customary law, leasehold tenure has been extended to a different set of land uses in order to accommodate changing needs. Initially, leases were only issued to land users who were not citizens of Botswana, or for specific business purposes. Subsequently, leasehold tenure was extended to cover grazing and commercial arable land, as well as to some residential land, to enable land holders to mortgage their land and secure finance from lending institutions.

Source: Mathuba, 1999

---

overrule specific local or indigenous land claims. The staff of Land Boards (rather than their members) are appointed by the Ministry of Local Government, Lands and Housing, and the improvement in communications in Botswana has resulted in much more rapid and regular instructions from central to local levels of government. Moreover, a larger number of district based representatives of central government institutions are now involved in the operations of the Land Boards and the technical groups which advise them.

Botswana's Tribal Grazing Lands Policy (TGLP) of 1975 sought to address a perceived problem of overgrazing in customary areas by encouraging herders to relocate their animals to fenced ranches. This created opportunities for the owners of large herds to establish private rights over land, but did not provide adequate extension and other services to ensure that technical improvements in range and stock management took place that were adapted to the new enclosed grazing regime. As a result, once the grazing on their own ranches was exhausted, TGLP ranchers simply returned their animals to communal grazing areas, placing further pressure on these common property resources (Segosebe,

---

Box 10.2: Botswana's Land Boards: accountability, criticisms and change

The Land Boards have been criticised by members of the public, Members of Parliament and Members of the House of Chiefs, for a number of shortcomings:

- The Act was considered inadequate to deal with the needs of modern society because it enshrined principles of tribal land;
- Board procedures are cumbersome and cause unnecessary delays in land allocation, as well as in the settlement of land disputes because of lengthy procedures involving the need for ministerial approval appeals;
- Boards are unable to enforce either their decisions or the provisions of the Act.

Originally, each Main Land Board had six members representing the District Council (Councillors), the Tribal Administration (Chief) and the Ministry of Local Government, Lands and Housing. The composition of membership has varied over the years and the numbers have increased. In 1989, both chiefs and councillors were removed from membership under an amendment to the Tribal Land Act in order to make the Boards as independent as possible of other local institutions. Since then, Main Land Boards have had twelve members while Subordinate Land Boards have had ten. Five are democratically elected by the people at the *Kgotla* (traditional assembly or meeting place). Another five members are nominated by the Minister of Local Government, Lands and Housing. The members elect the chairperson amongst themselves on a yearly basis. The two additional members on the Main Land Boards are *ex officio* members who represent the Minister of Commerce and Industry and Minister of Agriculture. Their role is to advise Board members on matters related to their respective Ministries.

The Minister of Lands is responsible for the overall operation of the Boards, and is answerable to Parliament. As the Minister nominates five of the Board members, so can he dismiss them.

The Tribal Land Act was further amended in 1993. The wording has changed such that land rights are now vested in the Boards for "the benefit of Citizens of Botswana" rather than for the "Tribesmen of the area", to the effect that they are now required to manage land in the national interest rather than more local tribal interests. The duties of the Boards have been expanded to include authorisation of change of use and land transfers, and Ministerial consent is no longer required. The amended Act has also made it possible for the Land Boards to cancel customary land rights they have granted, in cases where land has not been developed within the prescribed period or in accordance with the purpose for which it was granted.

Those who feel aggrieved by a decision of the Land Board may now either take their case to the new Lands Tribunal system set up in 1997, instead of the lengthy process of appeal to the Minister as before.

Source: Mathuba, 1999

1995; White, 1999). Although the resettlement strategy of the TGLP originally targeted "unused" lands beyond the commons, a component of the 1991 New Agricultural Policy now enables individuals and groups to enclose and fence land around water points, even in areas of common pasture (White, 1999).

The 1993 amendments to the Tribal Land Act (see Box 10.2) effectively abolished the concept of "tribesmanship", and required the Land Boards to administer tribal land in the interests of all the citizens of Botswana. Whilst curtailing the risk of discrimination in relation to land claims by members of particular tribal groups, this change has also had the effect of limiting the powers of the Land Boards in pursuing local development agendas (White,

1999) because the interests of local customary rights-holders are not necessarily a priority in a Land Board's decision making.

Despite the general shift towards local accountability resulting from the establishment of Land Boards, critics have argued that since 1975 there has been a slow but clear reversal of policy which has led to growing centralisation of land administration, the de-linking of communities from the land they occupy and own collectively, and the increasing privatisation of tenure arrangements (White, 1999). The main beneficiaries of this shift in policy have been the political and economic elite, who are the large cattle owners of the country. Accompanying this shift of policy, the distribution of wealth and income in Botswana has become more unequal in recent years.

The resource rights of indigenous groups, notably the Basarwa (*San* or *Bushmen*) to hunting, gathering and water resources, are not recognised as rightful claims by the land policy of Botswana. This has contributed to growing poverty amongst these communities (see for example Kashweeka, 1999). Land Boards have superimposed other customary and formal claims on the pre-existing rights of these indigenous groups, who have never had representation on land management institutions. The Basarwa are regarded as "tenants at will", with very limited rights, on the lands they have traditionally roamed, such as the Kalahari Game Reserve, which is now state land.

Although Botswana is a parliamentary democracy, political institutions are dominated by the administration, which, is largely staffed and controlled by the elite. Civil society in general and NGOs in particular are relatively weak and disorganised, and as a result there are few alternative voices to advocate in favour of the rural poor in national land policy. Neither are there independent checks and balances on the operation of the Land Boards at local level. Organisations supporting indigenous rights, however, recognise that land is a resource that is fundamental to the livelihoods and security of many rural people. They argue against the privatisation of traditional lands and for more equitable policies in relation to resource rights. Thus, for example, it is considered that local groups should receive priority over outsiders in the allocation of land leases for purposes of community-based wildlife management, tourism and hunting which offer rural communities new livelihood opportunities. In principle, the existence of Subordinate Land Boards now creates a degree of subsidiarity in relation to local decision making. In some cases, Land Boards have leased land to local community resource, management projects. However, in general, the Land Boards' operations tend to work against the devolution of local level.

LAND BOARDS ELSEWHERE

Namibia

In the context of long debated reforms to communal tenure, and a broadly similar agro-ecological context, Namibia is now adopting a similar approach to that of Botswana, which will involve the creation of Land Boards. Namibia's 1998 White Paper on National Land Policy states that Land Boards will be responsible for the survey and registration of all approved forms of land title in the area of their jurisdiction. They will also create zones for "National and Community development" and set limits on the amount of land which can be made available for leasehold. In addition, a Communal Land Bill has been drafted[1]. However, concerns have been raised as to how far these Boards can and will involve local communities effectively in land matters (Werner, 1999). The context within which the Communal Land Bill has eventually emerged is characterised by a variety of competing forces. Land policy development has been handled in a highly centralised way, with considerable delays, and the ruling elite are struggling to wrest power over land from traditional leaders. Meanwhile, in some areas, communal grazing land is being enclosed by large herders, anticipating the introduction of provision for private titling.

The Communal Land Bill (Government of Namibia, 1998) specifies the membership of the Land Boards to be appointed by the Minister. They will comprise representatives of each traditional authority in the area, farmers' organisations, the regional council, nature conservancies within the area, and nominees of Ministers responsible for regional government, land matters and environmental matters. Provision is also made for women's representatives, two of whom should be farmers and two of whom should have relevant technical expertise. Although no Board members are currently elected, a broader range of local representatives is involved than in Botswana, which may lead to fuller consideration of local interests in decision making, including those of women and ongoing community management projects in the area. Land Board members are required to disclose any personal interests that might have a bearing on matters relating to the Board's role.

The Boards are responsible for exercising control over how chiefs manage customary land rights, for leasehold allocations (which are also subject to the consent of traditional authorities) and for establishing and maintaining systems to register customary and leasehold land allocation and transfer. Thus, for

---

1 In February 2000, Namibia's Communal Land Bill passed into legislation to become the Communal Land Act. The new law has been criticised for granting too much power to traditional leaders, and for not incorporating the views and submisisons from NGOs (see also Chapter 7, this volume). Further details are not available at the time of going to press.

example, under the Bill, primary responsibility for the allocation of customary land rights still rests with traditional chiefs or their representatives at village level, for ratification by the Land Boards.

Namibia's Land Boards may draw some benefits from the experience gained by neighbouring Botswana, concerning both Land Boards and the development of nature conservancies as a source of rural livelihoods.

Uganda

Uganda's 1995 constitution provided for the devolution of authority over land management and administration, and the subsequent 1998 Land Act prescribed the institutional structures through which this is to be done. The Act required the establishment of Land Boards at district level throughout Uganda by January 1999, each with members to be appointed at district level for approval by the Minister responsible for lands. It has not proved possible to adhere to this timetable, with only 18 out of a total of 45 Land Boards having been appointed (Nsamba-Gayiiya, 1999). The overall institutional framework proposed by the Act is complex and includes Parish Land Committees, the institution of a Land Recorder at sub-county level (to record land allocations and transfers) and a system of land tribunals. All of these bodies are meant to be supported by full-time officials.

While this structure is designed to shift responsibility for land management to local level and provide for community involvement, it is a completely new set of institutions. It does not seek to build on existing land management arrangements at local level, nor does it provide for the representation of customary authorities, even at parish committee and tribunal level. It is hierarchical in nature, since the decisions taken at a lower level must be ratified by the Land Boards. Nor is it clear how much autonomy District Authorities will have in determining locally specific land policies and promulgating bye-laws, although this is desirable, given the great agro-ecological and socio-economic diversity found across Uganda, and the diverse tenure arrangements this has produced.

Despite the decentralisation programme which has been underway for the last five years, and the Act's devolutionary intent, its provisions have been centrally conceived. Neither has consultation taken place with local government as to the feasibility of the new structures, even though the Act requires them to be supported from district funds. It has now become clear that neither local nor central Government can afford to finance the full range of new institutions and their associated staff. Wider consultation about the priorities and practicalities of implementing the Act has now begun, and options for simplifying the institutional structure are being examined. However, this would require amendment to the Act, and the cost implications are still likely to remain very considerable.

The 1998 Act represents a challenging and ambitious programme. It seeks to provide security of tenure to all land users under a pluralistic tenure system, including customary tenure, leasehold and freehold, and makes provision for the conversion of customary tenure to formal title. The Act also provides for the protection of tenants' rights, and for the administration of a land fund, intended to support land acquisition by the landless and pay compensation to landlords. The responsibilities of Land Boards, and the procedures which they must follow, as prescribed by the Act, are complex and demanding. It is likely to be some time before Uganda can institute all these provisions and ensure an effective decentralised land management system which meets the needs of all land users.

CONCLUSIONS

The available evidence from the operation and impacts of Land Boards in Africa demonstrates a number of strengths and weaknesses in this approach.

Strengths

Land Boards offer a way of decentralising the implementation of national land policy by creating local institutions in which both government and local stakeholders can be represented. They also provide a way of removing customary land allocation from the absolute control of traditional chiefs, without rejecting the principles of customary land law, and allowing traditional leaders to retain some representation on the Board.

The allocation of land rights under both customary and formal tenure by the same institution allows the trade-offs and competition between the two systems to be kept in view. Land Boards can devise simple methods for recording customary land allocations and transfers, which meet local needs but stop short of detailed survey and registration. Boards can assess the needs for leasehold conversion in cases where a land user requires leasehold title as security against a bank loan, and examine any competing customary claims.

In common with the experience of the Land Commissions in the French-speaking countries of West Africa (see Chapter 13, this volume), Botswana's emphasis on local Land Boards as a means of land administration and gradual approach to policy reform demonstrate the viability of land management based on customary tenure and the development of local institutions, rather than a more centralised approach focusing on the perceived need to transform customary tenure.

Weaknesses

Land Boards have been shown to be subject to bureaucratic intervention and control. Given the weak development of civil society organisation and poor representation of many local communities, Land Boards tend to be dominated by local elites and central government interests. This may lead to the privatisation of customary land and the neglect of traditional claims to natural resources.

Land Boards are poorly equipped to resolve problems arising from overlapping rights and claims, and the needs of different ethnic groups. Wildlife, forest and water management issues, for example will all affect land claims, but Land Boards, as organs of a particular ministry, may not have the authority to address them.

The cost of setting up and staffing Land Boards is considerable, especially if they are to carry out all the tasks demanded of them as well as covering the whole country. A gradual, pilot approach to the development and operation of Land Boards, focusing on areas of greatest priority, is likely to prove more realistic and cost effective.

In conclusion, if Land Boards are to be made more effective as part of a land policy favouring the rural poor, a number of issues must be kept in mind. Provision needs to be made for representation of the range of different stakeholder groups, and must include both men and women, as well as different ethnic groups. Thought should be given to their capacity to engage effectively as members of the Board, to ensure that they are not dominated by the more vocal, better educated elite.

Land Boards can, in principle, function well as accountable, transparent institutions. However, their impact in practice also depends on the policies which they are required to implement. Sufficient local autonomy is needed in order to establish procedures, respond to applications for land, and formulate locally applicable land policies. Government needs to clarify the place of Land Boards within a wider system of devolved local government, the development planning process, and mechanisms for dispute resolution. Thus, to operate effectively, Land Boards need to be accompanied by a broader range of mutually supportive and consistent policy measures.

11

Registering Customary Rights

Camilla Toulmin and Julian Quan

INTRODUCTION

This chapter describes the experience and approach taken by several pro-grammes to manage customary rights. It draws on lessons from programmes to register customary rights both at the level of the individual or household, and at the collective, or village level. Examples of the first are taken from French-speaking West Africa, most particularly Ivory Coast and Niger, drawing sub-stantially from two papers presented at the DFID Workshop on Land Rights and Sustainable Development in Sub-Saharan Africa by Jean Rene Okoin and Moussa Yacouba respectively[1]. Cases of collective rights registration are de-scribed for Mozambique and South Africa. There are also considerable paral-lels with the establishment of Land Boards (see Chapter 10) as well as land reform activities in countries such as Uganda and Tanzania, described else-where in this book (see Chapters 6, 11 and 14). The registration of customary rights at either level is taking place as a means to provide land users with greater security. In practice, for individual registration programmes, such an improvement in security is not guaranteed for all rights-holders, because of the simplifications which registration inevitably introduces into a complex and dynamic set of practices. So far as registering collective title is concerned, while this may protect the rights of those able to claim membership of the community, such a registration process may well exclude the secondary rights of those who, as migrants or transhumant visitors, cannot assert a primary link to the village and its resources.

---

1 Though substantial reference is made to these papers, the analysis and interpretation of the material is entirely that of the main authors.

Why this interest in registering customary rights?

Registration of customary rights is being implemented in several African countries at both individual and community levels, and for a variety of reasons. First, in Ivory Coast, and Niger, the establishment of a register of individual plots is seen as being a means by which to provide greater security to land users and, thereby, encourage further investment in management and improvement of the land in question. Second, a register allows the state to identify more clearly where land is potentially available for other uses and provides a means by which it can be acquired and transferred. Thus, in Ivory Coast, land which is perceived as being "without an owner" *(sans maître)* can be acquired by the state, and under the new legislation of December 1998, any land not registered by 2008, will revert to state ownership[2]. In the case of Niger, land can be taken back from those who are not putting it 'to productive use' *(la mise en valeur)* and allocated to others. Third, in some cases, it has been linked, either implicitly or explicitly, to the establishment of a local taxation system. Such seems to have been one of the reasons for the Rural Land Plan[3] *(Plan Foncier Rural or PFR)* in Ivory Coast, but these two processes have subsequently been de-linked. This is to avoid people mis-reporting their land holdings, in order to minimise tax payments. Fourth, in some cases, registration programmes are a means to redress the legislative balance in favour of customary rights, their existence and strength having formerly been ignored. However, recognition of customary rights does not necessarily imply a similar acknowledgement of customary structures or chiefs.

Registration of customary rights at a collective level is being carried out for many of the same reasons, such as promoting greater security over resource management and hence more sustainable patterns of development. In some cases, the aim has been to reduce risks of conflict, through clarifying the rights of different user groups, as well as safeguarding local people's common interests in the resources around their community. The latter issue is of particular importance in an era of rapid change, and growing interest from outsiders in gaining access to land. The registration of collective rights also constitutes an important step towards establishing a decentralised system for land administration, which is heavily reliant on rural communities.

In colonial times, there was a pragmatic interest in recognising the customary authorities, given the need to rely on them for dispensing justice, collecting taxes, and mobilising labour. This also involved some recognition of their powers in relation to land. Some have argued that these prerogatives were

---

2 Loi no. 98-750 du 23 décembre 1998 relative au Domaine foncier rural.
3 The Plan Foncier Rural could also be translated as the Rural Tenure Plan. However, foncier conveys a broader set of concepts and issues than those of tenure alone. Hence we have chosen to use the phrase Rural Land Plan.

often an exaggeration of the actual powers a chief could exercise (Berry, 1993), but they were agreed to by the colonial administration because of the need to co-opt customary chiefs to manage much of the business of the colonial state. In West Africa, both the British and the French colonial governments carried out surveys of customary rights in the 1940s and 50s, to provide them with better understanding of local practice and institutions. Since Independence, there has been less evident recognition given to customary land tenure, with many governments considering that these systems provide an inadequate framework to ensure agricultural intensification, investment and development. Hence, many governments, with support from donors, have felt the need to move towards the registration of land holdings, through various titling programmes. Thus, for example, a major rationale for the Nigerian Land Use Decree was stated to be the inability of customary rights to provide the right incentives for agricultural investment and modernisation (Francis, 1984).

A parallel development in much of West Africa has been the emergence of the *gestion de terroir* (GT) approach, as a response to concerns about natural resource degradation and the need to transfer responsibility for village land use planning and management to the local community (Toulmin, 1994). However, a major difference exists between the registration of collective title as described for Mozambique and the South African Communal Property Associations, and the GT approach. In the latter case, there are no legal rights transferred, with villages remaining unable to control and manage access to the resources in their surrounding lands, since such rights have been retained by the forest service and other government bodies. Experience with local conventions in Mali (see Chapter 5) shows how groups are addressing this weakness by establishing a formal association able to make rules and ensure these are enforced.

REGISTERING INDIVIDUAL AND HOUSEHOLD RIGHTS

Ivory Coast's Rural Land Plan

Background to the land issue

The Ivory Coast faces a growing scarcity of land, due to rising population and the development of commercial agriculture. Given increasing competition and conflict over land, the government has been carrying out a pilot Rural Land Plan *(Plan Foncier Rural)* since 1990. This aims to register current patterns of use, whether customary or statutory, with a view to providing greater security, reducing risks of conflict, and generating greater economic development.

The population of Ivory Coast is almost 16 million, having doubled since

1980, and with a current growth rate of 3.5% a year. Migration into Ivory Coast has been substantial, with nearly one third of the Ivorian population having been born elsewhere. In the south and south-west of the country, conflicts over land largely concern competition between agricultural production, and use of land allocated as forest reserves. In northern areas, disputes between farmers and Peul herders from further north are more common (Bassett and Crummey, 1993). Migratory flows within Ivory Coast are also very significant, with a large number of people moving from the drier northern areas towards higher rainfall zones in the south and west. At the same time, refugees have fled across the frontier into south-west Ivory Coast from Liberia and Sierra Leone, putting further pressure on land availability.

The current situation regarding land in Ivory Coast must be seen in terms of its broader economic context. In the years following Independence, Ivory Coast experienced rapid economic growth. During the 1960s and 70s, the country pursued an open door policy in relation to migrants, who provided urgently needed labour to expand agricultural production, particularly of the main export crops – cocoa and coffee. The then President Houphouet Boigny maintained a policy of welcoming those from elsewhere, and allowing them rights of residence and to vote. Such a policy brought in large numbers of migrants, particularly from neighbouring Sahelian states, which had experienced serious droughts in the 1970s and 80s. These were not only seasonal migrants, who come for a few months before returning to farm in the Sahel in the rainy season, but also longer term migrants seeking land to settle and farm.

A significant number of plantations were established and developed by migrant farmers from the Sahel, who acquired the land from local people. Farmers from the village of Zaradougou in southern Mali provide an illustration of this process. In the early 1950s, young men migrated to Ivory Coast to help harvest coffee and cocoa. Several households bought land from local people and invested labour in establishing their own plantations of coffee, cocoa, and many fruit-trees. Now all but two households in Zaradougou have acquired plantations in Ivory Coast in the Aboisso, Daloa and Diva regions, and these holdings are managed as an integral part of the family's agricultural activities. Half the family workforce may stay in Ivory Coast for several years at a time, with earnings from these plantations contributing at least as much cash to the family purse as do their cotton fields in Mali (Brock and Coulibaly, 1999).

Claims by migrants to land are now being contested by Ivorians, for several reasons. In some cases, migrants face attempts by the local population to reinterpret the nature of the transactions by which they gained the land, such that "sales" are said now to have been "loans"; land which had been "sold" by a man, may be taken back by his heirs on his death, since the agreement is assumed to lapse once he dies; and some argue for the return of land, saying that

Box 11.1: Land and the state in Ivory Coast

Originally, land in Côte d'Ivoire belonged collectively to the village community or family, and its occupants only had use rights. When the French administration was set up, it decreed a "right of eminent domain" but, in view of the particular difficulties in enforcement it encountered, this claim to eminent domain was abandoned.

From 1900 to 1935, the French administration restricted its claims to land which was "vacant and had no master". As the notion of having "no master" was inappropriate within the context of Ivorian traditions, the government redefined both it and the notion of vacancy. Subsequently, the state would claim only land which had not been "put to productive use" *(mise en valeur)* for more than 10 years. However, protest movements intensified to such an extent that, in 1955, the French administration abandoned this claim too. After this date, the colonial state owned only that property to which it held formal title.

In 1956, the French National Assembly approved the move towards decentralisation, which would involve overseas populations more closely in managing their own affairs. As a result, land which was "vacant and had no master" was held to belong to the territories, rather than to France, with land use management defined as a matter for the local population and their authorities.

After Independence in 1960, the Ivory Coast inherited the rights and obligations of the French state. According to the decree of 1955, the government had abandoned its claim to land that was not mise en valeur. However, the government of Ivory Coast saw its role as trying to promote productive land use and was keen to reinstate such a claim as a state prerogative. The Commission on Land and Property Reform decided that "whenever under the current circumstances ... it appears that the State is best placed to take full advantage of the natural wealth of the Ivory Coast, the law must enable it to act in the public interest".

A law dated 20th March 1963 was drafted to bring in a new land and property code, and although it was approved unanimously by the National Assembly, was not enacted by the President of the Republic, since he judged it too ambitious for its time. Instead, he asked for further deliberations, but this second bill was not enacted either. In practice, formal law and customary law continued to co-exist within the country. However, formal law remains the only reference for the authorities in settlement of disputes, despite the fact that it applies to less than 2% of the rural area of the country.

A new law was finally passed on 23 December 1998[4] which defines the nature of rural land holdings and, while it recognises customary regimes, it sees these as being a transitional stage en route to a system of individual title. It also specifies that only Ivorian citizens can be land owners. Customary rights must be registered by 2008, all land not registered by this point will be considered as "without owner" and will thus revert to the state. Registration can be done either by an individual or collectively, such as villages, families, or local organisations.

Source: Okoin, 1999; Stamm, 2000

it had been wrongly sold by one member of the family without properly consulting the other members. In the last 10 years or so, the slackening in the economy and growing scarcity of land have led to tighter controls on migrant populations. The right of migrants to vote in Ivorian elections has been withdrawn, and in political circles it has become essential to demonstrate full Ivo-

---

4 Loi no. 98-750 au Domaine foncier rural

rian nationality. Equally, the need for extra labour to cultivate and harvest plantation crops has become less urgent than in years of boom, with increasing concern about youth unemployment and need to find work for them. At the same time the legislation of December 1998 expressly notes that land ownership can only be held by those of Ivorian nationality.

Origins and design of the Rural Land Plan

In 1988, in an attempt to address the problem posed by high levels of youth unemployment, the government launched a vast programme to try to resettle them on farmland. Difficulty in getting hold of fallow land, although it was assumed to be abundant and available, led the government to start an inventory of available land and landholding patterns. It very soon became clear, however, that apart from helping to understand rural landholding patterns and land availability, documentation on tenure was of great importance because it could serve as a tool to prevent and resolve tenure conflicts, while also providing a means to develop a land tenure code suited to rural conditions. At the same time, it could provide the basis for local taxation and rural development planning.

The Ministry of Agriculture and Livestock Resources (MINAGRA)[5] took the opportunity to begin a pilot Rural Land Plan (PFR) in 1990, following the decision of the Council of Ministers[6] to tackle the tenure issue, and with funding from the World Bank and French government (Okoin, 1999).

Due to funding constraints, the programme started in a pilot phase in only two areas, Korhogo and Beoumi, in the northern savannah region of Ivory Coast. Activities in the forest zone did not begin until later: in 1992 in the case of Abengourou and in 1994 for Soubre and Daloa. Hence, the results of the pilot programme have been spread out over several years, such that by the end of 1998, a total of 740,000 hectares had been covered, comprising 33,400 plots and involving a total of 334,100 people (Okoin, 1999). Following the 1994 programme evaluation, the government decided to extend the PFR throughout the country, as part of the National Village Land Use Management and Rural Capital Development Programme[7]. The process of implementing the PFR is complex and has generated a number of difficult issues, such as the sense of insecurity generated amongst lesser rights-holders and migrants, the simplification of complex and evolving rights through their being set down on paper, the time pressures imposed on the project as well as the costs of establishing and maintaining a register. In addition, the new law of December 1998 partially

---

5 Institutionally, the project is housed within MINAGRA. The National Technical Research and Development Office (BNETD) is responsible for implementing the Rural Land Use Plan and has set up an independent management unit.
6 Decision of 21 December 1988
7 Programme National de Gestion des Terroirs-Equipement Rurale

---

Box 11.2: Aims and methods of the *Plan Foncier Rural* (PFR).

The PFR aims to draw up a comprehensive inventory of both individual and collective, customary and modern rights; it records people's rights, as well as their equipment and farming practices used. The boundaries of landholdings are also being mapped.

There are two objectives:
- to provide a planning tool; and
- to draw up a legislative code governing rural tenure.

The PFR follows a number of stages. Firstly, studies of social and tenure issues in the project area are made. Secondly, campaigns at several different levels are launched to raise awareness and provide information to a range of different stakeholders. Thirdly, demographic surveys are conducted in each village to list the number of people by neighbourhood, lineage and family. This allows all potential holders of land rights within the village territory to be identified. A tenure survey is carried out to register rights-holders (whatever their social status, sex or national origin) and the extent of their rights, as well as to mark out the boundaries of their landholdings. A public notice phase follows, on completion of which the recorded information is ratified at village level. Finally, maintenance of the Rural Land Plan is planned to keep and update information on changes in landholdings.

Source: Okoin, 1999

---

undermines the approach of the PFR and its adherence to customary rights, by pushing for their transformation into private individual titles. Thus, customary rights once registered must be transformed into a *titre d'immatriculation* (registered title deed) within three years. These issues are discussed in more depth later in this chapter.

Niger's Rural Code

The government of Niger began work on developing a new Rural Code in 1986, when an ad-hoc Committee was set up with the task of conducting a wide-ranging debate about rural management systems. Its primary concern was to find ways to regulate management of and access to land, with a view to safeguarding the ecological balance and encouraging productive investment in land. The Committee viewed the drawing up of the Rural Code as a "long, long-term process", given the complexity and sensitivity of the issues involved. In order to ensure involvement by all relevant stakeholders, the decree setting up the National Committee also provided for regional and sub-regional committees at *arrondissement* and *département* levels[8], on which different groups are represented (Yacouba, 1999).

The National Committee drew up a framework document, covering issues such as access to and management of land, the role of customary practice, and conflict settlement. This was sent to different interest groups - farmers, herders,

---

8 Equivalent to District and Province, respectively.

NGOs, rural development projects and government technical services, and regional workshops were held in 1989 to debate the findings of these consultations. The results of these workshops were then brought together by the National Committee, which set up a team of national and international lawyers who were charged with drafting a text for the Rural Code.

The text suggested by the team was then sent back for discussion to all relevant interest groups and discussed again at a national seminar in 1990, which was also attended by donor agencies. Recommendations from this forum were incorporated into the draft which was subsequently enacted as a general framework of principles for future legislation *(loi-cadre)* by the government in 1993.

Box 11.3: Background to Niger

Niger is a Sahelian country of 10 million people, 85% of whom live in rural areas. Due to its position on the southern edge of the Sahara Desert, most of its land is unsuitable for cultivation, due to very low and highly erratic rainfall. Niger's arable area amounts to less than 15% of its territory, of which only an estimated 660 km2 is irrigated. The remaining area is used for seasonal grazing, when rainfall allows.

The agricultural sector is faced with serious problems of low returns, and high risks of degradation. Since the droughts of the 1970s and 80s, there has been rising concern over the future prospects for agriculture and rural development, with attention focused in particular on the reduction or disappearance of fallowing practices, the need to develop and spread more sustainable patterns of land use, and the inadequacy of the legal framework for management of natural resources. Hence, in 1986, a process was begun to draw up a Rural Code which would address the last of these three concerns.

Niger is one of the poorest countries in the world and has very limited economic opportunities. The collapse of uranium prices in the 1980s, which was its only significant mineral export, has hit the country's economy badly. The country remains highly dependent on external aid flows which constitute around half of the government budget revenues. There is a high level of outmigration to coastal nations such as Nigeria and Cameroon, particularly from Central and Eastern regions. Outmigration usually occurs on a seasonal or short term basis of a few years. Although women are also increasingly involved, in most cases it is the young men who migrate. As a result, women are taking on an increasingly important role in agricultural production.

Source: IIED, 1999

The Rural Code has aimed to address several objectives. First, land management in Niger is complex, due to the co-existence of customary law, Islamic law, and colonial regulations, as well as the laws and statutes of the State of Niger, introduced following Independence in 1960. Thus, the Rural Code aims to provide a synthesis of these different rules, the intention being that it should gradually take the place of all pre-existing legal rules, whether stemming from written or customary law. Second, the Code is meant to set out a legal framework conducive to the overall development of rural populations, and including the better management of resources - land, pasture, forests, animals and water resources – by providing rural land users with greater security over the resources on which they depend. Third, it aims to regulate areas of potential conflict, given the diverse cultures and forms of land use found in Niger, and the changing environmental and economic context.

Hence, the Rural Code has placed particular emphasis on seeing how best to clarify the rights and duties, obligations and sanctions, levels of competence and rights of appeal associated with different structures. It has tried to pay attention to the rights of marginal groups to own land, taking rural natural resources as part of the commonwealth of the nation *(patrimoine commun)* to which everyone in Niger has equal right of access, without discrimination on the grounds of sex or social origin. However, land must be shown to be put to productive use *(mise en valeur)* otherwise existing use rights may be transferred to another person.

Implementation of the Rural Code is closely linked to the parallel process of decentralisation, which is currently under way in Niger. Local land use management structures are meant to be established at *département, arrondissement,* and *commune* levels. Drawing up a rural register is an important element in the Rural Code process, and is the responsibility of the Land Commissions at *arrondissement* level.

These Land Commissions have both a consultative remit and decision-making power. Their opinion must be sought on all issues related to the determination of what constitutes "productive use of land" and the procedure for granting concessions which might lead to acquisition of ownership rights over the land concerned. Land Commissions also have the power to recognise and establish the content of tenure rights, as well as to transform concession rights into ownership rights. They have the general power to supervise development of land in the *arrondissement* or *commune*, and may also transfer to a third party land which is not being "put to productive use". However, they are not meant to get involved in conflict management, this task being left in the hands of existing structures, such as customary chiefs, and the police (Yacouba, 1999).

The Permanent Secretariat for the Rural Code has adopted a cautious approach to setting up Land Commissions, with pilots being established in eleven *départements* on a trial basis. A national campaign has been undertaken to make everyone in Niger aware of the content of the legislation and to reassure citizens as to its content. This has involved:

- publication and mass distribution of the legislation in the eight national languages;
- use of mass communications media: radio, TV, written press, audio-visual, etc;
- training, especially of the Commissions themselves, the regional administrative authorities, traditional chiefs, judges, and the other main parties involved in implementing the law;

●workshops for farmer and herder associations.

The Land Commission is meant to maintain and update the rural register *(Dossier rural)* under the authority of the *sous-préfet* or mayor. Registration of rights is done at the request of the user, in contrast to the systematic coverage pursued by the PFR in Ivory Coast. The register includes two separate documents:

●an overall map of the rural area showing the spread of tenure rights, as a result of surveys undertaken by the Land Commission;

●a file comprising the individual record cards made out in the name of each holder of rights. These cards should indicate the full identity of the holder.

All types of rights exercised over a natural resource can be registered, whether collective or individual. The entry entitles the applicant to the issue of an *attestation*, or certificate of ownership, provided that no opposition has been encountered during the survey in the field. In such an eventuality, the procedure is suspended until a court decision settles the dispute. The Land Commission is not a conflict settlement body, but an administrative structure, whose actions may be subject to appeal addressed to a higher authority (the *Préfet*[9]) or an appeal against abuse of power "according to the legal procedure" (Article 121 of the Code).

Box 11.4: Composition of the Land Commissions

According to the Rural Code, the Land Commission chaired by the *Sous-Préfet* or the Mayor shall be set up in each arrondissement or commune. It shall comprise the following persons:

The Permanent Rural Code Secretary;

The heads of the following municipal or arrondissement technical services:

● Planning

● Environment

● Wildlife, fishing and fish-farming

● Animal husbandry

● Agriculture

● Cadastral surveys and State property

● Rural engineering.

A representative of other municipal or arrondissement services as appropriate;

The customary authorities to whom the agenda is relevant;

One representative from each of the following groups: farmers, herders, women and young people;

Anyone else whose presence is deemed necessary

(Article 118 of the *loi-cadre*).

Source: Yacouba, 1999

As can be seen from Box 11.4, the Land Commissions are not elected bodies, but rather operate as technical services controlling use and management of land and natural resources. Where land users do not abide by the conditions agreed (e.g. failing to put land to productive use or doing so inadequately), the

---

9 The government appointed official responsible for administration at the level of the *département.*

owner or user may have their rights withdrawn for a set period. Land Commissions are clearly distinct from other organisations of rural civil society and elected bodies, such as producer associations, co-operatives, and village land-use management committees. Following the nation-wide elections held in February 1999, there are now 103 local government structures, each of which will require a Land Commission. However, given the need to test out the approach further, and limits on funding, it will be some time before each arrondissement can establish its own Land Commission.

CHALLENGES FACED BY THE REGISTRATION OF CUSTOMARY RIGHTS AT INDIVIDUAL LEVEL

A comparison of Ivory Coast and Niger

The cases of Ivory Coast and Niger show a somewhat different approach to registering customary rights. In both cases, a map and register of the relevant area are drawn up to identify the site of the holding, the rights-holders and the nature of rights held by different claimants. But in the case of Ivory Coast, the rights registered by the PFR do not constitute a claim to ownership, and must be transformed within three years of registration to become a fully legal title of property. In Niger, the certificate granted by the Land Commissions constitutes a title of "ownership". While both countries have adopted a pilot approach to test out the tools and approach, and the basis for an eventual nation-wide programme, in Ivory Coast the PFR has followed a systematic coverage of all rights holders, village by village. By contrast, in Niger, registration is done at the request of the land user. Nevertheless, a number of similar issues have emerged in Ivory Coast and Niger, which are outlined below. Many of the same problems have been encountered in other African countries, such as with the establishment of District Land Boards (see Chapter 10) and the implementation of land reform in Uganda (Mwebaza, 1999).

Registering rights in the context of decentralisation. Many countries in Africa are currently addressing both questions of land rights and decentralising government administration and provision of services (see Chapter 12 for a more detailed discussion). Newly elected district assemblies, or *communes rurales*, have been, or are in the process of being established, with new powers and responsibilities to test out. Many important questions remain unanswered regarding the roles and responsibilities of these new district assemblies, and how they will articulate their activities in relation to village level and customary structures. There are also important issues concerning how these assemblies will finance their activities, with fees from the granting of permits and allocation of rights over land as one possibly important source. In Ivory Coast, new local government structures were set up over the period 1978-85, with a wide range of responsibilities, including provision of education and public health services, and maintenance of local roads. Urban land use and planning has been retained as a central government responsibility, but in rural areas, communes have a role to play in the allocation of land. On the other hand, they have very limited financial autonomy and are highly dependent on central government for funds (Crook, 1996). In Niger, elections were held in 1999 for the 103 newly created decentralised assemblies, but it is unclear as yet what role they will exercise over land. Their capacity to raise significant funding is also likely to be very limited.

Generating insecurity. Rather than increasing security, the process of registering customary rights may generate increased uncertainty, and stir up dormant conflicts (Stamm, 2000). While reports of the PFR process in operation speak of an absence of open dispute when land is being registered, it is likely that outstanding conflicts will have been sorted out prior to the team's arrival (Okoin, 1999; Chauveau et al, 1998). The implementation of the PFR in Ivory Coast, in combination with the new law of 1998, seems to have opened up considerable uncertainty regarding the rights of migrant populations, since non-Ivorian people no longer have the right to be landholders. There is evidence of local farmers taking advantage of the insecurity engendered by the PFR process to take back lands which migrants had developed into profitable plantations. The registration process can also provide the means by which some people, or groups, can get their rights reinterpreted in ways which allow them to exclude others. Such cases can be seen from some of the Village Land Management *(gestion des terroirs)* programmes carried out in many parts of the West African Sahel, where settled village communities have used the project's mapping of village 'boundaries' as a tool to enable them to prevent access to village grazing lands by migrant herders. Recent research points to considerable pre-emptive behaviour by farmers in Niger, prior to the formal implementation of the Rural Code, with farmers aiming to clear as much land as possible, often in very rudimentary fashion, to demonstrate their "occupation and use" of the land (Lund, 1993; Batterbury et al, 1996). Equally, land under tenancy agreements has been taken back by land-owners who fear that adherence to the principle of "land to the tiller" may provide rights to tenants who might claim ownership of the land they are farming.

Simplification of complex rights. Programmes aimed at providing written title to land have been widely criticised for their damaging impacts on many groups, due to the simplification of rights which may occur through such titling activities, and the very skewed abilities of different groups to take advantage of such opportunities. Typically, those who benefit are those with contacts in the right places, a high level of education, and income to buy titles (see Chapter 3; Egbe, forthcoming). The registering of customary rights had been thought of as a means to avoid such adverse consequences. However, as will be seen below, many of the same difficulties arise in practice. Customary rights are frequently complex, depending greatly on the nature of the relationship between the land owner and user, and subject to re-negotiation over time, as conditions change and new opportunities develop. Yet the process of registration demands that rights be simplified in ways which then mean that they lose many of their most important elements, as well as their ability to evolve over time. Translation from a local language into French, or English, may further distort the nature of the transactions being described and written down (Chauveau et al, 1998). Thus, for example, in Ivory Coast, during the earlier part of the pilot phase, a simple classification of rights was used, which tried to fit all arrangements into two categories - land holder and land user. This process reduces a broad range of different arrangements to a few very simple ones. Many of the more marginal social groups may rely on access to resources through informal arrangements which may not have clearly defined European language equivalents and therefore may be particularly vulnerable to such a simplistic approach. Recently, it was decided to change the survey procedure to include a range of terms in local languages which would allow registration to bear a closer connection to current practice (Stamm, 2000).

Time pressures within a long term process. Clarifying the relations by which people gain access to land and other resources is, as noted for Niger, a very long term process (Yacouba, 1999). It takes a considerable amount of time to investigate the complex overlapping claims of different individuals and groups, particularly in areas which have accommodated a significant number of migrants. It also takes time to establish the legitimacy of new institutions with the different parties concerned, so that people understand how they work and are willing to abide by the decisions made. Programmes to register rights are often under pressure to work speedily to ensure they cover as large an area as possible, in a given time period. This can lead to a hasty treatment of inevitably complex issues, with the consequence that project staff are more concerned to meet targets than to do the work as carefully as needed. In the case of Ivory Coast, "external pressures to increase ... the area covered [by the programme] while reducing the time needed to a minimum, carries the risk that complex tenure situations will be simplified, leading to a reductionist view" (Stamm, 1998: 177). Yet despite such haste, on current performance, it will take a very considerable quantity of money and time to achieve nation-wide coverage of the PFR. For example, it has been estimated that it will take ten years to cover the whole of Ivory Coast, and this will only be possible if current resources and personnel are multiplied by a factor of six (Okoin, 1999).

The financial implications of registration. The establishment and mainte-nance of land registers require money. Estimates from Niger suggest an annual cost for running a Land Commission of around 40 million CFA francs (equiv-alent to US$ 64,000), with the rough cost per plot of land at approximately 1,000 CFA francs (US$ 1.60). This is viewed as good value for the plot holder, if it confers firm rights (Yacouba, 1999). For the PFR in Ivory Coast, the over-all cost of the project to the end of 1998 has been estimated at 3,447 million CFA francs (equivalent to US$ 5.5 million), which gives a cost of 4,700 CFA francs per hectare, the figure being lower in savannah areas and higher in the forest region, due to the larger holding sizes and easier survey work in the former (Okoin, 1999). Although much less expensive than establishing a full-scale cadastral survey, these sums are considerable, particularly for a very poor country like Niger, which means that the process is highly reliant on gaining funding from western donors, such as the World Bank, the French or US gov-ernments. This dependence makes the country vulnerable to changes in view amongst donors regarding land tenure. The process in Niger, for example, has been more than 90% reliant on funds from outside donors to establish the eleven pilot Land Commissions, and it will need further major support to enable it to gain nation-wide coverage. It must be remembered that registers require maintenance and updating, or they quickly lose their value as a record. Thus, it is not only necessary to find the capital sum involved in getting such registration systems established, but also the funds required for maintenance.

The ambivalent role of customary chiefs. In Niger, there is continued re-liance on the administration of justice by the customary authorities (mainly canton and village chiefs), who have powers to arbitrate between disputants. Since the state only pays them a minimal salary, the latter have a vested inter-est in arbitration of conflicts and the imposition of fines, even to the point where they may actively provoke disputes (Yacouba, 1999). The establish-ment and enforcement of clear laws are likely to bring a substantial reduction in the number of conflicts. As a result, some traditional chiefs view the Rural Code as a "fly in the ointment". Two previous attempts, in 1964 and 1970, to endow the country with progressive legislation failed due to the opposition of customary chiefs, who at that time held around 60% of the seats in the National Assemblies. This third attempt is proving more successful because the associ-ation of traditional chiefs has been involved in all stages of the process, and be-cause the new law provides that chiefs should be members of the Land Commissions as of right. This makes it easier to co-opt traditional chiefs into the process and limit the damage caused by those who oppose it (ibid.). In the case of Ivory Coast, customary chiefs are members of the local land registra-tion committee, but play no other formal role within the PFR process, nor in the provisions of the 1998 law.

REGISTERING COLLECTIVE RIGHTS[10]

There are various arrangements by which tenure systems can ascribe rights held in common to groups. In current African land law and policy making this is approached in two ways:

- by making villages or lineage groups the rights holders, and ascribing particular responsibilities to a customary authority, chief, village meeting, council of elders or village land committee, or
- where a group of individuals establishes a legal entity, such as a co-operative or communal property association, to guarantee individual and group rights in order to access land or to formalise pre-existing customary rights as joint owners or tenants.

Both of these approaches fall within the potential scope of Niger's Rural Code, where pastoral groups can gain recognition of their grazing homelands *(terroirs d'attache)* and local groups can establish firewood co-operatives with rights to manage and exploit their woodlands (see Box 5.5). They are also exemplified by approaches in Eastern and Southern Africa, as described below and in Chapter 13. In the case of Ivory Coast, the scope for registration of collective rights is much less evident, due to the overall thrust of the programme in favour of individual title.

Collective tenure arrangements, are particularly relevant to the question of *common property resource management.* Resources, such as pasture and surface water sources, are often used in common by local communities and are governed by a communal management system subject to customary rules. These resources are of great value to the incomes and livelihoods of rural people, yet are frequently ignored in land tenure debates. The changing approaches to management of common property are discussed more fully in Chapter 8.

Why support collective tenure arrangements?

Introducing collective tenure as a recognised legal form is one approach to registering customary rights and giving legal force to customary tenure systems. It serves to:

---

10 The term *collective tenure* is used here because it implies legal recognition of ownership rights which are not individual, and in distinction to the term *communal tenure*. This is frequently used, very loosely, to describe customary tenure systems, and can give rise to confusion in that these comprise both individual and collective sets of rights. *Communal tenure* is also, to some extent, a construct of colonial policy and language - in Southern Africa particularly, *communal areas* were in effect indigenous reservations, within which the state did not allocate individual or public property rights, leaving land management under the responsibility of traditional authorities or chiefs, according to modified customary, or *communal tenure* rules. Bruce (1999), prefers the term *community-based tenure*.

- vest formal tenure rights in a community, and avoid the need to register numerous sets of household, individual and subsidiary rights;
- defend community rights against outside or individualistic local interests (e.g. community land registration under the new Mozambique Land Act, *Conventions Locales* in francophone West Africa) (see Box 5.6);
- formalise and specify customary tenure rights held by a group over common property resources, as an alternative to the introduction of individualised rights or the development of open access;
- create group rights or shared ownership in circumstances where customary tenure arrangements have either broken down, or never existed (e.g. South African proposals for communal land associations).

As the example from Mozambique shows (see Box 11.5 below), relatively simple procedures for registering communal rights can be cost-effective in re-solving complex conflicts. The approach effectively devolves control to local communities and recognises that they are best placed to make decisions. It avoids the risk of generating disputes within the community which can occur if certain individuals start to register claims to land which others consider should remain under customary management. There is considerable reliance on customary practice as the best and safest bet for local land administration, and implicitly, in the existence of formal and informal procedures for resolution of internal community land disputes when they arise. The model does not cope well with changes and conflicts which may arise from the emergence of di-vergent interests within local communities (for instance between commercial producers, who may seek to acquire title in order to raise collateral for loans, and more subsistence-oriented households), or situations in which chiefs seek to sell off land for private gain, and cannot be trusted by communities. Nor would it work well in southern parts of Mozambique, where land is less abun-dant or cases where land is subject to overlapping sets of rights, resulting from successive phases of displacement and re-establishment of local communities during the war. However, community land registration is not intended to have universal application and, although communities are granted inalienable, her-itable and enforceable use rights, the state retains radical title to the land, and thus, the prerogative to intervene, should it wish to exert a strong interest.

In Mozambique, therefore, community land registration amounts to little more than a formal endorsement of and protection for use rights within func-tioning, informal customary systems that have retained sufficient local legiti-macy to be effective. The case of South Africa demonstrates the controversy that can be generated in relation to questions of collective tenure where radi-cal title or full ownership is at stake (see Box 11.6). Here, the question arises of whether groups should own land through formally established legal entities, through Tribal Authority structures or, as a compromise, as yet untested legal

---

Box 11.5: Community land registration in Mozambique

Under Mozambique's 1990 Constitution, radical title to all land is held by the state, but the use rights of individuals and groups are recognised. Although freehold rights cannot be bought and sold, the state can issue land concessions to private individuals and developers on a leasehold basis.

In debating the Land Bill (later to become the 1997 Land Act), Mozambique's inter-ministerial Land Commission recognised that the cost of individual registration of land plots throughout rural Mozambique would be very high and not justified by the benefits. The Commission considered the option of registering groups of plots in the names of Peasant Associations or co-operatives, but this would involve a dual bureaucratic process, whereby rural people would first need to establish a legal entity as land holder, and subsequently go through the registration process. In the light of submissions from farmers' organisations, the 1997 Land Law eventually provided for the registration of land by informally constituted rural communities, in a regime of co-ownership. This approach endorses customary ownership of village lands, and leaves the community to determine its own internal "customary" rules. Occupation of land by traditional family lineages was considered as a criterion for the collective registration of customary rights, but as a result of many years of civil war, social displacement and internal migration, many traditional communities are no longer intact. Nevertheless, new communities have arisen and, on the whole, these have proved remarkably robust and equitable in establishing rules for allocation of individual plots. Thus, while recognising customary occupation by kin groups, the law also allows for community registration by groups who have occupied a specific area for a minimum period of 10 years.

In practice, the Lands and Survey Organisation of Mozambique, DINAGECA, has begun registering community lands in northern Mozambique in order to safeguard local people's common interests in fallow and cultivated land, settlements, forests, pasture, water sources, and areas of cultural importance. The process involves a survey of resource utilisation, consultation with local communities and community leaders, using enlarged aerial photos to discuss boundaries, overall land availability and resource use, cadastral mapping, and entry into the Land Register. The process also aims to allow for population expansion in future. Common property resources and those whose use is governed by informal, community rules are all brought into the register, which would not be possible under an individual registration system.

Although cheaper than registration of individual plots, the process remains costly. As a result, land is targeted for community registration according to three criteria, which often overlap: areas in which there are high levels of tenure conflict (the primary conflicts have been with outsiders rather than internal to communities); areas with high potential for economic development; and areas where local groups have expressed an interest in registration.

Following registration, local communities acquire the right of consultation and veto on proposals by external investors for land development. State authorities cannot issue land concessions over their heads. Competition for land between local communities and external investors provided one impetus behind the new land law, and for a relatively speedy, low-cost approach to the registration of community land rights. The law now provides a reasonably solid basis for conflict reduction, and the eventual development of partnerships between communities and the private sector.

Sources: Quadros, 1999; Cuna Junior, 1999

---

concepts of common ownership, such as commonhold (see Chapter 13, this volume). The debate in South Africa has become highly politicised because Communal Property Associations (CPAs) represent a threat to the authority and vested interests of traditional leaders, who have been implacably opposed to the new measures. A history of abuse of power and community trust by traditional leaders, and use of tribal resources for personal gain have together generated much opposition and propelled the search for alternative forms of collective tenure. Abuse of power by customary chiefs on this scale have not been observed in Mozambique, where the simple transfer of land rights to communities remains a viable option.

Box 11.6: Communal Land Associations and their alternatives in South Africa

South Africa's Communal Property Associations Act of 1996 makes provision for group ownership, through the establishment of Communal Property Associations (CPAs) as land holding legal entities. The initial purpose of CPAs was to enable landless groups and people in receipt of land grants under South Africa's market-assisted land redistribution programme to pool their resources and acquire land as a joint asset. Under the Act, a set of rules and regulations for land ownership must be agreed by a two thirds majority of members, defined on a household basis. The rules must be written into a constitution and registered with the Department of Land Affairs (Ntsebeza, 1999).

In the former homelands, or communal areas, exist a complex set of overlapping rights and numerous land disputes, arising from a history of land alienation, forced removals and overcrowding. The post-apartheid government has sought to clarify land rights and enhance security of tenure by transferring land ownership to the land users. Where land was held and managed under "communal" systems, the initial thinking in drafting a land rights bill was that CPAs would provide the preferred vehicle for land ownership by groups because of the democratic safeguards that are built in (Claassens and Makopi, 1999). Test cases and consultations, however, have revealed a number of problems and divergent views, notably as to whether land should be transferred to legal entities, such as CPAs, or to tribal authority structures. Senior traditional leaders argue that traditional tribal systems have their own nature and rules, and should not be required to reconstitute themselves into new entities such as CPAs. On the other hand, many people have lost confidence in traditional systems, because of past abuses, and want to see more democratic, accountable structures established. In practice, where CPAs have been imposed on traditional societies, they have not worked; the new structures exist only on paper, there is no capacity to enforce the legal rights of CPA members, and they have proved irrelevant to the day-to-day management of land rights.

A compromise solution has been proposed in the draft Land Rights Bill, called customary *commonhold*. This new form would vest co-ownership of land in the members of tribes or local communities. The members would not need to create a new legal entity, but instead would choose or elect a structure to manage the land as a joint asset and deal with third parties (as occurs in well-functioning customary tenure systems), and set the rules determining community membership. Under this form of tenure, communities would be free to designate traditional structures as the bodies responsible for land management, where they retain legitimacy, or to appoint some other form of management committee. In this way, headmen, chiefs, or traditional leaders would be able to play a substantive role in land management, conducting business as usual. Ownership would not be transferred to them, however, thus commonhold would ensure the rights of community members are protected from possible abuse by chiefs.

Sources: Claassens and Makopi, 1999; Ntsebeza, 1999

At the root of the problem is the fact that during the apartheid era, customary law was interpreted so as to give legal land ownership to traditional leaders, rather than to community members (Claassens and Makopi, 1999; see Chapter 13, this volume). This has created an important issue of local governance in South Africa concerning how best to ensure a separation of powers of ownership and land rights management in the former homelands (Ntsebeza, 1999). Although the new administration in South Africa is reviewing the future of the Land Rights Bill, and the future of commonhold tenure is now uncertain, finding an answer to this question of local governance will remain important in seeking to establish secure land rights for communities as a whole, as well as their individual members.

Uganda's 1998 Land Act also makes provision for the establishment of Communal Land Associations (CLAs). In this case, CLAs are intended as the vehicle whereby communities can establish secure rights of tenure over common property resources, such as grazing land for pastoral groups, such as the Karamojong. The Act also specifies, however, that individual community members can apply in their own right for a certificate of customary ownership or for freehold title. This places an onus on the community to establish and register a CLA in order to pre-empt a process of land division into individual claims, which could see the privatisation of high value key resources, such as wetlands, at the expense of the broader system viability (see Box 11.7). The approach of community land survey and registration adopted in Mozambique might provide a simpler, more cost-effective solution to the problem of securing collective land rights.

In the case of Ivory Coast, the PFR has been part of the National Village Lands Management Programme (PNGT-ER) which aims to transfer responsibility regarding land use management to village level committees, though with no parallel transfer of powers. The focus of the PFR has been predominantly on the rights of those owning or using farmland, on an individual basis. Hence the question of collective rights has not been explicitly addressed. The new legislation of December 1998 allows for the possibility of villages to register their lands in their entirety, thus avoiding the risk of finding they are on lands declared as being 'sans maitre'. However, registration must be followed by immatriculation within three years and there is no provision for collective approaches to this latter process, since the village is not considered to constitute a legal entity.

In Niger, the Code Rural makes provision for rights over home grazing areas (terroirs d'attache) in both pastoral and agricultural zones. This is defined as territory which is determined and recognised by custom or documentary evidence as being the place where a given group of pastoralists live for the major part of the year and to which they return following migration, transhumance,

---

Box 11.7: Certificates of Customary Tenure: Uganda Land Act 1998

In Uganda, from 1998, any person, family or community holding land under customary tenure on former public land may acquire a certificate of *customary ownership* in respect of that land. These certificates are important in that they provide conclusive evidence of customary rights and interests in land. Subject to the limitations identified within each certificate, land may be sold, leased, mortgaged, pledged, etc. where the customs of the community allow. In addition, the Land Act provides that any person, family, community or association holding land under customary tenure on former public land has the option to convert the customary tenure into freehold. The reverse, conversion of freehold into customary tenure, is not possible however.

Communities practising communal tenure and who wish to use land as a group, may establish common land associations to manage and protect their interests in common land. Communal land associations may be reinforced by the establishment of common management schemes for grazing and watering of livestock, hunting, gathering woodfuel, building materials and other natural resources that any member of the community may gather for use of his or her family[11]. However, there are potential contradictions between provisions for communal land associations and individual certificates of customary ownership. Where people seek individual rights (on a customary or freehold basis) to land resources which are managed communally, this runs the risk of provoking local social conflict and upheaval.

The dispute settlement mechanisms provided for under the Act do not exclude the role of traditional authorities (see further Chapter 12). The role of traditional leaders in the dispute settlement system will be important because the registration of customary rights is likely to lead to a number of controversies which will require adjudication by authorities familiar with the local principles of customary law.

Source: Mwebaza, 1999

---

or nomadism. Pastoral groups are given neither ownership nor exclusive rights over this area, but are said to have "priority" rights, though it is unclear what this means since they must also guarantee access to water and grazing by third parties[12]. In addition, there are possibilities for people to form co-operative associations or local business groupings[13] which can then establish rights to manage and exploit common resources, such as woodlands, according to an agreed set of by-laws (IIED, 1999; see also Box 5.5 on firewood markets in Niger). Equally, promising approaches to decentralised natural resource management from across the Sahel are now emerging (Hilhorst and Coulibaly, 1999; and see Box 5.7).

Successful management of collective resources, in all the above cases, depends on having a legislative and administrative framework which recognises the role of local organisations in making rules and enforcing their application.

---

11 The provisions for Communal Land Associations were not included in any of the Bills preceding the final law, but were the direct result of the lobby and advocacy work of the Uganda Land Alliance and other interest groups. This focused on the need to integrate customary and statutory tenure generally, but also catered for specific needs of unique customary practices such as those of pastoralists. The Uganda Land Alliance is a consortium of local and international NGOs with the mission of ensuring that land policies and laws are reviewed to address land rights of the poor, and to protect access to land for the vulnerable and disadvantaged groups and individuals in Uganda.
12 Décret no. 97-007/PRN/MAG/EL du 10 janvier 1997 fixant le statut des Terroirs d'Attache des pasteurs.
13 Groupements d'interêt économique.

It also relies on the existence of strong local institutions able to manage the resources in question, monitor each others' behaviour, and resolve conflicts between users.

CONCLUSIONS

A judgement must be made about the comparative cost, effectiveness, and legitimacy of different ways of providing security for customary rights-holders. There are high costs to establishing new institutions for registering and managing land, as seen from the cases discussed here, despite their aim of providing a lower cost option than that involving a formal cadastral survey and titling programme. They also demonstrate that the process of individual registration generates almost as many problems as it solves. Consequently, it may be more worthwhile to focus such programmes only on those areas where such an approach is strongly needed. There are certainly some circumstances where land registration would be of considerable value, such as where indigenous tenure arrangements are absent or extinct; where there are frequent disputes between competing claims as a result, for example, of in-migration, or inter-group conflict which are not amenable to resolution by indigenous institutions; and where project interventions, such as intensive irrigation projects have led to extensive changes in production relations (IIED, 1999). In addition, in peri-urban areas throughout sub-Saharan Africa, the rapid increase in land values provides strong encouragement for people to establish firmer claim to the land they use, and ensure they can keep hold of it. In Niger, it is noted that some people are prepared to pay for a certificate "which would free them for good from incessant disputes and family quarrels" (Ouedraogo et al, 1996).

It may make sense for customary rights to be registered at a collective level in most situations, with individual rights registration reserved for areas of particular tension and difficulty (IIED, 1999). Thought must also be given to the likely impacts of such a process on different groups, particularly those holding secondary rights of access. As seen above, there may be circumstances where registration is appropriate, because of a vacuum in local power relations, or due to a rapid escalation in land values. But in other settings, such a process may bring more harm than good, and it may be better for governments to rely to a much greater extent on existing institutions and customary arrangements. Despite its apparent objectivity, registration is not a neutral procedure which leaves social relations unchanged in its wake. The actors involved in the registration of rights will usually try to position themselves in ways which will guarantee them a favourable outcome. However, this is not a win-win game, in which everyone can become better off. Local people may seize the opportunity associated with both individual and collective rights registration to re-define the nature of their rights over resources to block access to other users. As with formal titling programmes, it is often the better off, and educated classes which can best ensure that they emerge from registration with their se-curity improved. There may also be alternative ways of registering rights, which do not necessarily involve the cost and formality associated with Niger's Land Commissions and the PFR in Ivory Coast. Thus, for example, there is in-creasing reliance in Burkina Faso on drawing up a piece of paper recording a particular transaction in land, which is then witnessed by a government offi-cial (see Chapter 5). Better targeting of registration programmes, a willing-ness to experiment with a variety of mechanisms, and defining when best to go for individual versus collective approaches provide the three major chal-lenges for future programmes.

12

Decentralisation and Land Tenure

Camilla Toulmin

INTRODUCTION

Countries throughout Africa have been undertaking reforms aimed at decentralisation of certain administrative and other government functions, following a variety of different models. These processes are at various stages across the continent, some having started long ago, while others are still in the pipeline. Such moves to decentralise have usually been undertaken for political or administrative purposes and have not had questions of land tenure and natural resource management as central objectives of the reforms. However, the establishment of these new structures and the associated changes in the distribution of responsibilities between different levels of government have inevitably had impacts on how land is managed, the allocation of rights and the distribution of powers. This chapter draws on experience with decentralisation from South Africa, Ghana, Uganda, and several Sahelian cases.

There are various models evident from the case study material regarding the linkages between decentralised local government and land administration. In some cases, the elected local government body has powers of land allocation, amongst other mandates (as happens in Senegal). In other cases, the administration of land is dealt with by a separate body, such as a Land Board, often constituted partly from elected and partly from appointed members (as in Botswana). In yet other circumstances, decentralised local government may sit alongside a continued, formal role for customary chiefs in the administration of land (such as in Ghana). As will be seen below, there are differing consequences for the effective and transparent management of land associated with each of these models.

What is decentralisation?

Various terms are used to describe the different degrees by which powers and responsibilities are transferred from higher to lower levels of government, and the forms they take. *Decentralisation* in English, describes the general process involving the transfer of power from higher to lower levels of decision-making. In French-speaking countries it is defined more narrowly and refers to the definitive transfer of decision-making powers and executive authority from a higher to a lower authority, such as from central government to local level communes (Thomson and Coulibaly, 1994). *Deconcentration* describes a process whereby responsibility for certain administrative activities and provision of services is shifted from central to lower level structures within government, but with no transfer of decision-making powers involved. An example might be provided by the Ministry of Agriculture at central government level shifting certain functions to its regional offices. *Devolution* is a form of decentralisation which involves a transfer of power from a larger to a smaller unit, and may concern all powers or a selection of certain powers (Thomson and Coulibaly, 1994). For instance, in South Africa, there is a substantial devolution of powers from national government to state levels, which provides a degree of flexibility and diversity regarding aspects of policy. In this paper, we will use decentralisation to mean the devolution of powers to local level government structures. In most African settings, decentralisation has involved the establishment of new forms of local government, such as district assemblies, rural communes or municipal authorities. These have usually been constituted by a combination of elected and appointed members, and have been allocated both tasks devolved from above, and those transferred from customary structures at village and other levels. The authority these structures can exercise varies considerably, and depends partly on how they have been constituted, partly on their being perceived as broadly representative of the interests at stake, and partly on how well they carry out their mandate.

Where has the push for decentralisation come from?

The pressure in favour of decentralisation in Africa forms part of a broader global paradigm shift in favour of subsidiarity and local participation, and a move away from the all-powerful nation state. Adherence to a decentralised approach stems from various sources, such as donor pressure in favour of good government and democratisation, and cutbacks to central government budgets. In addition, it is also generally assumed that decentralisation should bring improved problem-solving capacity which is better adapted to local conditions, generating greater incentives for economic development, and improved provision of public services (Manor, 1998).

i. *Good governance and democratisation.* Establishing local government structures which are subject to periodic re-election is seen to be a means to create a more accountable and responsive system for providing basic services to the local population. Locating these structures at a relatively low level should permit easier contact between elected representatives and the electorate, and a greater responsiveness in terms of providing services than is possible through more centralised structures. Making these officials subject to periodic re-election should ensure that once elected they continue to maintain contact with their constituents, listen to the electorate and act in an accountable fashion. Decentralisation can also be seen as a way in which the particular circumstances and balance of interests in a given locality can best be addressed, though this also depends on the powers available at this level, and the extent to which decisions by local government and other structures remain firmly subject to approval at higher levels.

ii. *Clarifying jurisdictions between different forms of local governance.* The drive by governments to do away with traditional structures has also been an important motive behind the decentralisation process (see Box 12.2 on South Africa). In some cases, setting up new political structures, on democratic principles, has created opportunities for a fresh class of political activists, often younger, educated people, not connected to traditional structures of power. Such, for example, was the composition initially of the Committees for the Defence of the Revolution in Burkina Faso, following the take-over by Thomas Sankara. Decentralisation, in contrast to its espoused objectives, may also provide a means for central government to increase its involvement in local affairs. This is particularly important where party structures and the electoral system require a single list of candidates to be chosen by the party hierarchy. In other cases, governments have sought to incorporate customary authorities within the new system of local administration, such as the role allocated to traditional chiefs within the Land Commissions in Niger, with the aim of gaining their co-operation.

iii. *Cutbacks to national budgets* have been seen by some as the major driving force behind the current interest in decentralisation, since government hopes thereby to shift certain costs and responsibilities away from central government. In this sense, decentralisation can be seen as closely linked to and a consequence of programmes of structural adjustment, and the rethinking of state-level responsibilities and ambitions which these have involved. Establishing local government may also generate increased incentives for economic development, through the mobilisation of resources from the locality as well as from elsewhere (central government grants, access to donor funding, NGOs, etc.). By demonstrating a close link between tax payment and delivery of services, it is also hoped thereby to increase local tax raising capacity.

EXPERIENCE WITH DECENTRALISATION: EVIDENCE FROM PRACTICE

Decentralised systems of local government take a wide variety of forms, depending on history, political and institutional cultures, the purpose underlying the reforms, and the length of time since the process began. Equally, there are varying patterns regarding how far local government is involved in land administration. For example, local government in Uganda is based on a five-tier structure of elected local councils running down from District to Parish levels (Nsamba-Gayiiya, 1999). The legislation of 1998 also requires the creation of a large number of new Land Boards and Committees in Uganda. These have been designed to shift the focus of land management to the local level and provide for effective community involvement in land decisions. These institutions have had to be created from scratch and set in place almost immediately. Very little recognition has been given to the role of customary institutions and authorities in land rights management in the Land Act (see Box 12.5; Mwebaza 1999).

In Senegal, the Rural Councils are the lowest level of government and are responsible, first and foremost, for the allocation of use rights to land and resources, as well as for land use planning, i.e. the ability to reserve certain areas of the municipal land for specific purposes. In addition, they also have the power to regulate local markets, cattle routes and residential zoning patterns, and to finance local community projects through the rural council budget. Nevertheless, the state maintains considerable powers over decisions made by the Rural Council, which remains under the authority of the government's local administrator, or *sous-préfet* (Juul, 1999: 167).

The impacts and consequences of current decentralisation measures vary greatly depending on the extent to which these new forms of local government can acquire a sense of legitimacy vis-à-vis local people and other sources of local governance (such as traditional chiefs), how far central government supports the process in practice, as well as the extent to which they can actually carry out the activities expected of them. In some countries, these new forms of local government have an important mandate in relation to land, whereas elsewhere they have little power in this field. Decentralisation in many countries is a relatively recent policy shift, undertaken by many countries only in the late 1980s and 90s. This means it may take more than just a few years to start to see significant impacts from these institutional changes. Below, a number of issues are presented which relate to experience with decentralisation to date, and the impact of such reforms on questions of land administration.

Good governance, accountability, and the responsiveness of elected officials to local people

One of the main expressed purposes underlying decentralisation is to increase the responsiveness of local government activities, provision of services, and planning of development in ways which respond more closely to local people's priorities. Yet it is not clear how far, in practice, such capacity and willingness to listen and respond are actually fostered. For example, a survey of several communes in Ivory Coast showed that there were no regular means by which elected councillors met with their constituents. Equally, the priority actions put forward by councillors for the commune to undertake were frequently considerably at odds with the expressed priorities of local people (Crook, 1995). For instance, local councillors wanted to build town halls and secondary schools, while local people said they wanted roads, social infrastructure, markets, electricity and water. This disparity in expectations is due partly to limited contact with constituents but also to the lack of information amongst the general public regarding what local government has the mandate to deliver.

A survey of several Sahelian countries confirms the weak communication links existing between local councillors and their electorate. In some cases, independent candidates are not allowed to stand for local election, thereby ensuring that all candidates have to be members of one of the main parties and subject to their discipline and control (Ribot, 1999). This has led to the politicisation of rural council business, and a strong tendency for councillors to look upwards to their political masters rather than downwards to the local population.

In a study of District Assemblies in Ghana, which were established in 1988, the District Secretary (DS) who is appointed by central government was perceived to be the most important member of the Assembly, given his status as chairman of the executive committee and of the district administration (Ayee, 1996: 38). This research also notes a tendency amongst elected members of the District Assemblies to go along with the views expressed by the nominated members, who usually have a comparatively better level of education and professional experience. Indeed, in both the District Assemblies studied, the group of appointed members formed the hub around which local government activities revolved. This meant that local people saw no point in attending village meetings to discuss development priorities, since their views would carry no weight (Ayee, 1996).

Several writers have noted the need for some means to educate both the electorate and elected councillors regarding the responsibilities, duties and expectations of the various parties. This needs to recognise the importance of transferring practical skills and ways of communicating to enable local government officers and councillors to operate effectively, rather than focusing on more formal educational aspects alone (McCourt and Sola, 1999). For example, in Tanzania, a series of training events is underway aimed at introducing elected councillors to the four dimensions of their role: balancing the needs of various stakeholders (both local and national); the constitutional and legal requirements which define their areas of responsibility and power; technical skills such as financial management, strategic planning and running effective meetings; and leadership skills, to mobilise constituents, reflect the varied priorities of groups within the ward, and manage relationships with council staff (Taylor, 1999).

Equally, raising awareness within local community groups is an important task, given the need to ensure they understand the powers and mandate of new local government structures, and to provide checks on local government action. An example of this kind of activity can be seen from current work in Senegal being carried out by a couple of NGOs, who specialise in working on civic education with people newly literate in the local Fulfulde language (see Box 12:1). This example shows the importance of tailoring materials to the interests and capacities of newly literate people, and the wide range of skills of potential benefit to them (including financial management, and leadership skills). It also demonstrates the importance of strengthening capacity at village level, as a means to support the decentralisation process, while providing a means to balance the powers attributed to local government.

Experience from South Africa shows the difficulties faced by elected rural councillors, many of whom must cover a wide area of scattered villages and have few resources at their disposal. Many settlements are often inaccessible, with little or no transport or telephone links. In addition, the poor remuneration of councillors makes it difficult to attract people of calibre, an issue also raised by Kante (1997) pointing to the low level of educational qualifications and skills of local government staff in Senegal. In Tanzania, local government staff face great difficulties in carrying out their jobs effectively, and miss many of the most basic office necessities. As a result, of those surveyed, many reckoned to gain only some 20% of their income from salary, and spent only 10% of their day actually in the workplace (McCourt and Sola, 1999).

In the case of Uganda, new local government legislation came into force in 1997, creating new structures and bringing in many new people at local government level. This group of administrators had not been involved in the formulation of the new land law, despite their now being made responsible for its

> **Box 12.1: Community education for decentralisation in Senegal**
>
> i. *Local land use planning* consists of a training module to explore issues of resource tenure, access and management at the community level. The module is based on using participatory research and planning tools to help promote the shared management of common property resources. The training will enable community members to analyse their situation in relation to the existing tenure situation and the extent to which they have secure access to the resources necessary for their livelihoods. It will also explore ways in which they can improve this through negotiated, consensual arrangements with other user groups.
>
> ii. *Alternative conflict management and peace building* focuses on helping communities to analyse conflicts especially related to natural resource access, and to build local institutional capacity to manage disputes. The training provides support to communities in three areas:
>   - improved understanding of current legislation and administrative procedures regulating access to resources;
>   - ability to analyse conflicts between different resource users in order to be better equipped to manage them in a consensual manner; and,
>   - improved negotiation and mediation skills in order to identify win-win solutions to latent and actual conflict situations.
>
> iii. *Local organisational capacity building* seeks to reinforce the institutional capacity of community-based organisations and covers ten specific skills: ** Oral communication skills for community awareness raising exercises; ** Written communication skills for report writing, minute taking, etc.; ** Adult education to raise literacy levels; ** Group dynamics; ** Participatory learning; ** Financial management skills; ** Research and analytical skills; ** Planning skills; ** Organisational skills for implementing plans; and ** Leadership skills to help key resource people to work effectively within the community.
>
> iv. *Decentralisation training* has the purpose to inform and train local people and their elected officials in the legal and administrative provisions provided by the reform processes. Information is provided on the implications of, and the legal provisions within decentralisation legislation for natural resource management.
>
> Source: ARED/CERFLA, 1999

implementation. This has created a problem in terms of ensuring effective knowledge regarding the provisions of the legislation, as well as ensuring that they implement the law with enthusiasm (Mutyaba, 1999).

Clarifying jurisdictions between different forms of local governance

In many countries, the establishment of new district assemblies or councils has provided a means by which central government tries to bypass customary structures of authority, and break the power of traditional chiefs. Yet the legitimacy of new institutions and their ability to exercise power effectively take time to establish. Traditional ways of doing things cannot be changed over-night.

The role and powers of customary structures vary greatly between countries, and even between regions within given countries. In some cases, traditional structures of power appear to have lost their social legitimacy, as a result of failing in their customary responsibilities (see Box 12.2). Thus, for example, customary chiefs in Cameroon have started selling land which many people consider is not really their to sell, since it is held in trust for the larger clan (Egbe, forthcoming). In many parts of Ghana, paramount chiefs have retained important formal powers so that, for example, all land transactions must continue to be registered and validated by the Community Lands Secretariat. In peri-urban areas, there is evidence of customary chiefs colluding with property developers to take land for commercial purposes, while paying little or no compensation to displaced families. Although constitutional provisions debar the chiefs from receiving monetary considerations from the land purchasers, payment in the form of "drinks money" is a means of getting round this provision (Kasanga, 1999).

In some cases, customary chiefs have been adept in ensuring that they acquire power within newly created structures of power, and manage to get themselves elected to local government. In Burkina Faso, for example, it was found that the village level committees for managing land were usually controlled by the family of "notables"; though in contrast to the previous system, they were represented by an educated younger son, rather than by an elder (Faure, 1992).

The establishment of new local governmental structures raises many questions concerning the articulation between these and pre-existing structures. As Zimmermann notes, "one of the greatest challenges for each country's land policy ... is to make proper allowances for indigenous land principles amidst rapid change" (1999). It is important to ask how the rights and responsibilities of local government link to customary structures at village and other levels. In the case of Mali, de Leener (1999) notes the establishment of Rural Communes and their elected mayors and councillors now constitute a new set of actors seeking power within an already crowded field, and with whom village leaders will have to negotiate a new set of roles. In practice, in many circumstances, local councils will have to rely for day-to-day management on village level structures. Under the decentralisation legislation in Mali, rural communes are able to draw up contracts with lower level structures to take responsibility for managing certain resources. In some cases, where there are resources of considerable value, tensions are likely to develop between rural communes and local villages. For example, villages with a large area of land under fallow may find the commune eager to allocate these resources to others seeking farmland. Equally, villages with well-protected woodlands may find that the commune wishes to earn fees from sales of wood-cutting permits in what villagers have considered to be "their" woodland. It is not clear where the revenue from any such fees will be lodged. In Ghana, District Assemblies were made responsible for registering chainsaw operations and issuing licences for

> **Box 12.2: The abuse of power by traditional leaders in South Africa**
>
> Recognising the powers of traditional leaders has a number of far-reaching implications for control over land allocation, democratic local government and gender equality. Chiefly authority in South Africa is ascribed by lineage rather than achieved through election, and its patriarchal principles ensure that major decisions on land allocation and local government are almost invariably taken by men alone. Widespread abuse of power and corruption by traditional leaders, especially after the introduction of the Bantu Authorities Act in 1951 which led to self-government and "independence" of some Bantustans, is well documented. Although chiefs responded in a variety of ways to colonisation, the implementation of the Bantu Authorities Act firmly enlisted them as the local arm of the central state, thereby restricting their independence. As the apartheid state became vicious, so did many traditional leaders. Rather than winning reverence and legitimacy, traditional leaders became feared by most rural people.
>
> A feature of rural local government during the apartheid period, and to some extent the colonial period, was the concentration or fusion of administrative, judicial and executive power in a single functionary, the Tribal Authority. This fusion is well captured by Mamdani in what he calls "decentralised despotism" or the "bifurcated state", namely, the Native Authority:
>
> "Not only did the chief have the right to pass rules (bylaws) governing persons under his domain, he also executed all laws and was the administrator in "his" area, in which he settled all disputes. The authority of the chief thus fused in a single person all moments of power, judicial, legislative, executive, and administrative. This authority was like a clenched fist, necessary because the chief stood at the intersection of the market economy and the non-market one. The administrative justice and the administrative coercion that were the sum and substance of his authority lay behind a regime of extra-economic coercion, a regime that breathed life into a whole range of compulsions: forced labour, forced crops, forced sales, forced contributions, and forced removals" (Mamdani, 1996).
>
> It is now a constitutional requirement that elected local government structures be "established for the whole of the territory of the Republic", and that a person or community whose tenure of land is insecure as a result of racial laws or practices should have their tenure legally secured. Thus, rural elected councillors called Transitional Representative Councillors (TrepCs) have been elected in most of the former Bantustans, and the Department of Land Affairs is in the process of promulgating legislation that will create various options to ensure tenure security for rural people.
> Source: Ntsebeza, 1999

felling trees on farm land. However, this was done indiscriminately, since they were largely seen as a means of raising much needed revenues. In this way, timber operators increasingly encroached onto farming land, causing damage to the fields and felling trees with impunity (Amanor, forthcoming).

In Senegal, while land may be owned by the state, day-to-day management is devolved to elected rural councils, who establish local rules for the allocation and reallocation of land to rural users, according to their capacity to render the land productive. However, in practice, the reality may be somewhat different, since the Rural Council finds it difficult to exert its authority.

It is difficult to talk of rules in relation to the Rural Council, for among Fulanis, people do not follow what is written down. Formally it is the

Rural Council who should decide everything in relation to the management of the territory here. But that is not possible because of Fulani solidarity. People should make a request before settling in the area. But people just settle where they feel like. (Agropastoralist and Rural Council former President quoted in Juul, 1999)

It is not just a question of how local government articulates with customary structures, but also the distribution of powers within formal structures. At local government level in Tanzania, "legislation does not clearly spell out the division of functions and responsibilities between councillors and officers, resulting in overlapping of functions" (McCourt and Sola, 1999). There is also the issue of overlapping powers with those of other governmental structures. Again in Tanzania, reforms of local government over the last two decades have meant that despite the re-establishment of elected councils in 1984, other levels of government and party hierarchy continue to survive, so that there is considerable duplication of functions between councils, regional directorates, the party structure, and central government ministries (ibid.). In Uganda, tensions also exist between different levels of government, such as local government structures and national ministries regarding the management of forest reserves, and division of revenue derived from land fees (Nsamba-Gayiiya, 1999).

In several countries, rural councils can only play an advisory role, and require approval regarding the decisions they make from the government administrator at a higher level (Ribot, 1999). Equally, when it comes to managing certain resources, such as forests, decision-making and management may rest in the hands of the government's technical services with very little room for local councils to decide who can have access to such resources. This stems from an entrenched belief on the part of the government that it is too risky to hand over valuable resources to local people.

Financial autonomy and taxable capacity

Local government must raise funds in order to implement its priorities. It was noted earlier that one of the factors underlying the decentralisation process has been the cutbacks in central government budgets consequent on structural adjustment programmes, and the desire to shift certain costs from central to local levels. On a lesser scale this has been happening for some time in relation to the imposition of user charges for particular services, such as for veterinary care, or water fees (e.g. Ferlo bore-holes, in Senegal).

In practice, local government funding continues to rely heavily on central government grants, given the lack of any other options. In Southern Africa, wildlife revenues can provide a significant source of revenue for particular district councils and villages which have the good fortune to be host to large animal populations. Under the Communal Areas Management Programme for Indigenous Resources (CAMPFIRE) set up in Zimbabwe, rural communities directly receive income related to use and management of wildlife. An important lesson from CAMPFIRE has been that the management authority and rights to benefit need to be devolved to the lowest possible unit to have the maximum impact on people's behaviour with respect to conservation of natural resources. In some cases, Rural District Councils have held on to revenue and management rights, rather than devolving these to lower ward level (Jones, 1999: 4). In Namibia, 1996 legislation provides for rights over wildlife and tourism to be given to communal area residents who form a "conservancy", represented by an elected committee. The composition of these committees is entirely defined by the local communities and does not depend on local government approval. Whereas in the past, income generating opportunities with respect to wildlife resources have depended on the goodwill of government or the private sector, now the acquisition of conservancy status gives communities greater opportunities to generate income directly (Jones, 1999).

However, for many other areas, there are few resources on which tax revenue can be raised. Hence, local communes are bound to find themselves seriously constrained in terms of what they can undertake by the availability of revenue from higher levels. They may also often find very limited room for manoeuvre regarding their ability to vary tax rates according to circumstances.

With funds continuing to come mainly from central government, local councils will remain firmly indebted to national political concerns, with very limited room for autonomy. Elected officials are likely to take most heed from the places and people from which they gain their funds, further weakening the link between them and the local electorate. For example, Crook notes for Ivory Coast that after ten years of decentralisation, and despite cutbacks in central government funding of local communes, such funds still constituted 58% of total receipts. There were serious problems faced in trying to raise additional revenue from the local community, with some people considering that, since their candidate had not won the mayoral race, they therefore should not have to pay local taxes (1995). Even where "taxes" are being levied against provision of a service, such as water for livestock in Senegal, committees experience great difficulties in both raising revenue from water users and then ensuring that the funds received are allocated for bore-hole maintenance and upgrading (Juul, 1999).

Land taxes have been proposed by some as providing a basis for increased local government revenue. In the case of Senegal, Tano notes the difficulties being faced by rural councils in raising much money. Local councillors are caught in a bind, being reluctant to press their electors for tax payments while, equally, wanting resources to build social infrastructure and carry out development projects. He notes a marked contrast in tax raising performance between, on the one hand, the traditional levies which continue to be paid by many land users, such as the tithe and fees to the land chief and, on the other, government imposed taxes. One reason for the better performance of the former may be due to the role which such levies play in cementing social structures and relationships which people continue to value. Equally, each person within the hierarchy gains some part of the levy and, hence, has an interest in making it work. By contrast, the formal government tax system seems like "an alien system grafted onto a pattern of social organisation it hopes to transform" (Tano, forthcoming). At the same time, there is no particular incentive for those within the hierarchy to raise revenue, since they gain no share of this sum. In the case of Senegal, the absence of a market in land makes it difficult to assess its value and, hence, the level at which any land-based tax might be imposed, making such a system even harder to implement (ibid).

In the case of Ivory Coast, one of the initial goals of the Rural Land Plan (*Plan Foncier Rural,* PFR) was to provide the information necessary to set up a system of land taxation. However, this seems to have been abandoned at an early stage because of the worry that people would be tempted to give biased information regarding their holdings if they knew this would form the basis for subsequent tax assessment.

Impacts of decentralisation on allocation of land

Various models have been developed for managing the allocation of land at district and local government levels, such as Land Boards in Botswana, Land Commissions in Niger, and the Rural Council itself in Senegal. A key question concerns the extent to which there is a clear separation of powers between the local council and the land administration body. This separation is recognised by many as critically important in reducing possibilities for corrupt behaviour, as where elected officials use their powers to allocate land to reward political allies. Control over land and its allocation "empowers and legitimates local authorities..." (Ribot, 1999) by providing them with control over a very important asset for allocation to friends and clients. The temptations of using land allocation as a means of rewarding friends and allies has a long history, and often formed the basis of feudal regulation, such as found in Imperial Ethiopia. It remains of great importance, as can be seen by the conflicting views in South Africa, regarding whether to opt for tribal authorities, or elected local government structures as the body responsible for land administration (see Box 12.3 and Chapter 13).

Box 12.3: The strong need for the separation of powers: the case of South Africa

By establishing democratically elected local government with "development functions" and democracy in decision making regarding land, the intention of post-1994 South Africa is to introduce a separation of powers and democracy in the form of elected government and control over land, even in rural areas. At least on paper, this is a major departure from a single powerful Tribal Authority where almost none of the officials have been democratically elected. Of course, traditional leaders are not happy with this new system. They see rural elected councillors and the extension of democracy to land issues as deeply threatening attempts to undermine their political and economic powers. The refusal of traditional leaders to accept government policies and legislation is at the heart of current debate on tenure reform in South Africa's countryside.

Source: Ntsebeza, 1999

Land Boards provide a means of decentralising the management of land and land rights to district level, and below. Land Boards have authority to approve land allocations and transfers locally, according to specific, centrally established rules and procedures. Membership is usually drawn from central government representatives with a more limited number of elected representatives. Land Boards do not necessarily constitute a devolved form of authority over land matters, since they do not have the powers to determine district level policies, for example. Very often they substitute for, or supervise, land management by customary authorities at local level, and they may incorporate customary chiefs or their representatives as members. The extent to which the establishment of Land Boards constitutes an improvement in local management depends upon how representative is their membership and how transparent and accountable are their operations. In principle, by bringing land administration closer to the people, and with provision for local representatives, yet remaining independent of both local government and customary authorities, they offer opportunities to establish more open and effective governance in land matters. Land Boards are discussed more fully in Chapter 10.

In Niger, the Land Commissions are not elected bodies, but instead are formed by appointed representatives from the various technical service agencies. They perform a number of functions, including allocating land and registering title (see Chapter 11). However, at the same time traditional chiefs (canton and village chiefs) continue to play a role in settlement of disputes over many issues, including land, whereas the Commissions do not have a conflict resolution role. It is noted that chiefs value and exploit this role since they can gain revenue from the different parties to a dispute as part of the settlement process. While elections to new decentralised rural communes were held in February 1999, they are yet to be formally established.

In Uganda, the Land Act has created a very large number of new institutions for administering land, such as District Land Boards and a Land Committee for each Parish, gazetted urban area, and each division of Kampala city, as well as

---

Box 12.4: Managing land allocations in Senegal

In Senegal, Rural Councils were set up by legislation in 1972. Although originally one third of their members were appointed, since 1996 all councillors have been subject to election. In principle, they enjoy considerable authority over land, being responsible for the allocation of use rights over land, as well as land use planning, such as the marking out of cattle routes, and of residential zones, as well as financing development projects. In practice, however such powers are considerably muted. The president of the council is under the authority of the *sous-préfet* (the government administrator for a larger district). Large areas of land within the territory covered by the council are gazetted forest or game reserves, and therefore remain under the direct authority of the state, through the Forestry Services. The councils also dispose of few financial and logistical means by which to carry through their different responsibilities. The council budget is meant to come from a rural tax, but this is fixed by central government and is so limited that few, if any, development projects can be actually carried out.

The legal framework within which councils are meant to carry out their functions is both contradictory and ambiguous. The council agrees land allocations on the basis of whether the applicant is able to make good use of the land *(mettre en valeur)*. Some farmers have been able to make claims for very large areas of land which they have no means of farming, while others seize the opportunity of cultivating much larger tracts than those formally attributed. In contrast to cultivation, the grazing of land is not considered putting land to good use and, therefore, pastoralists have seen large areas of former grazing converted to farmland. Despite regulations on the prohibition to cultivate close to cattle tracks and wells, in practice these provisions are ignored. Certain powerful religious and commercial groups have benefited particularly from the willingness by local councils to turn a blind eye to the formal rules being broken.

Source: Juul, 1999

---

tribunals at district, sub-county and urban areas. However, there remains a major imbalance between the extensive legal provisions, and capacity on the ground to implement the new law. There is also a lack of clarity regarding the degree of autonomy that local government can exercise regarding land issues. Since 'land' is defined as constituting a national function under the Ugandan Constitution of 1995, it is not clear how much room for manoeuvre exists for local councils to vary regulations and by-laws according to local circumstances. Despite the difficulties in matching the high ambitions of the Land Act with limited local capacities, there has been great reluctance to use existing customary mechanisms, although these provide a well-tried and tested system of decision-making (see Box 12.5).

CONCLUSION

There are several potential models for the role of decentralised bodies in relation to land administration. The first involves the establishment of a new set of institutions, with a broad range of powers, including those to allocate and manage land. While this option has the advantage of starting afresh, the setting

---

Box 12.5: Integrating customary powers and local government roles in Uganda

In Uganda, in spite of the elaborate administration and dispute settlement mechanism set up under the Act, there is very little room provided for the involvement of traditional institutions. Land tribunals may pass on to traditional authorities the cases which they think fall within their jurisdiction, but this can only be done at the discretion of the tribunals. The same applies to the administrative set up. The Act only provides that "the parish committee may, in the exercise of its functions in relation to application for a certificate of customary ownership, refer any matter to any customary institution habitually accepted within the parish as an institution with functions over land for its advice and, where relevant, use it with or without adaptations."

Again the role of the traditional authorities is relegated to the periphery. They can only enter the administrative structure at the discretion of the parish land committee, which even then is not bound to accept their recommendations. For an Act which goes to great length to integrate customary with statutory tenure, it fails to utilise existing traditional institutions. Most tribes in Uganda have well-developed administrative and dispute settlement mechanisms, which the Act could have used, as shown below.

In Karamoja, land administration and dispute resolution are traditionally handled by the Ekokwe or Akiriket, an assembly of initiated male elders. These elders are well known and respected in their areas and follow clear procedures in their administration and dispute settlement mechanism, which also provides for appeals. The ultimate authority in Karamoja is the council of representatives from the ten territories (the Ekiriket and Ekitala). This body would therefore be the parallel for the district Land Board under the Land Act, with the assembly of elders, the Ekokwe or Akiriket, being parallel to the parish land committees under the Land Act.

In Gulu, dispute resolution is implemented independently of the Land Administration system. Locally appointed chiefs - Rwot Kweri (Chiefs of Hoes) - are responsible for allocating and verifying the boundaries of fields for cultivation while clan leaders (Rwodi Kaka) handle disputes. In Gulu, the highest authority is the senior clan leader, which coincides with the county level, which could well parallel the parish committees under the Act. Although the system does not have a parallel with the District Land Board, the parish parallel could well serve a useful function especially since it is at the parish level that the actual work of verifying peoples' rights in land will be carried out.

The failure to integrate traditional authorities into the administration of the Land Act is likely to lead to avoidable expenses in terms of time, money and human resources. Building on these and other available systems would have played a big role in the implementation of the Act especially on provisions relating to customary tenure. Customary systems do have problems of their own, notably the exclusion of women, the poor and the young in decision making. However, building on the existing infrastructure and adopting best practices while rejecting those which are inconsistent with good governance and natural justice, would have provided many benefits for the implementation of the Land Act especially at the initial stage.

Source: Mwebaza, 1999

---

up of these structures can be costly and slow, requiring considerable resources and personnel. They represent a substantial concentration of powers in a single structure, bringing risks of political patronage. Some checks may be provided through the role of higher level government administrators (as in the case of Senegal), or by continued *de facto* reliance on village chiefs for much day-to-day decision-making. But these new decentralised institutions may also find themselves in contest with customary sources of power and take a long while to establish their legitimacy amongst the population.

The second model involves the creation of a body at local level, separate from the local government administration, in the form of a Land Board or Land Commission. These structures are usually part-appointed and part-elected. Since they only deal with land allocation, they have the advantage of being less caught up in the broader range of activities and interests undertaken by local government. This should ensure some distance from the temptations of local politics and patronage. However, they may not adequately represent the priorities and views of all groups within the area, as well as being granted very limited authority.

A third model for local land management and decentralisation is based on customary leaders continuing to be responsible for land issues alongside an elected local government structure, which deals with service delivery and other matters. This model has the advantage of being familiar and cheap, since it does not require the establishment of new organisations. However, reliance on customary structures for land allocation is at potential risk from abuse of power by chiefs. They may also fail to listen to the views of those people who have lesser status in customary society, such as women, younger men, and recent settlers. There is also the risk of tension between the two systems of authority – one customary and based on heredity, the other elected – which may generate areas of overlapping jurisdiction.

Key factors underlying the choice between different options concern the need for a separation of powers to reduce the risks of corrupt practice; ways to ensure the needs of the broader population are given due weight; the constitution of a set of rules by which people agree to be bound which are known and understood and which clearly define the distribution of responsibilities between the different parties; and the cost of establishing and resourcing new institutions, in circumstances of tight budgetary constraints. In addition, ways to assure some level of accountability need to be addressed. Despite their apparent democratic appeal, there is no guarantee that elected officials will, in practice, listen and respond to the local population, since political processes and funding sources will mean they tend to look upwards, to higher levels of power.

There are unlikely to be perfect answers to the question of how best to organise local government and its responsibilities in relation to land, given differences in history, as well as economic, environmental and political circumstances. Second best solutions are inevitable in seeking a balance between building on existing structures while rendering them more representative, and avoiding the concentration of powers in a single structure, while preventing too wide a dispersion of powers and responsibilities amongst bodies which then contest each other's mandates. Whatever set of structures is chosen, attention should be paid to providing information, training and support to those at village level to ensure they know how powers are meant to be exercised and by whom. This should provide some guarantee that the potential benefits of decentralisation and land administration stand a chance of being achieved.

.

13

South African Proposals for Tenure Reform: The Draft Land Rights Bill

Aninka Claassens

Postscript: This chapter was first written in January 1999. In May 1999, the President of South Africa, Mr Thabo Mbeki, appointed a new Cabinet. He replaced the former Minister for Agriculture and Land Affairs, Mr Derek Hanekom, with a new Minister, Ms Thoko Didiza. Shortly after she had been appointed, the new Minister brought to a halt the work on the tenure proposals described in this paper. Instead, a new tenure framework is being developed providing, among other things, for the transfer of land to "tribes". No information about the proposed framework is yet available. The proposals described in the paper are therefore not the current proposals of the South African government through its Department of Land Affairs. The chapter describes the proposals and their status, as at February 1999.

INTRODUCTION

One of the most enduring legacies of colonialism and apartheid in South Africa is a dual system of property rights. The system of freehold title dominates the 80% of the country previously reserved for white people. However, a system of state ownership and permit based occupation applies in the 13% of the country which was formerly reserved for black South Africans[1]. This land is the former "homeland" areas and includes certain areas which were owned by the South African Development Trust (SADT) and were due to have been added to the homelands. Although there are significant differences between the

---

1 The other 7% is reserved for public purposes such as conservation and defence.

provinces, it is largely in the ex-homeland provinces that communal and traditional systems of land rights continue to operate. In some areas traditional
systems have all but disappeared or have been profoundly altered.

The degree of pressure and overcrowding on this land is exceptional even
by comparison with neighbouring countries in Southern Africa. In one of the
former homelands, QwaQwa, the population was over 320 people per square
km in 1980, and it has grown substantially since then[2]. This land pressure has
severely compromised the ability of indigenous systems of land rights to function effectively, in addition to the impacts of apartheid measures.

Clearly the first priority of land reform must be to change the 13% - 80%
disparity, so that black people are able to own substantial land in the 80% previously reserved for whites, and the pressure in the ex-homeland areas is re-
lieved. To this end, the Department of Land Affairs has three major
programmes. The first is redistribution, which focuses specifically on poor
black people acquiring land within the areas formerly reserved for whites. The
second is restitution, which aims to restore people to land from which they
were forcibly removed. Over three and half million people were removed from
land within the "white" 80% into the "black" 13%. Restitution therefore is
also redistributive. The third programme is tenure reform, which aims to alter
the nature of rights to land within the country as a whole. Various tenure laws
have been introduced to secure the occupation rights of farm workers and other
vulnerable people living on private land within the 80%[3].

Tenure problems in the "thirteen percent"

This chapter focuses on a particular aspect of tenure reform - the nature of
land rights in the 13%: the ex-homeland and SADT areas. About 12.7 million
people live in these areas which are by far the poorest parts of South Africa.

Virtually all the land in these ex-homeland areas is state owned[4], and there
is confusion and lack of clarity about the status of occupants' rights. Whilst
some people have permits to occupy the land under a system called "Permission to Occupy" (PTO)[5], this system has broken down entirely in some areas.
A significant proportion of people living in the ex-homeland areas do not have
PTOs or any other documented right to the land which could be used to show

---

2 This is compared with 17 people per square km in the "white" 80% at that time (Wilson and Ramphele, 1989: 37).
3 The Land Reform (Labour Tenants) Act of 1996 and the Extension of Security of Tenure Act of 1997.
4 There are some notable exceptions where groups of people or "tribes" managed to purchase land in these areas, or where previous governments awarded land as a reward for service in battles or other forms of "good behaviour". However the state prohibited black people from being able to own the land directly and it was (and still is) generally held "in trust on their behalf".
5 Introduced by the Bantu Areas Land Regulations. Proclamation no R188/1969.

the proof of tenure rights necessary to qualify for government housing subsidies, or papers that could be used in court to challenge evictions or confiscation of fields and other use rights. In any event, the PTO system is derived from apartheid. It provides only for permit-based rights which can be cancelled by the state, and which are inadequate for accessing loans or housing subsidies.

In South Africa, there are major disputes about who owns and controls communal land. In the Deeds Registers the land is generally shown as owned by the "Republic of South Africa". This has sometimes been interpreted by provincial governments to mean that the land can be used for housing projects, and by local governments to mean that they can allocate the land to people under individual title. Some government departments have assumed that since the land is state-owned, they can dispose of it or make it available to foreign investors in exchange for investment in infrastructure[6]. There has been strong resistance to these assumptions, and the actions based upon them. Occupants generally insist that the land belongs to them. They have accused the new government structures of continuing in the colonial and apartheid traditions of denying indigenous land rights and illegal confiscation of land.

The lack of clarity about the status of land rights jeopardises local development projects such as water schemes, schools, clinics and housing schemes. Traditional leaders oppose local government development initiatives on the grounds that they undermine pre-existing land rights, while local governments complain that traditional leaders act as gate-keepers and stop any form of development because it undermines their authority. Such disputes often lead either to violence, or to long delays.

In 1996, Parliament enacted the Interim Protection of Informal Land Rights Act as a holding measure to protect rights and interests in land which are not adequately protected in law, pending more far-reaching tenure reform measures. This Act provides that people holding informal rights to land cannot be deprived of that right except with their consent, or by expropriation (which implies the right to compensation)[7]. Furthermore, in 1997 the Minister of Land Affairs (as the nominal owner of much of the land in question) issued a document[8] to the provinces and to other departments which explained that he could not "sign off" any transactions in relation to communal areas which were not

---

6 One example was a development initiative in the Eastern Cape where the government planned to cede scenic areas of communal land to investors as tourism sites in exchange for the investors building a provincial road.
7 Informal rights are broadly defined to include permit based rights such as PTOs, trust beneficiaries, and occupation or use arising from "tribal, customary or indigenous law or practice", or from custom, usage or administrative practice as well as a catch all category of beneficial occupation of land for not less than 5 years.
8 Interim Procedures governing land development decisions which require the consent of the Minister of Land Affairs as nominal owner of the Land. (Document approved by the Policy Committee of the Department of Land Affairs on the 20 November 1997)

authorised by a majority of the occupants of the area. The document detailed a process of consultation which must be followed to ensure that the decision is representative of the majority of rights holders.

Rather than being proactive, these measures are protective; they maintain the status quo. However, there are many demands that the system of "feudal" ownership by the state be abolished in favour of a new system which clearly sets out the content of land rights in the former homeland areas. Many communities whose land is held in trust by the state demand that the land be transferred to them in direct ownership. Entrepreneurial farmers within communal areas demand that they be given title to areas which they currently cultivate. Traditional leaders demand that the land be transferred from the state to the tribal authorities, or to the tribes themselves[9]. Individuals in the communal systems demand stronger individual rights, both in order to be able to access state housing subsidies and loans, and because in some areas they complain of human rights abuses by traditional leaders under communal systems. This demand has been particularly strong from women, because of the way in which most traditional systems discriminate against them. Yet, in other instances, people support the communal system and want it to continue, but with stronger land rights and more democratic procedures.

The only thing that these various and sometimes conflicting demands have in common is that people want a transfer of rights from the state, and rights which are documented and secure so that they cannot be denied or interfered with. Of course, tenure security is more than just protection from interference. Benefits resulting from development must also be allocated. At the moment, money accruing from leases or transactions with third parties generally does not go to the community or people with informal rights, but accrues to the National Treasury because the land is considered a state asset. This inhibits not only transactions with investors, but also internal rental markets. Other forms of revenue, for example from mining or issuing PTOs to outsiders for business purposes, also accrues to the state[10]. The present government recognises that this is anomalous and unfair, and in some instances administrative arrangements have been made to redress this. However, changes to the law are necessary to deal with the issue of commercial land use comprehensively.

Another problem is that investors - whether local people or external agents - are loath to rely on the current option of PTO permits, which are in any event

---

9 Tribal Authorities are institutions set up under the Bantu Authorities Act of 1951. This legislation was widely and physically opposed by traditional leaders, rural communities and the ANC (African National Congress) when it was introduced because of the way in which it interfered with traditional systems, particularly as it was used to depose traditional leaders who opposed the government and replace them with "yes men".
10 The exception is where the land is registered as held in trust for a particular community or tribe - referred to under footnote 4. In such cases the land is considered private land and the revenue should accrue to the community or tribe. In many instances even this revenue is locked up in government trust accounts.

exceedingly difficult to obtain, because of the disintegration of the old land administration bureaucracy. Neither financial institutions nor the government housing subsidy scheme recognise PTOs as adequate security for loans or investment.

The Proposed Land Rights Bill - some challenges

The Ministry of Land Affairs has been keenly aware of the problems outlined above, and aware that land tenure constraints are inhibiting investment and development in the poorest parts of South Africa. However, as stated in the 1997 White Paper on Land Reform, land tenure reform will have far-reaching and perhaps unpredictable consequences and must be managed with care. Thus a two-year period (mid 1996-mid 1998) was set aside for investigation and consultation. Thereafter, the process of drafting legislation was begun to clarify the status of land rights in the ex-homeland areas and to enhance security of tenure. This resulted in draft legislative proposals known as the Land Rights Bill.

A critical challenge in the policy process was how to recognise and confirm underlying land rights in a way which provides real security, but does not undermine the social values and systems which provide a critical safety net for the poor. It was well understood that land titling schemes can lead to increased landlessness, either because the poor are excluded or because they sell their land in order to meet their basic survival needs[11].

A related challenge was to find a way of reconciling the Western system of property rights, based on exclusive ownership and registration, with more flexible and process-driven African systems of relative rights.

A DISCUSSION OF CHANGES DURING THE POLICY FORMULATION PROCESS

Issues of ownership

In South Africa, more than in many other African countries, the system of private ownership of land is dominant. This is not just because most land is privately owned, but because the economic and financial system is premised on this basis and neither recognises nor is geared towards other forms of land rights. The value of private ownership is also deeply entrenched at an ideological level. This is partly because of relatively recent experience of forced re-

---

11 This is a general problem in Africa (see Okoth-Ogendo, 1986).

movals[12] and massive government intervention in land rights. Many South Africans regard private ownership (whether group or individually held) as a "first class" system and the types of rights (such as PTOs) created for the ex-homeland areas, as second class rights. These other types of rights have never been registered within the national Deeds registry system, but only in "home-land' registries, many of which have not been maintained. Records have also been burnt or "lost" in periods of political instability (Claassens, 1991).

In this context, the initial thrust of policy was to transfer land out of the ownership by the State to the people. It was recognised that this raises a series of complex issues - in particular about individual as opposed to communal ownership, and to whom the land should be transferred. The thinking was that land would be transferred to those with *de facto* rights, according to actual practice. Thus, where individual rights existed on a *de facto* basis at a certain date, they would be transferred to those individuals. Where rights existed under communal systems they would be transferred to groups, but with substantial protections for members of a common property system. Furthermore, the form of group ownership should enable flexibility and future change in line with the views of the majority of members. A precedent for this model was created by the Communal Property Associations Act of 1996. This Act provides for group ownership but with strong rights for members and procedural protections against malpractice by the leaders of the CPA which were set out in law and in the constitution of each CPA.

These proposed reforms were tested in pilot schemes and a number of difficulties were raised:

• Which should be the "unit of ownership" in traditional areas? For example, should the land be transferred to "tribes" or "nations" consisting in some cases of hundreds of thousands of people, or should it be transferred to the village or headman level where most local decisions about land and resources are made? If land is vested at the level of the "paramount tribe" or "nation", smaller groups can always be outnumbered by the majority, even in decisions which affect particular localities. If land is vested in smaller units, then the prospective and inherent rights of members of the wider tribe are excluded, and this could be contrary to widely accepted values and practice.

• The problem also arises in areas where a "tribe" may have absorbed other sub-groups of people. Should the land be transferred to the large tribe or to a sub-group which can prove that it received a specific area as compensation for forced removal? Or should it be transferred to people who can show that their specific sub-group had collected money separately to pay for an area within the tribal boundaries?

---

12 Three and half million people were removed from their homes between 1960 and 1983 (see Platzky and Walker, 1985).

- Another issue pertains to the form of ownership. Should the land be owned by a democratic structure such as a Communal Property Association (CPA) or a carefully structured trust, or should the land be owned by the "tribe" or tribal authority structure?

The consultation process raised a further series of major difficulties, since decisions about such matters would have to be taken by the majority of people whose land rights would be affected by the proposed transfer:

- What constitutes a "majority" in disputed situations? The majority of people living within the area of a paramount tribe? Or the majority of those within a specific sub-area encompassed by the tribe who vehemently oppose transfer of their sub-area to that tribe and want it to be transferred to a smaller unit?

- There may be many different groups of people living within "tribal" areas. There could be people who were removed into the area and have a separate identity, but for the sake of security, loosely affiliated themselves to the dominant tribe. They may now vehemently oppose the registration of "their" land in the name of the tribe, but do not want to move away. There are also people who have lost all confidence in traditional systems, because of past serious and endemic abuses by traditional leaders in their areas. They insist that the new South Africa should be built on democratic structures and they want the land transferred to these democratic structures.

- Different interest groups have different views about the form of land holding. Often people in ANC branches and elected local councillors want the land to be vested in democratic structures such as communal property associations, or to be converted to individual ownership. Interestingly, traditional headmen often also support the transfer of land to village level units and do not generally oppose Communal Property Associations, perhaps because they are confident that traditional leaders will continue to play a key role within such structures. However, senior traditional leaders and their organisations generally oppose the transfer of land to smaller units and demand that transfer take place to their own large tribal units.

Therefore, the prospect of land transfer in the new South Africa creates high stakes for different interest groups. Land is often the only asset in rural, extremely impoverished ex-homeland areas, and semi-feudal relations continue to exist in many of these. Control over land remains a prime mechanism for exercising control over people.

In many areas, therefore, there are deep and intractable tensions between the new elected local government structures and traditional leaders. There has not been a systematic reconciliation of the functions of the different bodies, and so disputes arise about overlapping areas of jurisdiction. In this context ownership of the land is a high prize indeed, and in many areas the consultation process has unleashed unprecedented tensions, intimidation and the ever-present prospect of violence.

The pilot schemes also illuminated issues beyond the far-reaching impact of political disputes between elected and traditional structures, as follows:

- The process of consultation prior to transfer is necessarily intricate and time-consuming. It throws up endless boundary disputes, both geographical and social[13]. There are disputes between neighbouring groups and endemic disputes within groups about boundaries and units of land. The membership of the land holding group is also questioned - who qualifies as a co-owner, who does not? Before land transfer was on the agenda, some of these disputes hardly existed or were latent, but the irrevocable nature of land transfer is an effective alarm clock for latent social tensions.

- The important lesson is that land transfer, if enacted well, would be a very slow and intricate process that would require enormous resources to implement on a case by case basis. The intricate nature of the restitution process has already caused major delay and frustration for claimants. The Department of Land Affairs cannot afford a tenure programme which would take decades or centuries to meet its basic objectives.

- In the context of broader debates, the process of land transfer in South Africa illustrates the inherent difficulty in reconciling the exclusive nature of (western) title with African systems of land rights; in particular the "nested" nature of African systems of land rights. In many traditional systems sub groups "nest" within larger groups, so that a person has rights both at the local level, where certain key decisions about land rights are taken, and at higher levels up to the "paramountcy" or "nation" level. Different types of land issues are decided at different levels depending on the decision in question. Transfer of exclusive title to one or other level fundamentally undermines such systems. The prospect of transfer creates a conflict of interest between leaders at the different levels and opens unprecedented internal disputes.

Rethinking "upfront" land transfer as the fundamental mechanism of tenure reform

The Department of Land Affairs began to rethink whether up-front land transfers might in fact cause more disputes and problems than they are likely to solve. The proposed Land Rights Bill, therefore, addressed the dilemmas set out above by a shift in focus to the introduction of statutory land rights which would be introduced on a mass scale by the enactment of law.

---

13 Overlapping and multiple rights to land are not unique to South Africa (Berry, 1993).

Protected rights

It was proposed that a category of "protected rights" be created by law. The majority of people with stable land occupation in ex-homeland and SADT areas would qualify for protected rights. The basis for qualification would be their current *de facto* occupation and use of the land. Only those people whose *de facto* occupation or use was established by dubious means would be denied rights. Protected rights would have the status of property rights, in that the law would prohibit the deprivation of rights except with consent or by expropriation. It would also provide protected rights holders with decision making powers in respect of the land, and with the right to the benefits accruing from the land.

Whilst the nominal ownership of the land would continue to be vested in the Minister of Land Affairs, his or her powers would be constrained. Any decisions in respect of the land would have to be taken by the rights holders themselves.

Protected rights would vest in the individuals who use, occupy and have access to land. However, they would be dependent upon agreement by other people with shared rights in the land. In this sense they would be individual rights which are subject to group rules. Decisions affecting shared rights would have to be taken by a majority of rights holders. Determining what is meant by a "majority" would require membership of a "group" to be defined[14].

The proposal in the draft Bill was that "boundaries" must be seen as flexible. In other words, the boundary of the group would be determined with reference to who (which group of people) is affected by the particular decision. Thus, if the decision is about a change in grazing practice then the people affected by the change must be consulted, not the entire "tribe". Decisions affecting smaller numbers of people would require consultation of smaller groups, and those affecting lots of people would require that larger groups be consulted. It is intended that this approach would impact on the resolution of endemic disputes about who is entitled to represent whom. The intention is that such disputes be settled not by purely subjective or historical factors, but by a more objective test - what is the decision in question? Who is affected? Do the majority of those people endorse the decision or not?[15]

Under the proposals, protected rights could be registered. Complementary legislation to ensure that they could be registered within the Deeds Registry is being developed. It is envisaged that registration would not be mandatory but

---

14 The quantification of the group is a key difficulty in any land reform programme or law which attempts to provide statutory recognition of customary rights, particularly of communal rights. See for example the difficulties experienced in Mozambique in this regard (Kloek-Jenson, 1998).

15 Specific detail about the proposals is not appropriate in a paper such as this. Suffice to say that this formulation opens yet other problems about defining who exactly is "affected" by specific decisions. In an attempt to get a balance between those directly affected, and others (from the wider group) who have an interest in the decision at issue the draft Bill sets out that, while decisions affecting land rights must be made by a majority of those affected, the decisions must also be made with due regard to the interests of prospective rights holders and people who have reciprocal land rights and obligations with those directly affected.

demand-driven. It would be possible to register strong rights within parts of communal areas, for example housing development areas. In such cases, protected rights to housing sites would be registered as the property of particular families whilst common areas such as grazing land would remain unregistered. Protected rights would exist regardless of whether or not they were registered.

Land rights could be alienable if the majority of those affected so decide. In some areas, the majority of people believe that land should not be bought and sold, but elsewhere, this is accepted practice. The majority of rights holders could impose conditions on the sale of land rights, for example that rights be sold only to approved purchasers who agree to abide by group rules.

Transfer of ownership

These proposals do not imply that transfer of title from the state to rights holders would no longer be an avenue of tenure reform. The draft Bill also provides for the transfer of ownership to well-defined groups where there is a high degree of consensus.

However, this would be only be permitted after the group/tribe could show majority consensus about a unit of land, and agree on the entity in whom it would vest. Preliminary experiences from the pilot cases indicated that only rarely would the process of transferring title in communal areas not spark serious internal disputes concerning the boundaries of the land parcel and the identity of the proposed owner.

For those situations where there is sufficient consensus to proceed with the transfer, it was proposed that there be various options available. The current options for group ownership under South African law include trusts, companies and communal property associations (CPAs). However, there is a strongly held view that "tribes" have their own nature and rules and that it is absurd for them to have to reconstitute themselves as new entities such as trusts and CPAs (for an account of one disputed area see Ntsebeza and Buiten, 1998).

Furthermore, experience in redistribution projects has shown that CPAs, when imposed, exist on paper only, and can be irrelevant to the day-to-day operation of land rights. In some projects where the approach has been tried, there is serious abuse by traditional leaders who treat the land as their own personal asset. Lack of enforcement capacity has meant that the strong legal rights created under CPAs have proven ineffective. The desire to protect basic rights through the imposition of a new legal structure has been criticised as idealistic, where there is a lack of institutional capacity to enforce these rights (McIntosh, 1998).

On the other hand, to simply transfer land to "tribes" as governed by customary law was not an option. Abuse of power by traditional leaders is endemic in certain areas. In a recent court case Chief Lucas Mangope justified his personal appropriation of millions of rand obtained from mining revenues on tribal land on the basis that under customary law, traditional leaders are entitled to use tribal resources for personal purposes. Case law (as handed down by judges during the colonial period) gave ownership to traditional leaders rather than to the members of traditional systems (Klug, 1995). Indeed, there have been innumerable instances of leaders appropriating group assets for personal gain. There have also been problems concerning the land rights of women under customary systems (Mbatha and Albertyn, 1997). This is not to say that all customary systems are unjust. Many are highly participatory and manage land rights effectively, providing a valuable institutional asset in areas where there is an absence of state presence. The issue is not to make a value judgement about traditional systems in South Africa, but to build protection against potential abuse, of whatever kind, into mechanisms for group ownership.

In order to deal with these issues of transfer of ownership, the Minister of Land Affairs, as trustee and nominal owner of most of the land at issue, stated that it was his duty to ascertain that proper protections be put in place to protect basic human rights before land transfer could take place. Current legal options such as the Companies Act, trusts and CPAs have basic protections built into them, but these are not acceptable to some traditional societies. Thus, an alternative proposal concerning customary commonhold was developed and inserted into the Land Rights Bill.

Commonhold

Commonhold would be a new form of ownership created by the Land Rights Bill. It would provide that the land vests in the members of a tribe[16] or community as co-owners. At the moment, South African law requires that a group wishing to acquire land must either constitute itself as a legal entity or own the land in undivided shares. The problem with the system of undivided shares is that it requires the approval of each and every owner of an undivided share in order to ratify any decision or transaction in respect of the combined area. This makes dealing in the land or developing it virtually impossible. Commonhold would vest the land in the co-owners, but allow that decisions in respect of the land could be made on a majority basis. The co-owners would choose or elect a struc-

---

16 The word tribe is controversial in South Africa. Some traditional societies consider it a derogatory term preferring to use terms such as "nation" or "kingdom". Furthermore there are endless debates about what is a tribe, a unit at the level of the paramountcy? at the level of senior leader? at the level of the clan? etc. There are also deep historical disputes about whether certain groups of people are tribes, parts of tribes or sub-units of tribes. There is no direct translation or equivalent word in Southern African indigenous languages for the term "tribe". The Bill referred to communities rather than tribes as it is virtually impossible to find an acceptable definition of the word "tribe". "Tribes", were included under the definition of community.

ture to represent them in dealing with third parties and also to manage their joint asset on a day to day basis. However, if this structure entered into transactions which did not represent the views of the majority of co-owners the transaction would be void. Commonhold title would be endorsed on title deeds. Also, people or institutions acting on behalf of the co-owners would be bound to act in a capacity of a trustee in relation to the views and interests of co-owners.

The draft Bill sets out standards and procedures pertaining to democracy and equality which relate to all forms of joint land ownership created in terms of the bill, whether CPAs, trusts, or commonhold ownership. It also allows for individuals to have protected rights after transfer of the land, whether this be in commonhold or to a legal entity.

In summary, communities (including tribes) applying for transfer of ownership of state land could choose to form a CPA or other legal entity (including a trust), or they could choose to own the land in commonhold. Because commonhold would not require that they develop and adopt a constitution or trust deed it requires that those who choose commonhold must provide the following information in their application:

(i)   the shared rules governing qualification and disqualification for membership of the community;
(ii) a community resolution acknowledging the principles of land rights management contained in the bill; and
(iii) a list of the names of the members of the community.

The idea is that tribes and communities who qualify for transfer by showing majority support would not be forced to re-constitute themselves. They would continue to operate on the principle of "business as usual", except that they would be bound to respect the rights set out in the principles of land rights management and to abide by the terms of the law.

CAPACITY CONSTRAINTS

Like other African countries, South Africa faces major capacity constraints in implementing not just tenure reform, but land reform in general. The budget for land reform in 1997/8 was 579 million rand, which is less than 0.05% of the national budget. Budget cuts at the end of 1998 affected the Department of Land Affairs just as they affected other parts of government. The existing land reform budget is already fully committed to the two components of land reform which are underway, i.e. redistribution and restitution. Tenure reform in the communal areas is the latecomer, and very few resources were "left over" for it. Tenure reform has come late in the process because such reform is complex, and the policy formulation process needed to tread delicately around the fragile systems of vested interests and societal safety nets which exist in the poorest parts of South Africa.

Because of budgetary limitations, and because the Cabinet is committed to reducing rather than expanding the public service, the proposals have had to be pragmatic about capacity constraints. Rather than transferring ownership on a case-by-case basis (as originally proposed), there has been a move to create systems of protected rights by statute on a "blanket" basis. This transforms the status of rights in communal areas in one fell swoop by giving them the legal status of property rights. However, the mere existence of rights does not solve the problem of their enforcement (Cousins, 1997), nor of their day-to-day management, given that most protected rights will exist within a group context, and so will have to be exercised in accordance with group rules. It is envisaged that local institutions would choose the structure which would manage their land rights. They would have the option of endorsing existing structures or creating new ones. Such local structures would then be accredited by government to fulfil key functions as set out in the draft Land Rights Bill.

The decision to accredit existing structures which enjoy support, even if they are not "perfect" on the democracy or human rights front, reflected a pragmatic choice to build on existing capacity. Government does not have the resources to set up new structures on a massive scale. The draft Bill provides mechanisms to point existing structures in the right direction, and provides remedies for rights holders should the structures abrogate their powers. This is less ambitious than the other option of requiring traditional structures to reconstitute themselves into elected structures before they can be accredited. It is envisaged that tribal authorities which enjoy local support will be accredited and continue to play a key, and substantially enhanced, role in day-to-day land rights management. However, in areas where the tribal authorities are deeply unpopular or the old system has broken down, rights holders would either use other pre-existing structures (civics, development committees, or even the new elected local councils) or be assisted to set up new institutions.

The draft Bill is premised on the assumption that local officials would be available to help rights holders enforce their rights and to assist (and monitor) accredited structures. These officials would also have a key role to play in assisting to resolve disputes about overlapping rights, boundaries, and the delineation of disputed rights. They would have a pivotal role in the processes of accrediting local structures, and in the registration of rights. They would also play a "watchdog" role in relation to internal processes of alienation of land, deprivation of rights and the awarding of adequate compensation. In this regard, the Bill proposes that Land Rights Officer posts be created at a decentralised level, initially at the level of the old magisterial districts (smaller than the new rural councils).

It is also proposed that Land Rights Boards be established. These boards would be an attempt to bring together different interest groups in rural society and create a forum for co-operation in respect of land rights and development. These would include both traditional leaders and local councillors. Their functions would include dealing with disputes between structures, ensuring that rights holders were properly consulted, and recommending that extra resources be made available in overcrowded or disputed areas. Land Rights Officers and Land Rights Boards are the two institutions which would require substantial resources to establish and maintain.

Organising principle of the Bill: greater autonomy for more organised structures

The proposals were based on the principle that the more organised the rights holders are, the more responsibility could be transferred from government to local structures. Where there is a total breakdown or absence of local structures, officials would have to convene groups of rights holders to ascertain the views and decisions of the majority of rights holders. Where there are viable committees or structures which enjoy the support of the majority of rights holders, these would be accredited by government and would play a key role in the day to day management of land rights. Where rights holders have organised themselves into legal entities which meet specific criteria, the ownership of the land would be transferred to them if so requested.

Breakdown or absence of structures

In some cases, protected rights exist in areas where old structures have broken down, or where there are disputes. In such instances, it is proposed that the Land Rights Officer identify which rights holders would be affected by specific decisions and convene a process to establish the decision of the majority of rights holders. This process, by clarifying who holds rights and establishing the decision of rights holders, would assist where rights holders need to make quick decisions to take advantage of externally created opportunities related to investment or development in their areas. The Minister of Land Affairs, as nominal owner, would be able to enter into legally binding agreements with third parties on their behalf, but only on the instruction of those whose rights are implicated.

However, there would be a limit to the kinds of development which can proceed in the absence of accredited structures. For example, registration of rights and formalisation of transactions other than lease agreements would not be possible. This is because it would be beyond the capacity of over-stretched Land Rights Officers to step in where local institutions have failed or do not exist. Where there is insufficient cohesion and organisation to produce an accredited land rights structure, there is likely to be insufficient organisation and cohesion to sustain major development projects. The role of the Land Rights Officer in such situations would only be to assist right holders in taking the next step of applying for accreditation of their chosen structure.

Accredited structures

Procedures are proposed to test whether existing structures enjoy the support of the majority of rights holders before accreditation can take place. Accredited structures would then manage the day to day matters which affect communal land rights. They would play a key role in internal land allocation and in vouching for the status of rights holders who apply for the registration of their protected rights. Land rights would continue to vest in the rights holders, not in the structure, and so the structure would be bound to operate in terms of rules and decisions which reflect the views of the majority of rights holders.

Transfer of land to legal entities or in commonhold

The general principle behind these proposed reforms is that where groups are particularly well organised and cohesive, management of land would be transferred to them. Power is devolved from officials and the state as nominal owner of the land, to local structures (depending how representative and well-organised they are). Land rights management by accredited structures would be a "half way house" before the final and irrevocable transfer of the ownership of the land to the rights holders. It was anticipated that the high stakes entailed in land transfers and the likely disputes arising, would result in many groups of rights holders halting at the stage of accredited structures.

Immediate resource constraints

The draft Bill would have required significant resources. The anticipated budget to set up and run the process was 790 million rand over the first 7 years of its operation. On the assumption that it was to be set up and running throughout the country by year 2007, the running costs for that year were estimated to be 108 million rand. A key expense would be the costs of the Land Rights Officer posts and accompanying infrastructure. It is estimated that 348 posts and support posts will be required. Given that the people in these posts would be serving four to five million households, these figures were not considered excessive. The current chaotic and dysfunctional system of land administration in the ex-homeland areas, which would be replaced by the new proposals, employs 1,136 people.

However, given other priorities within the Department of Land Affairs and prior commitments, it appears extremely unlikely that such costs could be met within the current budget of the Department. Cabinet will have to be asked for additional resources and posts on the basis that the benefits, particularly the economic benefits, of the new proposals far outweigh the costs. Allocation of the necessary funds would be difficult in the current fiscal climate.

The old land administration system would have to be merged into a new system, which would create initial difficulties. The staff who used to issue PTOs have been scattered through different provincial government departments. With changes of government in 1994, land administration ended up in various provincial governments, but without a clear structure and without official posts. To rationalise the process would be complicated because of tensions between national government and provincial governments about the allocation of resources and workloads. Some of the people currently fulfilling the land administration function are steeped in the old ideology of land administration in which the state and traditional leaders were the only recognised players. However, there are provinces where excellent officials have been upholding citizen's rights despite the lack of structure, resources or institutional support from national government. It has been proposed that the Bill be tested in certain areas before being extended to the whole country, given all these resource constraints. An incidental (but important) benefit of this compromise is that it would enable a process of "testing" the new institutions and measures, and a chance to rectify mistakes before they have become widespread.

OVERLAPPING RIGHTS AND THE REDISTRIBUTIVE CONSEQUENCES OF TENURE REFORM

One of the most difficult aspects of tenure reform in South Africa is the problem of competing and overlapping rights to the same land. The complex tenurial situation in the reserves has arisen as a result of the arrival and acceptance of successive waves of people into areas that were already occupied by groups with long-established land rights. The new arrivals had often been forcibly removed or evicted from their farms elsewhere or may otherwise have been "refugees" from the apartheid system.

Against this background, if the proposed legislation were to attribute rights to land by virtue of current occupancy, without providing for compensation or additional land to be made available, recent arrivals would be attributed similar rights to the land as the historical owners. This would mean that by having accommodated desperate people, the earlier groups had effectively diminished their own rights in the land.

In some instances, a new equilibrium has been reached, and after much consultation, it was decided that it would be divisive to structure a law in a way which focuses on differences between people. However, in other cases, current land rights overlap to the extent that there is no functional security of tenure and where the status of different categories of rights holders is deeply disputed. In such cases, a process referred to as "unpacking" the overlapping rights is necessary. This involves all protected rights holders in the area being accommodated by a solution or "award" which provides different groups with land or resources commensurate with their vested interests in the land, whether these arise from long term historical occupation, or settlement following forced removals or farm evictions. The premise is that all people with established and stable occupation of land have protected rights which must be accommodated in the solution.

Historical claims would be taken into account in assessing the extent of underlying rights and so determining the area of additional land or other resources required to accommodate the interests of all parties. The awards would typically involve a combination of *in situ* confirmation of rights for some, and the provision of compensatory or additional land for others. In some cases "newcomers" might get *in situ* confirmation because of the numbers of people involved, whilst the historical occupants get additional land to compensate for the loss of their fields and grazing land. The awards would vary from case to case and the process is structured to elicit proposed solutions from the rights holders themselves.

It is envisaged that the Land Rights Boards would play a key role in prioritising which areas need to be "unpacked" in this way and referring them to the Department of Land Affairs to institute "Tenure Award" processes. The Boards would also review the solutions or awards which Land Affairs officials recommend and advise the Minister whether the awards adequately accommodate and balance the rights and interests of affected rights holders. One chapter of the proposed Bill sets out the mechanisms and procedure governing such tenure awards. This essentially involves redistributive mechanisms to make extra resources, particularly land, available where the confirmation of current rights of occupation would reinforce landlessness and poverty.

Because of the scale of overcrowding and overlapping rights, the redistributive consequences of the new tenure proposals are potentially very far reaching. The primary impact of tenure "redistribution" could well be to expand the current boundaries of densely settled areas and provide additional resources to existing communities rather than create new communities in distant areas (the classic redistribution model).

POSTSCRIPT AND CONCLUSION - IMPLICATIONS FOR OTHER AFRICAN COUNTRIES?

The proposals in South Africa's draft Land Rights Bill of 1999 described above would undoubtedly have been changed and adapted during the consultation and parliamentary process. The Bill would have been tested in selected districts before the legislation was extended to all communal areas. But a change of government thinking has now reduced the possibility of the Bill being passed into law. As at January 2000, the proposals have been shelved and policy for tenure reform has gone back to the drawing board.

Given that the proposals have not been implemented it would be presumptuous to suggest that they would provide solutions to the difficult tenure problems and dilemmas which South Africa shares with its neighbours elsewhere in Africa. However, it may be useful to draw out elements of the approach that were adopted in order to facilitate discussion of the possible relevance of this approach to other countries with similar problems.

- The Bill was a response to the need to have legally enforceable property rights which enable people to defend their land rights against incursions - whether by third parties, elites, or government. In South Africa as elsewhere, this must be done without destroying the systems which currently not only create and maintain land rights, but also provide a critical safety net for the poor.

- The main mechanism proposed to achieve this balance was the creation of high-content statutory rights which vest in the people occupying and using the land, and which are determined and quantified by reference to the actual exercise of the rights as it occurs in practice.

- In the proposals, the balance between individual and group rights was achieved by limiting the content of protected rights within communal situations such that they can only be exercised in accordance with group rules and group decisions.

- Defining the group or "community" of decision-makers and rights holders is always difficult. The proposal was that the boundaries of the decision making group shift depending on the decision or rule in question and who is affected by it. It was proposed that existing or new structures which enjoy majority support be accredited by government. These structures could play a key role in the day-to-day management of land rights and be accredited for specific areas. However, decision making processes which must enjoy the support of the majority of affected rights holders, would vary within the area and be defined by which group of rights holders were affected by the specific issue or decision.

- It was proposed that the law which creates and confers protected rights also sets out general principles concerning basic human rights which govern the way in which land rights are managed and held. The approach was that existing customary institutions which enjoy support would be recognised and accredited by government, but that rights holders have clear channels of redress should their basic human rights to equality and democratic decision making processes be abrogated.

- A key feature of the proposals was that they recognised and confirmed that various rights and interests may exist in respect of an area of land, and that ownership per se does not over-ride all other interests and claims. User and occupancy rights were proposed, as was protection against eviction unless certain procedures and criteria were complied with.

- Critical attention was given to the legacy of forced overcrowding and overlapping of land rights in the communal or ex-homeland areas. The process of clarifying rights can all too easily degenerate into a "winner takes all" contest and those with weaker rights find themselves entirely dispossessed by tenure reform. The Bill's approach was that all the various parties living on the land have some sort of vested interest, whether arising from long-term occupation, purchase, compensation for forced removals, or simple lack of alternatives when they were evicted from white farms. In the proposals, all such groupings would qualify for protected rights, and in situations where the degree of overlapping has led to conflict or materially affected the exercise of rights, the different groups would be entitled to alternatives or additional land. Historical and other factors would be taken into account in determining which group received what in the final settlement.

If the draft Bill had been submitted to the parliamentary process, one of the most controversial aspects would have been whether the proposals catered adequately for the interests of traditional leaders. There are those, both black and white, who opposed the proposals because they abhor communal systems and believe that individualisation and privatisation of land rights is the only "modern" way forward. But the more organised opposition was likely to come from those organisations which support the interests of senior traditional leaders (in particular Contralesa[17]).

Perhaps the greatest expression of rural resistance to apartheid was the widespread uprisings against the introduction of the Bantu Authorities Act in 1969 (Mbeki, 1964). This legislation still governs tribal authorities[18]. A prime fea-

---

17 Congress of Traditional Leaders of South Africa.

ture of rural apartheid was the deposition of respected traditional leaders and their replacement by those more prepared to co-operate with government. This process was uneven, and in some areas respected leaders managed to survive and traditional systems continue to operate relatively well. In some areas traditional systems are participatory and provide for important stability, but in others problems are endemic. In many rural areas no more effective alternative exists because of the weakness of rural local governments. There are areas where government is conspicuous by its absence and traditional systems, whether good, bad or middling, are the only institutions to which people can turn.

In assessing the potential response to perceived threats to traditional leaders under the proposed Act, it is not clear what position would have been taken by political parties which favour traditional systems (such as the Inkatha Freedom Party and the United Democratic Movement). On the one hand the draft Bill incorporated many of their key demands, in particular the legal recognition for indigenous land rights, and the acknowledgement of group based land rights. It also provided for institutional support to traditional institutions. However, it enabled people democratically to choose new structures to manage their land rights. Thus unpopular traditional leaders were *not guaranteed* a place in the system of land rights management, and steps could be taken against leaders (traditional or elected) who contravene basic human rights standards.

The draft Bill was scrapped before it was put to a vote in Parliament. As a result, we can only speculate whether any political parties would have supported legislation which, as we have outlined, aimed to bring indigenous and de facto land rights within the system of legally enforceable property rights for the first time in South Africa.

---

18 Its name has been changed to the Black Authorities Act

14

Land Policy in Africa:
Lessons from Recent Policy and
Implementation Processes

Robin Palmer

INTRODUCTION

In the 1990s, official land policy debates in Southern Africa have become
focused on two strategies: promoting freehold land markets to replace so-
called customary tenure zones and expanding "commercial farming"
through market mechanisms. These two strategies are expected to resolve
the escalating land problems. Yet, in the guise of promoting sustainable
land use, environmental care, new agricultural export crops and tourism,
large tracts of land are currently being alienated throughout the region. In
the last few years, market-based economic reforms and privatisation in
general are leading to a greater concentration of "foreign" and local elite
landownership rather than enhancing equitable land redistribution which
benefits the majority. (Moyo, forthcoming)

As the chapters elsewhere in this book amply illustrate, most countries in
sub-Saharan Africa are currently undertaking a variety of land reform initiatives[1]. This chapter is based on a review of policy processes and implementation of land reform in a number of African countries, most particularly Uganda,
Tanzania, South Africa and Mozambique. It draws on the work of Liz Alden
Wily and Martin Adams, who have shared their perspectives and extensive
experience with the author. It also makes reference to several papers presented

---

1 For a relevant literature survey, see Palmer (1997) and for the Oxfam GB website *Land Rights in Africa* (2000) en-
deavouring to keep tracking these events, see http://www.oxfam.org.uk/landrights/

at the DFID Workshop on Land Rights and Sustainable Development in Sub-Saharan Africa. The chapter endeavours to draw out some of the lessons that need to be learned from experience to date. It also emphasizes the contrast between countries such as South Africa, Zimbabwe and Namibia, which are concerned with land redistribution (or resettlement) and others elsewhere in Africa, where tenure reform has been the key issue (Palmer, 1998).

The actors

A characteristic of current land reform processes, in contrast to those of an earlier generation, has been the large number of actors involved. Civil society has expanded greatly since the days of one-party states and the Cold War, and the implications have been widely felt. The Uganda Land Alliance, for example, initially a coalition of concerned individuals, and later a formal NGO, has succeeded in both changing the nature of what was to become the Land Act of 1998 and in persuading the government to widen the consultation process which preceded it. In Mozambique, something very similar happened both during debates on the 1997 Land Law and the subsequent NGO Land Campaign, which sought to make rural people aware of their new rights, and how they could go about establishing them under the law (Negrão, 1999). Yet one needs to be aware that in much of Southern Africa, many NGOs are less than ten years old, were not involved in the struggle for Independence from which much of the impetus for reform stems, and are "dependent on external development agency funding of the land reform agenda" (Moyo, forthcoming).

In a context of straightened African government budgets, the role of donors has become more central. As one might expect, the legacy of colonial ties has meant that the British have been involved with land reform in Uganda, the Belgians in Rwanda, the French in Ivory Coast, and so on. In recent years, the UK's Department for International Development (DFID) has become increasingly engaged in supporting the process of land reform. In Uganda, DFID helped draft the Act, supported the Land Alliance and a workshop for MPs, and subsequently has been trying to help the Ugandan government think how best to implement the Act. Relations here have generally been amicable, in contrast to Zimbabwe, where controversies over land have dogged relations between the British and Zimbabwean governments from 1979 to the present (Palmer, 1990). While Zimbabwe may be an extreme case, it illustrates the point that foreign aid, in an area so politically contentious as land, can never be unproblematic, especially when it involves the ex-colonial power. In South Africa, it appears that DFID and other donors now believe in land reform rather more strongly than the new Minister of Lands. Nevertheless, it is worth remembering Sam Moyo's view that, in the eyes of many in Southern Africa, the real aim of donors is to block radical land reform, rather than to encourage it.

The role of foreign legal draftsmen, such as HWO Okoth-Ogendo and Patrick McAuslan, has also been key, but little open to public gaze. These lawyers are almost always confronted with formidable problems, but the kind of laws they draft do not always prove entirely appropriate to the local environment, nor practical when it comes to implementation.

Faced with a variety of pressures to devolve power, many African governments have gone along with the rhetoric in favour of popular participation and subsidiarity. In practice, however, many have been reluctant to go too far along this road. They might bend to NGO and donor pressures in favour of wider consultation, but many have yet to be persuaded of the real benefits to be gained by involving ordinary people in policy debate. Government officials are generally unwilling to pursue subsidiarity, for it may threaten their sources of patronage and challenge the habits of a lifetime. And, while politicians may be keen to get involved in land affairs, in a variety of ways, as recent experiences in the Kenyan Rift Valley and in Uganda illustrate, they tend to be less concerned about the practical implications of major policy changes.

However, while all these actors – government officials, donors, politicians, NGOs, and legal professionals - have focussed on the process of debating and passing laws and policies, they have failed to anticipate the many problems that would arise from trying to implement them.

POLICY PROCESSES

The policy processes that have driven land policy reform have been described by Okoth-Ogendo (1998) as follows:

> What we are witnessing is a search for the systematic articulation of national problems, vision, objectives and strategies about land as a central factor in development. The overriding concern in contemporary land policy reform appears to be the need to formulate a macro-level policy framework and complementary programmes about land: its ownership, distribution, utilisation, alienability, management and control.

He examines some of the factors driving such reforms and observes that, given massive colonial plunder of land and its devastating impact on agrarian systems and leadership structures, it is surprising that it has taken governments so long to confront the issues.

In former settler-controlled Africa, Okoth-Ogendo argues, "the main drivers were essentially political: the need to right historical wrongs, ensure equity as between different categories of citizens, and solidify the legitimacy of governments". More recently, donor agencies have entered the arena, putting economic arguments to the fore, and stressing "that rapid agricultural development in sub-Saharan Africa requires fundamental and deeply surgical changes in land policy and land law". But though economic drivers are now dominant, "we should expect social and cultural factors to intervene in an attempt to address issues of justice and equity in land relations" (Okoth-Ogendo 1998). Governments have tended to respond in one of four ways, as shown in Box 14.1.

Okoth-Ogendo sees three sets of substantive outcomes from these processes. The first are technocratic solutions requiring reorganisation of tenure which involves "conversion of customary holdings into private estates under individual title" (Kenya, Malawi, Zanzibar in the 1960s), reflecting dominant western beliefs concerning the magic of private property. The second, which occurs where the drivers are mainly political, concern radical measures ranging from "reorganisation of production relations to massive redistribution and restitution" (Kenya, Ethiopia, South Africa, Zimbabwe, at different times). The third are "reconstitutive of the past, or supportive of existing agrarian conditions" (Botswana, Swaziland, Lesotho), which are generally evolutionary in nature. Few countries have yet taken a holistic view of land policy reform, and those which have (Tanzania, South Africa, Malawi) "have found actual implementation slow, fraught with numerous political risks, cumbersome and expensive" (ibid).

A second analysis of land policy reform processes comes from the work of Alden Wily (forthcoming), which complements that of Okoth-Ogendo. She notes that:

> No matter where the intention to reform begins and with what level of modest objective, its scope quickly widens and becomes more complicated. Issues which the state wanted to avoid, or did not realise it would have to address, come into play. Moreover, this extends beyond the immediate realm of property. Each nation state finds itself having to tackle issues of governance, democratisation and state-people relations in general. The very notion of public trust comes under attack and in many states justifiably so. Tenure reform is notoriously destructive of the current social order. Inevitably, the expressed or real objectives of tenure reform themselves begin to change with a good deal of retrenchment as the implications of the task government has set itself, come to light. (ibid.)

Whilst each state has set its own unique agenda, each has also found itself having to tackle a remarkably common set of property issues:

Box 14.1: Four types of government response to land issues

First and least imaginatively, through bureaucratic "desk-top processes" designed "to anticipate or pre-empt relatively foreseeable consequences before these develop into unmanageable crises". Top officials tightly control and manage this process, which typically leads to "little more than broad statements of principles or policy prescriptions devoid of concrete strategies needed to resolve problems". Sometimes mere stop-gap measures are taken, especially in sectoral policies on land-based resources such as water, forestry, wildlife and the environment (Kenya, Tanzania, Malawi, Uganda).

A second approach is "the appointment of expert panels of inquiry, task forces and even sole investigators to prepare preliminary working documents". The premise is that "he basic problems are known, as are their possible solutions". So the purpose of the enquiry is to seek validation of a priori premises. Such mechanisms are often used at short notice to manage political stresses (Kenya, Zimbabwe), though the implementation rate from such processes has not been high.

The third approach is of broadly based, independent commissions of inquiry adopting participatory processes. This is much rarer (Tanzania, Malawi, Eritrea), takes the form of a long process, and runs the risk that governments may reject the findings on either political or economic grounds.

Fourth, there can be a combination of a bureaucratic approach and public discourse, with documents being drawn up for the explicit purpose of stimulating discussion (South Africa, Ethiopia). This works best "when there is substantial political capital [in the form of enhanced legitimacy] to be reaped from swift but popular action". Most countries in fact, now convinced that land policy reform is "fundamental to the sustainable management of development, have used a mixed bag of mechanisms and procedures to push this forward".

Source: Okoth-Ogendo, 1998

- How far, after all, should powers over property be vested in the state?
- How far should a market in land be permitted and prompted? And how freely should land be available to non-citizens?
- At what level of society and with what degree of autonomy from the executive should property relations be regulated, and with what level of popular participation?
- How may the plethora of land disputes be more swiftly and fairly resolved?
- How should unregistered, customary landholdings be handled? And with what objective in mind - abolition of the regime as a whole, its conversion into rights of freehold or leasehold, continued "trusteeship" or ownership by the state, or recognition 'as is'? (ibid.).

Alden Wily argues that simple recognition of customary landholdings tends to be the most problematic. She argues: "if there were a single point of radicalism in tenure reform as occurring in sub-Saharan Africa, it is this; *for the first time in one hundred years, states are slowly being forced to recognise customary rights in land (and therefore customary regimes) as legal in their own right*" (ibid.).

Land reform everywhere also has to deal with new concerns arising from the last few decades of great social and economic change, in particular:

- the position of women as property holders, a group which had been widely dispossessed in the changes of the last century, despite their role as primary producers of agricultural wealth;
- the position of farm workers or tenants in property holding;
- the untenured urban poor, those still-growing millions of citizens in the sub-continent which land law regards as 'squatters';
- pastoralists and others who pursue land use and therefore tenure regimes least amenable to the strictures of imported notions of land holding;
- and integral to many of the above, a new concern is the need to make provision for common property. (ibid.)

As a consequence, old doctrines and dogma relating to titling are being questioned. Previously, recording, registration, and the issue of titles were inseparable from the individualisation of the ownership of that property. Alden Wily argues that the damage this has done to domestic property relations on the continent has been immense, quite aside from the constraint this has placed upon group and community tenure. As discussed earlier in this book, the link has now been broken (see Chapter 3). Whilst certification remains deeply rooted within strategies for improving land security throughout the region, it is no longer necessarily for the purpose of individualisation (see Chapter 11).

The very notion of what constitutes "private property" has begun to expand its conventional boundaries to embrace a simple - and traditional - idea that spouses, families, clans, groups and communities may also own private property. Accordingly, new tenure laws in South Africa, Mozambique, Uganda and Tanzania in particular, make provision for two or more persons, groups, associations and communities, as "legal persons" or "entities", to hold and register land (Alden Wily, forthcoming; Ntsebeza, 1999).

The certification process itself is also changing. For example, in Mozambique, certification may be verbal and verbally endorsed. In Tanzania, the community itself may conduct the adjudication, recording and registration process. Remarkably, in both these countries, it is now recognised that customary rights in land may exist in perpetuity, rendering such rights superior to other forms of tenure available - "a pleasing reversal of fortune for the rural majority" (Alden Wily, forthcoming).

Consultation: where does it lead?

One of the key issues in the development of such wide-reaching reforms is the degree of participation or consultation which different governments - and donors - either encourage or permit. According to Alden Wily, "for the most part, the process of reform has been centrally-driven, defined and delivered,

Box 14.2: The Presidential Commission on Land Policy in Malawi

The importance of detailed planning before commencing an inquiry into such complex issues as land was one of the main lessons which arose from the experience of the Presidential Commission on Land Policy Reform in Malawi.

Factors to be considered at the design stage: A lot of thought was put into the design of appropriate operational tools and procedures for consultation. The Commission was aware that expectations of land redistribution had been raised during the multiparty electoral campaign of 1994 and had to take particular care to present itself as a sort of research organisation and not the promised land distribution agency. It was also recognised that it was as important to conduct an inquiry as it was to be seen to have conducted one. For this reason, 237 public meetings were heard (so that there was a meeting in each area under a chief) despite the fact that, according to a statistical sampling approach, 70 meetings would have been sufficient to provide the same results. Limitations of time and resources meant that careful budgeting of the US$1.2m and scheduling over 12 months had to be planned in order to produce credible land policy recommendations. Finally, the Commission were aware that Malawians, in particular the villagers, were suffering from 'inquiry fatigue'. Several studies and consultations had been embarked upon by various government bodies and NGOs. To villagers, it seemed that all these studies and consultations were being conducted by the same organisation. Many were puzzled as to why the government keeps sending its people to ask questions that they have already been asked. "Don't government people consult each other?" was a frequent remark.

Public Hearings: As all land in Malawi is initially administered by chiefs, a meeting was scheduled for each area under a chief. Land Commissioners held briefing sessions for the District Commissioners, local chiefs and other district heads of government. Subsequently, the District Commissioners and chiefs visited each area to announce the coming meeting, its purpose, format and how to prepare in advance. It was originally envisaged to hear traditional leaders, women, estate owners separately before consulting the community as a whole. However, this format was invariably rejected by local people in order to save time, in the interests of transparency (of the traditional leaders in particular) and due to the perceived impropriety of Commissioners sitting down to talk with groups of "other people's wives" in private.

After this series of public hearings, written submissions were sought from the public and thereafter from particular stakeholder groups. Special meetings followed up the issues raised from these submissions, and three regional workshops were held to discuss the Commission's preliminary report and co-validate the findings. A national workshop was scheduled to discuss emerging proposals to come up with possible recommendations. In addition, the Commission made a review of existing studies, and commissioned additional reports. Travel to four countries in the region and at least one country outside the region was originally planned but, due to funding constraints, this did not take place.

Based on the Malawian experience, a checklist at the design stage should include the following:
- Take stock of available resources;
- Analyse resource demands implicit in the terms of reference;
- List additional resources needed;
- Analyse pressure of available time on resources;
- Determine the composition of the support staff;
- Determine an appropriate code of conduct for Commissioners and support staff.

Source: Harawa, 1999

and such popular participation as has occurred, has been in the vein of 'consultation' of which note is, or is not, taken, according to the will of state". Rwanda, Ethiopia, Tanzania provide examples where public consultation appear to have been deliberately limited. Here, "the common position appears to be that matters of property are too political, too powerful in their implications to be left even in part to those who have most stake in the matter, the ordinary, and mainly peasant landholder" (Alden Wily, forthcoming).

Why should governments start from the local level when designing new legal paradigms in property relations? Alden Wily argues that the singular advantage "is that it tackles social legitimacy, commitment and cost all in one go. As a matter of course, it leads to community-based solutions and institutional development as part of a slowly accruing process which adds up to more genuine reform in property relations than a nationally designed and imposed 'big bang' transformation may ever achieve" (ibid.). Thus, the landholders themselves have the opportunity to become actors, not just beneficiaries or casualties of government's decisions which are likely fundamentally to affect their rights. The lack of such involvement has been felt in several countries (such as Eritrea, Ethiopia, Uganda, Zambia, Namibia and Zimbabwe) where new legal paradigms in property relations have proven to be unworkable, over-expensive, and unwanted by the supposed clients, at least in the form currently offered (ibid.; Moyo, forthcoming).

Consultation itself comes in varying degrees in the matter of tenure reform. Perhaps the most genuine consultative process so far has taken place in the case of Mozambique. As Negrão (1998) observes, "from the beginning, there was participation of civil society in the land debate. NGOs, churches and associations all discussed how best to guarantee access to and the possession of land by the family sector. The spectre of war preoccupied everyone, either because of the resettlement, which was underway, or because of land grabbing which threatened the peace that had been achieved". For this reason, the Land Law was developed as much as a consensus building exercise as a reform of the law (Negrão, 1998). Another example of a land reform process involving a high degree of public consultation comes from Malawi (see Box 14.2). However at the time of writing, it is not yet clear whether or how the President intends to follow up the recommendations that have been formulated in the course of the consultation process.

An interesting example of the limitations to consultation comes from Mandivamba Rukuni, chair of the 1994 Commission of Inquiry into Appropriate Agricultural Land Tenure Systems in Zimbabwe (Government of Zimbabwe, 1994). In a recent interview, Rukuni argues that a one-off commission "doesn't have much impact" unless the government puts in place "a more permanent arrangement to learn continually from people and involve them in reforming the land tenure system. [Otherwise], a Commission of Inquiry becomes almost like a political gimmick". However, consultation should not be confused with "the inherent constitutional rights of people for civic participation through communication with government on a continual basis" (Haramata, 1999).

According to Rukuni, the Zimbabwean bureaucracy was generally sceptical about the Commission's Report, both because it was difficult to implement and it requires them to do more work than they usually do. It also requires central ministerial departments to give up some of their powers over budgets and management of staff. In their reaction to the report, politicians were, on the whole, more honest. They sought political gain, were quick to pick out the elements from which they could gain politically, and wanted to see particular things done but not the rest. Unfortunately, this approach tends to produce a patchy, inherently inconsistent programme (Haramata, 1999).

Public participation, as Okoth-Ogendo concludes, is now essential to satisfactory land policy reform and debate between government and the diverse range of stakeholders should ideally be engaged throughout. The Ugandan and South African processes demonstrate the advantage of "informed public discourse at any stage of the exercise". Public participation has become "so crucial that donors are now insisting on and actively demanding its incorporation into all land policy reform exercises however limited these may be" (Okoth-Ogendo, 1998). Governments need to learn how to engage with the public in a constructive and well-defined manner. For example, in the case of Uganda, Nsamba Gayiiya (1999) notes the participatory approach is still new, so that commitment to it and to the devolution of authority over land management needs strengthening.

Alden Wily and Mbaya summarise the extent of public consultation in the formulation of new land policies and laws in Box 14.3 below. This shows the very varied experience and practice between countries ranging from cases where there has been no public involvement at all, to cases such as South Africa, Malawi and Mozambique where considerable time and effort has been invested in getting public inputs into the process.

IMPLEMENTATION PROCESSES

Implementation of new land laws and policies has proved problematic, which is not unexpected, given the contentious and highly political nature of land, and current financial constraints on governments. The challenges encountered by countries such as Uganda, Tanzania and South Africa can provide useful lessons for others, as can the relative ease of the process followed by countries such as Mozambique. However, it should be remembered that rushing to early

---

Box 14.3: Extent of public consultation in formulation of new policies and laws.

Uganda	Limited consultation until Bill gazetted in March 1998, followed by active input from Uganda Land Alliance
Tanzania	Consultation began well with 1991-2 Commission, but dwindled thereafter
Rwanda	None
Eritrea	None
Mozambique	High level of consultation
Malawi	High level of consultation by Land Policy Commission
Zambia	Mixed
Zimbabwe	Limited
South Africa	High level of consultation at times
Namibia	High at times, limited at others. Decision-making centralised despite periodic conferences and consultation
Lesotho	Some consultation
Swaziland	Substantial consultation

Source: Alden Wily with Mbaya, forthcoming

---

judgements about the process of land reform may not be helpful and indeed may often be misleading, given Kinsey's recent findings on Zimbabwe (1999)[2].

In addition to these formal, legal, public processes, other far less formal and more spontaneous processes are also underway. Sam Moyo has directed our attention to what amounts to a "silent class struggle"[3] over land in Southern Africa, in which the poor and landless in countries such as South Africa (especially in KwaZulu-Natal), Zimbabwe and Namibia are invading land. Occasionally, as in Zimbabwe, though illegal, this is happening with the apparent support of politicians seeking votes. Those who resort to land invasions and the like are doing so because they are impatient with the formal processes which have not delivered for them. While there is as yet little documentation of these processes, Moyo (forthcoming) believes:

> The majority of rural people who continue to subsist on marginal lands are increasingly exerting their collective powers to resolve the land question on their own through organised strategies of land occupations, popular protests, renegotiating their electoral votes and other forms of resistance. Recently, illegal squatting or land occupations, albeit of a sporadic nature, have been more influential in keeping the land redistribution issue on the agenda than formal organisations of civil society or their community-based counterparts.

---

2 Kinsey argues that negative assessments of Zimbabwe's land reform programme are premature and have used inappropriate criteria. He argues one is ill-advised to attempt a comprehensive evaluation of the benefits of resettlement in less than a generation. He shows that the programme has, after a lag, resulted in both higher incomes and more equally distributed incomes, that genuine poverty reduction through resettlement is possible, and that broad based land reform can lead to declining levels of inequality.

3 The allusion is to Issa Shivji's classic work on Tanzania, *The Silent Class Struggle* (Dar es Salaam, 1974).

These events are little understood "because of the inability of most official discourse to deal with the illegal and underground aspects of mobilising for reform" (Moyo, forthcoming). There is also considerable recent land grabbing, often in the guise of eco-tourism, and mining development, as well as the recent settlement of land by white South African farmers in neighbouring countries (Moyo, 1998; Palmer, 1998).

Uganda

Turning to the formal processes of land reform, Uganda provides perhaps the prime example of recent legislation and implementation (see Box 14.4). Here, a comprehensive Land Act was passed in 1998 following a relatively open process of consultation, in which the Uganda Land Alliance (a coalition of local NGOs "lobbying for fair land laws") and DFID (as a major donor) played important roles at different times. Vigorous debate ensued within the Ugandan Parliament before the Act was passed by the deadline of 30th June 1998, which had been imposed by the 1995 Constitution. Yet, for all the good intentions, the Act has proved difficult to implement in its current form.

First and foremost, while a large amount of energy went into lobbying in order to get the best possible deal for the various stakeholders within the legislation as it progressed through Parliament, little thought was given to the costs of implementation, which in the event have proved to be very large. The funding needed to finance land titling and ownership transfer alone has been estimated as in excess of Ush 700 billion or UK£280 million (Government of Uganda, 1999). The Implementation Study Report of September 1999, funded by DFID, concludes that "the implementation of the Uganda Land Act of 1998 is beyond the current capacity of the government budget. Even if the resources for its implementation could be raised, the costs would outweigh the envisaged economic benefits of the reform, at least in the foreseeable future". It was considered unlikely to have a significant positive impact on the supply of commercial bank farm credit over the medium term "due to the unwillingness of almost all commercial banks to lend to farmers." It "was also unlikely to have major impacts on farm production through improved tenure security", while one unexpected short-term impact was that the Act "had itself created new uncertainties as to the allocation of rights over some urban and rural land… A vacuum exists in land administration and, especially, dispute resolution. Disputes which would previously have been settled quickly at a local level are now persisting… There has also been a degree of land-grabbing by opportunists in the hope of acquiring a certificate" (Government of Uganda, 1999).

Adams stresses that "it is important to record that the Implementation Study found that the Uganda Land Act, 1998 *is a major step forward in equitable*

Box 14.4: Land reform in Uganda

Tenure reform began in 1988 with the establishment of a committee under the Ministry of Agriculture to look into ways to increase security of tenure and to make land more freely available for investment. Research into tenure systems was conducted with the support of USAID and the Wisconsin Land Tenure Center. From 1993, four Bills were drafted. By 1995, the new Constitution of Uganda had set the policy framework, with a strong orientation towards the democratisation of property relations. This was manifest in the removal of root title from the state and its vesting directly in landholders. Democratisation was to be furthered through the removal of authority over property titling and transfer from government to district level autonomous Land Boards. Dispute resolution was to be similarly removed from the Government-supported judiciary into a regime of independent land tribunals.

The Land Bill was eventually gazetted in early 1998 and enacted in mid-1998. The Land Act included a rigorous timetable for establishing the new institutional framework for new land management and dispute resolution, and a funding mechanism to support the capacity of local people to benefit from its provisions (e.g. to title their land, or to buy out landlords under the mailo system).

In carrying through this set of measures, Uganda has faced the difficulty of not having formulated at the start an overall land policy. The Land Act was based on the preliminary studies and Constitutional provisions. These were primarily derived from country-wide consultations during the consultative exercise leading to the drafting of the Constitution. Therefore unlike other countries, Uganda did not commence its land reform process with the formulation of a systematic policy on land. Rather policy development was more or less thrust upon government as the emotive nature of land issues begun to tear through the political process.

Sources: Alden Wily with Mbaya, forthcoming; Nsamba-Gayiiya, 1999; Mwebaza, 1999

---

land tenure reform. As with all land-related legislation, amendments will be needed to make the law more workable. The amendments proposed by the Implementation Study Report do not represent major changes in direction. They aim to provide more flexibility in implementation. This is necessary because of the budgetary constraints and the specific requirements of the different regions of Uganda…The study found that it would be important to monitor the Act's impact over time, not just in isolation, but in conjunction with other developments in the economy. If unfettered, the provisions of the Act could cause growing inequality in farmland distribution and could prejudice the government's poverty alleviation targets. At that stage, further policy reform with respect to the terms on which land was held might become appropriate, e.g. the introduction of a progressive tax on titled land. Other elements of the impact which it would be important to monitor included the extent to which certificates of title and land registers were kept up to date and the efficacy and equity of the new dispute settlement structures (Adams, forthcoming).

Despite the challenges made apparent by this report, the government of Uganda and DFID have confirmed their commitment to the Act over the long term, given that land reform should not be considered a quick fix. Early lessons from the process so far demonstrate the need for careful thought regard-

---

Box 14.5: Lessons from the Ugandan experience

The passage of Uganda's tenure reform legislation was not preceded by a financial and economic appraisal nor were the budgetary implications the subject of rigorous review. As a result, no provision was made in the budget for its implementation. When the Bill became law, the responsible implementing agencies were without the necessary staff and funds to implement it. Previous laws and institutions were swept away in the new law but no arrangements had been put in place to manage the transition. Amendments to the Land Act are now being drafted to allow courts to hear disputes until the new tribunals are in place, and to reduce the number of Land Boards and Committees needed for tenure administration.

The Act covers the entire country. Inadequate attention was paid to the very significant regional differences in land tenure and land use, which range from intensive smallholder arable production to extensive pastoral rangelands, which, in turn, called for different implementation strategies and arrangements. Some areas were urgently in need of land tenure reform, while others were not.

The most valuable lesson which Uganda has learnt since the passing of the new law is the importance of the use of the bottom up approach to land matters. The Land Bill faced many problems because it was developed in a top-down fashion. The report of the Parliamentary Sessional Committee on the Land Bill stated: "From our own experiences during the public consultations we held, it was apparent that peoples' indignation with the Bill was because of their ignorance of its contents and what it aims to achieve... It is therefore important that the government should before introducing any law, make widespread consultations with the people and get their trust".

Government is now giving greater priority to sensitisation (i.e. letting everyone know what the new land law says, what it does not say, what role it plays in the land reform, what is going to change and how, what kind of timeframe may be expected and what the law means for the different stakeholders). To this end, a Sensitisation Focus Group has been established, comprising representatives of the government, NGOs and private media. The group will oversee the production and dissemination of information to the local people.

The Sensitisation Programme faces various challenges and constraints. Key among these are:
- Uganda is a multi-ethnic society with a multitude of vernacular languages. This poses the difficulty of choosing which local languages to use to simplify and translate the Land Act.
- There are widespread misconceptions of the law amongst the public.
- Pressure to move forward with the programme without due regard to adequate planning.
- The existence of insecurity in some parts of the country.
- Budgetary constraints.

The key statutory bodies and other stakeholders will need to engage in serious dialogue to resolve some of these issues.

Sources: Alden Wily with Mbaya, forthcoming; Adams, forthcoming; Nsamba Gayiiya, 1999

---

ing how best to take forward the provisions of the Land Act. Equally, the process and objectives of land reform must be set within the broader context of promoting agricultural development, and measures to alleviate poverty in a more systematic fashion. Some lessons from the Ugandan experience are drawn in Box 14.5.

The case of Uganda illustrates clearly the need for strategic planning, to assess how much institutional change is really necessary to achieve the goals set out by the Land Act and to enable the costs of such reforms to be compared with the likely risks and benefits (Alden Wily, forthcoming).

Tanzania

In Tanzania, public consultation was far more limited than in Uganda. The two 1999 Acts - the Land Act and the Village Land Act - were drafted by Patrick McAuslan under funding from DFID. The Acts are extremely long and comprehensive in a deliberate attempt to restrict the capacity of local officials for corrupt implementation[4].

The government recognises that the enactment of these laws marks the start of a long land tenure reform process which will last several decades (Government of Tanzania, 1999). The Ministry of Lands has formed an Implementation Committee which has prepared an Action Plan to address the immediate and long term measures necessary for "operationalising" the new legislation, focusing initially in areas where land disputes are particularly acute. Pilot schemes were also a feature of the early land reform initiatives in South Africa (see below). Box 14.6 below outlines the approach followed by the land reform process in Tanzania, and the innovative decision to vest land management responsibilities in the existing Village Councils.

For Alden Wily, the point of the Village Land Act is to devolve land administration, so that it is carried out "by the village, at the village, for the village", the social, spatial and legal institutional foundation of rural Tanzanian society for the last twenty five years. She notes further that the Tanzanian land reform may therefore ultimately work better than elsewhere because the institutions upon which it will depend are already subject to popular direction through meetings of the Village Assembly. The main challenge for the Ministry of Lands will be to change its approach towards providing advice, rather than trying to take over management of village lands itself (Alden Wily, 1998; forthcoming).

South Africa

In South Africa, the obstacles to land reform have been many, not least from the continued strength of "organised agriculture" (composed mainly of white commercial farmers). Here, as in Zimbabwe and Namibia, the continued intransigence of white farmers and their attempts to block land reform are likely to prove disastrous to them in the long term.

The post-apartheid government launched a highly ambitious programme of land restitution, redistribution and tenure reform (see Box 14.7). An entirely

---

4 For more detailed critiques, see Palmer (1999) and Shivji (1999).

Box 14.6: Land reform in Tanzania

Attention to tenure matters in Tanzania began in 1989-90 with the establishment of a Technical Committee in the Ministry of Lands, Housing and Urban Development to draft new Urban Land Policy. This was quickly overtaken by a Ministerial recommendation to establish a Presidential Commission of Inquiry into Land Matters. This began in January 1991 and presented its final report in January 1993. To achieve its objective, the 12-man Commission travelled widely in the country, holding 277 meetings attended by 80,000 people. The prime recommendations of the Commission to vest root title of most of the country in respective village communities, and to remove control over tenure administration from the executive into an autonomous Land Commission met with no support from government and the lengthy report remained unpublished.

Nonetheless, in 1993, the Ministry drew up a position paper and draft National Land Policy which drew heavily upon most other aspects of the Commission's recommendations. Though this was the subject of a public workshop in January 1995 it was approved by Parliament in August 1995 without any real public consultation.

A final draft Land Bill was presented in November 1996, and remained uncirculated until late 1998 at which point, the extremely lengthy draft was gazetted as two proposed laws, a Land Bill and a Village Land Bill. A limited amount of public discussion ensued immediately before its debate in Parliament in February 1999, where the two laws received full support. A commencement date for the law has not yet been set, since the government is keen to await the results of the upcoming election (2000).

The need to conduct a thorough and comprehensive information and education programme on the law is especially critical in Tanzania. This is because the centre-piece (and main innovation) of the new tenure laws is the devolution of a great deal of authority and administration over land to the grassroots, in what is arguably a unique form of tenure democratisation. Unlike Uganda, Tanzania has chosen to use the existing and well-established village governance machinery for tenure administration and local dispute resolution, rather than depositing these functions in district level agencies. The Village Council is the body elected democratically by the community, at meetings of the Village Assembly which brings together all adult village residents. So called "village lands" encompass the vast majority of land in the country. The Land Act and Village Land Act designate the Village Councils as land managers, responsible for guiding community decisions as to the distribution of land within the village into household, clan, community or other lands, and their adjudication, registration and titling. The importance of clear, accurate and comprehensive guidance to villagers will thus be clear. This 'democratisation' of control over property relations should simplify implementation of the reform, increase accountability in local land matters, and cost a great deal less than is anticipated in the concurrent reform process in neighbouring Uganda.

The Tanzanian laws were subject to very limited public consultation in their formulation. However, whilst disappointment has been expressed at the failure of the government to release its ultimate ownership and control over land, there is widespread approval for its handling of customary rights in land, the devolution of administration as noted above, and the express support in principle and procedure given to the security of women, urban 'squatters', and pastoralists. Significant innovations have been made to retain and develop the capacity of groups to hold land securely in common into the 21st century. At this point, the main question facing the reform is the extent to which political will and central government willingness to release powers as suggested in the new laws, will be realised.

Source: Alden Wily with Mbaya, forthcoming

Box 14.7: Land reform in South Africa

Prior to the elections in 1994, the African National Congress set out its proposals for land reform in the policy framework for the Reconstruction and Development Programme (RDP). It stated that land reform was to be the central and driving force of a programme of rural development. Land reform was to redress the injustices of forced removals and the historical denial of access to land; ensure security of tenure for rural dwellers; eliminate overcrowding and to supply residential and productive land to the poorest section of the rural population; to raise incomes and productivity; and, through the provision of support services, to build the economy by generating large-scale employment and increase rural incomes. As anticipated in the 1994 policy framework, the government's response has had three major elements:

Land Restitution covers cases of forced removals, which took place after 1913. They are dealt with by a Land Claims Court and Commission, established under the Restitution of Land Rights Act, 22 of 1994. By the cut-off date in March 1999, over 60,000 claims by groups and individuals had been lodged. By March 2000, some 1,450 property claims, mostly in urban areas, had been settled and about 300 rejected. Amendments to the Act in 1999 provided for simpler administrative processes for the resolution of cases. A major outstanding issue is the level of compensation to which claimants should be entitled. The high cost of compensation is in danger of swallowing up the budget at the cost of other land reform components.

Land tenure reform has been addressed by laws, which aim to improve tenure security and to accommodate diverse forms of tenure, including communal tenure. The Communal Property Associations Act 1996 enables a group of people to acquire, hold and manage property under a written constitution. The Land Reform (Labour Tenants) Act 1996 provides for the purchase of land by labour tenants and the provision of a subsidy for that purpose. The Extension of Security of Tenure Act 1997 helps people to obtain stronger rights to the land on which they are living or on land close by. It also lays down certain steps that owners and persons in charge of the land must follow before they can evict people. The Interim Protection of Informal Land Rights Act 1996 protects those with insecure tenure, pending longer term reforms. The proposed Land Rights Bill, covering the rights of people living on state land in the former homelands, was to have finalised the programme of tenure reform, set out in the 1997 White Paper on South African Land Policy. However, the measure was overtaken by the elections in mid-1999 (see Chapter 13).

Land Redistribution aims to provide the poor with residential and productive land. It started with a two-year pilot exercise to devise, test and demonstrate arrangements for a national programme, which began in 1997. The legal instrument to allocate a government subsidy to 'qualifying persons' for rural land, housing and infrastructure stems from 1993 under the Provision of Certain Land for Settlement Act. The Act, amended and renamed in 1998, had provided some 700,000 hectares to over 55,000 households by the end of 1999. Major outstanding issues are: who should qualify; the extent to which government should intervene in a 'market-based' and 'demand-led' process; and the co-ordination of government agencies in the planning and implementation of land redistribution projects.

While having achieved a considerable amount, in terms of the RDP policy framework, South Africa's land reform programme has failed to meet expectations. It has faced serious fiscal constraints, receiving less than 0.4 per cent of the government budget, over the financial years 1994/5-1998/9. Under the Constitution, landowners are entitled to market-related compensation. The Constitution also sets out the distribution of responsibilities for land reform, which are not easily co-ordinated. While the national government is responsible for land acquisition, the provincial and local spheres are meant to provide services for settlement and agriculture. Constraints have arisen from the weak organisation of rural people and the lack of capacity of governmental agencies, whose personnel lack experience and training.

Source: Adams, pers. comm.

new Department of Land Affairs (DLA) was created to drive the process, and early attention was focussed on difficult problem areas. Although some felt that this served to slow the pace of land reform elsewhere in the country, Adams (1999a) disagrees. The Land Reform Pilot Programme (LRPP) ran from 1994-96 and was, he argues, of immense help. It operated in nine pilot districts and was concerned with land redistribution only. The pilot districts were very often those with major restitution and redistribution problems. This experience enabled the DLA to devise, test and demonstrate the required systems and procedures for the national land redistribution programme. By the end of the pilot programme, all the provincial offices of the DLA were up and running and working on province-wide redistribution programmes learning from the pilot districts. A thorough and independent review of the LRPP in August 1996 concluded that a considerable amount was achieved in meeting its objectives. Rather than delaying the process, this interim pilot phase forced DLA staff "to get on with the job from day one rather than indulge in philosophising. It was a period of frenetic activity by a handful of people and proved a very useful learning experience" (Adams, 1999a).

In June 1999, following a change in the Minister responsible for Lands and Agriculture, the Land Rights Bill which aimed to sort out tenure problems in the former homelands was shelved (see Chapter 13). Instead, the new South African government plans to give greater weight to redistribution of freehold land to "progressive" African farmers. However, experience from Zimbabwe and Namibia suggests that the issue of tenure reform in the communal areas will continue to recur, and that the historic opportunity afforded by the abolition of apartheid to redress the wrongs meted out to the landless and poor had been lost.

But there are other major issues which must also be tackled. The South African government has looked favourably at the prevailing World Bank model of market-assisted land reform. Yet in the South African context there are fundamental constraints to such a demand-led, market-based approach to land reform. The scope that this approach provides for securing sustainable rural livelihoods for poor people has proved very limited. It clearly needs to be complemented by a supply side component involving acquisition of land by government when it becomes available at favourable prices for later redistribution to the rural poor. This is necessary because poor people in South Africa are simply not in a position to organise themselves to gain access to funds for land acquisition, settlement and production on any significant scale.

The performance of South Africa's land reform programme needs to be seen within the contexts of the huge constraints imposed by the inherited apartheid structures, and lack of experience of the new state structures, compounded by the absence of effective local government structures. Land advocacy NGOs have not been able to articulate the priorities and perspectives of different stake-holders as effectively as needed. At the same time, there have been major shifts in political support for land reform, a characteristic not uncommon in situations where a nation has recently achieved majority rule.

Mozambique

In Mozambique, a more modest enabling law has proved much more feasible to implement in practice than the new legislation in South Africa, Tanzania or Uganda. This was partly due to the participatory processes surrounding the making of the 1997 Land Law (see Box 14.8), partly because of the successful Land Campaign by NGOs, and partly because NGOs have actively sought partnerships, rather than confrontation, with new investors and the business sector (Negrão, 1998).

Those organising the Land Campaign believed that "the effective application of the law would depend to a large extent on the knowledge rural families held about the law". The Campaign did not attempt to substitute for the voice of small farmers, but rather "to inform the producers, as well as the operators and businessmen, about the rights and duties of each according to the new Bill" (Negrão, 1999). The organisers produced and disseminated 15,000 copies of a *Manual to Better Understanding of the New Land Law*. As well as disseminating information about the new law, the Campaign sought to promote justice by enforcing application of the law and to stimulate discussion between the family and commercial sectors occupying the same area. The most sensitive point was the recognition of rights to land occupation on the basis of oral proof; it was necessary for all citizens to have knowledge of this legal measure so as to avoid conflicts and the violation of the fundamental right to land. After two years, 114 of the 128 districts and 280 of the 385 administrative posts existing in the country had already been covered. Around 15,000 volunteers had been trained as activists in the Land Campaign – these included young people, religious workers, teachers, extensionists and NGO staff, in an authentic movement of national unity (ibid.).

In its second year, the Campaign stressed the fact that consultation with local communities was obligatory where applications are made by outsiders to acquire land in rural areas and it sought to inform citizens about the ways in which consultation with the state should be carried out. This concern arose from a series of cases in which officials had limited themselves to collecting only a few signatures as a token attempt to fulfil the consultation requirements. In addition, there are a growing number of cases of corruption in urban and peri-urban land matters. While the Campaign advised citizens to register their land, they acknowledge that, in practice, the capacity to do this does not always

Box 14.8: Land reform in Mozambique

As in all African states, land ownership matters have been central to the battle for Independence in Mozambique. In 1979, the state promulgated a land law which vested land in itself, earmarked areas for socialist-oriented enterprise and restricted rural families to certain areas to encourage agricultural co-operative development and provide labour for state enterprises. The 1979 and 1986 land laws permitted individuals to title their land and established titles issued by Government as the only mechanism for foreign access to land. Demand for land accelerated in the late 1980s, as a result of the successful negotiation between Renamo and the Government and the introduction of the economic reconstruction programme. White farmers from South Africa and especially Zimbabwe represented a significant source of interest in land acquisition, resulting in a strong concessionaire culture whereby lands were leased by the government to foreigners for certain productive uses.

In 1992, the Land Tenure Center of Wisconsin, contracted by USAID to examine tenure issues, organised the First National Land Conference in Mozambique. This was undertaken in conjunction with the Government's Land Commission established the previous year and now named the Inter-ministerial Land Commission within the Ministry of Agriculture. A subsequent Conference was held in May 1994.

In October 1995, Government approved a National Lands Policy and an Implementation Strategy. A draft land law was prepared in January 1996, which was circulated to 200 institutions, experts, NGOs and the media. Working teams were sent to all ten provinces. A Technical Secretariat presented the findings and submissions to a third Land Conference held in June 1996, which was attended by 226 participants drawn from all public and private sectors. The resulting Working Document formed the basis for the Bill, considered by an open public session, two parliamentary committees and various other bodies, but not without conflict and delays (debate of the Bill was delayed three times in 1997). NGOs played a critical role in mobilising pro-peasant support. The Act was finally passed on 31 July 1997. Regulations under the law were subsequently developed through a series of working groups with widely inclusive non-governmental participation and finally approved by Cabinet in December 1998.

In the interim, a range of national and foreign NGOs and academics founded a National Committee to launch a Land Campaign. Its aim has been to disseminate the new law, to promote justice by enforcing the application of the new law and to stimulate discussion between the family and commercial sectors which occupy the same land areas. Promoting the rights of women in land, the right of communities to participate in tenure-related decision making and encouraging group action on land matters, have been important thrusts of the campaign. Manuals, leaflets, videos, comic books and plays have been developed. The Campaign operates in many areas of the country and continues into 2000.

Pursuant to the mode of Portuguese law, the new Land Law, 1997, is a concise set of articles, setting out principles with minimal detail or procedural guidance (and in this respect, a strong contrast to the highly detailed and prescriptive Tanzanian Land Act, 1999). Nonetheless, its promulgation was marked by concern regarding ambiguities and lacunae, concerns not entirely remedied by the Regulations of the following year. In 1997, Kloeck-Jensen observed that the law neither met the ambitions of most citizens nor met the keenest of the donor community to create a clear legal environment for the development of private property and a free market in land. At the same time, "the law devolves more authority and autonomy to private investors and assumes a more conciliatory approach towards capital, both foreign and national". Negrão (1999) concludes that the considerable consultation process had the effect of diluting consistent policy and rendering the law "more a platform for understanding between the different actors and interests" (i.e. a compromise) than a strategy of reform. The strong lobbying stance of Renamo appears to have constrained 'pro-peasant' developments.

A key change provided by the law is the requirement that communities participate in the administration of natural resources and the resolution of conflicts (Arts. 10 and 21). This does not extend however to a right of veto. Another critical change is that communities, as well as individuals, may hold land and may obtain legal title (Art. 7). Verbal evidence is accepted in the law as the basis of a recognised right in land. Application of the law is proving less satisfactory, however, partly through the absence of clear community organisation and representation, and partly through the retention of complex and expensive titling procedures, unfavourable to the poor majority.

Sources: Alden Wily with Mbaya, forthcoming

exist. The Campaign is being replaced by a Forum which is expected to focus its attention on the key issues of community land, women's land rights within the family, and the buying and selling of land in peri-urban areas.

CONCLUSIONS

In many ways, it is too early to make a judgement regarding the success of land reforms in Africa. Certainly, the new land laws are proving difficult to implement, but this is neither surprising nor necessarily a problem. The passage into law of such fundamental reforms is a considerable achievement in itself. In many parts of Africa, the issue of tenure reform is likely to grow in importance, given rising pressures on land, the development of new economic opportunities and the struggle between competing institutions for the mandate to allocate access to land. The material presented in this and other chapters has illustrated the wide range of models for designing a policy process and implementation of land reform measures, the choices each model implies, and the difficulties raised in putting them into practice. Experience from across Africa also shows the need to set the land question within a broader policy framework aimed at promoting agricultural growth, and addressing poverty, while providing a mechanism for monitoring and amending the implementation process, as need be.

In October 1997, President Museveni of Uganda urged his countrymen to "decide now on this issue. This land reform thing should be resolved now"[5]. His call echoed many earlier attempts by British colonial administrators to find 'final' solutions to land problems. But experience from across the range of African countries suggests that there are no final solutions and that we are dealing here with long-term processes of social and economic change, with open and hidden struggles, and with much contestation. While most donors and

5 *Sunday Vision*, 12 October 1997.

NGOs take a consciously apolitical stance, they need to be fully aware of the political issues at stake.

Conflicts over land are made even more complex in societies experiencing "deepening differentiation along racial, class, ethnic and gender lines" as attempts at redistribution are thwarted by an increasing concentration of land by new black and foreign elites. For Moyo, "unequal ownership of and access to land are, increasingly, a central threat to stability in Southern Africa". These are the major issues and are more important than "the legal form of tenure that concerns elites, some governments and some donors" (Moyo, forthcoming). Elsewhere, such a "deepening differentiation" is, as yet, less evident and the need to clarify the status of different forms of land tenure remains a high priority.

The dependence of governments and NGOs on donor funds and expertise is doubtless inevitable in present circumstances. This gives donors a difficult role to play. They need to steer a careful line between encouraging more imaginative forms of land reform, which opens up debate regarding the diverse options available on the one hand, and remaining sensitive to political constraints on the other. The cases of Uganda and Tanzania show that donors should aim particularly to strengthen capacities at national and especially at local levels. A promising step in this direction, following the Sunningdale (February 1999)[6] and Addis Ababa (January 2000)[7] workshops, has been DFID's encouragement of the development of African-owned networks on land tenure and policy in East, West, Southern and the Horn of Africa. Here, the aim is to listen to and facilitate requests for networks aimed at "continued learning, information exchange, collaborative research and capacity building for policy debate and practical implementation involving both governments and civil society". DFID seems genuinely committed to 'letting go' of these processes rather than seeking to direct them. This is very important because, as Sam Moyo told the Addis workshop, such networks are in reality political, not just technical, processes. Their success will depend in part on their ability to engage effectively with government and civil society in their respective countries and in part on how sensitively donors, such as DFID, respond to these networks in the future as they grow. Welcoming this networking process, Okoth-Ogendo cautioned the Addis workshop that while sharing experiences and networking were clearly valuable, African countries have yet to develop a culture of exchange and there is a need to develop capacity for rigorous comparative analyses to help both policy makers and researchers examine the different options to be considered.

What is the future vision of land reform in Africa? The policy of "sub-

---

6 DFID, Land Rights and Sustainable Development in Sub-Saharan Africa: Lessons and Ways Forward in Land Tenure Policy: Report of a Delegate Workshop on Land Tenure Policy in African Nations, Sunningdale Park Conference Centre, Berkshire, England, 16-19 February 1999.
7 NRI, OSSREA and DFID, Networking on Lands Issues in Sub-Saharan Africa, Report of the Workshop held on 24-26 January 2000, Imperial Hotel, Addis Ababa, Ethiopia.

sidiarity" in land management is often adhered to in the rhetoric of governments, meaning a commitment that decisions on land management and control should be taken at the lowest levels possible. But are governments ready to let go of this valuable resource so easily? Adams draws attention to "the persistent manner in which politicians manipulate and control access to land in order to further party and personal interests and so retain the balance of power. Politicians may tolerate bottom-up participatory processes in other areas, but not in matters which require them to relinquish control (directly or indirectly) over land allocation. Any analysis of processes of land reform, including tenure reform, should not be divorced from an analysis of the political processes at work" (Adams, pers.comm).

Tenure reform itself however is only part of a wider struggle to achieve sustainable livelihoods. Many of the long-term answers to land and rural livelihoods must inevitably lie off the land, in the gradual shift of people and resources away from agriculture towards a more diversified set of economic activities (Bryceson and Jamal, 1997). Failure to find substantial alternatives to small-scale farming will lead to a progressive impoverishment of people and the land on which they depend - hence the need to set the land question within the broader context of national strategies to address poverty and develop more sustainable livelihoods.

Appendix 1: Final Statement of the Workshop on Land Tenure Networking in Sub-Saharan Africa, Imperial Hotel, Addis Ababa, 24-26 January 2000

THE PURPOSE OF THE WORKSHOP

The purpose of the workshop was "to develop a practical framework for a programme of African driven network activities on land tenure and land policy for continued learning information exchange, collaborative research and capacity building for policy debate and practical implementation involving governments and civil society."

The workshop, which was organised and hosted by OSSREA, was attended by participants from eighteen African countries; namely Burkina Faso, Cameroon, Ethiopia, Ghana, Kenya, Malawi, Mozambique, Namibia, Nigeria, Rwanda, Senegal, South Africa, Sudan, Swaziland, Tanzania, Uganda, Zambia, Zimbabwe and Southern Africa. The following donor and international support organisations: DFID, GTZ, French Co-operation, SIDA, UN-FAO, IUCN, World Bank, the IFAD Popular Coalition to Eradicate Hunger and Poverty, NRI, OXFAM, UN-ECA, CILSS and IIED also participated. The workshop was sponsored by DFID.

BROAD AREAS OF ASSESSMENT

After two days of deliberation both in plenary and in sub-regional caucuses, the workshop agreed as follows:

289

Assessment of need

Note was taken of the fact that over the past decade, the vast majority of African countries have initiated programmes of policy development, legislative reform, administrative restructuring and conflict management on issues relating to land, land rights, and land use. Despite differences in colonial experience, language, culture and environment, it was observed that these programmes are directed at remarkably similar issues and problems as are the preliminary prescriptions emerging from specific country-level processes. Nevertheless, there is little evidence that individual African countries and regions are drawing on each others' experiences. Need exists, therefore, for the establishment of mechanisms which would facilitate active networking by both governments and civil society, including practitioners, scholars and policy makers at national, sub-regional and regional (i.e. continent wide) levels.

Mission and objectives

It was agreed, therefore, that interactive networks be established at each of these levels. The mission of such networks would be:

to build an enabling environment for the formulation and implementation of people-centred land policies, laws and structures necessary for the eradication of poverty and the promotion of sustainable livelihoods in Africa.

The primary objectives arising from that mission which networks must strive to achieve are to:
- develop capacity for reciprocal learning, exchange of expertise and comparative research and analysis;
- build information systems at all levels for use by governments, NGOs, community based organisation and researchers;
- provide support services to these stakeholders in their efforts to influence and improve decision-making about and implementation of land policies and laws;
- facilitate regional (i.e. including sub-regional and national) co-operation in all issues relating to land policy development.

Thematic approach and activities

Note was taken of the fact that land issues in Africa arise in complex political economic, cultural and environmental contexts and that these are dynamic and vary from country to country and from one sub-region to the next. It was agreed, therefore, that the thematic approaches and specific activities that can be undertaken by networks can only be identified in terms of broad categories.

It was agreed that, as a starting points, focus be disected at the following broad themes:

- land policy and legislative development strategies,
- improving tenure systems and protecting land rights (whether customary, statutory, common property based, or individual),
- environmental security and conflict management, and
- gender dimensions of land rights protection.

Consistent with these themes, the specific activities which networks should strive to undertake would include:

- the establishment, maintenance and periodic update of information systems on each of these themes;
- the facilitation of regular exchange of information and materials through workshops, consultations, exchange visits and electronic interaction, drawing on local, national, sub-regional and regional developments;
- the publication of newsletters, fact sheets and bulletins (including the development and management of web-sites) reporting on land issues at all levels;
- encouragement of collaborative research within and between sub-regions, and
- carefully targeted advocacy on issues of topical interest.

Structure, membership and management

Having recognised the need for networking at all levels, the workshop agreed that the structural framework and membership of networks be guided by the following principles:

- the need to engage governments and civil society organisations in the networking process;
- the need to work towards structures and processes independent of but drawing legitimacy from the stakeholders which support and constitute the membership of any given network;
- the desirability and feasibility of initiating networking activities first at the sub-regional level, supported by strong national networking arrangements
- the need to identify a co-ordinating framework (whether an individual, institution or committee) at each of those levels, and
- the development of vertical and horizontal linkages, amongst stakeholders (including governments) at all three levels.

It was further agreed that details relating to the components of networking structures, management dynamics and logistical arrangements at all levels should grow on the basis of need, circumstance, resources and infrastructure.

In this regard it was agreed that at the regional level (i.e. Africa -wide) the priorities in the short term would be the management of information and exchange of expertise.

Immediate next steps

It was agreed that immediate next steps should consist of the following activities:

- identification and/or refinement of sub-regional needs and priorities
- the development of projects for initial networking activities and further sub-regional consultations and
- the development of comprehensive inventories of national, sub-regional and regional stakeholders, resources and expertise
- the progressive launch of network activities on the basis of subsidiarity. (i.e. from national to sub-regional and regional level; beginning at the lowest level appropriate for specific activities)

Forward planning

- The need to designate an organisation to perform residual functions involving information, monitoring and interim co-ordination was recognised. In particular there is a need to reconvene a similar regional workshop in the next twelve months. It was resolved that until more permanent arrangements are agreed upon OSSREA should continue to perform those functions.

THE QUESTION OF CORPORATE NAME

The workshop agreed on the need for a corporate or working name for networking at the regional (continental) and sub-regional levels, encompassing a board range of land issues (including tenure, land rights, land use and land policy).

It was proposed therefore that the network be called simply LANDNET AFRICA.

Each sub-regional component could then be referred to by its geographic position such as LANDNET AFRICA-East (or Southern, North, West, Horn etc.)

However, it was recognised that the sub-regional networks would need to agree on their own specific designations and exact geographical scope.

Appendix 2: Networks and Resources

A number of organisations, networks and programmes dealing specifically in land matters were identified by studies on land tenure networking which were carried out in mid-1999. The consultants who conducted the studies are now acting as interim sub-regional coordinators of the Africa Land Tenure Network:

East Africa Coordinator
Michael Ochieng Odhiambo
Resources Conflict Institute (RECONCILE)
Printing House Road, PO Box 7150
Nakuru, Kenya
Tel: +254 37 44940
Fax: +254 37 212865
Email: reconcile@net2000ke.com

Horn of Africa Coordinator
Prof. Abdel Ghaffar M. Ahmed
Organization for Social Science Research in
Eastern and Southern Africa (OSSREA)
PO Box 31971
Addis Ababa, Ethiopia
Tel: +251 1 553281/551163
Fax: +251 1 551399
Email: ossrea@telecom.net.et
Website: www.ossrea.org

Southern Africa Coordinator
Sue Mbaya
94 Harare Drive
Marlborough
Harare, Zimbabwe
Tel: +263 91 223 873
Tel/Fax: +263 4 300 340
Email: mbayas@internet.co.zw

West Africa Coordinator
Hubert Ouédraogo
05 BP 6082 Ouagadougou 05
Burkina Faso
Tel: +226 31 30 33
Fax: +226 38 31 33
Email: o.hubert@fasonet.bf

Organisations/Programmes/Networks

East Africa

Resources Conflict Institute (RECONCILE)
Printing House Road, PO Box 7150, Nakuru,
Kenya
Tel: +254 37 44940 Fax: +254 37 212865
Email: reconcile@net2000ke.com
Contact person: Michael Ochieng Odhiambo

Kenya Land Alliance
c/o RECONCILE (as above)
Contact person: Damaris Adhoch

IUCN - East Africa Regional Office
PO Box 68200, Nairobi, Kenya
Tel: +284 2 890605/6/7 Fax: +284 2 890615
Email: egb@iucnearo.org
Contact person: Ed Barrow

Uganda Land Alliance
PO Box 26990 Kampala, Uganda
Tel/fax: +256 41 531824
Email: ula@infocom.co.ug
Contact person: Rose Mwebaza

HAKIARDHI – the Land Rights Research and
Resources Institute
PO Box 75885
Dar es Salaam, Tanzania
Tel/Fax: +255 51 152448
Email: hakiardhi@raha.com
Contact person: Deus Kibamba

Arid Lands and Resource Management
Research Network (ALARM)
The Regional Secretariat
c/o Centre for Basic Research
15 Baskerville Avenue, Kololo, PO Box 9863,
Kampala, Uganda
Tel: +256 41 342987/231228
Fax: +256 41 235413
Email: CBR@imul.com
Contact person: Frank Muhereza

Horn of Africa

Organization for Social Science Research in Eastern and Southern Africa (OSSREA)
PO Box 31971, Addis Ababa, Ethiopia
Tel: +251 1 553281/551163 Fax: +251 1 551399
Email: ossrea@telecom.net.et
Website: www.ossrea.org
Director: Prof. Abdel Ghaffar M. Ahmed

Southern Africa

ZERO Regional Environment Organisation
PO Box 5338, Harare, Zimbabwe
Tel: +263 4 791333 / 700030
Fax: +263 4 720 405
Email: zero@internet.co.zw
Contact person: Nelson Marongwe

National Land Committee (NLC)
PO Box 30944, Braamfontein 2017, South Africa
Tel: +27 11 403 3803 Fax: +27 11 339 6315
Email: NLC@nw.apc.org
Contact person: Asma Hassan
Email: asma@nlc.co.zw

Southern Africa Regional Institute for Policy
Studies (SARIPS)
PO Box 111, Mount Pleasant
Harare, Zimbabwe
Tel: +263 4 702 882 Fax: +263 4 732 735
Email: sapesmps@africaonline.co.zw
Director: Prof. Sam Moyo

Programme for Land and Agrarian Studies
(PLAAS)
School of Government
University of the Western Cape
Private Bag X17, Bellville 7535
Western Cape Province, South Africa
Tel: +27 21 959 3961 / 3739
Fax: +27 21 959 3732
Email: nemmett@uwc.ac.za
Director: Prof. Ben Cousins
Email: bcousins@uwc.ac.za

West Africa

Groupe de Recherche et d'Action sur le Foncier (GRAF)
05 BP 6082
Ouagadougou, Burkina Faso
Tel: +226 33 07 14 Fax: +226 38 31 33
Email: o.hubert@fasonet.bf
Website: graf.citeweb.net
Contact person: Hubert Ouédraogo

Plan Foncier Rural
04, BP 945 Abidjan 04, Côte d'Ivoire
Tel: +225 22 44 43 44 / 44 18 32
Fax: +225 22 44 43 30
Contact person: Yeho Kolo

Association Avenir, Espace et Société (Observatoire du foncier)
BP E 217, Bamako, Mali
Tel: +223 23 05 95 Fax: +223 23 05 19
Contact person: Samba Soumaré

Groupe de Recherche sur l'Etat, la Décentralisation et le Foncier (GREDEF)
BP 84 Bamako, Mali
Tel: +223 22 27 74 Fax: +223 22 75 88
Email: cnrst@spider.toolnet.org
Contact person: Bréhima Kassibo

Secrétariat Permanent du Code Rural, Niger
BP 13611 Niamey, Niger
Tel: +227 73 20 93
Contact person: Maÿ-Moussa Abari

UFR Sciences Juridiques et Politiques
Université Gaston Berger de Saint-Louis
BP 234, St Louis, Sénégal
Tel: +221 961 22 01 / 961 23 02
Fax: +221 961 18 84
Contact person: Samba Traoré

IIED Sahel Programme
BP 5579, Dakar, Senegal
Tel: +221 824 4417 Fax: +221 824 4413
Email: iiedsen@telecomplus.sn
Contact person: Bara Guèye

Institute for Land Management and Development
University of Science and Technology
Kumasi, Ghana
Tel/fax: +233 51 60454
Director: Prof Kasim Kasanga

Northern based organisations

International Institute for Environment and Development (IIED)
3 Endsleigh Street
London WC1H 0DD, UK
Tel: +44 20 7388 2117 Fax: +44 20 7388 2826
Email: drylands@iied.org Website: www.iied.org
Contact person: Camilla Toulmin / Judy Longbottom

IIED-Drylands Programme
4 Hanover Street, Edinburgh EH2 2EN, UK.
Tel: +44 131 624 7040 Fax:+44 131 624 7050

Natural Resources Institute (NRI)
Land and Natural Resource Tenure Programme
Central Avenue, Chatham Maritime,
Kent ME4 4TB, UK
Tel: +44 1634 883163 Fax: +44 1634 883377
Email: r.burchell@gre.ac.uk Website: www.nri.org
Contact person: Julian Quan / Ruth Burchell

Oxfam GB
274 Banbury Road, Oxford, OX2 7DZ, UK
Tel: +44 1865 312221 Fax: +44 1865 312600
Email: rpalmer@oxfam.org.uk
Website: www.oxfam.org.uk/landrights
Land Policy Adviser: Robin Palmer

Department for International Development (DFID)
Rural Livelihoods Department
94 Victoria Street, London SW1E 5JL, UK
Tel: +44 20 7917 7000 Fax: +44 20 7917 0105
Email: livelihoods@dfid.gov.uk
Website: www.livelihoods.org
Contact person: Jane Clarke

Overseas Development Institute (ODI)
Portland House, Stag Place, London SW1E 5DP, UK
Tel: +44 20 7393 1600 Fax: +44 20 7393 1699
Email: c.boyd@odi.org.uk

African Studies Centre
PO Box 9555, 2300 Leiden
The Netherlands
Tel: +31 71 527 3372 Fax: +31 71 527 3344
Email: asc@fsw.leidenuniv.nl
Website: asc.leidenuniv.nl
Director: Gerti Hesseling
Contact person: Marcel Rutten
Email: rutten@fsw.leidenuniv.nl

Groupe de Recherche et d'Echanges Technologiques (GRET)
211-213 Rue La Fayette, 75010 Paris, France
Tel: +33 1 40 05 61 61 Fax: +33 1 40 05 61 10
Email: lavignedelville@gret.org
Website: www.gret.org
Contact person: Philippe Lavigne Delville

Association pour la promotion des recherches et études foncières en Afrique (APREFA)
S/c LAJP, 9 rue Mahler, 75004 Paris, Cedex, France
Tel: +33 1 44 78 33 80 Fax: +33 1 40 78 33 33
Email: lajp@univ-paris1.fr
Director: Alain Rochegude

GTZ
PO Box 5180, 65726 Eschborn, Germany
Tel: +49 6196 791 484 Fax: +49 6196 797153
Email: willi.zimmermann@gtz.de
Website: www.gtz.de
Contact person: Willi Zimmermann

Agrarian Reform Network (ARnet)
Popular Coalition to Eradicate Hunger and Poverty
IFAD, 107, Via del Serafico
00142 Rome, Italy
Tel: +39 06 5459 2445 Fax: +39 06 504 3463
Email: coalition@ifad.org
Website: www.ifad.org/coalition
Contact person: Bruce Moore

Land Tenure Center (LTC)
University of Wisconsin-Madison
1357 University Avenue, Madison
WI 53715, USA
Tel: +1 608 262 3657 Fax: +1 608 262 2141
Email: hmjacobs@facstaff.wisc.edu
Website: www.wisc.edu/ltc
Contact person: Harvey Jacobs (Director)
or Senior Reseacher and Lecturer: John Bruce
(at the World Bank until 9/2001)
Email: jwbruce@facstaff.wisc.edu

World Bank Land Policy Network
Land Policy and Administration Team
1818 H Street, NW
Washington, DC 20433, USA
Website: www.worldbank.org/landpolicy
Contact person: John Bruce
Tel: + 1 202 458 7668
Email: jwbruce@worldbank.org

Bibliography

Abel, N (1993) "Reducing cattle numbers on southern african communal range: is it worth it?" in Behnke, R H, Scoones, I and Kervan, C (eds) *Range ecology at disequilibrium: new models of natural variability and pastoral adaptation in African savannas*, Overseas Development Institute, International Institute for Environment and Development, Commonwealth Secretariat, London

Abudulai, S (forthcoming) "Land rights, land use dynamics and policy in peri-urban Tamale, Ghana" in Lavigne Delville, P, Toulmin, C and Traore, S (eds) *Gaining or giving ground? Dynamics of resource tenure in West Africa*, Earthscan, London

Adams, M (1993) "Options for land reform in Namibia", *Land Use Policy,* 10(3) pp 191-196

Adams, M (1995) "Land reform; new seeds on old ground" *Natural Resource Perspectives,* No 6, Overseas Development Institute, London

Adams, M (1999) *Setbacks to tenure reform in the ex-homelands of South Africa,* in Oxfam GB, Land Rights in Africa, website: www.oxfam.org.uk/landrights/

Adams, M (forthcoming) *Economist's guide to land reform*, work in progress

Adams, M, and Devitt, P (1992) "Grappling with land reform in Namibia", *Pastoral Development Network,* 32, Overseas Development Institute, London

Adams, M, Cassidy, E, Cusworth, J, Lowcock, M and Tempest, F (1996) *ODA Land appraisal mission to Zimbabwe,* British Development Division in Central Africa, ODA, October

Adams, M, Cousins, B and Manona, S (1999a) "Land tenure and economic development in rural South Africa: constraints and opportunities", National Conference on *Land and Agrarian Reform in South Africa*, 26-28 July 1999. Also published as Working Paper 125, Overseas Development Institute, London

Adams, M, Sibanda, S and Turner, S (1999b) "Land tenure reform and rural livelihoods in southern Africa", *Natural Resource Perspectives*, No 39, Overseas Development Institute, London

Agbosu, L K (1990) "Land registration in Ghana: past, present and the future", *Journal of African Law*, 34, pp 104– 27

Ainslie, A (1998) "Wading in: the realities of land tenure reform in the communal areas of the Eastern Cape Province, South Africa", Paper presented at the *7th Conference of the International Association for the Study of Common Property*, Vancouver, Canada, 10-14 June

Alberts, R, Fourie, C P, Dahl Højgaard, J, Shitundeni, A, Corbet, J and Latsky, F (1996) *Land management and local level registries*, Ministry of Lands, Resettlement and Rehabilitation, Windhoek

Alden Wily, L (1998) "The village, villagers and the Village Land Bill", Paper prepared for the *Land Management and Natural Resources Programme*, Arusha Region, November

Alden Wily, L (forthcoming) *Changing property relations of state and people: a critical review of land reform in Eastern and Southern Africa at the turn of the century*, work in progress

Alden Wily, L with Mbaya, S (forthcoming) *A study of land, people and forests: the impact of property relations on community involvement in forest management* (IUCN)

Alston, L J, Libecap, G D and Schneider, R (1996) "The determinants and impact of property rights: land titles on the Brazilian frontier", *The Journal of Law, Economics, and Organization*, 12(1), pp 25-61

Andre, C (1989) *Evolution des systèmes d'exploitation et des droits fonciers: le cas du Rwanda*, unpublished master thesis, Faculté des Sciences Economiques et Sociales, Namur, Belgium

Andre, C and Platteau, J P (1998) "Land relations under unbearable stress: Rwanda caught in the Malthusian trap", *Journal of Economic Behavior and Organization*, 34(1), pp 1-47

Arnold, M and Townson, I (1998) "Assessing the potential of forest product activities to contribute to rural income in Africa", *Natural Resource Perspectives* No. 37, Overseas Development Institute, London

Assier-Andrieu, L (ed) (1990) *Une France coutumière; enquête sur les "usages locaux" et leur codification (XIIXe-XXe siècles)* Editions du CNRS, Paris

Atwood, D A (1990) "Land registration in Africa: the impact on agricultural production", *World Development*, 18(5), pp 659-671

Ault, D E and Rutman, G L (1979) "The development of individual rights to property in tribal Africa", *Journal of Law and Economics*, 22(1), pp 163-182

Baland, J M and Platteau, J P (1996) *Halting degradation of natural resources – is there a role for rural communities?*, Clarendon Press, Oxford

Barrett, J C (1992) "The economic role of cattle in communal farming systems in Zimbabwe", *Pastoral Development Network*, Paper 32b, ODI, London

Barrows, R and Roth, M (1989) "Land tenure and investment in African Agriculture: theory and evidence", *Land Tenure Center Paper* N° 136, University of Wisconsin Press, Madison

Barzel, Y (1989) *Economic analysis of property rights,* Cambridge University Press, Cambridge

Bassett, T J (1993) "Introduction: the land question and agricultural transformation in sub-Saharan Africa", in Bassett, T J and Crummey, D E (eds) *Land in African agrarian systems,* pp 3-31, University of Wisconsin Press, Madison

Bassett, T J and Crummey, D E (eds) (1993) *Land in African agrarian systems,* University of Wisconsin Press, Wisconsin

Batterbury, S P J, Warren, A and Waughray, D (1996) *Social and environmental relationships, land use and land degradation in southwestern Niger,* Final report to the ESCR Global Environment Change Programme, Brunel University, Department of Geography and Earth Sciences, Uxbridge

Bayart, J F (1989) *L'etat en Afrique,* Fayard, Paris

Behnke, R H (1994) N*atural resource management in pastoral Africa,* Commonwealth Secretariat, London

Behnke, R H and Scoones, I (1993) "Rethinking range ecology: implications for range management in Africa", in Behnke, R H, Scoones, I and Kervan, C (eds) *Range ecology at disequilibrium: new models of natural variability and pastoral adaptation in African savannas,* Overseas Development Institute, International Institute for Environment and Development, Commonwealth Secretariat, London

Benneh, G (1987) "Land tenure and agroforestry land use systems in Ghana", in Raintree, J B *Land, trees and tenure,* Proceedings of an International Workshop on Tenure Issues in Agroforestry, Land Tenure Centre, Wisconsin, USA

Bentsi-Enchill, K (1975) "The traditional legal systems of Africa", in Lawson, F H (Chief Editor) Property and Trust, Chapter 2, Section IV, Vol. VI *International Encyclopedia of Comparative Law,* the Hague, pp 68–101

van den Berg, A (1999) "Women farmers in search of land security in northern Cameroon", Paper presented at the *Conference on Land Tenure Models for 21st Century Africa*, the Netherlands, 8-10 September

Berkes, F (1989) *Common property resources: ecology and community-based sustainable development*, Belhaven Press, London

Berry, S (1984) "The food crisis and agrarian change in Africa: a review essay", *African Studies Review*, 27(2), pp 59-112

Berry, S (1988) "Concentration without privatization? some consequences of changing patterns of rural land control in Africa", in Downs, R E and Reyna, S P (eds) *Land and society in contemporary Africa*, pp 53-75, University Press of New England, Hanover and London

Berry, S (1990) "Land tenure and agricultural performance in Africa: report on a conference", Report on *Conference on Rural Land Tenure, Credit, Agricultural Investment, and Farm Productivity,* Nairobi, June 4-8

Berry, S (1993) *No condition is permanent, the social dynamics of agrarian change in sub-Saharan Africa,* University of Wisconsin Press, Madison

Berry, S (1994) "Resource access and management as historical processes – conceptual and methodological issues", in Marcussen, H and Lund, C (eds) *Access, control and management of natural resources in sub-Saharan Africa – methodological considerations,* Occasional Paper No. 13, International Development Studies, Roskilde University, Roskilde

Bertrand, A (1996) "Négociation patrimoniale plutôt que gestion de terroirs", in Le Roy et al (eds) *La sécurisation foncière en Afrique,* Karthala, Paris

Bertrand, A (1998) "L'exemple des marchés ruraux du bois-énergie au Niger" in Lavigne Delville, P (ed) *Quelles politiques foncières en Afrique rurale? réconcilier pratiques, légitimité et légalité,* Ministère de la Coopération/Karthala, Paris

Besley, T (1995) "Property rights and investment incentives: theory and evidence from Ghana", *Journal of Political Economy,* 103(5), pp 903-937

Binswanger, H P, Deininger, K and Feder, G (1995) "Power, distortions, revolt and reform in agricultural land relations", in Behrman, J and Srinivasan, T N (eds) *Handbook of development economics,* 3B, pp 2659-2772, Elsevier, Amsterdam

Biot, Y (1993) "How long can high stocking densities be maintained?" in Behnke, R H, Scoones, I and Kervan, C (eds) *Range ecology at disequilibrium: new models of natural variability and pastoral adaptation in African savannas,* Overseas Development Institute, International Institute for Environment and Development, Commonwealth Secretariat, London

Bishop, J and Scoones, I (1994) "Beer and baskets: the economics of women's livelihoods in Ngamiland, Botswana", *Sustainable Agriculture Programme Research Series,* 3(1), International Institute for Environment and Development, London

Blundo, G (1996) "Gérer les conflits fonciers au Sénégal: le rôle de l'administration locale dans le sud-est du bassin arachidier", in Tersiguel, P and Becker, C (eds) *Développement durable au Sahel,* pp 103-122, Karthala/Sociétés, espaces, temps, Paris/Dakar

Boserup, E (1965) *The conditions of agricultural growth: the economics of agrarian change under population pressure,* Allen and Unwin, London

Bouju, J (1998) "Contrôle foncier et conflits pour les ressources: l'accès aux bas-fonds aménagés comme enjeu de pouvoir local", in *Aménagement et mise en valeur des bas-fonds au Mali,* Actes du séminaire de Sikasso, CIRAD/CBF, Montpelier

Bradbury, M, Fisher, S and Lane, C (1995) *Working with pastoralist NGOs and land conflict in Tanzania,* IIED, London

Brasselle, A S, Gaspart, F and Platteau, J P (1998) "Land tenure security and investment incentives: further puzzling evidence from Burkina Faso", *Cahiers de recherche,* CRED (Centre de Recherche en Economie du Développement), Department of Economics, University of Namur, Belgium

von Braun, J and Webb, P J R (1989) "The impact of new crop technology on the agricultural division of labor in a West African setting", *Economic Development and Cultural Change,* 37(3), pp 513-534

Brock, K and Coulibaly, N (1999) "Sustainable rural livelihoods in Mali", *Research Report 35,* IDS, Sussex, UK

Bromley, D W (1989) "Property relations and economic development: the other land reform", *World Development,* (17) 6, pp 867-877

Bruce, J (1999) "African tenure models at the turn of the century: individual property and common property models", Paper prepared for a conference on *Land Tenure Models for 21st century Africa,* 8-10 September 1999, the Hague, the Netherlands

Bruce, J W (1986) "Land tenure issues in project design and strategies for agricultural development in sub-Saharan Africa', *Land Tenure Center Paper,* 128, University of Wisconsin Press, Madison

Bruce, J W (1988) "A perspective on indigenous land tenure systems and land concentration", in Downs, R E and Reyna, S P (eds) *Land and society in contemporary Africa,* pp 23-52, University Press of New England, Hanover and London

Bruce, J W (1993) "Do indigenous tenure systems constrain agricultural development" in Bassett, T J and Crummey, D E (eds) *Land in african agrarian systems,* University of Wisconsin Press, Wisconsin

Bruce, J and Migot-Adholla, S E (1994) *Searching for land tenure security in Africa,* World Bank, Washington

Bruce, J W and Migot-Adholla, S E (eds) (1994) *Searching for land tenure security in Africa,* Kendall/Hunt Publishing Company, Iowa

Bruce, J W et al (1994) "The findings and their policy implications: institutional adaptation or replacement" in Bruce, J and Migot-Adholla, S (eds) *Searching for land tenure security in Africa,* Kendall/Hunt Publishing Company, Iowa

Bryceson, D (1997) "De-agrarianisation in sub-Saharan Africa: acknowledging the inevitable", in Bryceson, D and Jamal, V (eds) *Farewell to farms, de-agrarianisation and employment in Africa,* African Studies Centre, Leiden

Bryceson, D F and Jamal, V (1997) *Farewell to farms: de-agrarianisation and employment in Africa,* Research Series 10, African Studies Centre, Leiden

Campbell, B M, Luckert, M and Scoones, I (1997) "Local-level valuation of savannah resources: a case study from Zimbabwe", *Economic Botany,* 51 (1) pp 59-77

Carney, D (1998) "Implementing the sustainable rural livelihoods approach", in Carney, D (ed) *Sustainable rural livelihoods - what contribution can we make?* Department for International Development, London

Carney, D and Farrington, J (1998) *Natural resource management and institutional change,* Routledge, London and New York

Carter, M R (1997) "Environment, technology, and the social articulation of risk in West African agriculture", *Economic Development and Cultural Change,* 45(3), pp 557-590

Carter, M R, Wiebe, K D and Blarel, B (1994) "Tenure security for whom? differential effects of land policy in Kenya", in Bruce, J W and Migot-Adholla, S E (eds) *Searching for land tenure security in Africa,* pp 141-168 Kendall/Hunt Publishing Cy,, Dubuque, Iowa

Chambers, R (1997) *Whose reality counts? Putting the first last,* Intermediate Technology Publications, London

Charnock, M (1991) "Paradigms, policies and property: a review of the customary law of land tenure", in Mann, K and Roberts, R (eds) *Law in colonial Africa,* London

Chauveau, J P (1997) "Jeu foncier, institutions d'accès à la ressource et usage de la ressource", in Contamin, B and Memel-Foté, H (eds) Le *modèle ivoirien en crise,* GIDIS/Karthala, Paris/Abidjan

Chauveau, J P (1998) "La logique des systèmes coutumiers", in Lavigne Delville, P (ed) *Quelles politiques foncières en Afrique rurale? réconcilier pratiques, légitimité et légalité,* Ministère de la Coopération/Karthala, Paris

Chauveau, J P, Bosc, P M and Pescay, M (1998) "Le plan foncier rural en Côte d'Ivoire" in Lavigne Delville, P (ed) *Quelles politiques foncières en Afrique rurale? réconcilier pratiques, légitimité et légalité,* Ministère de la Coopération/Karthala, Paris

Chidzero, B T (1961), *Tanganyika and international trusteeship,* Oxford University Press

Ciriacy-Wantrup, S V and Bishop, R C (1975) "Common property as a concept in natural resource policy", *Natural Resources Journal,* 15, pp 713-727

Claassens, A (1991) "For whites only - land ownership in South Africa", in: de Klerk (ed) *A harvest of discontent. The land question in South Africa.* Idasa, Cape Town.

Claassens, A (1999) "Land rights and local decision making processes: proposals for tenure reform", Paper presented at the *National Conference on Land and Agrarian Reform in South Africa,* Broederstroom, July, National Land Committee and Programme for Land and Agrarian Studies, University of the Western Cape

Claassens, A and Makopi, S (1999) "South African proposals for tenure reform: the draft Land Rights Bill - key principles and changes in thinking as the bill evolved", Paper presented at the DFID workshop on *Land Rights and Sustainable Development in Sub-Saharan Africa; Lessons and Ways Forward in Land Tenure Policy,* Sunningdale, UK, 16-19 Feb

Clarke J , Cavendish, W and Coote, C (1996) "Rural households and Miombo woodlands: use, value and management", in Campbell, B M (ed) *The Miombo in transition: woodlands and welfare in Africa,* Centre for International Forestry Research, Bogor

Coldham, S (1978) "The effect of registration of title upon customary land rights in Kenya", *Journal of African Law,* 22(2), pp 91-111

Collier, P (1983) "Malfunctioning of African rural factor markets: theory and a Kenyan example", *Oxford Bulletin of Economics and Statistics,* 45(2), pp 141-171

Comby, J (1998) "La gestation de la propriété", in Lavigne Delville, P (ed) *Quelles politiques foncières en Afrique rurale? réconcilier pratiques, légitimité et légalité,* Ministère de la Coopération/Karthala, Paris

Constantin, F (1998) "Un enjeu de pouvoirs: la gestion des ressources naturelles entre participation et développement durable", in Lavigne Delville, P (ed) *Quelles politiques foncières en Afrique rurale? réconcilier pratiques, légitimité et légalité,* Ministère de la Coopération/Karthala, Paris

Cooper, B M (1997) *Marriage in Maradi, gender and culture in a Hausa society in Niger, 1900-1989,* Social history of Africa series, James Currey, Oxford

Cousins, B (1992) "Room for dancing on: grazing schemes in the communal lands of Zimbabwe", *CASS Occasional Paper* NRM 4/1992, Centre for Applied Social Sciences, University of Zimbabwe, Harare

Cousins, B (1996) "Livestock production and common property struggles in South Africa's agrarian reform", *Journal of Peasant Studies,* 23 (2/3), pp 166-208

Cousins, B (1997) "How do rights become real? formal and informal institutions in South Africa's land reform", *IDS Bulletin,* 28 (4), pp 59-68, Institute of Development Studies, Sussex, UK

Cousins, B (1997) Unpublished material presented to the Africa Regional Meeting of ODA's Natural Resources Advisers and Field Managers, Cape Town, January

Cousins, B (1999) "Invisible capital: the contribution of communal rangelands to rural livelihoods in South Africa", *Development Southern Africa,* 16(2), pp 299-318

Crook, R (1996) "Democracy, participation and responsiveness: a case study of relations between the Ivorian communes and their citizens", *Public Administration,* 74(4) Winter

Cross, C (1998) "Rural land tenure reform: surrounded by hungry allocators", *Indicator*, 4 (2), University of Natal, Durban

Crousse, B (1991) "L'influence des réglementations foncières modernes dans l'aménagement de la vallée; objectifs, contenus, résultats et conflits sur la rive mauritanienne", in Crousse, Mathieu and Seck (eds) *La vallée du Sénégal, évaluations et perspectives d'une décennie d'aménagements,* Karthala, Paris

Cuna Junior, A (1999) "Community land delineation: a case study from Montepuez, Mozambique", Paper presented at the DFID workshop, *Land Rights and Sustainable Development in Sub-Saharan Africa: Lessons and Ways Forward in Land Tenure Policy*, Sunningdale, UK, 16-19 Feb

David, R (1995) "Changing places: women, resource management and migration in the Sahel", *Case studies from Senegal, Burkina Faso, Mali and Sudan* ESRC/SOS Sahel, London

De Ridder, N and Wagenaar, K T (1986) "Energy and protein balances in traditional livestock systems and ranching in eastern Botswana", *Agricultural Systems,* 20, pp 1-16

De Zeeuw, F (1997) "Borrowing of land, security of tenure and sustainable land use in Burkina Faso", *Development and Change*, 28(3), pp 583-595

Deere, C and León, M (1999) "Institutional reform of agriculture under neoliberalism: the impact of women's and indigenous movements", Paper presented at the workshop *Land in Latin America: New Context, New Claims, and New Concepts,* CEDLA, Amsterdam, 26-27 May

Deininger, K (1998) *The evolution of the World Bank's land policy,* World Bank mimeo, Washington, DC

Deininger, K and Feder, G (1999) "Land policy in developing countries", *Rural Development Note* No. 3, World Bank, Washington, DC

Deininger, K and Squire, L (1997) "Economic growth and income inequality: re-examining the links", *Finance and Development,* March, pp 38- 41

Demsetz, H (1967) "Toward a theory of property rights", *American Economic Review*, 57(2), pp 347-359

Derman, B (1990) "The unsettling of the Zambezi Valley: an examination of the mid-Zambezi rural development project", *Seminar Paper,* Centre for Applied Social Sciences, University of Zimbabwe, Harare

Devereaux, S (1996) "Fuzzy entitlements and common property resources: struggles over rights to communal land in Namibia", *IDS Working Paper* 44, Institute of Development Studies, Sussex, UK

DFID (1999) "Land rights and sustainable development in sub-Saharan Africa: lessons and ways forward in land tenure policy", *Report of a delegate workshop on land tenure policy in African nations,* Sunningdale, UK, 16-19 Feb

Diallo, Y (1996) "Transition démocratique, changements fonciers et gestion des ressources naturelles au Mali", in Mathieu, P et al (eds) *Démocratie, enjeux fonciers et pratiques locales en Afrique Cahiers africains,* No 23-24, Institut africain/L'Harmattan, Paris

Didiza, T (2000) *Discussion document on strategic planning by the Minister of Agriculture and Land Affairs,* Workshop held on 11 February, 2000 at the 'Africa Window', Pretoria

DLA (1998) "Update on draft Land Rights Bill", *Tenure Newsletter,* No 2, Department of Land Affairs, Pretoria

DLA Review (1999) McIntosh, A, Barnard, J, Wellman, G, Sejake, S, Cliffe, L, and Palmer, R, *Review of the Land Reform Pilot Programme in South Africa,* for South African Department of Land Affairs, Department for International Development, the European Union and Danida (Pretoria: Department of Land Affairs, November).

Doornbos, M R (1975) "Land tenure and political conflict in Ankole, Uganda", *Journal of Development Studies,* 12(1), pp 54-74

Dorner, P and Saliba, B (1981) "Interventions in land markets to benefit the poor", *Land Tenure Center Paper* No 74, University of Wisconsin, Madison

Dorner, P (1972) *Land reform and economic development,* Penguin, Harmondsworth

Downs, R E and Reyna, S P (eds) (1988) *Land and society in contemporary Africa,* University Press of New England, Hanover and London

Dzumbira, K (1999) "Women and land tenure policy in African nations", Paper presented at the DFID workshop on *Land Rights and Sustainable Development in Sub-Saharan Africa: Lessons and Ways Forward in Land Tenure Policy,* Sunningdale, UK, 16-19 Feb

Edwards, P and Abivardi, C (1998) "The value of biodiversity: where ecology and economy blend", *Biological Conservation,* 83 (3), pp 239-246

Egbe, S (forthcoming) "Forest tenure and access to forest resources in Cameroon", in Lavigne Delville, P, Toulmin, C and Traore, S (eds) *Gaining or giving ground? dynamics of resource tenure in West Africa,* Earthscan, London

Eicher, C K and Baker, D C (1982) "Research on agricultural development in sub-Saharan Africa: a critical survey", *MSU International Development Paper* No 1, Dept of Agricultural Economics, Michigan State University

El Ghonemy, M R (1990) *The political economy of rural poverty: the case for land reform,* Routledge, London/New York

El Ghonemy, M R (1994) *Land reform and rural development in North Africa, Land reform, land settlement and cooperatives,* FAO, Rome

Ellis, F (1999) "Rural livelihood diversity in developing countries: evidence and policy implications", *Natural Resource Perspectives,* No 40, Overseas Development Institute, London

Engelhard, P and Ben Abdallah, T (1986) *Enjeux de l'après-barrage - vallée du Sénégal,* ENDA et République Française, Ministère de la Coopération, Dakar

Fabricius, C, Koch, E and Magome, H (1999) *Community wildlife management in Southern Africa: challenging the assumptions of Eden,* Draft final report for IIED, International Institute for Environment and Development, London

Falloux, F (1987) "Land management, titling and tenancy", in Davis, T J and Schirmer, I A (eds) *Sustainability issues in agricultural development-proceedings of the seventh agricultural sector symposium,* pp 190-208, World Bank, Washington, DC

Feder, G (1987) "Land ownership security and farm productivity: evidence from Thailand", *Journal of Development Studies,* 24 (1), pp 16-30

Feder, G (1993) "The economics of land and titling in Thailand", in Hoff, K, Braverman, A and Stiglitz, J E (eds) *The economics of rural organization –theory, practice, and policy,* pp 259-68, Oxford University Press (Published for the World Bank), New York

Feder, G, and Feeny, D (1991) "Land tenure and property rights: theory and implications for development policy", *The World Bank Economic Review,* 5 (1), pp 135-53

Feder, G and Nishio, A (1997) "The benefits of land registration and titling – economic and social perspectives", World Bank (mimeo), Washington, DC

Feder, G, and Noronha, R (1987) "Land rights systems and agricultural development in sub-Saharan Africa", *Research Observer,* 2 (2), pp 143-169

Feder, G, Onchan, T, Chalamwong, Y and Hongladarom, C (1988) *Land policies and farm productivity in Thailand,* Johns Hopkins University Press (for the World Bank), Baltimore

Firmin-Sellers, K (1996) *The transformation of property rights in the Gold Coast – an empirical analysis applying rational choice theory,* Cambridge University Press, Cambridge

Fortmann, L and Nabane, N (1992) "The fruits of their labours: gender, property and trees in Mhondoro District", *CASS Occasional Paper Series –* NRM 6/1992, Centre for Applied Social Sciences, University of Zimbabwe, Harare

Francis, P (1984) "For the use and common benefit of all Nigerians: consequences of the 1978 land nationalisation", *Africa,* 54 (3), pp 5-28

Franklin, A S (1995) *Land law in Lesotho: the politics of the 1979 Land Act,* Aldershot

Friedman, J, Jimenez, E and Mayo, S K (1988) "The demand for tenure security in developing countries", *Journal of Development Economics,* 29 (2), pp 185-198

Frimpong, K (1986) "The administration of tribal lands in Botswana", *Journal of African Law,* 30, pp 51–74

Frimpong, K (1993) "Post-independence land legislation and the process of land tenure reform in Botswana" XXVI CILSA, pp 385–395

Frost, P and Madondo, A (1999) "Improving rural livelihoods in semi-arid regions through management of micro-catchments", *IES Working Paper* No. 12, Institute for Environmental Studies, University of Zimbabwe, Harare

Gado, B A (1996) "Le code rural au Niger, une réforme prometteuse, une application difficile", in Mathieu, P et al (ed) D*émocratie, enjeux fonciers et pratiques locales en Afrique,* no.23-24, Cahiers africains, Institut africain/L'Harmattan, Paris

Gastellu, J M (1982) "Droit d'usage et propriété privée", in Le Bris, E, Le Roy, E and Leimdorfer, F (eds) E*njeux fonciers en Afrique noire*, pp 269-279, ORSTOM and Karthala, Paris

Giri, J (1983) *Le Sahel demain,* Karthala, Paris

Glazier, J (1985) *Land and the uses of tradition among the Mbeere of Kenya,* MD, University Press of America, Lanham

Goheen, M (1988) "Land accumulation and local control: the manipulation of symbols and power in Nso, Cameroon", in Downs, R E and Reyna, S P (eds) *Land and society in contemporary Africa,* pp 280-308, University Press of New England, Hanover & London

Golan, E H (1990) "Land tenure reform in Senegal: an economic study from the Peanut Basin", *Land Tenure Center Paper* No.101, University of Wisconsin, Madison

Gore, C (1993) "Entitlement relations and 'unruly' social practices: a comment on the work of Amartya Sen", *Journal of Development Studies,* 29 (3), pp 429-460

Gourou, P (1991) *L'Afrique tropicale: nain ou géant agricole?,* Paris

Government of Malawi (1999) *Report of the Presidential Commission on Land Policy Reform* (under the chairmanship of P M Saidi), Lilongwe

Government of Namibia (1998) *The latest draft of the Communal Land Reform Bill for the Honourable Minister's Attention*, Oct.

Government of Tanzania (1991) *Report of the Presidential Commission of Enquiry into Land Matters* (under the chairmanship of Issa G Shivji), Dar es Salaam

Government of Tanzania (1999) *Land reforms in Tanzania: development and implementation of the national Land Policy 1995,* Ministry of Lands and Human Settlements Development, Dar es Salaam, November

Government of Uganda (1999) *Report of the Land Act Implementation Study,* September, Kampala

Government of Zimbabwe (1994) *Report of the Commission of Enquiry into Appropriate Agricultural Land Tenure Systems* (under the chairmanship of M. Rukuni), 3 volumes, Government Printer, Harare

Government of Zimbabwe (1998) *National Land Policy Framework,* Department of Lands, Ministry of Lands and Agriculture, November 26

Green, J K (1987) "Evaluating the impact of consolidation of holdings, individualisation of tenure, and registration of title: lessons from Kenya", *Land Tenure Centre Paper* 129, University of Wisconsin, Madison

Hagberg, S (1998) "Between peace and justice: dispute settlement between Kaboro agriculturalists and Fulbe agro-pastoralists in Burkina Faso", *Uppsala Studies in Cultural Anthropology*, no 25, Uppsala

Haramata (1999) "Interview with Mandivamba Rukuni", *Haramata*, 35, October, pp 6-7

Harawa, V (1999) "The Presidential Commission of Inquiry on Land Policy Reform in Malawi: operational design and consultation approach", Paper presented at the DFID workshop on *Land Rights and Sustainable Development in Sub-Saharan Africa: Lessons and Ways Forward in Land Tenure Policy,* Sunningdale, UK, 16-19 Feb

Hardin, G (1968) "The tragedy of the commons", *Science*, 162, pp 1243-1248

Harrison, P (1987) *The greening of Africa,* Paladin Grafton Books, London

Haugerud, A (1983) "The consequences of land tenure reform among smallholders in the Kenya Highlands", *Rural Africana,* No 15-16, Winter-Spring, pp 65-89

Hilhorst, T and Coulibaly, N (1998) "Elaborating a local convention for managing village woodlands in southern Mali", *Drylands Issue Paper,* no. 78, IIED, London

Hoben, A (1988) "The political economy of land tenure in Somalia", in Downs, R E and Reyna, S P (eds) *Land and society in contemporary Africa,* pp 192-220, University Press of New England, Hanover & London

Hyden, G (1983) *No shortcuts to progress – African development management in perspective,* University of California Press, Berkeley & Los Angeles

IIED (1995) *The hidden harvest - the value of wild resources in agricultural systems - a summary,* International Institute for Environment and Development, London

IIED (1997) "Valuing the hidden harvest: methodological approaches for local-level economic analysis of wild resources", *Sustainable Agriculture Programme Research Series,* 3(4), International Institute for Environment and Development, London

IIED (1999) *Land tenure and resource access in West Africa: issues and opportunities for the next twenty five years,* International Institute for Environment and Development, London

Ilius, A and O'Connor, T (1999) "On the relevance of non-equilibrium concepts to arid and semiarid grazing systems", *Ecological Applications,* 9(3), pp 798-813

Jacobs, S (1999) "Gender, class and democracy in Zimbabwe's land resettlement programme", *Occasional paper series, Land Reform and Agrarian Change in Southern Africa*, No 11, University of Western Cape

Johnson, O E G (1972) "Economic analysis, the legal framework and land tenure systems", *Journal of Law and Economics,* 15(1), pp 259-76

Jones, B (1999) "Rights, revenues and resources: the problems and potential of conservancies as community wildlife management institutions in Namibia", Unpublished report for *Evaluating Eden Project,* IIED, London

Jones, C (1996) "Plus ça change, plus ça reste le meme? the new Zanzibar land law project", *Journal of African Law,* 40, pp 19–42

Juul, K (1999) "Tubes, tenure and turbulence: the effects of drought related migration on tenure systems and resources management in northern Senegal", *PhD Dissertation, International Development Studies,* Roskilde University Centre, March

Kasanga, K (1999) "The development of land markets in peri-urban Kumasi, Ghana", Paper presented at the DFID Workshop on *Land Rights and Sustainable Development in Sub-Saharan Africa: Lessons and Ways Forward in Land Tenure Policy,* Sunningdale, UK, 16-19 Feb

Kashweeka, R (1999) "Linkages between land tenure, land distribution, poverty and sustainable development: the Botswana experience", Ditshwanelo – the Botswana Centre for Human Rights, Paper submitted to the DFID Workshop on *Land Rights and Sustainable Development in Sub-Saharan Africa: Lessons and Ways Forward in Land Tenure Policy,* Sunningdale, UK, 16-19 Feb

Kaunda, M (1986-92) "Ownership of property rights in land in the first two Republics of Zambia: an evaluation of restrictions on free alienation and some lessons for the future", *Zambian Law Journal,* pp 61–73

Keita, Y (1998) "De l'essai d'un bilan des législations foncières en Afrique de 1960 à 1990", in Lavigne Delville, P (ed) *Quelles politiques foncières en Afrique rurale? réconcilier pratiques, légitimité et légalité,* Ministère de la Coopération/Karthala, Paris

Kepe, T (1997) "Communities, entitlements and nature reserves: the case of the Wild Coast, South Africa", *IDS Bulletin,* 28(4), pp 47-58, Institute of Development Studies, Sussex, UK

Kerner, D O (1988) "Land scarcity and rights of control in the development of commercial farming in northeast Tanzania", in Downs, R E and Reyna, S P (eds) *Land and society in contemporary Africa,* pp 159-191, University Press of New England, Hanover & London

Kesse, M M (forthcoming) "Co-management: a participatory approach to sustainable forest management: the case of gazetted forests in Côte d'Ivoire", in Lavigne Delville, P, Toulmin, C and Traore, S (eds) *Gaining or giving ground: dynamics of resource tenure in West Africa,* Earthscan, London

Kinsey, B H (1999) "Land reform, growth and equity: emerging evidence from Zimbabwe's resettlement programme", *Journal of Southern African Studies,* 25 (2), pp 173-96

Kloeck-Jensen, S (1998) "Locating the community: local communities and the administration of land and other natural resources in Mozambique", Proceedings of the *International Conference on Land Tenure in the Developing World,* 27-29 January 1998, University of Cape Town, Cape Town

Kludze, A K P (1974) "The modern Ghanaian law of mortgages", *XI University of Ghana Law Journal,* pp 1–19.

Klug, H (1995) "Defining the property rights of others: political power, indigenous tenure and the construction of customary law", *Working Paper 23,* Centre for Applied Legal Studies, University of the Witwatersrand

Knox, A (1996) "Nigeria country profile", in Elbow, K et al, (eds) *Land tenure profiles,* Land Tenure Centre, Madison

Koehn, P (1983) "State land allocation and class formation in Nigeria", *Journal of Modern African Studies,* 21(3)

Kolawole, A (forthcoming) "Access to agricultural and pastoral resources in Nigeria: an overview", in Lavigne Delville, P, Toulmin, C and Traore, S (eds) *Gaining or giving ground? dynamics of resource tenure in West Africa,* Earthscan, London

Kone, M, Basserie, V and Chauveau, J P (1999) "'Petits reçus' et 'conventions': les procédures locales de formalisation des droits fonciers et les attentes de 'papiers'", Case study in Centre-West Ivory Coast, in Lavigne Delville, P and Mathieu, P (eds) *Formalisation des contrats et des transactions: repérage des pratiques populaires d'usage de l'écrit dans les transactions foncières en Afrique rurale,* Document de travail, GRET/IED, Paris/Louvain

Kunze, D, Waibel, H and Runge-Metzger, A (1998) "Sustainable land use by women as agricultural producers? the case of Northern Burkina Faso", *Advances in Geoecology,* 31, pp 1469-1477

Lane, C and Moorehead, R (1995) "New directions in African range management, natural resource tenure and policy" in Scoones, I (ed) *Living with uncertainty: new directions in pastoral development in Africa,* Intermediate Technology Publications, London

Lane, C (1998) (ed) *Custodians of the commons, pastoral land tenure in East and West Africa,* Earthscan, London

Lavigne Delville, P (1998a) *Rural land tenure, renewable resources and development in Africa,* Coll Rapports d'études Ministère des Affaires Etrangères - Coopération et francophonie, Paris

Lavigne Delville, P (1998b) "La sécurisation de l'accès aux ressources, par le titre ou l'inscription dans la communauté?", in Lavigne Delville, P (ed) *Quelles politiques foncières en Afrique rurale? réconcilier pratiques, légitimité et légalité,* Ministère de la Coopération/Karthala, Paris

Lavigne Delville, P (1999) "Harmonising formal law and customary land rights in French-speaking West Africa", *Drylands Issue Paper,* No. 86, International Institute for Environment and Development, London

Lavigne Delville, P (ed) (1998) *Quelles politiques foncières en Afrique rurale? réconcilier pratiques, légitimité et légalité,* Ministère de la Coopération/Karthala, Paris

Lavigne Delville, P and Chauveau, J P (1998) "Conclusion", in Lavigne Delville, P (ed) *Quelles politiques foncières en Afrique rurale? réconcilier pratiques, légitimité et légalité,* Ministère de la Coopération/Karthala, Paris

Lavigne Delville, P and Karsenty, A (1998) "Des dynamiques plurielles", in Lavigne Delville, P (ed) *Quelles politiques foncières en Afrique rurale? réconcilier pratiques, légitimité et légalité,* Ministère de la Coopération/Karthala, Paris

Lavigne Delville, P and Mathieu, P (eds) (1999) *Formalisation des contrats et des transactions: repérage des pratiques populaires d'usage de l'écrit dans les transactions foncières en Afrique rurale,* Working Document GRET/IIED, Paris/Louvain

Lavigne Delville, P, Toulmin, C and Traore, S (eds) (forthcoming) *Gaining or giving ground? dynamics of resource tenure in West Africa,* Earthscan, London

Lawry, S W (1990) "Tenure policy toward common property natural resources in sub-Saharan Africa", *Natural Resources Journal,* 30, pp 403-422

Lawry, S W (1993) "Transactions in cropland held under customary tenure in Lesotho", in Bassett, T J and Crummey, D E (eds) *Land in African agrarian systems*, pp 57-74, University of Wisconsin Press, Madison

Le Roy, E (1979) "Réforme foncière et stratégique du développement - réflexion à partir de l'exemple sénégalais", *African Perspectives,* 1, pp 67-81

Le Roy, E (1987) *La réforme du droit de la terre dans certains pays d'Afrique francophone,* Etudes législatives, FAO, Rome

Le Roy, E (1996a) "La théorie des maîtrises foncières", in Le Roy, E et al (eds) *La sécurisation foncière en Afrique, pour une gestion viable des ressources renouvelables,* Karthala, Paris

Le Roy, E (1996b) "Des autorités foncières légitimées, autonomes et gestionnaires", in Le Roy, E et al (eds) *La sécurisation foncière en Afrique,* pp 239-250 Karthala, Paris

Le Roy, E (1997) "La sécurité foncière dans un contexte africain de marchandisation imparfaite de la terre", in Blanc-Pamard and Cambrézy (coord) *Terre, terroir, territoire, les tensions foncière, coll dynamique des systèmes agraires* pp 455-472, Orstom, Paris

Le Roy, E (1998a) "Les orientations des réformes foncières depuis le début des années quatre-vingt dix", in Lavigne Delville, P (ed) *Quelles politiques foncières en Afrique rurale? réconcilier pratiques, légitimité et légalité,* Ministère de la Coopération/Karthala, Paris

Le Roy, E (1998b) "Faire-valoirs indirects et droits délégués, premier état des lieux", in Lavigne Delville, P (ed) *Quelles politiques foncières en Afrique rurale? réconcilier pratiques, légitimité et légalité* Ministère, de la Coopération/Karthala, Paris

Le Roy, E, Karsenty, A and Bertrand, A (1996) *La sécurisation foncière en Afrique: pour une gestion viable des ressources renouvelables,* Karthala, Paris

Leach, M, Mearns, R and Scoones, I (1997) "Environmental entitlements: a framework for understanding the institutional dynamics of environmental change", *IDS Discussion Paper,* 359, Institute of Development Studies, Sussex, UK

Leservoisier, O (1994) *La question foncière en Mauritanie –terres et pouvoirs dans la région du Gorgol,* Editions L'Harmattan, Paris

Levin, R (1997) *When the sleeping grass awakens: land and power in Swaziland,* Witswatersrand University Press, Johannesburg

Lewis, W A (1955) *The theory of economic growth,* George Allen and Unwin Ltd, London

Leys, C (1994) "Confronting the African tragedy", *New Left Review*, 204, pp 33-47

Lipton, M (1993) "Land reform as commenced business: the evidence against stopping", *World Development*, 21(4), pp 641-657

Lipton, M and Maxwell, S (1992) "The new poverty agenda: an overview", *Discussion Paper 306,* Institute of Development Studies, Sussex, UK

Longway, M H C S (1999) "Tanzania: legal land reforms against gender discrimination", Paper presented at the DFID Workshop on *Land Rights and Sustainable Development in Sub-Saharan Africa: Lessons and Ways Forward in Land Tenure Policy,* Sunningdale, UK, 16-19 Feb

Lund, C (1993) "Waiting for the Rural Code: perspectives on a land tenure reform in Niger", *Drylands Issue Paper,* No. 44, IIED, London

Lund, C (1996) "Compétition pour les juridictions et manœuvres politiques", in Mathieu, P et al (eds), *Démocratie, enjeux fonciers et pratiques locales en Afrique,* no 23-24, *Cahiers africains,* Institut africain/L'Harmattan, Paris

Lund, C (1998) *Law, power and politics in Niger: land struggles and the rural code,* APAD, LIT Verlag, Hamburg

Mackenzie, F (1993) " 'A piece of land never shrinks': reconceptualizing land tenure in a smallholding district, Kenya", in Bassett, T J and Crummey, D E (eds) *Land in African agrarian systems*, pp 194-221, University of Wisconsin Press, Madison, Wisconsin

Maine, Sir Henry (1861) *Ancient law,* Murray, London

Mair, L (1974) *African societies,* Cambridge University Press, Cambridge

Maletsky, C (2000) "Namibian Land Reform Bill unopposed; legislation does not include input from non-governmental organisations, *Farmers Business Day*, February 18, 2000, Johannesburg

Mamdani, M (1996) *Citizen and subject contemporary Africa and the legacy of late colonialism*, Princeton University Press, Princeton

Mathieu, P (1991) "De la maîtrise de l'eau au contrôle de la terre", in Le Bris, E, Le Roy, E and Mathieu, P (eds) *L'appropriation de la terre en afrique noire*, pp 61-76, Karthala, Paris

Mathieu, P (1995) "Le foncier et la gestion des ressources naturelles" in Mathieu, P and Laurent, P J (eds) *Actions locales, enjeux fonciers et gestion de l'environnement au sahel*, no. 27, pp 46-59, Cahiers du CIDEP

Mathieu, P (1996) "La sécurisation foncière entre compromis et conflits: un processus politique?" in Mathieu, P et al (eds) *Démocratie, enjeux fonciers et pratiques locales en Afrique,* no. 23-24, *Cahiers africains,* Institut africain/L'Harmattan, Paris

Mathieu, P (1999) "Les paysans, la terre, l'etat et le marché: sécurisation et formalisation endogène des transactions foncières en Afrique", in Lavigne Delville, P and Mathieu, P (eds), *Formalisation des contrats et des transactions: repérage des pratiques populaires d'usage de l'écrit dans les transactions foncières en Afrique rurale,* Document de travail GRET/IIED, Paris/Louvain

Mathieu, P, Laurent, P J, Mafikiri Tsongo and Mugangu, S (1997) "Compétition foncière, confusion politique et violence au Kivu: des dérives irréversibles ?" *Politique Africaine*, n°67, pp 130-136

Mathuba, B M (1999) "Land boards and customary land administration in Botswana", Paper presented at the DFID Workshop on *Land Rights and Sustainable Development in Sub-Saharan Africa: Lessons and Ways Forward in Land Tenure Policy,* Sunningdale, UK, 16-19 Feb

Matlon, P (1994) "Indigenous land use systems and investments in soil fertility in Burkina Faso", in Bruce, J W and Migot-Adholla, S E (eds) *Searching for land tenure security in Africa*, pp 41-69, Kendall/Hunt Publishing Cy, Dubuque, Iowa

Matose, F (1997) "Conflicts around forest reserves in Zimbabwe: what prospects for community management?", *IDS Bulletin*, 28(4), pp 69-78, Institute of Development Studies, Sussex, UK

Matowanyika, J (1999) "Land and the pursuit of sustainable development pathways for Southern Africa: an overview", Paper presented at the DFID Workshop on *Land Rights and Sustainable Development in Sub-Saharan Africa: Lessons and Ways Forward in Land Tenure Policy,* Sunningdale, UK, 16-19 Feb

Mbatha, L and Albertyn, C (1997) "Land allocation practices in Taung and Braklaagte", Research conducted by the *Gender Research Project*, Centre for Applied Legal Studies (Wits University) for the Department of Land Affairs, June 1997

Mbeki, G (1964) *South Africa: the peasants' revolt*, Penguin, Hammondsworth

McAuslan, P (1998) "Making law work: restructuring land relations in Africa", *Development and Change*, 29, pp 527–552

McAuslan, P (forthcoming) "As good as it gets: politics and markets in the making of Uganda's land act"; in *Bringing the law back in,* a paper first given at a workshop on land market reforms in Latin America, Africa and Eastern Europe at the Lincoln Institute of Land Policy, July 1998, Cambridge, Massachusetts

McAuslan, P (forthcoming) "The best laid schemes o' mice an' men: reflections on the diaspora of English planning law in Africa and Asia", in B*ringing the law back in*

McCay, B J and Acheson, J M (eds) (1987) *The question of the commons: the culture and ecology of communal resources,* University of Arizona Press, Tuscon

McIntosh, A (1998) *The involvement of tribal authorities in the land redistribution programme, KwaZulu-Natal province*, Case study report prepared for the Land and Agricultural Policy Centre, Wits.

Médard, C (1996) " Les conflits 'ethniques' au Kenya: une question de votes ou de terres?" *Afrique contemporaine* n° spécial, 4° trimestre, pp 62-74

Meer, S (ed) (1997) *Women, land and authority: perspectives from South Africa,* David Philip, Oxfam , National Land Committee, Cape Town

Migot-Adholla, S E (1999) "Principles of the World Bank's land policy", Slide presentation at the DFID Workshop on *Land Rights and Sustainable Development in Sub-Saharan Africa: Lessons and Ways Forward in Land Tenure Policy,* Sunningdale, UK, 16-19 Feb

Migot-Adholla, S E, Hazell, P, Blarel, B and Place, F (1991) "Indigenous land rights systems in sub-Saharan Africa: a constraint on policy?", *World Bank Economic Review*, 5(1), pp 155-175

Migot-Adholla, S E, Benneh, G, Place, F and Atsu, S (1994a) "Land, security of tenure, and productivity in Ghana", in Bruce, J W and Migot-Adholla, S W (eds) *Searching for land tenure security in Africa*, pp 97-118, Kendall/Hunt Publishing Co, Dubuque, Iowa

Migot-Adholla, S E, Place, F and Oluoch-Kosura, W (1994b) "Security of tenure and land productivity in Kenya", in Bruce, J and Migot-Adholla, S E (eds) *Searching for land tenure security in Africa,* Kendall/Hunt, Iowa

Mill, J S (1848) *Principles of political economy – with some of their applications to social philosophy*, Reprints of Economic Classics, Augustus M Kelley, New-York (1965)

Mongbo, R L (forthcoming) "Land availability and the land tenure regime in rural Benin", in Lavigne Delville, P, Toulmin, C and Traore, S (eds) *Gaining or giving ground? dynamics of resource tenure in West Africa*, Earthscan, London

Moor, G M (1996) *Tenure security and productivity in the Zimbabwean small farm sector: implications for South Africa*, Department of Agricultural Economics, University of Natal, Pietermaritzburg

Moore, D (1996) "Clear waters and muddied histories: competing claims to the Kaerezi River in Zimbabwe's Eastern Highlands", *PLAAS Occasional Papers Series,* No 1, Programme for Land and Agrarian Studies, University of the Western Cape, Cape Town

Moore, S F (1998) "Changing African land tenure: reflections on the incapacities of the state", *European Journal of Development Research,* 10(2), pp 33-49

Moore, S M (1975) *Law as process: an anthropological approach,* Routledge, Henley and Boston and Kegan Paul, London

Moorehead, R (1997) "Structural chaos: community and state management of common property in Mali", *Pastoral Land Tenure Monograph,* No 3, IIED Drylands, London

Moyo, S (1995) *The land question in Zimbabwe,* SAPES Books, Harare

Moyo, S (1998) "Land entitlements and growing poverty in Southern Africa", *Southern Africa Political and Economic Monthly,* 11(5), pp 15-22.

Moyo, S (1999) "The political economy of land acquisition in Zimbabwe: the 1997-98 case study", Paper submitted to the DFID Workshop on *Land Rights and Sustainable Development in Sub-Saharan Africa: Lessons and Ways Forward in Land Tenure Policy,* Sunningdale, UK, 16-19 Feb

Moyo, S (forthcoming) *The land question and land reform in Southern Africa*

Murombedzi, J (1991) "Decentralising common property management: a case study of the Nyaminyami District Council of Zimbabwe's wildlife management programme, *Drylands Issue Paper,* No 30, International Institute of Environment and Development, London

Murphree, M W M (1993) "Communities as resource management institutions", *IIED Gatekeeper Series* No. 36, International Institute for Environment and Development, London

Murphree, M W M (1996) *Wildlife in sustainable development; approaches to community participation,* Presentation to the ODA African Wildlife Consultation, April, Sunningdale, UK

Murphree, M W M (1997) "Congruent objectives, competing interests and strategic compromise: concept and process in the evolution of Zimbabwe's CAMPFIRE Programme", Paper presented at the *Conference on Representing Communities: Histories and Politics of Community-Based Resource Management,* June, Helen Georgia, USA

Mutyaba, B (1999) "Land law reform in Uganda: policy and legislative processes", Paper presented at the DFID Workshop on *Land Rights and Sustainable Development in Sub-Saharan Africa: Lessons and Ways Forward in Land Tenure Policy,* Sunningdale, UK, 16-19 Feb

Mwebaza, R (1999) "Integrating statutory and customary tenure systems in policy and legislation: the Uganda case" Paper presented at the DFID Workshop on *Land Rights and Sustainable Development in Sub-Saharan Africa: Lessons and Ways Forward in Land Tenure Policy,* Sunningdale, UK, 16-19 Feb

Nabane, N (1994) "A gender sensitive analysis of a community based wildlife utilisation initiative in Zimbabwe's Zambesi Valley", *CASS Occasional Paper Series* – NRM 1994, Centre for Applied Social Sciences, University of Zimbabwe, Harare

National Research Council (1986) *Proceedings of the Conference on Common Property,* Resource Management, National Academy Press, Washington, DC

Negrão, J (1998) "Land and rural development in Mozambique", African Studies Association of the UK, Biennial Conference: *Comparisons and Transitions,* SOAS, University of London, 14-16 September

Negrão, J (1999) *The Mozambican Land Campaign, 1997-99,* workshop on The Associative Movement, Maputo, 14 December, in Oxfam GB, Land Rights in Africa, website: www.oxfam.org.uk/landrights

NEPRU (Namibia Economic Policy Research Unit) (1991) *Briefing papers for the National Land Reform Conference,* NEPRU, Windhoek

Netherlands Development Assistance (NEDA) (1997a) "Gender and environment; a delicate balance between profit and loss", *Women and Development Working Paper*, No. 1, Ministry of Foreign Affairs, the Hague

Netherlands Development Assistance (NEDA) (1997b) "Rights of women to the natural resources land and water', *Women and Development Working Paper,* No. 2, Ministry of Foreign Affairs, the Hague

Ng'ong'ola, C (1992) "Land problems in some peri-urban villages in Botswana and problems of conception, description and transformation of 'tribal' land tenure", (1992) *Journal of African Law*, 36, pp 140–67

Niamir-Fuller, M (1994) "Natural resource management at local- level" in *Pastoral natural resource management and policy,* Proceedings of the Subregional Workshop, Dec. 1993, UNSO, Arusha, New York

Noronha, R (1985) A *review of the literature on land tenure systems in sub-Saharan Africa*, Research Unit of the Agriculture and Rural Development Department, Report No: ARU 43, World Bank, Washington, DC

North, D C (1990) *Institutions, institutional change and economic performance,* Cambridge University Press, Cambridge

Nsamba-Gayiiya, E (1999) "The complexities of implementing land tenure reforms: tasks ahead for Uganda", Paper presented at the DFID Workshop on *Land Rights and Sustainable Development in Sub-Saharan Africa: Lessons and Ways Forward in Land Tenure Policy,* Sunningdale, UK, 16-19 Feb

Nsamba-Gayiiya, E (1999b) "Implementing land tenure reform in Uganda: A Complex Task Ahead", *Drylands Issue Paper,* No 84, International Institute for Environment and Development, London

Ntsebeza, L (1999a) "Land tenure reform in South Africa: an example from the Eastern Cape Province", *Drylands Issue Paper*, No 82, International Institute for Environment and Development, London

Ntsebeza, L (1999b) "South Africa's land tenure reform programme in the former Bantustans: the example of the Eastern Cape province", Paper presented at the DFID Workshop on *Land Rights and Sustainable Development in Sub-Saharan Africa: Lessons and Ways Forward in Land Tenure Policy,* Sunningdale, UK, 16-19 Feb

Ntsebeza, L and Buiten, E (1998) "Resolution of land ownership and governance issues in the Tshezi communal area in Mqanduli, Eastern Cape Province", Report prepared for the Department of Land Affairs

Okoin, J R M (1999) "Côte d'Ivoire's rural land-use plan: an innovative approach towards an appropriate rural land tenure code", Paper presented at the DFID Workshop on *Land Rights and Sustainable Development in Sub-Saharan Africa: Lessons and Ways Forward in Land Tenure Policy,* Sunningdale, UK, 16-19 Feb

Okoth-Ogendo, H W O (1969) "Land tenure and agricultural development in Kenya and Tanzania - a comparative study", *Journal of the Denning Law Society*, Dar es Salaam

Okoth-Ogendo, H W O (1976) "African land tenure reform", in Hayer, J, Maitha, J K and Senga, W M (eds) *Agricultural development in Kenya: an economic assessment*, pp 124-142, Oxford University Press, Nairobi

Okoth-Ogendo, H W O (1982) "The perils of land tenure reform", Paper presented at the workshop on *Land Policy and Agricultural Production in Eastern and Southern African Countries*, Gaborone, Botswana

Okoth-Ogendo, H W O (1986) "The perils of land tenure reform: the case of Kenya", in Arntzen J W et al (eds) *Land Policy and agriculture in Eastern and Southern Africa,* United Nations University, Tokyo

Okoth-Ogendo, H W O (1989) "Some issues of theory in the study of tenure relations in African agriculture", *Africa*, 59 (1), pp 6-17

Okoth-Ogendo, H W O (1991) *Tenants of the crown: evolution of agrarian law and institutions in Kenya,* ACTS Press

Okoth-Ogendo, H W O (1993) "Agrarian reform in sub-Saharan Africa", in Bassett, T J and Crummey, D E (eds) *Land in African agrarian systems*, University of Wisconsin Press

Okoth-Ogendo, H W O (1998a) "Land policy reforms in East and Southern Africa: a comparative analysis of drivers, processes and outcomes", Paper for an *International Conference on Land Tenure in the Developing World,* Cape Town, South Africa, also delivered at a *Public Policy Debate on Land Reforms in Africa* organised by the African Centre for Technology Studies at the Nairobi Safari Club, 20 May.

Okoth-Ogendo, H W O (1998b) "Implementing land legislation in Uganda: drawing on Comparative Experiences", Paper for a DFID *Technical Workshop on Uganda's Land Act,* Jinja, Uganda

Okoth-Ogendo, H W O (1998c) "Legislating land rights for the poor: a preliminary assessment of Uganda's Land Act 1998", Paper for the *Uganda Land Alliance Workshop,* Mukono, Uganda

Okoth-Ogendo, H W O and Tumushabe, G (1999) *Governing the environment,* ACTS Press

Olivier de Sardan, J P (1984) *Les sociétés songhay-zarma (Niger, Mali), chefs, guerriers, esclaves, paysans,* Karthala, Paris

Ostrom, E (1990) *Governing the commons: the evolution of institutions for collective action,* Cambridge University Press, Cambridge

Ouedraogo, H and Toulmin, C (1999) "Tenure rights and sustainable development in West Africa Paper", Paper presented at the DFID workshop on *Land Rights and Sustainable Development in Sub-Saharan Africa: Lessons and Ways Forward in Land Tenure Policy,* Sunningdale, UK, 16-19 Feb

Ouedraogo, H, Faure, A, Christophersen, K, Lund, C and Mathieu, P (1996) "Evaluation des mechanismes de mise en oeuvre du code rural a travers l'-experience des commissions foncieres test de Maïne–Soroa et Mirriah rapport final", unpublished final report August 1996

Ovonji-Odida, I (1999) "Land law reform: challenges and opportunities for securing women's land rights in Uganda", Paper presented at the DFID workshop on *Land Rights and Sustainable Development in Sub-Saharan Africa: Lessons and Ways Forward in Land Tenure Policy,* Sunningdale, UK, 16-19 Feb

Oxfam GB (2000) *Land rights in Africa,* www.oxfam.org.uk/landrights/

Palmer, R (1990) "Land reform in Zimbabwe, 1980-1990", *African Affairs,* 89, pp 163-81.

Palmer, R (1997) *Contested lands in Southern and Eastern Africa: a literature survey,* Working Paper, Oxfam UK, Oxford and Ireland

Palmer, R (1998) *Mugabe's 'land grab' in regional perspective,* Centre of African Studies, University of London, SOAS, and the Britain Zimbabwe Society with the support of the Zimbabwe High Commission, Conference on Land Reform in Zimbabwe - The Way Forward, SOAS, 11 March

Palmer, R (1999a) *Learning lessons from land reform in Africa,* Workshop on Land Use and Villagisation in Rwanda, Kigali, 20-21 September, in Oxfam GB, *Land Rights in Africa,* www.oxfam.org.uk/landrights/

Palmer, R (1999b) *The Tanzanian Land Acts 1999: an analysis of the analyses,* in Oxfam GB, Land Rights in Africa, www.oxfam.org.uk/landrights/

Pastoral Development Network (1992) *Newsletter,* No 32, Overseas Development Institute, London

Peters, P (1987) "Embedded systems and rooted models: the grazing lands of Botswana and the commons debate", in McCay, B J and Acheson, J M (eds) *The question of the commons: the culture and ecology of communal resources,* University of Arizona Press, Tucson

Peters, P (1994) *Dividing the commons politics, policy and culture in Botswana,* University Press of Virginia, Charlottesville and London

Peters, P (1997) "Commentary on Rocheleau: shared spaces", *Common Property Resource Digest,* No 40, pp 10-11

Peters, P (1998) "The erosion of commons and the emergence of property: problems for social analysis", in Hunt, R C and Gilman, A (eds) *Property in economic context,* Monographs in Economic Anthropology, No 14, University Press of America, Lanham, New York, Oxford

Piermay, P L (1986) "L'espace, un enjeu nouveau", in Crousse, B et al (eds) *Espaces disputés en Afrique noire,* Karthala, Paris

Pinckney, T C and Kimuyu, P K (1994) "Land tenure reform in East Africa: good, bad, or unimportant?", *Journal of African Economies,* 3 (1), pp 1-28

Platteau, J P (1990) "The food crisis in Africa: a comparative structural analysis", in Drèze, J and Sen, A (eds) *The political economy of hunger, 2: famine prevention,* pp 279-387, Clarendon Press, Oxford

Platteau, J P (1992) "Land reform and structural adjustment in sub-Saharan Africa: controversies and guidelines", *Economic and Social Development Paper* 107, Report prepared for the Policy Analysis Division, FAO, Rome

Platteau, J P (1993) "Réforme agraire et ajustement structurel en Afrique subsaharienne: controverses et orientations", *Etude développement économique et social* 107, FAO, Rome

Platteau, J P (1996) "The evolutionary theory of land rights as applied to sub-Saharan Africa: a critical assessment", *Development and Change,* 27(1), pp 29-86

Platteau, J P (1997) "Mutual insurance as an elusive concept in traditional rural communities", *Journal of Development Studies*

Platzky, L and Walker, C (1985) *The surplus people: forced removals in South Africa,* Ravan Braamfontein

Quadros, M C (1999) "The land policy and legislative process in Mozambique", Paper presented at the DFID Workshop on *Land Rights and Sustainable Development in Sub-Saharan Africa: Lessons and Ways Forward in Land Tenure Policy,* Sunningdale, UK, 16-19 Feb

Quan, J F (1997) "The importance of land tenure to poverty eradication and sustainable development in sub-Saharan Africa", *Background report for the 1997 UK government White Paper on International Development,* July, DFID, London

Quan, J F (1998) "Land tenure and sustainable rural livelihoods", in Carney, D (ed) *Sustainable rural livelihoods: what contribution can we make?* Department for International Development, London

Quan, J F (1998) *Issues in African land policy: experiences from Southern Africa,* Natural Resources Institute, Chatham, UK

Quesnel, A and Wimard, P (1996) *Recompositions familiales et transformations agraires, une lecture de cas africains et mexicain,* Documents de recherche no 1 Equipe Transition de la fécondité et santé de la reproduction, Orstom, Paris

Rahmato, D (1999) "Land and rural poverty in Ethiopia", Paper presented at the DFID workshop on *Land Rights and Sustainable Development in Sub-Saharan Africa: Lessons and Ways Forward in Land Tenure Policy,* Sunningdale, UK, 16-19 Feb

Raynaut, C and Lavigne Delville, P (1997) "Transformation des rapports sociaux et dynamique d'usage des ressources: (2) l'émancipation de la force de travail", in Raynaut, C (ed) *Sahels, diversité et dynamiques des relations sociétés-nature,* pp 315-346 Karthala, Paris

Reardon, T, Delgado, C and Matlon, P (1992) "Determinants and effects of income diversification amongst farm households in Burkina Faso", *Journal of Development Studies,* 28 (2), pp 264-296

Riddell, J C, Salacuse, J W and Tabachnick, D (1987) "The national land law of Zaire and indigenous land tenure in central Bandundu, Zaire", *Land Tenure Center Paper,* No 92, University of Wisconsin, Madison

Rihoy, E (ed) (1995) *The commons without the tragedy? strategies for community-based natural resources management in Southern Africa,* SADC, Lilongwe

Rocheleau, D and Ross, L (1995) "Trees as tools, trees as text: struggles over resources in Zambrana-Chacuey, Dominican Republic", *Antipode,* 27 (4), pp 407-428

Roth, M (1993) "Somalia land policies and tenure impacts: the case of the Lower Shebelle", in Bassett, T J and Crummey, D E (eds) *Land in African agrarian systems,* pp 298-325, The University of Wisconsin Press, Madison, Wisconsin

Rugege, S (1995) "Conflict resolution in African customary law", *Africa Notes,* Oct.

Runge, C F (1986) "Common property and collective action in economic development", *World Development,* 14 (5), pp 623-635

Sachs, A and Welch, A (1990) *Liberating the law: creating popular justice in Mozambique,* London

Sandford, S (1983) *Management of pastoral development in the Third World,* John Wiley in association with Overseas Development Institute, London

Sawadogo, J-P, Stamm, V, Ouédraogo, R S and Ouédraogo, D (1998) "Local perceptions of indigenous land tenure systems: the cause of peasants, women and dignitaries in a rural province of Burkina Faso"

Schlager, E and Ostrom, E (1992) "Property-rights regimes and natural resources: a conceptual analysis", *Land Economics,* 68 (3), pp 249-262

Scogings, P, De Bruyn, T and Vetter, S (1999) "Grazing into the future: policy making for South African communal rangelands", *Development Southern Africa,* 16 (3), pp 403-414

Scoones, I and Wilson, K (1989) "Households, lineage groups and ecological dynamics: issues for livestock research and development in Zimbabwe's communal lands", in Cousins, B (ed) *People, land and livestock,* Proceedings of a workshop on the Socio-economic Dimensions of Livestock Production in the Communal Lands of Zimbabwe, GTZ and Centre for Applied Social Sciences, University of Zimbabwe, Harare

Scoones, I (ed) (1995) *Living with uncertainty: new directions in pastoral development in Africa,* Intermediate Technology Publications, London

Scoones, I et al (1996) *Hazards and opportunities: farming livelihoods in dryland africa: lessons from Zimbabwe,* Zed Books / International Institute for Environment and Development, London

Segosebe, E M (1995) "Land tenure reforms in Botswana: a case study with special reference to the tribal grazing land policy", Paper prepared for *BATLA Annual Conference*, Maun, Botswana, July

Shackleton S, van Maltitz, G and Evans, J (1998) "Factors, conditions and criteria for the successful management of natural resources held under a common property regime: a South African perspective', *Occasional Paper 8*, Programme for Land and Agrarian Studies, University of the Western Cape, Cape Town

Shackleton, C M (1993) "Are the communal lands in need of saving?", *Development Southern Africa*, 10(1)

Shackleton, S, Shackleton, C and Cousins, B (1999) "The economic value of land and natural resources to rural livelihoods: case studies from South Africa", Paper presented at the *National Conference on Land and Agrarian Reform in South Africa*, National Land Committee and Programme for Land and Agrarian Studies, University of the Western Cape, Broederstroom, July

Shepherd, A (1999) "Rural development and poverty reduction at the end of the century: lessons for South Africa", Paper presented at the *National Conference on Land and Agrarian Reform in South Africa,* National Land Committee and Programme for Land and Agrarian Studies, University of the Western Cape, Broederstroom, July

Shipton, P (1988) "The Kenyan land tenure reform: misunderstandings in the public creation of private property", in Downs, R E and Reyna, S P (eds) *Land and society in contemporary Africa*, pp 91-135, University Press of New England, Hanover & London

Shipton, P (1989) "Land and the limits of individualism: population growth and tenure reforms south of the Sahara", *Development Discussion Paper* No 320, Harvard Institute for International Development, Cambridge, MA

Shivji, I (1998) *Not yet democracy: reforming land tenure in Tanzania,* IIED, London

Shivji, I (1999) *The Land Acts 1999: a cause for celebration or a celebration of a cause?*, Keynote Address to the Workshop on Land held at Morogoro, 19-20 February.

Sjaastad, E (1998) *Land tenure and land use in Zambia – cases from the Northern and Southern Provinces*, PHd Thesis, Agricultural University of Norway, As (mimeo)

Sklar, R L (1979) "The nature of class domination in Africa", *Journal of Modern African Studies*, 17(4), pp 531-552

Stamm, V (1998) *Structures foncières et politiques foncières en Afrique de l'Ouest*, l'Harmattan, Paris

Stamm, V (2000) "Land tenure policy: an innovative approach from Côte d'Ivoire" *Drylands Issue Paper* No 91, IIED, London

Stringer, R (1989) "Farmland transfers and the role of land banks in Latin America", *Land Tenure Center Paper,* No 131, University of Madison, Wisconsin

Swallow, B M (1996) "Understanding the multiple functions of common property regimes: examples from rangelands", Paper presented at *Sixth Annual Conference of the International Association for the Study of Common Property,* Berkeley, 5-8 June

Swift, J (1995) "Dynamic ecological systems and the administration of pastoral development", in Scoones, I (ed) *Living with uncertainty: new directions in pastoral development in Africa,* Intermediate Technology Publications, London

Sylla, D (1995) "Pastoral organisations for uncertain environments", in Scoones, I (ed) *Living with uncertainty: new directions in pastoral development in Africa,* Intermediate Technology Publications, London

Tallet, B (1998) "Au Burkina Faso, les CVGT ont-ils été des instances locales de gestion foncière?" in Lavigne Delville, P (ed) *Quelles politiques foncières en Afrique rurale? réconcilier pratiques, légitimité et légalité,* Ministère de la Coopération/Karthala, Paris

Tallet, B (1999) "Le certificat de palabre comme instrument dans les transactions fonciers (Burkina Faso)", in Lavigne Delville, P and Mathieu, P (eds) *Formalisation des contrats et des transactions* GRET/IIED Working paper, Paris/Louvain

Tenure Newsletter (1998) *Update on draft Land Rights Bill,* 2, pp 1-1998

Thebaud, B (1995) "Land tenure, environmental degradation and desertification in Africa: some thoughts based on the Sahelian example", *Drylands Issue Paper*, No. 57, IIED, London

Toulmin, C (1994) *Gestion des terroirs: concept and development,* UNDP/UNSO

TRAC (1994) *The rural women's movement: holding the knife on the sharp side,* Transvaal Rural Action Committee, Johannesburg

Traore, S (1997) "Les législations et les pratiques locales en matière de foncier et de gestion des ressources naturelles au Sénégal", in Tersiguel, P and Becker, C (eds) *Développement durable au Sahel,* pp 89-102, Karthala/Sociétés, espaces, temps, Paris/Dakar

Traore, S forthcoming "Straying fields: difficulties in enforcing the customary principle of shared pastoral land management in the Ferlo (Senegal)", in Lavigne Delville, P, Toulmin, C and Traore, S (eds) *Gaining or giving ground? dynamics of resource tenure in West Africa,* Earthscan, London

Twaib, F (1996) "The dilemma of the customary landholder: the conflict between customary and statutory rights of occupancy in Tanzania", in Debusmann, R and Arnold, S (eds) *Land law and land ownership in Africa,* Bayreuth

Tyler, G, El-Ghonemy, M R and Couvreur, Y (1993) "Alleviating poverty through agricultural growth", *Journal of Development Studies,* 29 (2), pp 358-364

UNDP (1993) *Workshop summary and recommendations: the future of land tenure in Lesotho,* UNDP, Maseru

UNDP (1999) *Human development report,* UNDP, Oxford

Vandergeest, P (1997) "Rethinking property", *Common Property Resource Digest,* 41, pp 4-6

Vedeld, T (1992) "Local institution-building and resource management in the West African Sahel", *Pastoral Development Network, No. 33c,* Overseas Development Institute, London

van der Walt, A J (1995) "Tradition on trial: a critical analysis of the civil-law tradition in South Africa property law", *South African Journal of Human Rights,* 11-12, pp 169–206

van der Walt, A J (1998) *The constitutional property clause,* Cape Town

Weber, J (1998) "Perspectives de gestion patrimoniale des ressources renouvelables", in Lavigne Delville, P (ed) *Quelles politiques foncières pour l'Afrique rurale,* Karthala/Coopération française, Paris

Weitzman, M (1993) "Economic transition – can theory help?", *European Economic Review,* 37, pp 549-555

Werner, W (1997) "Land reform in Namibia: the first seven years", *NEPRU Working Paper,* No 61, NEPRU, Windhoek

Werner, W (1999) "Land policy development and popular participation: the case of Namibia", Namibian Economic Policy Research Unit (NEPRU), Paper submitted to the DFID workshop on *Land Rights and Sustainable Development in Sub-Saharan Africa: Lessons and Ways Forward in Land Tenure Policy,* Sunningdale, UK, 16-19 Feb

West, H (1972) *Land policy in Buganda,* Cambridge

White, R (1999) "Livestock and land tenure in Botswana", Paper presented at a conference on *Land Tenure Models for 21st century Africa,* African Studies Centre, the Netherlands, Sept

Williams, T (1998) "Multiple uses of common pool resources in semi-arid West Africa; a survey of existing practices and options for sustainable resource management", *Natural Resource Perspectives,* No. 38, Overseas Development Institute, London

Wilson and Ramphele (1989) "Uprooting poverty: the South African Challenge", WW Norton

Winter, M (1998) "Decentralised natural resource management in the Sahel: overview and analysis", *Drylands Issue Paper* No 81, IIED, London

Wolf, E (1982) *Europe and the people without history,* University of California Press, Berkeley

Woodman, G (1988) "Land title registration without prejudice: the Ghana land title registration law 1986", *Journal of African Law*, pp 119–135

World Bank (1974) *Land reform,* World Bank Development Series, Washington, DC

World Bank (1982) *Sub-Saharan Africa - from crisis to sustainable growth,* World Bank, Washington, DC

World Bank (1990) *World development report,* World Bank, Washington, DC

Yacouba, M (1999) "Niger's experiences in decentralised management of natural resources", Paper presented at the DFID workshop on *Land Rights and Sustainable Development in Sub-Saharan Africa: Lessons and Ways Forward in Land Tenure Policy,* Sunningdale, UK, 16-19 Feb

Young, C (1986) "Africa's Colonial Legacy", in Berg, R J and Whitaker, J S (eds) *Strategies for African development,* pp 25-51, University of California Press, Berkeley

Zimmerman, W (1999) "Land tenure in development cooperation", Paper presented at the DFID workshop on *Land Rights and Sustainable Development in Sub-Saharan Africa: Lessons and Ways Forward in Land Tenure Policy,* Sunningdale, UK, 16-19 Feb